The Diaspora's Role in Africa

Africans living in the diaspora have a unique position as potential agents of change in helping to address Africa's political and socioeconomic challenges. In addition to sending financial remittances, their multiple, hybrid identities in and out of geographical and psychocultural spaces allow them to play a role as cultural and political ambassadors to foster social change and sustainable development back in their African homelands. However, this hybrid position is not without challenges, and this book reflects some of the conundrums faced by members of the diaspora as they negotiate their relationships with their home countries.

The author uses her lived experiences and empirical research to ask: are members of the diaspora conduits of Western cultural hegemony at the cost of their traditional preservation and meaningful development in Africa? How does the Western media's portrayal of Africa as the "Dark Continent" in the 21st century influence their decision-making process to invest back home? How could African nations' governments manage their relationships with citizens abroad to motivate them to invest in their home countries? How do some citizen-residents in Africa and African Diaspora communities perceive each other in the context of Africa's development? How could the African Diaspora collaborate with citizen-residents across growth sectors to impact Africa's development? The book hopes to inspire agents of change within the diaspora and features diverse African entrepreneurs' success stories and their experiences of tackling these challenges.

The book will be of interest to aspiring entrepreneurs, researchers across African studies, and the expanding and vibrant field of diaspora research.

Stella-Monica N. Mpande is an award-winning multifaceted business and media professional, entrepreneur, and critical communications, cultural, and media scholar. Born in English-speaking Uganda, raised in French-speaking Côte d'Ivoire, prior to relocating to the United States, Dr Mpande's transcultural upbringing influences her works and personal experiences.

Dr Mpande has taught at Howard University, where she earned her PhD, and at Johns Hopkins University as full-time faculty and a program coordinator. Her research in African development, diasporic affairs, diversity and inclusion, communications, and relationship management has been published in several articles and books. Dr Mpande's versatile professional experiences in broadcast journalism, public relations, global marketing communications and advertising, the performance arts, ethics, and compliance have led to her global career with Fortune 500 companies, as well as international development and multilateral development organizations. Currently, she is an Ethics Officer at the World Bank Group.

Rethinking Development

Rethinking Development offers accessible and thought-provoking overviews of contemporary topics in international development and aid. Providing original empirical and analytical insights, the books in this series push thinking in new directions by challenging current conceptualizations and developing new ones.

This is a dynamic and inspiring series for all those engaged with today's debates surrounding development issues, whether they be students, scholars, policy makers and practitioners internationally. These interdisciplinary books provide an invaluable resource for discussion in advanced undergraduate and postgraduate courses in development studies as well as in anthropology, economics, politics, geography, media studies and sociology.

Southern-Led Development Finance
Solutions from the Global South
Edited by Diana Barrowclough, Kevin P. Gallagher and Richard Kozul-Wright

Introducing Forced Migration
Patricia Hynes

Mobile Technology and Social Transformations
Access to Knowledge in Global Contexts
Edited by Stefanie Felsberger and Ramesh Subramanian

Prevention of Violence Against Women and Girls
Mainstreaming in Development Programmes
Tamsin Bradley and Janet Gruber

Global Development and Learning in the Age of Neoliberalism
Stephen McCloskey

The Diaspora's Role in Africa
Transculturalism, Challenges, and Development
Stella-Monica N. Mpande

For more information about this series, please visit: www.routledge.com/Rethinking-Development/book-series/RDVPT

The Diaspora's Role in Africa

Transculturalism, Challenges, and Development

Stella-Monica N. Mpande

Routledge
Taylor & Francis Group
LONDON AND NEW YORK

First published 2022
by Routledge
2 Park Square, Milton Park, Abingdon, Oxon OX14 4RN

and by Routledge
605 Third Avenue, New York, NY 10158

Routledge is an imprint of the Taylor & Francis Group, an informa business

British Library Cataloguing-in-Publication Data
A catalogue record for this book is available from the British Library

Library of Congress Cataloging-in-Publication Data
Names: Mpande, Stella-Monica N., author.
Title: The diaspora's role in Africa: transculturalism, challenges and development/Stella-Monica N. Mpande.
Description: Abingdon, Oxon; New York, NY: Routledge, 2022. |
Includes bibliographical references and index.
Subjects: LCSH: Economic development–Social aspects–Africa. |
African diaspora–Economic aspects. | Entrepreneurship–Africa. |
Africa–Emigration and immigration–Economic aspects.
Classification: LCC HC800.Z9 E44597 2022 (print) |
LCC HC800.Z9 (ebook) | DDC 330.96–dc23
LC record available at https://lccn.loc.gov/2021019335
LC ebook record available at https://lccn.loc.gov/2021019336

ISBN: 978-1-138-49194-6 (hbk)
ISBN: 978-1-032-10651-9 (pbk)
ISBN: 978-1-351-03166-0 (ebk)

DOI: 10.4324/9781351031660

Typeset in Bembo
by Deanta Global Publishing Services, Chennai, India

DEDICATION

I dedicate this book to:

My father, Emmanuel K. N. Mpande, the fearless warrior who trains me to fight relentlessly, break barriers, advocate for what right, and to dream bigger than life itself—because your big dreams, genius mind, love and tenacity have transformed generations and planted the seed of my journey that make me what I am … and birthed this book.

My mother, Proscovia E. N. Mpande, the phenomenal angel whose unfathomable strength and wisdom chart my path on every mountain I climb and obstacle I face—your passion, love, spirit, and strength ignite my core. Thank you for saving my life every single day.

Cheryl and Caroline, my best friends, God's gifts to my life, and talented, mover-and-shaker forever ride-and-die fighters to the end: My story is your story is our story and we are recreating narratives …

Paul, my dedicated brother-in-law, whose resilience and commitment to truth propel Africa to new heights … Thank you for believing in me.

Victoria and Violet, God's darling angels and future global leaders—take the legacy higher.

Thank you all for your infinite sacrifices, your leadership, and your selfless sacrifices—Your love, prayers, strength, and ceaseless support motivate, inspire, and guide me.

This book is also dedicated to the many change-agents, leaders, and future generations of Africa's vibrant soldiers, warriors, and community—including those I interviewed.

Keep charting the path ahead!

Finally, to You, Beloved Mother Africa:

May your vast land, heart, wisdom, grace, and riches forever be honored, revered, protected, preserved, and cherished!

Contents

Figures

Foreword

In my long period living in the United States, I have come across members of the African diaspora who seek to return to Africa and start a business. Sometimes, their dream is to start a small business, and at other times it involves being part of a big business. Those dreams lead to a prevalent question in the African diaspora: how do I enter the African business environment after having been away from Africa for a long period? There are no easy answers. About a decade ago, a friend who shared those dreams left Washington, D.C. to start a small business in Enugu, Nigeria. A few years later, he was back in the United States with his family. He did not realize his dream. Returning to the United States disappointed meant starting his life all over again. I wish now that he had read *The Diaspora's Role in Africa: Transculturalism, Challenges, and Development!* Unfortunately, the book has come late for him, but there are numerous others who now have the advantage of having this resourceful book to help them navigate the African business environment.

Crucially, it is heartwarming that Dr Stella-Monica Mpande is the author of this important book. I have known her for over a decade, and her passion, without an iota of doubt, is how Africans in the diaspora can contribute economically to the African homeland. Her dissertation was related to that topic. Her business ideas are Africa-focused. Her passion for Africa-focused business is obvious in so many other ways. Sometimes I think, and now believe, that Africa-based businesses encapsulate her dream.

Reading through the book, there is no doubt that Dr Mpande breathes Africa-based business. She has organized the book thoughtfully, bearing in mind the general need of Africans in the diaspora who seek to return home to start a business. The book, clearly, has that audience in mind. Stella-Monica reminds the African diaspora that she "felt frustrated in (her) unsatisfactory attempts to identify information hubs, resources or advice to guide (her) efforts to actively contribute more toward the development of (her) African homeland." It is that kinship with the African diaspora who seek to start a business upon return to Africa that makes this book a compelling source for starting a business in Africa.

Dr Mpande starts off with an important conversation with the African diaspora. It is a warm opening section where she acknowledges the identity crisis that confronts a decision to return to Africa with a plan to start a business. It is a situation that questions the worth of indigenous ideas and cautions about the savior complex that dominate the returnee. The second unit of the book delves into multiple business sectors including agribusiness, startup funding, financial technology, and telecommunications. There are also chapters on infrastructure with details on healthcare and education; creative and culture economics in several entertainment industries; and on leisure, hospitality, and real estate. In essence, she covers a wide range of industries. Most startups would readily think about the issues covered in the opening two units, but it is the third unit that no business startup should ever ignore. This unit addresses challenges that are usual with startups in Africa. Unfortunately, most new businesses do not learn about those challenges until they are in the thick of difficulties. The four chapters in this unit address different types of challenges and is a bonus for startups. The final unit offers recommendations and tips that should make the expectant African diaspora confident that a venture into Africa is not in vain. As added bonus, in several sections of the book, Dr. Mpande asks questions that make the reader think deeply in preparation to confront challenges.

While I am not an entrepreneur, I have authored scores of books—some academic and others of general interest. I also read, avidly, books on multiple topics on Africa. I boldly state that *The Diaspora's Role in Africa: Transculturalism, Challenges, and Development* stands out. It is written in a way to satisfy both the expectant entrepreneur and the inquisitive academic. It is a tough combination, but Dr Mpande craftly provides answers to seemingly disparate audiences. I am glad to have the opportunity to read the book, and I wish that you embrace a similar opportunity.

Thank you.

Chuka Onwumechili, Ph.D.
Editor of *The Howard Journal of Communications*
Previous positions held:
Interim Dean, School of Communications—Howard University
Editorial Board—Communication & Sports Journal
Governing Board—International Association of Communication & Sports
Vice-President—Digital Bridge Institute, Nigeria
Published several books and academic journals and featured in various media publications.
Selected media appearances in:
The Conversation
Africa Today program on TVC News, Nigeria
The Heat, television program on the China Global Television Network (CTGN)

Foreword

Having been on an entrepreneurial journey over two decades and built a successful, multimillion-dollar toy empire that is renowned for its Unity Doll African-themed toys, my passion to contribute toward improving my compatriots and Africa's development runs extremely deep. With no prior experience at the tender age of 18 years old, but with a lot of heart and confidence, I embarked on my adventurous, life-transformative journey to create a new niche market and build what has evolved into the present-day Auldon Group. Personally, I sought to revive a childhood dream; globally, I sought to effect a paradigm shift to replace Eurocentric beauty standards with African indigenous values and perspectives. I found it crucial to empower Africans, especially the younger generation, to celebrate their unique beauty, embrace their cultural identities, and preserve their rich history. But my passion and concern for the growth of the African continent expands beyond her vibrant, booming creative and cultural economy.

This book, *The Diaspora's Role in Africa: Transculturalism, Challenges, and Development*, clearly speaks in line with that passion for the continent's rise. Similar to my inspiration with my businesses and broader goals, the book aims to position Africa as a leader at the center and forefront of her development agenda. Hence, I am inspired to write this foreword for such a great piece, which articulates adequate resources for easy reference so that diasporic Africans can join that quest toward a collective effort in raising Africa up through diaspora involvement.

As an African, I have always seen and known Africa as a continent with vast human and natural resources. Yet, at the same time, Africa struggles to attain her full potential as compared to other continents. A myriad of challenges stemming from socioeconomic to volatile political conditions within African countries have largely impacted the continent's growth trajectory over the decades. This calls for a dedicated approach from all actors in and out of Africa to help fix the slide and move the needle of complex issues impacting the continent.

So, with my immense passion for Africa's growth, I could not have been more elated to write a foreword for this book. The book is written to address the diaspora's conflicted role in African development, looking at transculturalism and resistance and charting the road ahead for a greater Africa. The author, Dr Stella-Monica Mpande, who is a pan-Africanist and also identifies as Ugandan-Ivorian-American, presents her own self-reflexivities in this book. Occasionally combining wit with deep introspection, she uses some of her lived experiences as a diasporic African to assist other diasporic Africans toward contributing to their nation's welfare through this book. In essence, Dr Mpande's honesty in presenting various experiences and posing critical questions allows audiences in and outside of Africa to connect with her.

In fact, Dr Mpande's ability to immediately connect with others is a personal attribute that I admire and that is also a strong asset in creating a rapport with her readers. Even with her numerous accomplishments since an early age, Dr Mpande is accessible and relatable to her audiences. She sincerely values others' unique journey and incorporates their perspectives on Africa's development agenda in this book. Hence, I was also humbled by her genuine interest in my own story and journey. But it is also Dr Mpande's compelling background that qualifies her unique approach to this subject matter. Despite having resided outside the continent for quite some time, Dr Mpande still retains her "African touch." Whether it is through her casual switch to "pidgin" dialects or her various projects related to Africa, she maintains a deep connection with home. She is equally passionate about empowering Africans within and outside of the continent to develop Africa. In her efforts to support both groups' contributions and strengthen their collaborations, she also attempts to mitigate some of their foreseeable challenges.

For instance, Dr Mpande acknowledges that many diasporic Africans who exhibit strong entrepreneurial orientation, and similarly crave lifting the continent beyond its present stage, face some frustrations. One of those frustrations is the lack of satisfactory information or adequate resource guides for meaningful development. This book provides a readily accessible repository of materials, which catalogues Africa's growth sectors and industries. Hence, the entrepreneurial prowess of a diasporic African can flourish and begin to approach the much-needed changes the continent so needs.

Aside the diasporic African and their development quest and agenda for the continent, this book made reference to the term *citizen-resident*, which is used to describe some Africans who reside in their home countries but yet transact businesses globally. This term, *citizen-resident*, is worth mentioning in this foreword because it is very relatable to me. The use of this term also demonstrates that this book encompasses both diasporic Africans and resident citizens who are keen on developing Africa. Dr Mpande makes a deliberate attempt to equip both groups with the necessary resources and building blocks to work together to actualize that common goal.

Ultimately, the importance of the gainful involvement—both economically and politically—of Africa's teeming diaspora community and resident citizens in radically transforming Africa into a world leader cannot be overemphasized.

So naturally, this book also touched on African diasporic involvement in politics in and illustrated opportunities for political participation by diaspora communities. The African diaspora's involvement could address some of the challenges surrounding the continent's political scene that inhibit the African diaspora's decisions to be involved politically in their respective countries. My personal experience as an astute entrepreneur who set up and grew a toy firm in the heart of Idumota—the rowdy commercial nerve center of the cosmopolitan city of Lagos, Nigeria—afforded me firsthand knowledge of some of the various challenges Africans face. But even as some eke out a living amidst tribulations in their respective communities, Africans have also shown themselves to be a resilient collective that can take charge of their environments! These personal experiences elicit my thoughts: for Africa to meet and attain her full potential, successful entrepreneurs should be duty-bound to prepare themselves for a life of service through active politics. Politicians make society's choices, which may either enhance or impede their businesses.

In conclusion, I must say that today's Africa calls for more involvement of her diaspora community who have proven and distinguished themselves in their host countries as energetic, resilient, and creative. I include within this community Dr Mpande, whom I regard to be a role model and a good reflection of what young Africans should aspire to. I strongly believe we could achieve a common goal in emancipating Africa from the shackles of numerous challenges and enable her to flourish. However, a concerted effort by concerned diasporic African and resident citizens who are willing to make that significant contribution is key. Africa needs a firm diasporic engagement to deliver sustainable development solutions to optimally boost development and place the continent on a growth trajectory. To achieve this, her diaspora community must have adequate resources for easy reference, which this book provides.

Paul Orajiaka
CEO: Auldon Group

Paul Orajiaka has won numerous awards and notable recognitions.
A select recent few include:

- 2019 Ashoka Africa Entrepreneurship Award—Social Entrepreneur of the Year (Africa)
- 2018 AACSB Influential Leaders Award—The Association to Advance Collegiate Schools of Business (AACSB)
- 2016 All Africa Business Leaders Award
- 2016 Global Titan CEO Award (Regional Winner and Country Winner in the SME sector—West Africa)

Paul Orajiaka has also been featured in numerous media outlets.
A select few include *Forbes International*, *Forbes Africa*, *CNBC*, *BBC News*, *BusinessBecause*, *BusinessDay*, *Vanguard News*, *How We Made It in Africa*, *The African Exponent*, and *Bella Naija*.

Preface

I've been told many times by friends and strangers to write several kinds of books—but I don't think writing an academic book on Africa's development was at the forefront of anyone's mind—certainly not mine! After all, my lived experiences in Africa's development scene did not reflect those of my parents, who had lived and worked across African countries as an agro-economist (father), surgical nurse (mother), and entrepreneurs, representing a family whose history lineage spanned leaders who have pioneered movements in Africa's political, socioeconomic, and cultural development scenes. So, what would I write about?

But I learned quickly that a lot of my educational and professional background, entrepreneurial initiatives, career experiences, and my own lived transcultural and transnational experiences as a member of African diaspora communities within several host countries and African countries I called "home" over the past few decades, have long been writing this book for me! Ultimately, my personal and professional experiences and my role as a target audience of this book equipped me to own my articulation of the problematizations I introduce and guide my writing approach of the phenomenon under investigation in this book.

My scholarly writing endeavors about the African diaspora's contribution toward Africa's development began in 2011, and over the years, culminated in conference presentations, published journal articles and book chapters, panel discussions, and, ultimately, the 2015 doctorate dissertation *Relationship Management of the "Brain Circulation" Phenomenon: The Case of the Ugandan Government and Its Ugandan Diaspora in the United States*. Therefore, I am very proud to say that the publication of my first sole-authored book, *The Diaspora's Role in Africa: Transculturalism, Challenges, and Development* in 2021 marks a 10-year, full-circle academic writing endeavor on a subject-matter that I have lived my whole life!

Hence, written partly as a critical autoethnography, this book fuses some of my personal anecdotes of autobiographical transnational experiences with critical theory and philosophy to connect to broader socioeconomic, cultural, and political understandings of global development.

Interestingly, in my perpetual quest to motivate the African diaspora to contribute toward or invest in Africa's development, I have developed and disseminated other media products and launched initiatives that also represent my own investment in and contributions towards Africa's development. I am also proud to acknowledge this book as one of my efforts to globalize the product of knowledge—a journey that I felt spiritually called to pursue for both my own development and the development of my global community.

Therefore, one of my goals with this book is to build and foster a community of like-minded, like-spirited brethren and sistren on a complex journey that could also, at times, be quite lonely and perplexing! It is not always easy to locate and access comprehensive resources or a one-stop shop that answers personal and practical questions about one's efforts in contributing "back home." It is also complex when trying to even answer the question "Where's home?" The journey becomes more complicated to navigate amongst a climate of distrust, particularly amongst some community leaders and self-titled influencers who may invest more in their brands and performances as "development pioneers" or "influencers" than on actual development work. Sadly, this trend has further incited ego-battles, greed, corruption, and unclear intentions and has also hindered potential collaborative efforts between and within African diaspora and African homeland communities. I pray that together, we may recognize that the road towards developing Africa is not a race but a collective, global effort that spans across geographical borders and generations, transcending space and time, connecting history to present-day in the 21st century.

This leads me to why this book is also an ode to history's iconic revolutionary thinkers and pragmatists of Africa's decolonization and liberation struggles, ranging from Kwame Nkrumah, Julius Nyerere, Frantz Fanon, and Albert Memmi to my own ancestors, professors. and mentors, including the late Dr Sulayman Nyang. All of these leaders have equipped me with intellectual weapons and tools to ignite my activism and strengthen my commitment towards "decolonizing my mind," and a charge to commit to the development of my local and global communities in body, mind, and spirit.

Various factors, including colonial legacies, governance, migration and globalization forces, and other influences may impact the African diaspora's role in contributing towards their nation's development agenda. As a result, this book also contributes to the transdisciplinary fields of global cultural studies, postcolonial studies, Africa studies, development studies, and other disciplines by adopting a critical lens to explore some of the complex dynamics that impact Africa's development.

And at the heart of references to critical theory, colonial, or governance legacies, or dynamics between citizen-residents and diaspora groups, the terms *normative* or *dominant* may refer to European-centered ideologies or to other ideologies and frameworks, based on the context and analysis of the particular phenomenon under investigation. Ultimately, the goal is not to pit any particular group against another, nor incite a "Black versus White" battle. Instead, I employ critical theory and frameworks to problematize and analyze the phenomenon under investigation; identify the root issues of the problem; illustrate how structures, power dynamics, and socio-economic, political, cultural, and historical factors contribute to the status quo of the problem; and unleash emancipatory potential by offering alternative perspectives and tools to address the observed phenomenon or to raise questions about the way forward. I am also aware that a potential audience of this book also includes change-agents who may represent diverse racial and ethnic backgrounds, cultural belongings, or skin color but share similar worldviews and critical approaches towards this subject-matter.

Therefore, I humbly implore the broader global community of scholars and practitioners to collaborate further towards strengthening the nexus of critical theory and international development, scholastically and pragmatically. As the field of global studies vastly expands, the world requires newer sites of knowledge production and dissemination to answer critical questions and solve critical problems in our daily, lived realities. If you don't believe me, ask the "Year of 2020"!

Clearly, little did I know that the critical theoretical paradigms and discussion questions raised in each chapter, as well as the data-driven insights from my interviews, would have greater meaning amidst the global Covid-19 pandemic and global protests for racial justice and against police brutality, particularly in the "Year of 2020." Some of the topics that I raised in the book—Black representation and identity, Africa's sustainable development in growth sectors, power-imbalanced structures and systems, racism and prejudice—were transpiring as protests in my hometown of Washington D.C., as breaking news headlines on my TV screen or as "trending topics" on my social media feeds. In short, what I call the "Year of 2020," also dubbed by many the "Year of the Awakening" and the "Year of the Revolution," dramatically increased the relevance and heightened the urgency of this book for its target audiences!

I strongly believe that the "new normal" that the Year of 2020 positioned us for transcends digital and technological advancements that inform "new ways of doing business." The "new normal" challenges us individually and collectively to be inclusive of alternative paradigms that may better inform how we diagnose issues, problem-solve, and collaborate with each other. The "new normal" dares us to question the status quo and replace normative ideological and cultural systems, processes, and methodologies with newer knowledge systems and processes, especially if they may result in life-transformative breakthrough solutions in our health, educational, legal, business, and international development across the globe. The "new normal" enlists the global community to collaborate together and commit towards practices that are ethical, right, equitable, and transparent. The "new normal" invites us to operate from and for the core of human freedom. And is human freedom not what any personal or communal development strives to achieve?

It is my sincere hope that you will find this book useful in generating discourse regarding development and in drawing connections between theory and practice. I especially hope that this book will guide your own self-reflexive journey towards Africa's development and inspire you to further revolutionize and positively transform our broader global community. After all, the road to Africa's sustainable development merges two forks: one that seeks to heal and liberate itself from the grip of the historical and contemporary detrimental effects of oppression, and the other that strives to create new ideologies, new narratives, and new legacies that will carve a booming, vibrant continent of Mother Africa!

Acknowledgments

First, I would like to thank the Almighty Father for His abundant love, blessings, and guidance, and for equipping me to do all that He has called me to do. I am humbled and immensely grateful for the motivation, encouragement, and gifts of so many angels—the most amazing family and angels of friends—that God has blessed me with so that I may endure to the very end of this journey. Thank you, Father! Our journey continues …

I would love to thank Dr Chuka Onwumechili for his incredible mentoring, encouragement, patience, and guidance on my journey. It is amazing to know that after more than 10 years, your mentorship still inspires my endeavors outside the classroom. Thank you for relentlessly challenging me to push farther, for being a rock, and for rejuvenating me with a renewed energy that inspired me to leap further ahead!

I would love to thank all of my research participants all over the world who graciously offered their time, insights, and positive support with this endeavor. Your perspectives, your voices, and your hearts are captured in this work that reflects the essence of your spirit, your vision, and mission as leaders, sons, and daughters of Mother Africa! I pray that I have made you all proud. I pray that you all are also proud of yourselves for joining me in this process!

I would love to thank my amazing team at Routledge for their unbelievable patience, encouragement, and support in this endeavor. We have persisted through the years and I sincerely appreciate your enthusiasm and passion that ignited this project and belief in me.

Lastly, I would like to thank my family, supportive global community, and close friends who have encouraged me, inspired me, and reminded me to share my voice and perspectives with the world. I also thank you all for checking in on me regularly and for reminding me to breathe fresh air, eat, drink, and partake in healthy human behaviors to ensure I am still alive.

Introduction

*During one of my childhood visits to Uganda, a few kids called me a "Black American," especially because of my so-called "American" accent and because of the fact that I also cannot speak Luganda fluently—despite understanding it fluently. In French-speaking Ivory Coast, they referred to me as an "*étranger*" (foreigner) or "*Anglophone*" (English-speaker). In America, I have been told that I'm not Black enough, or that I act White; others had "corrected" them: I was not African enough. Despite having lived in America for 20 years, I generally refer to myself as "Ugandan-Ivorian"—although I self-identify more as a pan-Africanist, and only recently self-identified more as Ugandan-Ivorian-American. But when I speak English, French, adopt a Spanish accent with a few phrases I mastered, or float seamlessly in different circles with various forms of pidgin, I can see the creases in their forehead tighten; they struggle to pinpoint my "true" identity. Then I await their two simple, yet loaded questions: "So, what are you? And where do you call 'home'?"*

For many of us Africans living in the diaspora, our multiple, cultural hybrid identities and acquired specialized skillsets empower us with a potential to leverage the intercultural competence needed to thrive and excel in numerous social and professional settings—particularly in the West. Ironically, sometimes the ability to apply these skills to developing our African homelands is our challenge. Although a number of us have returned to our homelands, many of us still reside in the diaspora, yet seek to remain connected to, invest in and/or also return to our African homelands. However, we are faced with psychocultural, socioeconomic and political challenges and conflicts that stem from within ourselves, our host countries, and our African homelands. Unless our tug-of-wars are effectively addressed, we will continue to remain a largely untapped source of power that has yet to fully transform Africa as a global force to be reckoned with.

Over the years and through countless stories I have been told, some of the diaspora's conflicts and challenges became clear to me. Many members of diverse Diaspora communities all over the world have expressed to me at least one of, or several of the following conflicts and challenges they grapple with when trying to identify with, invest in, or relocate to their African "home":

- *Some of us who do not reside in our African home nation(s) feel burdened with the task of justifying or manifesting our value-add in an African country, whose cultures, values, traditions, languages, and people may be as psychologically foreign to us as the host country we physically reside in.*

DOI: 10.4324/9781351031660-101

- *Some of us who have resided in highly industrialized Westernized societies may have gained decent incomes, can afford luxury-brand goods and luxury services, and even lead multi-million-dollar business operations. Hence, we question our sanity in forfeiting such high levels of comfort for what we may (albeit, falsely) imagine may be less comforting upon our return to our African homelands. We can also thank the media's history-long commitment to presenting Africa as a single war-torn country with levels of debilitating poverty and corruption that do little to further inspire us to buy a one-way plane ticket and relocate to the continent.*
- *Some of us may have moved to the West and experienced socioeconomic hardship and challenges that illustrate many migrants' struggles in a foreign country—unbeknownst to others who may believe that living outside of Africa is easy and reflects TV's "white picket fences" or episodes of "The Fresh Prince of Bel-Air." Little do they know that some of us struggle to stay afloat and confront prejudices of our host lands, seeking to make ends meet and support our families back in our African home countries.*
- *And then, there are those of us in the diaspora who desire a stake in the governance of our African homelands beyond merely sending remittances home. However, we may choose to self-censor our political voices to ensure safety.*

Yet, we strive to work through these conflicts and seek to remain connected to our African homelands because ultimately, we care about our "home".

So, in response to the earlier questions, "What are you? And where do you call 'home'?" I answer: I am a restless sojourner who balances on a global pendulum, creating new happy mediums that connect me to wherever I live now and African home lands—a mesh of all the worlds that I call home—although Africa remains my heart …

Objectives of the book

This book seeks to inspire, empower, challenge, and guide younger generations of students, scholars, and practitioners, particularly in the African diaspora, to contribute towards the development of their African home countries by placing emphasis on a critical approach.

More specifically, this book speaks to the younger generation of the African diaspora and future entrepreneurs, scholars, and practitioners that have a heart for Africa's development, but struggle to identify a starting point because of their unfamiliarity with their African home country ("I don't have a lay of the land so how do I start?"), or because they question the value of their cultural hybrid identities in Africa's development agenda ("I've been told I'm not African enough, so what's out there for me?").

These sentiments commonly articulate some of the diasporic identity experiences of belonging to multiple cultural worlds. While some diaspora have made peace with their "fluid" and "hybrid" cultural identities and proudly tick all the boxes or none of the boxes and tick "other," some still face potential "identity crises" that weaken their African national ties and dissuade them from fully participating in their African national development agenda. But articulating an African identity is challenging. Forces of colonial legacies, globalization, migration, and technology in the 21st century, which continuously alter, construct, and define African and African diaspora identities, present additional challenges. Another challenge is that numerous paradigms that have sought to explain and address diasporic cultural identities are normative and prescriptive, and fail to contextualize the realities and transnational experiences of ethnic and racial minority and underrepresented groups.

Hence, in light of these challenges, this book seeks to motivate the African diaspora to contribute towards or invest in their African home nation's development through a critical lens by

(i) drawing relations between cultural identities and their importance to Africa's development;
(ii) identifying some of Africa's top industries/growth sectors for the diaspora to explore, and adopting critical approaches in their pursuit of practical development opportunities they explore when collaborating with citizen-residents in Africa and other stakeholders;
(iii) addressing some challenges that potentially hinder the diaspora's role in their African homeland's national development and how to mitigate them;
(iv) proposing recommendations and guidelines for fostering an enabling environment and collaborative relationship-building between citizen-residents and the African diaspora.

Although there are various online and tangible resources that offer readers practical step-by-step guidelines of how to invest in or start entrepreneurial businesses in Africa, I learned early on in my journey that prior to seeking practical guidelines about entrepreneurism or contributing towards my African home country, I needed to have a "lay of the land," given my physical absence from on-the-ground realities in my identified African home countries. I also needed to confront the realities of my own relationship to my homeland. I often reiterated the same questions: What were my unique opportunities and unique challenges as a member of the diaspora community? What approach would I need to adopt to ensure that I was not perceived as a foreign investor whose intentions may be misunderstood, especially since I was expected to respect and loyally uphold some of the cultural norms of my African home country communities? How could I ensure that I was not a "part of the problem" and instead, a part of the solution? What did it mean for me to practically approach development in a way that was "we"-centric and not "I"-centric?

Hence, this book sets a foundation for its target African diaspora audiences at three levels. First, this book challenges them (the African diaspora in particular) to recognize how their identity impacts their approach towards development opportunities in Africa. Second, this book serves as a guidebook that offers audiences general but useful information on "lay of the land," on-the-ground realities across Africa's vast development scene. Third, this book equips its audiences with critical analytical thinking tools and recommendations, illustrated with case studies and examples, to guide how they may approach practical development opportunities in Africa.

The research methodological approach

Given the magnitude of this endeavor and the many layers of a topic that seeks to create a nexus between identity and development, I adopt a multi-methodological approach within and across different chapters. More specifically. I interweave exploratory, descriptive, explanatory, and critical research methodologies and approaches to fulfill the objectives outlined in this book.

As an *exploratory* study, I raise key issues and raise questions that unveil various tugs-of-war that may impact the African diaspora's role in contributing towards or investing in Africa's development agenda. I also introduce new angles from theoretical and application perspectives to help readers draw connections between topics of diasporic cultural identity and Africa's development to help improve their understanding of this complex phenomenon.

At times, I utilize a *descriptive approach* to further expand our understanding and provide greater clarity of the issues under investigation. I accomplish this by creating new sets of categories and classifications and adapting new models of community cultural wealth, relationship management frameworks, and other concepts to fill in missing parts of prior research, or by discovering more research to simulate new explanations surrounding the nexus of transcultural identity and development.

Other times, I delve into an *explanatory approach* that aims to provide a greater in-depth understanding of the phenomena. Therefore, I extend theories and concepts into new issues to explain cause-and-why dynamics and relationships, and I also draw connections to link various topics under common themes of diasporic identities, media representation and stereotypes, and other issues.

Lastly, I engage in a *critical approach* by adopting a critical lens that investigates the nexus between transnational or transcultural identity and Africa's development. Across various chapters, I engage in critical inquiries, adopt a critical autoethnography, adapt models and frameworks with critical perspectives (African diaspora community cultural wealth, relationship management theoretical framework), or employ other critical methods to question and challenge conventional and normative conceptual and theoretical frameworks, epistemologies, and methods that are assumed to be best practice standards, factual, or norms of the status quo. I inquire, examine, or expose hegemonic colonial strongholds that govern the realities that we take for granted in media, political dynamics, cultural clashes between the host and African homelands, and relational tensions between citizen-residents and the African diaspora.

Acknowledging the role of power and social position in phenomena, particularly within fields of knowledge production and dissemination, I attempt to reveal the sociohistorical context, present social critiques, and reveal critical meanings of the African diaspora's transnational or transcultural experiences as they relate to race, culture, class, and various forms of oppression that impact their identity formation. I also use a critical lens in my efforts to strengthen the nexus between migrants of African, diasporic, and transcultural identities and their role in Africa's development, particularly in the 21st century. While I present the conflicts and contradictions that characterize this phenomenon under investigation, I also present the emancipatory potential across various disciplines in an attempt to reverse inequalities, inequities and power imbalances that maintain the structural problem. Ultimately, the goal of this book is to liberate and empower those marginalized by social, cultural, and political forces of oppression to be pivotal, conscious actors, and change-agents with a critical role to play in Africa's development.

So this leads to another research question—a proverbial elephant in the room: How do I address the biases that may impact the research and perspectives in the book, given my role as a participant and researcher? I appreciate the perspective on the complexities of evidence-based qualitative research given by Thorne (2009), who asserts that (italicized in this book)

> Principally, that our challenge is not to try and convince that qualitative work reflects objective, opinion-free neutrality. *Rather, it is to better articulate the unique value that qualitatively derived knowledge can play within a system that measures impact through an evidence-based decision-making lens.* Although it may be more difficult to quantify the impact of qualitative research, we should resist the temptation to reach for a positivist tape measure to solve this problem. To do so will lead us to become apologists for the subjectivity that is the very strength of interpretive work.
>
> (Galdas, 2017, para. 12)

Throughout the book, I present my own self-reflexivities and consider the unique value of my own cultural lived experiences that shed a unique lens on a lesser-researched phenomenon. Some scholars have emphasized the urgent need to expand theories and epistemologies of global diaspora and international development studies that reflect perspectives of underrepresented ethnic and racial groups. In this book, I utilize my experiences and those of others as vital data that contribute knowledge and information and respond to gaps in broader bodies of work. The subjectivity that I present contributes to the strength of the interpretive work and attempts to respond to scholars' criticisms about insufficient representation or works from ethnic and racial groups in this particular space.

I also reduce the chances of participant and researcher bias in my interview with my participants of a preliminary study I conducted, before and during the interview process. I achieved this by soliciting feedback from a third party for unbiased opinions and by framing and structuring the interview skillfully.

Value propositions of the book

Diaspora studies have increasingly found their niche in academic literature, focusing primarily on our historical and cultural origins, roles in society, use of technology in constructing our identities, and the impact of our remittances in our home nations' development. Studies relating to migrants' intercultural communication have illustrated the diaspora's efforts to acculturate in foreign countries while striving to maintain our cultural ties with our birth origins. However, there are a few shortcomings and missed opportunities in the way diaspora studies are usually approached and presented to audiences, which I seek to address in this book.

Value #1: A transdisciplinary approach

Most diaspora studies limit their focus on diaspora works to one particular phenomenon, such as cultural identity, media imperialism, brain circulation, or political participation. But, given the fluid, porous intersectionalities that characterize diasporic subjects, more diaspora case studies should strive to integrate multiple themes within multi-methodological, transdisciplinary analyses. Such an approach would extract newer phenomena that diverse audiences could apply in their fields of expertise. Case in point: This book aims to integrate these multiple themes into a holistic, larger narrative that draws various connections. It draws connections between the diaspora's transcultural identities and relationships between their host country and homeland, as well as with their potential to effectively contribute towards international development, contextualized within Africa.

Value #2: Infusion of interdisciplinarity with critical theory

Second, greater emphasis is usually placed on descriptive, statistical, and methodological analyses of the phenomenology of the diaspora. Instead, more emphasis should be placed on developing more critical inquiry in diaspora studies in rarely discussed contexts. Such inquiry should also combine theoretical and practical implications to develop data-driven solutions that can be implemented at the micro and macro levels of society to address contemporary challenges. Case in point: This book interweaves various critical theories within pragmatic, interdisciplinary discussions of the diaspora's roles in business, sociocultural, economic, and political development in Africa. Ultimately, such infusions increase our breadth and depth of understanding of the complex diaspora phenomenon and expand our "emancipatory worldview [to] include vital human agency and creativity" (Sumner, 2003, p. 4). Sumner (2003) also emphasized that

> The infusion of interdisciplinarity with critical theory can create a kind of critical interdisciplinarity that is powerful enough to address crucial global issues. Interdisciplinarity itself opens up "new, hybrid spaces" (Massey, 1999, p. 5) such as cultural studies or rural studies. Looking at interdisciplinarity relationally adds the potential of negotiation between these new, hybrid spaces and traditional disciplines. Fusing a critical perspective onto this relational interdisciplinarity gives it the license, one might say, to use

> these new, hybrid spaces to critically investigate complex contemporary issues. Two of those issues—globalization and sustainability—can illustrate this idea (p. 8).

Indeed, we address how factors related to globalization further shape the African diaspora's cultural hybrid identities and their roles in contributing towards Africa's sustainable development in the global economy.

Value #3: Practical guide and overview of Africa's growth sectors and industries

Third, I—like many diaspora brethren and sistren I have met—have also felt frustrated in my unsatisfactory attempts to identify information hubs, resources, or advice to guide my efforts to actively contribute more towards the development of my African homeland. This book, therefore, includes a repository of an overview of Africa's growth sectors and industries—a "lay of the land." It also includes general guidelines, tips, and approaches from entrepreneurs, citizen-residents, and active change-agents in the African community to guide an approach to investing in or contributing towards Africa's development.

Value #4: Newer explorations between the African diaspora and citizen-residents in Africa

Fourth, the book introduces a less-discussed phenomenon of inquiry in African studies: the relationship between Africans living in Africa and Africans living in the diaspora. While some romanticize an ideal that seeks to unify a pan-African, Black identity collective, there are differences that exist within peoples of African descent that may cause tension, or even fragment their relationships with each other. This reality should also be considered, especially if it holds global implications that may affect their ability to collaborate towards a region's development.

Hence, this book presents the findings of a preliminary study I conducted in the course of writing this book that sought to explore the perceptions between citizen-residents in Africa and Africans in the diaspora. These perceptions serve as a baseline for a future robust in-depth study on revealing their relationships and how they could be managed effectively towards their joint efforts in African nations' development.

Value #5: Discussion questions with self-reflexive and transdisciplinary objectives

Fifth, I present discussion questions at the end of each chapter of the first three units to promote in-depth understandings of real-world global development issues. To address the complex dynamics of the 21st century, some discussion questions encourage readers' self-reflexivity. Their self-reflexivities may be useful, as they conduct independent research projects through the lens of policy makers, researchers, government officials, entrepreneurs, and other roles that comprise the key stakeholders in Africa's burgeoning and vivid development scene.

Other questions reflect transdisciplinary objectives that challenge readers to implement various disciplines in problem-solving and develop innovative, cross-cutting solutions. Hence, students may simulate real-life experiences when collaborating across teams on case-study workshops.

Ultimately, students of diverse backgrounds and professional disciplines are encouraged to read this book together. For instance, there is great value in creating teams comprised of business, healthcare, engineering, art, journalism, and history professionals who may collaborate together and adapt newly discovered skills to critical problem-solving. Such an approach seeks to fulfill the transdisciplinary objectives that stem from an integration of their unique backgrounds, competencies, and professional experiences.

Value #6: Author is representative of the target audience

Another value that is important to acknowledge is that I, personally, am also a target audience of the information I researched and am disseminating. I seek to assist individuals who desire to contribute towards their nation's welfare but have not resided in an African country for years, and whose diasporic identity is further influenced by transcultural and transnational experiences and upbringing. Many in this position seek an overview, or "lay of the land" to know where to begin!

So, I structured the objectives of the book around personal questions that I also framed as a checklist:

- If I wanted to anticipate potential outcomes of my re-acculturation experience in an African country, or if I sought guidance on how to leverage my competencies and skills towards Africa's development while residing in my host country, would this book offer me any guidance?
- If I wanted to know the growth industries and sectors in Africa and sought some ideas for how to get involved or issues to be mindful of, would this book assist me in that endeavor?
- If I needed tips on building relationships and networks with citizen-residents at home, would this book inform me of what to expect, including any potential forms of resistance, biases, and complexes to be mindful of?
- And *after* I read this book, would this book position me to think critically about my roles and intentions in investing in and contributing towards Africa's development? More specifically, would I be encouraged to think about being socially and ethically conscious in my efforts towards contributing towards development?

In my pursuit of authenticity and representation, I seek to humanize and pragmatize the complex phenomenon of Africa's development and the roles that various stakeholders can play.

Value #7: Contribution to Africa's knowledge economy and critical scholarship

This leads to the final value proposition. In writing this book to (i) motivate the African diaspora to invest in and contribute towards Africa's development with (ii) a critical lens and (iii) to engage with and collaborate with citizen-residents in Africa, I, too, was doing the same all along! This book is (i) a *knowledge product* about the African diaspora's roles in Africa's development and contributes towards the knowledge economy of Africa, (ii) *written with a critical lens and (iii) by a member of the African diaspo*ra who also *engaged with other Africans in the diaspora and citizen-residents in Africa.*

Also representing the emancipatory potential of critical scholarship, this book privileges the authentic voices of diverse Africans who have historically been misrepresented, underrepresented, or spoken for by others in subject matters on various platforms.

Given that the goal of this book is to motivate the African diaspora to invest in or contribute towards their nations' development, I came to a surprising revelation that in the making of this book, I was "walking the talk" and putting my words in practice!

Characterizing the "African diaspora" in this book

Terms such as *diaspora* and *migration* are merely a few of the terms closely associated with this phenomenon. However, the precise definition of the term *diaspora* remains controversial, as various historical, political, economic and/or social conditions account for different characterizations of the dispersals of unique groups. This book refers to Blunt's (2003) conceptualization of the term as both a construct of geography and self-identity:

> The term "diaspora" is inherently geographical, implying a scattering of people over space and transnational connections between people and places. Geography clearly lies at the heart of diaspora both as a concept and as lived experience, encompassing the contested interplay of place, home, culture and identity through migration and resettlement,
>
> (Rios & Adiv, 2010, p. 2; Blunt, 2003, p. 282)

Closely associated with the historical dispersion of the Jewish people who were exiled from Israel, the term *diaspora* has expanded since the 1960s to include various ethnic groups and broader dispersals. Today, *diaspora* refers to "expatriates, expellees, political refugees, alien residents, immigrants and ethnic and rational minorities" (Hickman, 2005, p. 119).

Rios and Adiv (2010) review literature and the evolution of various scholars' use of the term diaspora, which they classify in frameworks within and outside the scope of geographical contexts. Various scholars, including Saffran (1991),

Cohen (1997), Vertovek (1999), and Butler (2001) have expanded the realm of the meaning of *diaspora* to include "collective mythology of homeland" (Rios & Adiv, 2010, p. 3); consistent relationship with the homeland; collective trauma; affiliation to nation-states through social, cultural, and economic ties; type of consciousness; mode of cultural production; and more (Rios & Adiv, 2010).

Complementary to the notion of the diaspora is the term, transnationalism—another term with no universally agreed definition. However, Tedeschi et al. (2020) identified some key common variables that 'transnationalism' conveys:

> type of actors involved (organisations or private citizens); the type of activities (sociocultural, economic, political); the degree of integration/segregation; the degree of cosmopolitanism (whether the actors involved have built meaningful connections with more than two countries, rather than only with the country of origin and the current host country); the degree of emotional belonging (to what extent the individuals feel that they belong to one rather than another country); and the degree/intensity of connections with the home (or other) country.
>
> (Tedeschi et al., 2020, p. 6)

As such, Tedeschi et al. (2020) propose that transnationalism can best be described as such:

> transnationalism "from below" (from the viewpoint of individuals and civil society) concerns cross-border (sociocultural, political, and/or economic) activities, practices, and behaviours that are meaningful, affect the identity and sense of belonging of people, and are carried out on a regular (not exceptional) basis in the everyday lives of individuals—even though this latter criterion can be questioned.
>
> (Tedeschi et al., 2020, p. 13)

Ultimately, this postmodern paradigm highlights a dynamic state of negotiations and seeming contradictions that accompany a borderless, unfixed, hybrid identity that transgresses physical boundaries of nationalism and ethnicity. This is a departure from Edward Said's binary divisions of identity as being either "Occidental" or "Oriental," depicting the separation of the Western and Eastern worlds, respectively. Closely connected to the postmodern paradigm of cultural hybridity is Homi Bhabha's notion of the "third space"— an "in-between," interstitial, liminal space of colliding cultures. According to Homi Bhabha, "the process of cultural hybridity gives rise to something different, something new and unrecognizable, a new area of negotiation of meaning and representation" (Rutherford, 1990, p. 211).

Significantly, Werbner (2000) criticizes the diaspora typologies and classifications that limit discussions to either a diaspora's ethno-relational connections or diasporic dualities (Hickman, 2005, p. 120). "The challenge is 'to disclose how the tension between these two tendencies is played out in actual situations'" (Hickman, 2005, p. 120; Werbner, 2000, p. 5).

This book illustrates some of the various tensions, or tugs-of-war, which stem from the cultural hybrid identities and dualities that the African diaspora possess and how these tensions are manifested in their desire or ability to contribute towards Africa's development agenda.

It is also important to recognize the spectrum of diversity and range of experiences that exist within any diaspora group or any cultural community. The diaspora is not a monolithic group; neither are Africans. Although I use the general terms *African diaspora, citizen-residents*, or *Africa* to specify that the scope of the target groups or locale under investigation is of the African continent, I also acknowledge the multiplicity and plurality of experiences and cultural connotations that cannot be generalized to a homogenic "African diaspora," "African citizen-resident," or the African continent. I am aware that there are unique variations that speak to specific regions, cultural groups, and countries across Africa and of her diaspora.

Furthermore, Mitchell (1997) observes that "some authors take issue with what they see as an idealization of a type, and call for grounding notions of transnationalism in the actual experiences of migrating people" (Rios & Adiv, 2010, p. 4; Mitchell, 1997a). Staeheli et al. (2002) also observe that terms like *transnational* and *transnationalism* seem limited to academia, and are not used by immigrants or service providers (Rios & Adiv, 2010). As such, this book is largely inspired by my own unique experiences as a Third Culture Kid (TCK) and those of others whose similar backgrounds and experiences may reflect commonalities of our "hybrid, transgressive or translocal" nature (Rios & Adiv, 2010, p. 4). This book also grounds notions of transnationalism, transculturalism, diaspora, identity, and development in the actual experiences shared by other African diaspora and citizen-residents in Africa who participated in interviews for this book.

Migration patterns of the African diaspora in this book: An overview

The African diaspora that are targeted in this book are those that emigrated from Africa between the 20th and 21st centuries. Migration in the 20th century characterized the period of the decolonization of Africa or resulting African independence movements when numerous African countries gained independence from their former British and other European colonies. The struggle for African countries to gain political stability and economic growth in their new independent states reinforced a surge of emigration within and from Africa. Up until the 21st century, various drivers of globalization, such as employment, the internationalization of education, conflict, war and postcolonial or neocolonial ties account for continued migration patterns.

In 2012, the World Bank estimated the global, continental dispersion of the African diaspora to be 39 million in North America; 113 million in Latin America; 13.6 million in the Caribbean; and 3.5 million in Europe (Kajunju, 2013, para. 3).

More specifically, the United States witnessed an increase of African immigrants from 80,000 in 1970 to 881,000 in 2000 and about 2.1 million in 2015, accounting for "4.8% of the U.S. immigrant population in 2015, up from 0.8% in 1970" (Anderson, 2017, para. 2). In a comparative analysis of other major groups that arrived in the United States between 2012 and 2017, the growth rate for African emigration increased the fastest from 2000 to 2013 by 41% (Anderson, 2017, para. 3). By 2018 81 percent of sub-Saharan Africans in the United States came from Eastern and Western Africa (Echeverria-Estrada & Batalova, 2018). As of 2018, "Nigeria, Ethiopia, Ghana, and Kenya and Somolia comprised the top five sending countries, accounting for 54% of the foreign-born sub-Saharan African population in the United States" (Echeverria-Estrada & Batalova, 2018, para. 4).

However, Flahaux and De Haas (2016) caution that African migration patterns—particularly from Sub-Saharan Africa to Maghreb and Europe—have been erroneously reported and fueled by assumptions and journalistic sensationalism on the part of the media, politicians, and scholars. These contribute to various misleading narratives about African migration patterns, including that they are higher and more irregular than that of other groups; a source of international terrorism; prone to be erratic and must be managed through stricter immigrant policies and border controls; and the result of development failures that must be remedied through foreign aid and remittances (Flahaux & De Haas, 2016).

To illustrate these misconceptions, Flahaux and De Haas (2016) cite numerous scholars' works and empirical evidence to argue that African migration patterns are not irregular—there is actually more intracontinental African migration than extracontinental migration. Furthermore, in addition to migrating to the Gulf, the Americas, and the United Kingdom, Africans migrate extracontinentally with valid travel documentation (Flahaux & De Haas, 2016). Lastly, micro-evidence also indicates that the search for improved lifestyle, family, education, and work is the major driver of African migration as poverty and conflict are (Flahaux & De Haas, 2016).

The emergence of newer databases—albeit with limitations—may facilitate the analysis of more comprehensive migration patterns. Additional factors that shape migration patterns include people's aspirations and capabilities; nations' political processes, which result in visa restrictive policies; structural development trends; and desirable immigration opportunities in new destinations like the United States, Canada, and Australia that are akin to those of former colonial powers (Flahaux & De Haas, 2016).

To delve into analyses of various African migration patterns would go beyond the scope of this book. Despite the different migration patterns that may characterize the unique backgrounds of any member of the African diaspora of specific nations, my focus is to address the African diaspora's collective outcome: leveraging their resulting cultural hybrid identities to serve effectively as change-agents in their collaborations with citizen-residents in Africa and various stakeholders in contribution towards Africa's sustainable development.

Conceptualizing the "African diaspora" in this book

Amongst a highly contested debate amongst scholars is a universally agreed-upon conceptualization of the term *African diaspora*, especially when examined through various racial and political ideologies and theoretical and historical constructs. The emergence of the African diaspora can be traced to several time periods or waves in history, depending on the scope and goals of discourse. Of the most commonly discussed is the involuntary emigration of 25–30 million Africans predominantly from Western and Central Africa to the Americas, the Caribbean, and Europe between the 1500s and 1830s in the transatlantic (triangular) slave trade (UNESCO.org). Descendants of these slaves comprise the global dispersion of African-American or Black American, Caribbean, Afro-European, Afro-Latin American, or Black Latin American populations that are generally regarded as part of the Black or African diaspora.

In this book, however, the conceptualization of the term *African diaspora* and any related phrase(s) addressing Africans in the diaspora, narrows its scope to three fundamental, interrelated features:

1) It is inclusive of those originating in both Sub-Saharan Africa and northern African countries;
2) It refers to migrants and/or the descendants of migrants who emigrated voluntarily to any region outside of the African continent between the 20th and 21st centuries. These migrants include but are not limited to professionals, students, refugees, exhibit diverse backgrounds and a plethora of skill sets and educational levels, and
3) It is adapted partially from the definition used by the African Union (AU), a continental union that seeks to promote sustainable development, democratic governance, peace, and solidarity in Africa through the economic, political and sociocultural, integration of its 55 countries and their peoples. As of 2005, the AU's working definition of the African diaspora is "peoples of African descent and heritage living outside the continent, irrespective of their citizenship, and who remain committed to contribute to the development of the continent and the building of the African Union" (Africa Union, 2018, para. 3).

Underscoring the third feature above, this book particularly addresses the African diaspora who desire and intend to contribute towards or invest in their African homeland. Hence, the discussions related to decolonization, diasporic cultural identity, and re-acculturation (Unit 1); an overview of growth sectors in Africa to consider for development (Unit 2); challenges they may confront that may potentially hinder their endeavors (Unit 3); and tips and guidelines to consider in pursuit of development (Unit 4) all rest on the premise that the African diaspora desire and yearn to connect with, invest in, and contribute towards their African home country's development agenda.

Occasionally, the phrase *in the diaspora* may also be used in the book to generally represent the conceptual space or territory of residence outside of the African home country.

Conceptualizing "citizen-resident" Africans in this book

In addition to the African diaspora, the book will also refer to another group of Africans that are essential in Africa's development agenda: citizen-residents in Africa. The term *citizen-residents in Africa* will be used to identify national citizens of an African country who also reside in their home country, and may not necessarily have permanently migrated to or left their homeland. This term also refers to those that have made their African home country their home base, but may still conduct business globally, operating from their African home country as permanent residents.

The distinction between the African diaspora and citizen-residents in Africa is particularly significant when discussing their relationships and opportunities for collaboration or strategic partnership in Africa's development.

The following section presents an overview of African migration patterns that contextualize the emergence of the African diaspora that have been conceptualized in this book.

The structure of the book

Structured into four units, this book is organized to reflect the tug-of-war journey of the target audience who (i) seeks validation that their diasporic or transcultural identities give them license to contribute towards or invest in Africa's development agenda; (ii) desires to get a sense of the "lay of the land" and wants to explore possible entry points across Africa's different sectors and industries; (iii) confronts internal and external challenges that may dissuade them from pursuing development opportunities in Africa; and (iv) seeks guidelines, tips, and first-hand account experiences from industry experts and those on the ground who are actively contributing to Africa's development agenda.

Each chapter presents some key concepts, theoretical frameworks and terms, case studies, industry experts' insights or personal anecdotes to further contextualize the chapter. Furthermore, each chapter in Units 1–3 also ends with a chapter review of key concepts and practical discussion questions that encourage readers to conduct additional research and collaborate with others towards problem-solving.

The last unit (Unit 4) highlights findings of a study I conducted with citizen-residents and the African diaspora to gain first-hand accounts of their experiences with development and to explore the dynamics of their relationship to strengthen their collaboration in nation-building efforts.

Below is a breakdown of the units and chapters:

Unit 1: Exploring the nexus of national and cultural identities and development in Africa

This unit introduces the complex dimensions of cultural diasporic identities with a focus on the African diaspora and its relevance in Africa's development agenda. In Chapter 1, "Diaspora's Identity "Crises": War of the Paradigms," I introduce some of the debates surrounding some normative cultural and diasporic identity theories and concepts that are grounded in Eurocentric ideologies. I also illustrate how alternative paradigms such as Southern theory—particularly decoloniality—exemplify a useful approach to exploring African diasporic identities and other complexes, transnational experiences of minority ethnic, racial, and cultural groups. I also argue that alternative paradigms may innovatively contribute towards transdisciplinary approaches, relating to citizenry, nationhood, and identity and socioeconomic, political, and cultural development.

In Chapter 2, "The African Diaspora, The African Personality, and an African Human Development Paradigm: Exploring Their Nexus," I explore how some scholars, philosophers, and African political thought leaders have conceptualized the African identity or *African Personality* and have acknowledged its vitality in developing Africa. I draw connections between the African Personality and its relevance for the African diaspora's role in contributing towards Africa's development, particularly when applied to a human development paradigm.

In Chapter 3, "The African Diaspora Community Cultural Wealth Model (ADCCWM): A Proposal to Leverage the Cultural Capital of the African Diaspora in Development," I address a misconception that by virtue of their hybrid identities, the African diaspora may inherently suffer cultural deficiencies that result in their limited ability to contribute towards their African countries' development agenda. As a result, some organizations in the host or African home countries may fail to effectively leverage the diaspora's competencies and integrate them in community or national development agendas, or may exclude African diaspora from decision-making opportunities that may, otherwise, benefit from their input. Therefore, I adapt Yosso's (2005) concept of community cultural wealth, originally coined by Daniel G. Solórzano, and introduce the African Diaspora Community Cultural Wealth framework (ADCCW) to propose ways to leverage the various forms of cultural capital that the African diaspora already possess and effectively implement them within Africa's development agenda.

Unit 2: Exploring development opportunities in Africa: The brain circulation phenomenon and growth sectors and industries in Africa

This unit targets those who seek value in learning more about each of the different sectors, their growth trends in key countries, and any guidelines or observations to consider in how to approach the industry. In Chapter 4,

"Migration Postulates: Brain Drain, Brain Gain, Brain Circulation," I introduce the brain circulation phenomenon as one of the newer migration postulates to have evolved from the brain drain–brain gain dynamic. The African diaspora leverage the brain circulation phenomenon to maintain socioeconomic, political, and cultural ties with their homelands as they reside in their host countries and contribute to their African nations' development.

However, some diaspora who are interested in maintaining these ties may be unfamiliar with some of the on-the-ground realities that would be valuable to inform them of ways to participate in their nations' welfare. It is also difficult to identify information hubs that could inform the diaspora about some of Africa's growth sectors to inform their decision-making in investments and opportunities to contribute towards nation-building in their African home country. Hence, Chapters 5 through 8 attempt to fulfill one goal of this book: to present a one-stop shop or repository that identifies some of the top-performing industries and sectors driving growth in Africa.

To achieve this, I categorize each of the industries and growth sectors that share commonalities to facilitate any cross-references for analyses, especially when discussing the impact of the Covid-19 pandemic. Chapter 5, "An Overview of Growth Sectors and Industries in Africa—Part I: Exploring Industrialization," discusses industrialization, with a focus on agriculture and agribusiness (with a subcategory of food and gastronomy), startup funding, fintech, and telecommunications; Chapter 6, "An Overview of Growth Sectors and Industries in Africa—Part II: Exploring Infrastructure," addresses infrastructure, with a focus on economic infrastructure (energy, transport, water/sanitation, extractive industries) and social infrastructure (healthcare, pharmacy, and education); Chapter 7, "An Overview of Growth Sectors and Industries in Africa—Part III: Exploring the Creative and Cultural Economy," discusses the creative and culture economies (music, film, fashion, apparel, retail, luxury, and sports); and Chapter 8, "An Overview of Growth Sectors and Industries in Africa—Part IV: Exploring Leisure and Hospitality," explores leisure and hospitality (tourism and real-estate industries).

Each of these chapters provides a snapshot of relevant data, current trends, breakthroughs, and developments, illustrated with examples from various African countries. When relevant, I also interweave critical theories, concepts, or inquiries in my observation of industry trends to prompt readers to consider alternative ways they may support Africa's development. Hence, I also offer suggestions and recommendations within each sector or industry to help the new diaspora entrepreneur consider new startups or investment opportunities in collaboration with citizen-residents on the ground.

Lastly, each sector concludes with a discussion of how it has been impacted by the Covid-19 pandemic. Viewpoints and valuable insight from entrepreneurs or industry experts are also shared throughout the sections, including those with whom I conducted interviews for the purpose of this book.

Unit 3: Challenges and conundra for the African diaspora in approaching development in Africa

The African diaspora confront several challenges that may affect their desire or ability to effectively contribute to their nations' development. In Chapter 9, "Managing Cultural Conundrums 101: Cultural Shifts, Cultural Contracts, Cultural Clash!" I explore the "double-edged sword" of the diaspora's hybrid identities that may result in cultural clashes between their African country's indigenous cultures and Western cultures. At times, the African diaspora's perceived "Whiteness" may even result in cultural misconceptions with some citizen-residents in their African home country who may question their authenticity and intentions. This chapter explains some of the cultural identity shifts, cultural contract types, coping mechanisms, and cultural clashes the African diaspora may experience in their re-acculturation processes upon re-entry into their African home countries from the West.

In Chapter 10, "The Miseducation of the African Diaspora by Western Media," I present a critical autoethnography of my own experience with Western media and its influence on my approach towards Africa's development. I relate my experience to other studies to draw a link between media framing and its potential to shape identities and self-concepts, influence investment decisions, and affect relationship-building between key stakeholders—all of which potentially impact Africa's development. In Chapter 11, "It's Not Just Politics ... Or Is It? Engaging the African Diaspora in Africa's Political Affairs," I introduce some of the challenges surrounding political dynamics that may affect the African diaspora's decisions to participate politically in their home countries.

Unit 4: Recommendations and tips for development in Africa

In this unit, I uncover some of the findings of a preliminary, co-orientational analytical study I conducted in the course of writing this book to assess some sentiments that may characterize the relationships between citizen-residents in African countries and the African diaspora. I also reveal some of their insights in collaborating towards developing Africa.

In Chapter 12, "Relationship Status: 'It's Complicated'—Addressing Relational Dynamics between the African Diaspora and Citizen-Residents in Africa," I unearth some of the misunderstandings and misperceptions between some African diaspora and citizen-residents in Africa that may complicate their collaboration towards nation-building, as well as their proposed strategies towards developing resolutions. In Chapter 13, "Relationship-Management Theory: Harnessing Relationships between the African Diaspora and Key Stakeholders to Motivate the Diaspora to Invest in or Contribute towards their Nations' Development," I explore how policy makers could implement critical analytical frameworks that incorporate cultural lenses to effectively engage the African diaspora in their African home nations. Specifically, I introduce my proposed alteration of the relationship-management theoretical framework from my 2015 case study to assess and manage relationships between the African diaspora, citizen-residents, or other designated organization-public relationships in the context of national development.

In Chapter 14, "Guidelines and Recommendations to Foster African Diaspora Engagement with their African Homelands," I present additional findings of the study I conducted in writing this book, which offers recommendations and guidelines to strengthen networks and promote collaborations between the African diaspora and citizen-residents. I also present recommendations for fostering an enabling environment that promotes investments, entrepreneurial opportunities, and contributions from the African diaspora towards Africa's development.

I conclude the book with Chapter 15, "A Critical Road Ahead in Africa's Development: Reflexive Highlights and a Call for Pan-Africanism?" This chapter reflects on notable requisites for Africa's development, based on recurrent themes emerging throughout the chapters. I also reflect on the significance of what I dub the "Year of 2020" in the context of pan-Africanism and Africa's development. The Year of 2020 introduced the global Covid-19 pandemic, which revealed racial and ethnic systemic health and social disparities within countries and across the globe. Furthermore, global protests against police brutality and racism forced nations to confront their legacies of colonialism and governance. Africans on the African continent and across the broader diaspora relied on solidarity and allyship collaborators to support their communities' welfare in their host country and in their African homelands. Ultimately, in light of these illuminations of the Year 2020, I leave audiences to ponder: Would a pan-African approach be relevant in transforming paradigms to catapult Africa's development to newer levels of success in the 21st century and ahead?

So welcome ... our transnational journey begins!

References

Anderson, M. (2017, February 14). *African immigrant population in U.S. steadily climbs*. Pew Research Center. https://www.pewresearch.org/fact-tank/2017/02/14/african-immigrant-population-in-u-s-steadily-climbs/

Blunt, A. (2003). Geographies of diaspora and mixed descent: Anglo-Indians in India and Britain. *International Journal of Population Geography*, *9*(1), 281–294.

Butler, K. (2001). Defining diaspora, refining a discourse. *Diaspora*, *10*(1), 189–220.

Cohen, R. (1997). *Global diasporas: An introduction*. London: UCL Press.

Echeverria-Estrada, C., & Batalova, J. (2019, November 6). Sub-Saharan African Immigrants in the United States. https://www.migrationpolicy.org/article/sub-saharan-african-immigrants-united-states-2018.

Flahaux, M. L., & De Haas, H. (2016). African migration: Trends, patterns, drivers. *CMS*, *4*(1), 1. doi:10.1186/s40878-015-0015-6

Galdas, P. (2017). Revisiting bias in qualitative research. *International Journal of Qualitative Methods*, *16*(1), 160940691774899. doi:10.1177/1609406917748992

Hickman, M. (2005). Migration and diaspora. In: J. Cleary & C. Connolly (Eds.), *The Cambridge Companion to Modern Irish Culture* (Cambridge Companions to Culture, pp. 117–136). Cambridge: Cambridge University Press. doi:10.1017/CCOL052182009X.007

Kajunju, B. S. A. T. C. (2013, November 1). Africa's secret weapon: The diaspora. *CNN.* https://edition.cnn.com/2013/11/01/opinion/africas-secret-weapon-diaspora/index.html

Massey, D. (1999). Negotiating disciplinary boundaries. *Current Sociology*, *47*(4), 5–12.

Mitchell, K. (1997a). Transnational discourse: Bringing geography back in. *Antipode*, *29*(2), 101–114.

Rios, M., & Adiv, N. (2010). *Geographies of Diaspora: A Review.* Davis, CA: UC Davis Center for Regional Change

Rutheford, J. (1990). The third space. Interview with Homi Bhabha. In J. Rutherford (Ed.), *Identity: Community, Culture, Difference* (pp. 207–221). London: Lawrence & Wishart.

Safran, W. (1991). Diasporas in modern societies: Myths of homeland and return. *Diaspora*, *1*(1), 83–89.

Staeheli, L. A., Ledwith, V., Ormond, M., Reed, K., Sumpter, A., & Trudeau, D. (2002). Immigration, the internet, and spaces of politics. *Political Geography*, *21*(1), 989–1012.

Sumner, J. (2003). Relations of suspicion: Critical theory and interdisciplinary research. *History of Intellectual Culture*, *3*(1), 1–12. https://core.ac.uk/download/pdf/328007624.pdf

Tedeschi, M., Vorobeva, E., & Jauhiainen, J. S. (2020, August 9). Transnationalism: Current debates and new perspectives. *GeoJournal.* doi:10.1007/s10708-020-10271-8

The Diaspora Division (2018). Africa Union. https://au.int/en/diaspora-division#:%7E:text=The%20African%20Union%20defines%20the,constitutive%20act%20declare

Thorne, S. (2009). The role of qualitative research within an evidence-based context: Can metasynthesis be the answer? *International Journal of Nursing Studies*, *46*(4), 569–575. doi:10.1016/j.ijnurstu.2008.05.001

Vertovec, S. (1999). Three meanings of diaspora, exemplified by South Asian religions. *Diaspora*, *6*(3), 3–36.

Werbner, P. (2000). Introduction: The materiality of diaspora—Between aesthetic and "real" politics. *Diaspora: A Journal of Transnational Studies*, *9*(1), 5–20. doi:10.1353/dsp.2000.0010

Yosso, T. J. (2005). Whose culture has capital? A critical race theory discussion of community cultural wealth. *Race Ethnicity and Education*, *8*(1), 69–91. doi:10.1080/1361332052000341006

Unit 1

This unit introduces the complex dimensions of cultural diasporic identities with focus on the African diaspora. In Chapter 1, I introduce some of the debates surrounding some normative cultural and diasporic identity theories and concepts, as well as illustrating how alternative paradigms such as Southern theory—particularly decoloniality—exemplify a useful approach to exploring African diasporic identities and other complex, transnational experiences of minority ethnic, racial and cultural groups. I argue that alternative paradigms may innovatively integrate transdisciplinary fields, relating to citizenry, nationhood, identity, and socioeconomic, political, and cultural development.

In Chapter 2, I explore how some scholars, philosophers, and African political thought leaders have conceptualized the African identity, or *African Personality*, and acknowledged its vitality in developing Africa. I draw connections between the African Personality and its relevance for the African diaspora's role in contributing towards Africa's development, particularly when applied towards a human development paradigm.

In Chapter 3, I explore how the African diaspora may effectively leverage various forms of cultural capital in their pursuit of development opportunities in their African homeland as a result of their diasporic identities that grant them a laissez-passer between their host countries and African homelands.

DOI: 10.4324/9781351031660-1

1 Diaspora's identity "crises"

War of the paradigms

Migrations of Africans within and outside of Africa—particularly in the 21st century—have resulted in newly formed communities and newer cultural and political identifications with their new, host countries. Meanwhile, the consequent emergence of multiple and hybrid identities of Africans continue to reconfigure the face and identity of Africa and her descendants. These reconfigurations may impact their ties to Africa and connectivity to issues central to Africa's development. While buzzword concepts and theories like "multiculturalism," "interculturalism," and "superdiversity" have dominated much of the field of global and cultural studies for decades, they have been contested for being prescriptive and failing to articulate the unique, complex transnational experiences of underrepresented, "minority" diasporic ethnic, racial, and cultural groups.

This chapter will introduce some of the debates surrounding some normative cultural and diasporic identity theories and concepts and will offer an alternative theoretical approach towards characterizing African diasporic identities. It is important to identify new alternative paradigms and theories that speak to the unique ontological frameworks and epistemologies of people of African descent. New knowledge systems that support new frameworks, models, research designs, and methods may lead us closer to predicting, explaining, and understanding complex behaviors of diverse ethnic and racial cultural groups of African descent in various contexts, including development.

Triggered by an internal struggle

I will never forget that day in 1995 when on summer vacation in Uganda when a few strangers on the street fondly told me that I look like a "nigger." I immediately learned that their use of the term "nigger" was equivalent to "nigga," which I learned that they equated to "Black American." But why was I taken aback? After all, they had offered me a compliment and form of praise. Someone eventually explained to me: I did not come across as a Ugandan because of my alleged American accent and "look"—despite the fact that I was born in Uganda to Ugandan parents. I realized that some Africans back home did not distinguish between "nigger" and "nigga," as the term "nigga" had become embraced, acknowledged, and understood as a term of endearment and self-acceptance

DOI: 10.4324/9781351031660-2

and a communal identifier by some African-Americans, which was also prevalent and shared amongst masses across media platforms, including music, and TV/film. For some who appropriated the word and did not acknowledge the history of the term, or who were unaware of the controversial debate of who was permitted to use "nigga" versus "nigger," it was a term that was supposed to be endearing to me in that context. Why? Because I was an outsider—a foreigner, and specifically an "American"—which apparently carried valuable social capital in that particular locale. In their minds, they complimented me. But I remember thinking in that moment, their casual reference to me as a "nigger" had insulted me—and themselves. And how ironic that my African community had called me a "nigger."

Fast forward to my freshman year of college at the University of North Carolina at Chapel Hill, I was assigned a "minority" advisor—in addition to the undergraduate "general" advisor. At first, I jokingly concluded that my "minority" label was attributed to my status as a freshman—a label that I believed I would discard by my sophomore year—at latest, my junior year. Hence, I misunderstood the hesitation of my Caucasian suitemates when I suggested they also "adopt" my minority advisor as theirs because she was pretty cool. Finally, a suitemate exasperatedly told me, "Stella-Monica, we can't have minority advisors. The reason you have a minority advisor is because you're Black." And just like that, my "Blackness" hit me like a ton of bricks. In typical Spike Lee film style, an imaginary camera zoomed into my face and I was officially baptized, "Black in America." Now, don't get me wrong—I always knew I was Black. But somehow, being Black as it was pronounced for me in America reflected a different texture and shade from what I already knew my Blackness to be in Africa.

And then, a third significant Black pronouncement and self-identification hit me again during my first Masters program. This time an Asian international student tried to compliment me for being "different from most Black people." She found comfort in that I was "articulate," "proper," and "relatable," and she appreciated feeling that she could "talk to me." Again, another compliment attempt gone sour.

Over the years, I have come to acknowledge that my identity carried various connotations that required context. Little did I know that every year in America would further enrich my knowledge of my complex identity and present me with diverse shades, hues, and saturations of the terms "Black," "transculturalism," and "diaspora" over the next 20 years. I am proudly Black because of the pigment of my skin. I am proudly Black because I share many experiences that accompany the rich history of my skin color with others globally who share the same Black melanin. But which variable I chose to first identify with varied, depending on who I was around. Sometimes I do not identify as "Black" first. I may self-identify first as "African." For most of my life, I self-identified as "Ugandan-Ivorian." Honestly, depending on my locale or mood, I would also just identify as being from the last state or city in the USA I lived in, e.g. "New York" or "Los Angeles"—which also spared me lengthy chit chats with inquisitive minds if I was moody! But technically, it was always more accurate to just identify as "foreigner." Despite having lived in America for 20 years, I only more recently started to self-define as "African/African-American" or "American"—only because I still feel like a foreigner in a country that I have spent the majority of my life in. And I accepted that no matter what country I travel or return to, I will always be a foreigner. But yet, I felt that

America was my home. As was anywhere in Africa. And when I travel around the world in Europe, Asia, or South America, I also quickly feel a sense of "home" because there is an immediate nostalgic familiarity in the language, expressions, or culture that mirrored how I grew up and the international networks that are my family. When I meet anyone in the world from any walk in life, we connect quickly—there is a part of "me" I see in their world and they in my world.

Because I am foreigner everywhere, the world is my home anywhere ... and Africa is my heart ...

The clash of diasporic identity theories

An overview of "classic" diasporic identity theories and concepts

As Africans are further "removed" from their homelands of origin and gravitate towards the diaspora, there is a sense that their African identity becomes more "diluted." Apparently, their identity becomes increasingly "concentrated" with more other cultural influences. This reinforces the debate that the impact of globalization further results in serious personality and identity crises for the individual and the collective people of a region. These crises, arguably, aggravate the ability for a diasporic African to develop a political, economic, or social consciousness about his or her African home country. In so doing, some admit to or are accused of losing their "African card" or "Black card" and are perceived to be no different from foreigners who have their own personal and business agenda when seeking to contribute towards, or invest in, our African home countries.

Over the past decades, scholars, researchers, policymakers, and political institutions have developed different paradigms, theoretical frameworks, and concepts across different subjects and fields to predict, explain, or understand diasporic identity formations of populations' migration patterns. Evidently, migrations of Africans within the continent, and especially overseas, have led to newly formed communities and newer cultural and political identifications with our new, host countries. Stuart Hall recognized that globalization has resulted in two contradictory, or competitive, trends: (i) the trend towards assimilation and homogenization of cultures, as well as (ii) the reassertion of identities, e.g., national, ethnic, and religious, that center around localism. Hall also recognized that in the era of globalization, diasporic communication refers increasingly to those of "*cultural hybrid identities*," especially as identities become increasingly blurred. Cultural identity regards hybrid identities as the source of diasporic communication, as identities no longer subscribe to Edward Said's binary divisions of Occidentalism (Western worlds) or Orientalism (Eastern worlds). Shome and Hegde (2002) are amongst the postcolonial scholars who also critique this notion. They argue that the "West–East, North–South divide ... does not work as well in contemporary times, in which the lines separating the East from the West, and the North from the South, are increasingly becoming porous under conditions of globalization" (Shome and Hegde, 2002, p. 257). These porous boundaries redefine the geographical spaces and result in newer cultural and hybrid identities (Shome & Hegde, 2002, p. 257). Homi Bhabha also recognized the emergence of a third space—an interstitial space between the first space of the colonized, and the second space of the colonizer. Shome and Hegde (2002) add that fourth, fifth, and additional spaces are just as reasonable as postcolonial migrations further blur points of origin, as newer hybrid identities are further separated from their original homelands.

As newer hybrid identities emerge and form, they require new theoretical frameworks to support their analyses. Hence, different scholars still grapple with identifying the most accurate concepts and theoretical frameworks that optimally describe the nuances of a diaspora member's cultural identity, nationhood, and citizenship. *Cultural identity* refers to how someone defines themselves through the different cultural lenses and experiences that have influenced them. Therefore, it should not be shocking that problems may arise when the cultural lenses that a person uses to define themselves or others are questioned. Different ideologies would shape and filter the lenses and experiences through which one identifies another and self-identifies.

The following section presents an overview of some debates and discussions that critically acclaim and highly contest popular theories and concepts of cultural identities. These discussions ground the argument for new, uncharted conceptual frameworks of diaspora identity formations to be explored.

Multiculturalism, interculturalism, transculturalism, and superdiversity: Praise and critiques

Associated with normative theories, multiculturalism and interculturalism continue to undergo historically rooted debates, resulting in no universally agreed definition at present. These terms were originally developed in Canada to recognize the English and French languages of a bilingual country (Kastoryano, 2018).

Arguably, and perhaps simply, *multiculturalism* acknowledges the co-existence of numerous cultures that are simultaneously present and do not compete with each other; each cultural group separately asserts itself and is, ideally, given equal attention. However, as several scholars point out, multiculturalism does not imply the integration or the assimilation of these different cultures.

In fact, multiculturalism has been critiqued by many scholars over the years. Also described as "politics of tension" (Taylor, 1994), multiculturalism implies notions of "tribalism and groupism" (Brubaker, 2002), and has been "perceived as a threat to national identity" (Kastoryano, 2018, p. 1). Shome (2012) also critiques the limitations of multiculturalism when applied in global contexts in her assertion that "the conceptual logics and frameworks informing our engagements with multiculturalism (both in scholarship and public discourse) often remain situated within a nation-centred ethos of citizenship, justice, rights, and identity, and also in West-centric assumptions about "freedom", "belonging", and "democracy" (p. 145).

Multiculturalism has also been contested for reinforcing a homogeneity of cultures and giving the impression that cultural groups are static and fixed through their commitment to cultural assertions and to reinforcements of distinct, cultural silos. In her work *Multiculturalism without Culture*, Anne Phillips argues about the cultural homogenization of multiculturalism:

> Multiculturalism appears not as a cultural liberator but as a cultural straightjacket, forcing those described as members of a minority cultural group into a regime of authenticity, denying them the chance to cross cultural borders, borrow cultural influences, define and redefine themselves
>
> (Grosu, 2012, p. 107; Phillips, 2007, p. 14).

Additional viewpoints share this perspective, including that of Ndholvu (2015), who criticizes multiculturalism for perpetuating underpinnings of "racial hierarchies, inequalities, social and the social stigmatization of indigenous and immigrant minorities" (Ndhlovu, 2015, p. 30). Ndholvu (2015) argues that these underpinnings have resulted in the isolation of groups, stereotypes, and marginalization. The concept also fails to effectively capture the emergence of newer complex identities and cultures that more realistically reflect the unprecedented nature of present-day transnationalism (Ndhlovu, 2015).

Interculturalism, on the other hand, is postmulticulturalism, and spread across Europe in reaction to multiculturalism. Adopted within policy instruments, including the European Commission/Council of Europe "Intercultural Cities" program in 2008, the initiative described interculturalism as "'a concept that promotes policies and practices that encourage interaction, understanding and respect between different cultures and ethnic groups'" (Farrar, 2012, n.p.; Wood, 2009, p.11). Unlike multiculturalism, interculturalism reinforced contact between the different cultures and interactions through interpersonal dialogue, assumed to occur within a locale. Zappato-Barrero (2017) also adds that there is a "sharing of a common project, or even inter-dependence, where to reach an expectation or purpose people are reliant upon others' actions" (para. 22). However, interculturalism has been critiqued as a variant of multiculturalism. Both concepts have also been critiqued for failing to articulate the experiences of "minority" ethnic and cultural groups that are immersed in "majority"-group environments.

Challenging both multiculturalism and interculturalism is *transculturalism*, a term that was coined in 1945 by Fernando Ortiz Fernández, a Cuban anthropologist, to describe the evolution of Cuban culture. Transculturalism represented a new, synthesized "common" culture that results from "a cultural group's departure from its past and its preference for new, present outside influences" (Ardelean, 2018, p. 282; Fernandez, 1940). Associated with a rejection of cultural boundaries (Ardelean, 2018, p. 283; Tassinari, 1999, p. 46), transculturalism is a complex process of the merging, fusion, and integration of cultures into a resulting new, undefined, boundary-less cultural identity. Cuccioletta (2002) frames this altered cultural identity as "cosmopolitan citizenship" in his definition of transculturalism:

> Transculturalism, places the concept of culture at the center of a redefinition of the nation-state or even the disappearance of the nation-state. This process of recognizing oneself in the other leads inevitably to a cosmopolitan citizenship. This citizenship, independent of political structures and institutions, develops each individual in the understanding that one's culture is multiple, métis and that each human experience and existence is due to the contact with other, who in reality is like, oneself
>
> (para. 30).

Transculturalism is also associated with "seeing oneself in the other," which suggests an egalitarian approach to and perspective on how these groups should interact (Ardelean, 2018, p. 283). As such, transculturalism emphasizes the impact of borderless territories and incorporates psychological and emotional bonds that migrants experience vis-à-vis their multiple cultural experiences.

And therein lies a major difference. At macro and micro levels, multiculturalism and interculturalism are generally recognized as *theoretical concepts*—through narratives or political paradigms—that prescribe ideologies or describe sociological structures and intergroup processes of racial and ethnic groups and the management of their cultural diversity. Deviating from multiculturalism and interculturalism, however, transculturalism, related to transnationalism (see Introduction), describes the *experiences* of migrants and minorities resettling across nation-states. These experiences illustrate migrants' negotiations of emerging, evolving transnational identities and solidarities, impacted by their increased mobilization and information and communication technology (ICT), resulting in the "intense and complex ongoing ties that migrants uphold with their country of origin and the cultural, social, economic, political and ideological transfers that occur between the departure and the receiving country and beyond" (Kastoryano, 2018, p. 6). As a result, transnationalism and transculturalism challenge "founding principles of nation-states with regard to territoriality, citizenship, and membership to a single political community" (Kastoryano, 2018, p. 6). Transculturalism challenges the normative theories of multiculturalism and interculturalism, which are confined and limited to boundaries of national societies and geographical space (Kastoryano, 2018).

Associated closely with transnationalism and transculturalism, *third-culture kids* (TCK) represent another cultural identity of those whose mélanges of cultural identities transcend geographical borders—an outcome of transnationalism. In short, one may recognize a TCK by the infamous long, complicated response to the simplest, yet hardest question: "Where are you from?" The answers usually ramble with age-marked shout-outs to random countries and travel documents: "Well, I was born in Country X. My dad is from Country Y and my mom is from Country Z. However, when I was 12, I lived in Country P, but 3 years later, I moved to Country J. My passports, however, are..."

In the 1950s, sociologists Ruth Hill Useem and John Useem coined the term "third culture" to describe the "interstitial culture and lifestyle shared by expatriates" (Lee, 2011, p. 6), which differed from their "first culture (home or passport culture) and second culture (host culture)" (Lee, 2011, p. 6).

David Pollock and TCK Ruth Van Reken expanded on the conceptualization of a TCK:

> A person who has spent a significant part of his or her developmental years outside the parents' culture. The TCK builds relationships to all cultures, while not having full ownership in any. Although elements from each culture are assimilated into the TCK's life experience, the sense of belonging is in relationship to others of similar background
>
> (Lee, 2011, p. 7).

Greatly influenced by additional cultural dimensions of "home," many TCKs generally define a sense of "home" through relationships and connections with others that identify with similar upbringings and psycho-emotional and sociological patterns. These individuals rely on their heterogeneous, diverse, cultural backgrounds to contribute towards their sense of self. They are usually characterized as individuals of high mobility and rapid adaptability to any geographical environment, further accentuated by the impact of globalization.

At first glance, transculturalism appears to effectively respond to the deficits of multiculturalism and interculturalism that many scholars may agree upon. Cuccioletta (2002) hails transculturalism for its celebration of a "cosmopolitan citizenship" that acknowledges individuals' multiple identities that can be linked to their own cultural heritage, host country, and various local and global geographical spaces (Grosu, 2012). Roy L. Brooks acknowledges the "convergence" of cultures where "each social group" contributes "something of value to a new, blended mainstream culture" (Grosu, 2012, p. 108; Brooks, 2012; p. 24–25). However, transculturalism has also been criticized by various scholars and doctrines. Brooks (2012) perceives a dilemma: Transculturalism reinforces cultural hegemony and results in individuals surrendering their own cultural identities, losing their cultural markers, and adopting new identities in this new cultural melting pot (Grosu, 2012, p. 108; Brooks, 2012, p. 25).

In 2006, Vertovek conceptualized an alternative paradigm through the diasporic identity concept of *superdiversity*—also in response to the limitations of multiculturalism and normative theories. Rooted in observations made on the basis of migration data in Britain and the European Union, superdiversity acknowledges two main developments: the wider range and variety of resources that migrants transfer and exchange in their daily interactions with other individuals and organizations, as well as the greater accessibility to ICT that grants the individual greater exposure to various networks and information (Ndhlovu, 2015; *Diggit Magazine*, n.d.).

However, superdiversity has also been contested for various reasons from various scholars, including reinforcing the same challenges that it purports to alleviate! Also referred to as "colonial matrices of power" and "global imperial designs" by Quijano (2000), superdiversity has been criticized by various scholars for many reasons: (i) In addition to having a confusing prefix, "super," superdiversity falsely alludes to a romantic idealism of equality with references to pluralism and tolerance, when it really only serves to reinforce exclusive practices and promote elitism; (ii) it fails to address the daily, lived realities of individuals—particularly in a globally asymmetrical world; and (iii) superdiversity superficially refers to almost any migratory pattern under globalization as a new phenomenon of "superdiversity" without taking into account various migratory patterns and behaviors like "barter trade, adventures, seasonal pastoral migrations" (Ndhlovu, 2015, p. 34) that had already existed in premodern and precolonial civilizations in African societies or in the Middle Ages.

Ndhlovu (2015) also criticizes multiculturalism, cosmopolitanism, and superdiversity similarly for deceptively and institutionally covering up the exclusion of cultural groups, and for imposing repeated messages like "shared humanity" and "individuals seeing others as themselves" as though to force a theoretical ideal that arguably lacks grounding and reality.

Scholars have generally critiqued the aforementioned theories as universalist, normative, or exclusive for not acknowledging lived realities from other cultural groups. Hence, there has been a push to illustrate how experiences of transnationalism and transculturalism result in the emergence of newer, multiple cultural identities. Echoing the sentiments of numerous scholars and practitioners in the field, such a pursuit requires a transdisciplinary approach in addressing complexities of representation and identity.

Decoloniality: An approach to uncovering the African diasporic cultural identity

Enter *Southern theory*—a new "world" social science theory that questions universalism and acknowledges the Global South (developing nations) as a knowledge producer to further understand society, one whose "knowledge systems should be recognized and included in" discourse on development, "social progress," (p. 35) and human welfare (Ndholvu, 2015).

Without seeking to displace theoretical frameworks from the Global North (developed nations) that have their own place, nor seeking to assert its own theoretical assumptions as the singular authority on all matters related to diasporic identity, Southern theory offers a newer, revolutionary alternative paradigm (Ndholvu, 2015). Southern theory recognizes the intricate dynamics of knowledge, power, democracy and identity that reflect the "experiences of the majority of the world's populations" (Ndhlovu, 2015, p. 35).

Connected to Southern theory is *decoloniality*, also known as *decolonial epistemology*, which privileges a new, alternative site of knowledge production that prompts one to question, critique, and challenge hegemonic, dominant ideals and normative assumptions. Decoloniality offers a multipronged approach to more clearly understanding diasporic identity formations—particularly of "minority" ethnic, racial, and cultural groups—whose complexities and nuances may not be effectively addressed through homogenizing and simplistic normative theories like multiculturalism and superdiversity (Ndhlovu, 2015). Ultimately, decoloniality calls for deployment and new methods to generate "alternative knowledges," conceptualizations and theoretical frameworks of cultural identities that "both counter and complement dominant Euro-American epistemologies" (Ndhlovu, 2015, p. 37).

Hence, to explore new conceptual frameworks of cultural diasporic identities, Ndhlovu (2015) identifies three cornerstones of coloniality to be dismantled for a psychological liberation from Euro-American hegemonies:

> (i) *coloniality of power*, which references contemporary forms of colonial legacy—evident in social discrimination, social order and invisible hierarchies in culture and language—that still grip non-Western, formerly colonized subjects in matrices of power and supplant their worldview with those of the West; (ii) *coloniality of knowledge*, which privileges the Eurocentric knowledge production and as a default for valid theory and knowledge, and (iii) *coloniality of being*, which refers to colonialists' use of Western theories and colonial imaginaries of racism to construct cultural and identity categories that dehumanized and re-identified colonial subjects, leading to present-day binary conceptualizations and understandings of "us" versus "them," "Global South" versus "Global North," and "developed" versus "developing"—which are further reinforced through colonial technologies. (Ndhlovu, 2015)

The African diasporic identity is layered with innumerable influences that trace its origins to coloniality and that have become even more complicated amidst forces of contemporary forces of globalization since postcolonialization. Various scholars and sociologists over the decades have reflected on the impact of racial, political, and social hierarchies created by European colonialism on African diasporic identity formations across the globe and the diaspora's self-concept. Their accounts in their works of nonfiction illustrate different forms of coloniality of power, coloniality of knowledge, and coloniality of being that invite new and diverse discourses on African diasporic cultural identity formations.

Ndlovu-Gatsheni (2012) refers to the coloniality of power in his African decolonization project to reveal African people's entanglement "within the colonial matrix of power underpinning asymmetrically structured global social order," and he "laments those African scholars who are oblivious to the 'invisible hierarchies of … linguistic and racial arrangements underpinning imperial global designs within which African struggles for decolonisation took place'" (Ndhlovu, 2015, p. 36; 2012, 74).

Frantz Fanon, a French West Indian psychiatrist and political philosopher from the French colony of Martinique, has famously depicted the grips of coloniality throughout his various works. Fanon (1986) responds to challenges stemming from coloniality of knowledge when he problematizes the dominance and hegemony of Eurocentric knowledge systems that result in their assumed, principal site of knowledge production and dissemination (Ndhlovu, 2015). In *Black Skin, White Masks*, Fanon (1952) details his lived experienced as a Black man who is granted approval only after adopting European linguistic, cultural, and knowledge systems:

> To speak a language is to appropriate its world and culture. The Antillean who wants to be white will succeed, since he will have adopted the cultural tool of language. I can remember just over a year ago in Lyon, following a lecture where I had drawn a parallel between black and European poetry, a French comrade telling me enthusiastically: "Basically, you're a white man." The fact I had studied such an interesting question in the white man's language gave me my credentials.
>
> (Fanon, 1952, p. 21)

In one of his famous works, the nonfiction account *The Colonizer and the Colonized*, French-Tunisian writer Albert Memmi details the impact of colonialism on Tunisians. Epitomizing the problematizations of coloniality of being, Memmi (1967) affirms the re-creation of his new identity, based on the transformative pervasiveness of the colonial system:

> I was Tunisian, therefore colonized. I discovered that few aspects of my life and my personality were untouched by this fact. Not only my own thoughts, my passions and my conduct, but also the conduct of others toward me was affected.
>
> (Memmi, 1967, iii)

Other examples of coloniality of being "otherize" and create identities of subjugated populations through "bifurcated terms" (Ndhlovu, 2015, p. 36). An example includes the outdated references to "First World" countries (Western countries) that were more developed and distinguished from "Third World" countries (Africa, Asia, Latin America). These terms reflected the geopolitical world during the Cold War that arguably and the "otherization" of an imposed categorization—which the coloniality of being addresses. Indeed, the term became controversial for its derogatory, insulting, and condescending connotations of "poor" and "sub-standard" and was replaced with "developed" (formerly First World) and "developing" (formerly Third World). Miriam Makeba, a famous South African musician and icon, famously lamented in reference to these distinguishing polarizations:

> And why is our music called world music? I think people are being polite. What they want to say is that it's Third World music. Like they use to call us underdeveloped countries, now it has changed to developing countries, it's much more polite
>
> (Klaus Kästle—nationsonline.org., n.d., para. 1).

Also epitomizing the coloniality of being is William E. B. Du Bois, who illuminates the impact of an imposed "otherization" on contemporary global diaspora cultural identities and one's self-concept, particularly when describing African-Americans' struggle in oppressive conditions in the United States of America. Through his concept of *double-consciousness*, Du Bois presents his living experience in a world with no consciousness that permits him to only see himself through the revelation of the other world. Du Bois vividly paints the duality of "his two-ness,—an American, a Negro; two souls, two thoughts, two unreconciled strivings; two warring ideals in one dark body" (The Atlantic, 2020, para. 3). Notably, Du Bois highlights the identity conflict in his struggle: He seeks to reconcile separate identities as the American that he wishes to not Africanize, and also as the African whose blood that he wishes to not bleach "in a flood of white Americanism" (The Atlantic, 2020, para. 3)—all the while seeking to preserve the opportunities of self-development that he is aware that each racial identity offers.

So, while decoloniality introduces a school of thought in this field, decoloniality still requires further conceptualization and examination. In their book *On Decoloniality: Concepts, Analytics, Praxis*, Mignolo and Walters (2018) accentuate that "decoloniality is not a done deal, a condition to be reached, or a stage of critical enlightenment. It is also not an abstract academic paradigm, that is, a paradigm and postulate devoid of struggle and praxis" (jstor.org, n.d., para. 13).

Like many critical paradigms or alternative schools of thought, decoloniality—as a process, as a positioning, or however it may eventually become conceptualized—underscores a key message: For one to reveal truth or accuracy about global human experiences, one must first be willing and then able to see, hear, question, and challenge the most subtle assumptions that are concealed within our daily interactions and that are (re)produced through hegemonic knowledge systems. This is an individual journey as much as it is a collective endeavor. Mignolo and Walters (2018) also reference Bob Marley's "Redemption Song" to highlight each individual's responsibility in decolonial liberation.

But be forewarned: When put into practice, one also must be prepared to encounter resistance from those that question an agitation to the status quo. Such resistance ranges from common criticisms, including accusations of "making everything a race issue" or for perpetuating stereotypes, such as the "angry Black man," "angry Black woman," and other labels designed by systemic architectures to resist, frustrate, and alienate the woke, conscious mind. Memmi, Du Bois, Fanon, and many others in the global community of sociologists, scholars, and critical thinkers from previous decades until the present day stress a valid point: Very little is untouched by the colonial legacies that have infiltrated every fiber of our society.

But any conscious effort towards unlocking critical insights is a first step to revolutionizing our society.

> The point of greater significance about decoloniality is that it is "an-other thought" that seeks to inaugurate "an-other logic," "an-other language"

> and "an-other thinking" that has the potential to liberate ex-colonized people's minds from the clutches of Euro-American epistemological hegemonies. (Ndhlovu, 2015, p. 38; Mignolo, 2007)

The goal of an "an-other thinking" is to translate those thoughts into action so that "an-other behavior" can lead to an-other reality and an-other set of lived, valid experiences.

Contextualizing the TCK-cultural diasporic identity formation for an alternative paradigm

It would be interesting to see how scholars' critiques of cosmopolitan citizenship as a normative ideology may be challenged when described by the voices and from the perspectives of TCK and transcultural individuals, including, for instance, those whose fundamental upbringings in international schools took place in sub-Saharan African countries. Different geographical contexts that carry unique sociohistorical dynamics may re-conceptualize the make-up of "majority-minority" groups. For instance, ethnic divisions and economic class divisions may be more predominant than racial divisions within many African countries, whereas race divisions that influence social and economic status may be the more predominant, glaring social dividers in Europe or the United States, for instance. Hence, transcultural individuals of African descent or other culturally represented ethnic groups that may have comprised the majority group in one host country may not have been subjected to ethnic, racial, or gender discrimination. But suddenly, when thrust into another host country, these individuals are automatically labeled and treated as "minority status groups" or "majority status groups," accounting for new personal and professional self-concepts and experiences.

Such is the fate of many transcultural individuals of varied ethnic descent and of mixed race or mixed ethnicity. Some may be raised within international community school settings across the world, given their parents' occupations and constant mobility as international civil servants, diplomats, ambassadors, religious missionaries, political figures, military officers, or global heads of multinational or transnational corporate firms. For many of these individuals, their sense of diasporic cultural identity may illustrate that of the TCK. As a result, they may feel little pressure to limit themselves to one particular racial, ethnic, or cultural identifier. Instead, they may claim all of their punctuated and hyphenated identities, e.g., Russian/Brazilian-Senegalese, or vaguely respond with "I'm all sorts of stuff." In short, their sense of identity is less about tangible national country borders and instead focuses more on their relationships to their surroundings and those of similar mind and experience.

Another factor affecting their identity is connected to what accounts for a TCK's experiences of "culture shock." Many adapt quickly to the cultural and traditional norms of their new host environments. Hence, they embrace and associate "change" with "stability," as they routinely adapt to new host countries. However, particularly for those who have resided in environments with heterogeneous cultures, they may experience a different sort of "culture shock" when thrust into an environment that reinforces ethnic, racial, or cultural divides. This form of "culture shock" may pressurize the TCK to "pick" and "declare" their cultural identity, label their race, and align with a cultural group that falls within a fixed, static, limited prescribed range of options. Ironically, this pressure may even stem from other diaspora groups of their parents' home nation, who yet may not have had a transnational or transcultural upbringing that mirrors that of the TCK. I remember in my case, I was told by some Africans on my college campus that I was not "African enough," by some African-Americans that I was not "Black" enough, and by other groups that I was more "American"—even though I had never lived in America up until that time. Ultimately, these pressures usually stem from those who may have had limited exposure to the cultural identifiers than what TCK have grown up with. As a result, the TCK may grow frustrated with their "new" stereotypes or become confused about why their new society expects them to act apprehensive around individuals who are "Black," "White", "Mixed," "Muslim," "Jewish," "LGBT," or "other." These same cultural identifiers and markers that embraced friends' and family members' differences in previous host countries have now been redefined as "triggers for concern" in a new host environment. These terms now evoke new heavily loaded emotions with associations, meanings, stereotypes, and biases that trace to historical, political or socioeconomic contexts of the new host country.

These cultural shifts hold very significant implications in the global context of community development, nation-building, and social cohesion. Many TCK normalize a self-concept of "fitting outside a box," "redefining the box" and embodying "diversity inclusion." But this utopic bubble threatens to burst open when TCK are thrust into diverse environments with a low tolerance of inclusion. When their racial, ethnic, and cultural identifiers move from their "blind spot" or "rearview mirrors" to the windshield and side-view mirrors, this cultural shift may affect their interactions and self-concept because it contradicts the values that shaped their identities and their understandings of the world.

There is great value in the experience of the TCK who has an opportunity to play an active and leadership role in community development of their new environmental surroundings. If TCK's transnational experiences formed during phases of early child development, then their school pedagogy and family upbringing may have raised them to effectively embrace diversity inclusion and manage—not fear—cultural, racial, religious and ethnic differences. These influences may shape their psychological, emotional, and social development and contribute to high emotional quotients (EQ) that guide their interactions with others.

And perhaps this is why the term "identity crisis" may be problematic when applied to transcultural or transnational individuals' concepts of ethnic, cultural or national identity—regardless of their ethnic descent. The term carries a connotation that suggests a problem, when the problem only resides with those of limited cultural exposure who impose their restrictions on others with more diverse global experiences and more expansive worldviews. Hence, the problem is not to do with one's transcultural identity—nor is it in a state of crisis. Many solutions and opportunities can arise for TCK who can leverage their backgrounds to serve as role models in their communities. Their cultural affinities may position them to teach tolerance for diversity, equity and inclusion of marginalized groups; foster environments that nurture a sense of belonging for everyone; promote conflict resolution; develop paradigms that aim to empower communities; improve human welfare and bridge socioeconomic, cultural, and political divides between host and homeland countries.

Various factors continue to influence and shape African diasporic cultural identity formations. Southern theory represents one of several theories that introduces social thought processes like decoloniality and other alternative paradigms in transdisciplinary studies. But the emergence of TCK or other transnational identity formations reinforces an increasingly urgent need to discover other analytical tools.

Perhaps one could reflect on Fanon's (1952) observation:

> There is a dramatic conflict in what is commonly called the human sciences. Should we postulate a typical human reality and describe its psychic modalities, taking into account only the imperfections, or should we not rather make a constant, solid endeavor to understand man in an ever changing light? (goodreads.com)

The world needs newer additional theories, critical paradigms, and epistemologies to address the complexities of our rapidly transforming global world, their impact on our identities, and our roles in our nations' development agendas.

Chapter summary

Key concepts

cultural hybrid identities	interculturalism	Third-Culture Kids (TCK)
cultural identity	multiculturalism	Southern theory
decoloniality/decolonial epistemology	transculturalism	
double-consciousness	transnationalism	

Discussion questions

Imagine you were conducting a sociological study of transcultural or transnational students in your class.

1) A) Identify some of the strengths and challenges that a person of transcultural or transnational background may experience within their personal or professional capacity.
B) How can these strengths be leveraged to build teams and benefit a community? How can these unique challenges be converted into strengths and opportunities to benefit a community?
C) How could their upbringing and experiences influence their perspective on contemporary societal issues? Select any issue that is of relevance to your community.
D) Identify and explain a theoretical perspective to address an angle of the contemporary societal issue you identified above. Why did you select that particular theory? Explain how it is useful to apply to an issue in community development. What are the limitations of this theory? Present any alternative paradigms that also address this societal issue.

References

Ardelean, C. (2018). Cultural integration in Europe: From nationalism to multiculturalism and transculturalism. *Synergy, 14*(2), 276–286. http://www.synergy.ase.ro/issues/2018-vol14-no-2/10-Carmen-Ardelean.pdf

The Atlantic. (2020, June 24). *W. E. B. Du Bois on Black "Double-Consciousness."* https://www.theatlantic.com/magazine/archive/1897/08/strivings-of-the-negro-people/305446/

Brooks, R. L. 2012. "Cultural Diversity: It's All About the Mainstream", in *Monist* 95.1: 17–32.

Brubaker, R. (2002). Ethnicity without groups. *Archives Européennes de Sociologie, 43*(2), 163–189.

Cuccioletta, D. (2001–2002). Multiculturalism or Transculturalism: Towards a Cosmopolitan Citizenship. *LONDON JOURNAL OF CANADIAN STUDIES*. Published. https://is.muni.cz/el/1421/podzim2013/CJVA1M/43514039/reading_3_Transculturality.pdf

Fanon, F. (1952). *Black Skin, White Masks*. New York: Grove Press.

Fanon, F. (1986). *The wretched of the earth*. New York: Grove Press.

Farrar, M. (2012). 'Interculturalism' or 'critical multiculturalism': Which discourse works best? In: M. Farrar (Ed.), *Debating Multiculturalism 1*. London: Dialogue Society.

Fernandez, Ortiz F. 1940. *Contrapunteo cubano del tabaco y el azúcar*. Translated into English 1995, *Cuban Counterpoint: Tobacco and Sugar*, Durham and London: Duke University Press.

Fukayama, F. (2018, November 27). In an age of identity politics, inclusive national identity matters more than ever. *ABC Religion & Ethics*. https://www.abc.net.au/religion/why-national-identity-matters/10559382

Grosu, L. (2012). Multiculturalism or transculturalism? Views on cultural diversity. *Synergy, 8*(2), 102–111. https://synergy.ase.ro/issues/2012-vol8-no2/06-lucia-mihaela-grosu-multiculturalism-or-transculturalism-views-on-cultural-diversity.pdf

Kastoryano, R. (2018). Multiculturalism and interculturalism: Redefining nationhood and solidarity. *Comparative Migration Studies, 6*(1), 1–11. doi:10.1186/s40878-018-0082-6

Kästle, Klaus—Nationsonline.org. (n.d.). First, Second, and Third World countries. *Nations Online Project.* Https://Www.Nationsonline.Org/Oneworld/Third_world_countries.Htm

Lee, S. (2011). Third culture kids: Global nomads in search of a home. CAMD Scholar Project. https://panet.andover.edu/bbcswebdav/institution/CAMD/CAMDModule/CAMDScholars/SeyoungLee.pdf

Memmi, A. (1967). *The Colonizer and the Colonized.* Boston, MA: Beacon Press.

Ndhlovu, F. (2015). A decolonial critique of diaspora identity theories and the notion of superdiversity. *Diaspora Studies, 9*(1), 28–40. doi:10.1080/09739572.2015.1088612

Ndlovu-Gatsheni, S.(2012). Fiftieth anniversary of decolonisation in Africa: A moment of celebration or critical reflection? *Third World Quarterly, 33*(1), 71–89. https://www.jstor.org/stable/41341212

Mignolo, W. (2007). Coloniality of power and de-colonial thinking. *Cultural Studies, 21*(2–3), 155–167. https://doi.org/10.1080/09502380601162498

Mignolo, W. & Walsh, C. (2018). *On Decoloniality: Concepts, Analytics, Praxis.* Durham; London: Duke University Press. doi:10.2307/j.ctv11g9616

Phillips, A. (2007). *Multiculturalism without Culture.* Princeton New Jersey: Princeton University Press.

Quijano, A. (2000). Coloniality of Power, Eurocentrism and latin America. *Nepantla, 1*(3), 533–580.

Shome, R., & Hegde, R. (2002). Postcolonial approaches to communication: Charting the terrain, engaging the intersections. *Communication Theory, 12*(3), (249–270). ISSN 1050-3293

Shome, R. (2012). Mapping the Limits of Multiculturalism in the Context of Globalization. *International Journal of Communication, 6,* 144–165. https://ijoc.org/index.php/ijoc/article/viewFile/1184/689

Tassinari, L. 1999. *Utopies par le Hublot,* Carte Blanche: Outremont.

Taylor, C. (1994). The politics of recognition. In A. Gutmann (Ed.), Multiculturalism: examining the politics of recognition. Princeton: Princeton University Press.

Wood, Phil (ed.) (2009) *Intercultural Cities – Towards a model for intercultural integration,* Strasburg: Council of Europe Publishing.

Zapata-Barrero, R. (2017). Interculturalism in the post-multicultural debate: A defence. *CMS, 5*(1), 14. doi:10.1186/s40878-017-0057-z

2 The African diaspora, the African Personality, and an African human development paradigm

Exploring their nexus

There is generally a link assumed between the strength of a person's national identity and their desire and ability to invest in, or contribute toward, their nation's welfare. But what does this mean for the African diaspora who have been raised outside of their African homeland? If their sense of national identity in relation to their African home country is weakened, would a weak link to their home country lessen their role in participating in Africa's development?

This chapter explores how some scholars, philosophers, and African political thought leaders have conceptualized the African identity or African Personality and acknowledged its vitality in developing Africa. I draw connections between the African Personality and its relevance for the African diaspora's role in contributing toward Africa's development, particularly when applied to a human development paradigm.

Identity and national development: Why should we care?

Migration, colonialism, and slavery have long affected the self-perception of Africans and have led to the emergence of new identity categorizations. Dynamic globalization forces in the 21st century continue to affect Africans' self-definitions, self-concept, and interpretations of their relationships to the rest of the world. Present-day migrations of Africans within the continent, and especially overseas, have led to newly formed communities and newer cultural and political identifications with their new, host countries. The consequent emergence of multiple and hybrid identities of Africans continue to reconfigure the face of Africa. So now, what does it mean to become an African? Who is an African? The impact of "modernization" on Africa continues to produce generations of diasporic Africans and individuals of diverse, hybrid cultural identities of African descent. For some, the result is a cascade of 'personality crises' of the individual and of the collective people. These crises, arguably, may aggravate the desire or ability of a diasporic African to develop or strengthen a political, economic, or social consciousness about his or her African home country. A weakened national identity or weakened consciousness about one's nation may weaken ties and connections to that nation, resulting in apathy toward contributing to, or investing in, one's country.

DOI: 10.4324/9781351031660-3

Generally, the African diaspora rely on their cultural connections and pyscho-emotional affections to maintain their ties with their African home country while residing in their host countries. Despite poverty levels, corruption practices, or any other challenges occurring within their home country, African diaspora who have strong ties to their African country will typically engage in an activity to maintain the connection with their country.

Fukuyama (2018) outlines six key points about the importance of nations fostering an inclusive national identity among its citizens that supports a nation's political order (italicized in the original article). According to Fukuyama (2018), an inclusive national identity reinforces and fosters a nation's

(i) *physical security* by allowing the country to unify and increase its solidarity and mobilizing it to protect its self-interests—otherwise the country becomes prone to foreign attack and is more vulnerable;
(ii) *quality of government*, especially if there is less emphasis on ethnic or political party preferences and the government prioritizes the wider, public interests of its diverse nation over its own (ethnic) preferences;
(iii) *economic development*, particularly as the "elites" of the country dedicate their resources toward the nation's economic development and forfeit their own personal needs—as epitomized more by the "elites" of Japan, South Korea, and China, whose "kind of public-directedness was key to the success of the 'developmental state' in these and other rapidly modernizing economies; it was much less common in such regions as sub-Saharan Africa, the Middle East and Latin America" (para. 21). Furthermore, commonalities built around nationhood support thriving economies that grant citizens access to wide markets that are not constrained by the identities by buyers or sellers—"provided, of course, that national identity does not become the basis for protectionism against other nations" (para. 21);
(iv) *social capital* among diverse citizens, whose shared values and informal norms help them to cooperate and participate in economic and political spaces;
(v) *strong safety nets* that "mitigate economic inequality," reinforced by citizens who identify each other as extended family members with whom they trust and support through social programs;
(vi) *a liberal democracy* that represents an implicit contract between citizens, their government, and among themselves that they believe is legitimate and binds them "as [being] part of the same polity, [otherwise], the system will not function" (para. 24).

The reasons aforementioned reinforce the significance of promoting an inclusive African identity among Africans to promote Africa's political and socioeconomic development. Such a collective identity has been the mantle of a pan-African consciousness that many African leaders and political thinkers articulated (see Chapter 13). Articulating an inclusive African identity, which I also reference in this chapter as the African Personality, suggests that Africans within the continent and in the diaspora may be empowered with an agency to own their own narrative from hegemonic grips, define their own identities on their own terms, and own their own resources, resulting in the collective strength and vitality of the African continent. However, how can one approach the feat of articulating the African identity in the 21st century when different nations across the continent reflect diverse approaches to leadership and different qualities of governance that result in national divisions, ethnic and religious factions, weakened national security, weakened economies, and, ultimately, rapid emigration and the continual dispersion of their citizens in the diaspora that reconfigure Africans' self-identity?

Reconfiguration of Africans' self-identity

To be born an African, one finds oneself within the limitations of a political narrative, characterized by the constraints of a political geography, shaped by Western-defined boundaries of the African continent—54 independent states and neighboring islands. The immediate result of Africa's diverse communal tapestry includes traditional, Euro-Christian/Western, and Arab-Islamic African societies.

The history of slavery and colonialism redefined this concept of "African" people and their "personality," which were affected by relocations, separations from the motherland, and, ultimately, from the cultural world of their ancestors. According to Dukor (2010):

> Africans of the first half of this century have begun to search for their identity because they had the feeling that they had lost it. The three factors which led to this feeling were; slavery, colonialism and racialism of all these, racialism is said to be the source of the colonialism and slavery. It was because Africans were considered racially inferior and culturally uncivilized that both Arabs and Europeans felt a moral justification in expiating them by reducing them to slavery. Therefore the heart of the whole problem of African identity lies in Racialism.
>
> (p. 159; Ndubuisi, 2013, p. 224)

The culmination of these relocations and separations resulted in present-day African diasporic formations of African-American or Black American, Caribbean, Afro-European, Latin American and other African-descent groups in the Middle East and Asia. These diasporas have formed their own cultural values and traditions, yet are all linked to a common originating, ancestral point in the African continent.

So, given these culturally-hybrid "selves," is it still possible to articulate an *African Personality* for Africans in the 21st century? Interestingly, Frantz Fanon (1952) also raised this dilemma:

> All colonized people—in other words—people in whom an inferiority complex has taken root, whose local cultural originality has been

> committed to the grave—position themselves in relation to the civilizing language: i.e., the metropolitan culture. The more the colonized has assimilated the cultural values of the metropolis, the more he will have escaped the bush. The more he rejects his blackness and the bush, the whiter he will become.
>
> (Fanon, 1952, p. 3)

The rapidly expanding global economy in the 21st century further accounts for the mobility of individuals who relocate to foreign countries in search of improved living conditions. One significant consequence of the high mobility and migrations from Africa to the Western world and other regions is immigrants' transformed psychological connection with, and identification of, "self" and "other." In what context is such an individual the "other" or the "self" in the new surroundings? A transcultural African's self-identification and/or psychological connection as the "other" is further challenged and consistently contextualized differently when he or she migrates to another geographical region, is educated by that particular system, and acclimates to the ways, thought patterns, and norms of that region's cultural group. Hence, the dynamics are more complex because such an individual relates to at least three or more distinct cultures simultaneously—at times from birth. As an immigrant of a new geographic and cultural setting, his or her negotiation and adoption of foreign practices gradually become ingrained into his or her lifestyle. His or her "personality" contributes to an individual identity and self-concept that reflects a mélange of ideologies and thought-consciousness patterns of Europeans, Latin Americans, Europeans, and Americans simultaneously, ones that differ from those of his/her indigenous, African parents, and first-generation Americans of African descent—possibly even second-generation Africans as well.

So what exactly is the African identity, or African Personality, and what does it mean for the African diaspora?

Approaching the African Personality/African identity

The African Personality presents a concept, ideology, and set of worldviews of what it means to be African—a highly difficult feat that has evolved into various conceptualizations and approaches over the centuries and innumerable debates about its conceptualization.

Although defining the African identity or African Personality transcends the scope of this chapter, it is helpful to understand how certain orientations toward explaining the African Personality influenced Africa's independence, is alluded to in some of Africa's development paradigms, and raises critical questions for its relevance in the 21st century.

In his critique of various scholars' approaches to defining the African identity, Tembo (2016) highlights four conceptual orientations that various scholars and leaders have generally used to approach the African identity: (i) the "need to uphold [indigenous] African cultures and values" (p. 103); (ii) presenting

Africanity as ontologically opposed to Western-ness; (iii) "the homogenization of individual and collective sociopolitical and cultural agency of black people into the notion of African Personality or identity"; and (iv) representing issues that are relevant to specific portions of the African continent as being representative to all people of the entire African continent.

I expound further on these aforementioned orientations to thematize my discussions and observations of the work of different scholars, philosophers, and African political thought leaders who have conceptualized the African identity.

Upholding indigenous African cultures and values

Many assume that the fundamental approach toward the African Personality begins by stripping away any trace of colonial strongholds from the individual to reflect a pure extract of the indigenous African. Perhaps this is clearly illustrated when Ndubuisi (2013) quotes Jean Paul Sartre's description of man's "existential integrity" as "the original purity of his existence" (p. 226) to note that the "search for identity is a mission back to the root, to become fully conscious of himself as an African" (p. 226)—a cornerstone for social, economic, self and holistic development that integrates the "resources of [one's] being, culture and world" (p. 226).

Whereas debates ensue about employing methodologies toward this endeavor that may inherently reflect a Eurocentric hermeneutic approach that counteracts the goal, this perspective reinforces that of many scholars and philosophers who seek to incorporate African worldviews and indigenous perspectives into new alternative paradigms, epistemologies, and knowledge systems.

African ontology, African metaphysics: African philosophy

Various scholars have conceptualized the African identity through African ontology, which some argue is a foundation for African philosophy. Intertwining threads of communalism and spirituality, the African ontological significance of relationism is illustrated in human connections, as well as in an inseparable oneness of the physical and spiritual world. Whereas some scholars argue that *African ontology* is anthropocentric, with an emphasis on humans as preceding that of a God, others acknowledge a spiritual reverence of a "*vital force*" that characterizes the "being" as central to the African identity.

Ngangah (2019) addresses this argument in a comparative analysis of Western and African concepts of "being" that observes Tempels' (1959) illustration of "vital force" in African ontology. The "vital force" comprises an interrelation of human spirits (namely ancestors) and non-human spirits (nature) within an ontological hierarchy that forms communities' worship and social systems, as well as outlining social practices and a moral order that are institutionalized through laws, customs, and taboos that permit or prohibit specific actions (Ngangah, 2019).

An underlying framework is thus highlighted that "ensures that human beings' governance of the human and non-human forces, under God, is spiritually and socially streamlined. That framework is founded on the communal understanding that all beings are spiritually interrelated forces that exact consequential influence on all individuals within a given spiritual, ethical and social order" (Ngangah, 2019, p. 51).

Ngangah (2019) uses this backdrop to distinguish the "superiority of communal force over the individual's force" (p. 53) as the criteria that differentiates the African ontology of personhood from the *Western ontology* of personhood. In the West, an individual is defined as set apart from their community; in Africa, society determines or defines the personhood of an individual only after societal expectations, performance of social obligations, demonstration of competence, and other criteria have been met that mark society's approval of that individual's conduct and relationships with other community members (Ngangah, 2019).

Other scholars and African political leaders similarly reference African metaphysics and African traditional worldviews that pronounce a "*we-existence*" (p. 229), which opposes the Eurocentric emphasis of the autonomous individual, "I" (Ndubuisi, 2013). The communal characteristic of African identity, as always "being with others" (p. 225), is rooted in networks, community, and family, which Julius Nyerere, first president of Tanzania, referred to as the "African brotherhood" (Ndubuisi, 2013, p. 224). Illustrations of this communal network within the cultural prisms in African communities have also been presented in various African contexts that continuously embody the "*Ubuntu*" philosophy, an Nguni Bantu concept that refers to humanity, centered in its premise "I am, because we are," or Kenya's "*Harambee*" in Swahili, which translates to "all pull together."

Kwame Nkrumah, first president of Ghana, and Leopold Senghor, first president of Senegal, also regarded the African Personality as a composite of energetic forces of matter that are linked to a dynamic spirit—an ontological philosophy that accounts for a set of moral orders, ethical codes, and expressive outlets in a communal manner that are distinctively African. Ultimately, African ontology recognizes how African identity rests on communal connection that transcends other humans and blends between invisible and visible realities (Ndubuisi, 2013).

Sociopolitical and cultural agency of Black people

The African Personality has been approached through its relations to nationalism, political and economic independence, cultural assertions, and Marxism, and it has even been criticized when attempts were made to extract specific characteristics to depict the African.

Perhaps one would regard tribalism in Africa as a source of pure, authentic African tradition that depicts the systems, structures, and practices of a unique society. However, in *What is a Tribe*, Mahmood Mamdani (2019) presents the manipulation of tribes as colonial restructures of native conglomerations, designed to advance and facilitate colonialists' direct and indirect rules. Their introduction of class levels and systems in tribes led to a system that was congruent to a divided, politically led, racial system in other parts of the world. Hence, the term "tribal identity" was synonymous with, and comprised of, political and cultural identity that were linked to administrative practices designed by colonists. To date, some view the word "tribe" and all related terms as derogatory and condescending.

The correlation between one's cultural or national identity and political identity reinforce the postcolonial effects on one's sense of self—which may explain why scholars and leaders have linked the conceptualization of the African Personality to African political thought, and why African leaders, including Kwame Nkrumah and Julius Nyerere, linked the conceptualization of the African Personality to a political agenda.

African political thought "refers to the original ideas, values, and blueprints for a better Africa that inform African political systems and institutions from the ancient period (Kush, sixth century BCE) to the present" (Martin, 2012, p. 1). African political thought also refers to political theories and ideologies originated from African scholars and politicians in their various literature—from speeches to policy statements—that "inform political action ...[and] provide practical solutions to political, economic, social, and cultural problems, and it varies according to historical circumstances and a constantly changing African and world political environment" (Martin, 2012, p. 1).

Kwame Nkrumah (1964), president of Ghana and revolutionary leader who led the Gold Coast to independence from Britain in 1957, presents the African Personality as one that highlights the traditional prong of African society that is related to an African conscience, presented through a philosophical *Consciencism* that seeks to interweave specific elements of African, Euro-Christian, and Islamic into an African Personality (Nkrumah,1964). The strength of the African Personality revolved around an independence from colonial powers and strongholds, especially in regards to political decision-making, and a self-reliance in terms of social, economic, and cultural action (Nkrumah,1964, p. 103).

In a 1958 speech, Sekou Touré (1959), Guinean political leader and Guinea's first political president, expressed similar sentiments to Nkrumah's reference to socialism as the antithesis of capitalism and framework for egalitarianism. Touré also reinforced the need for Africans to actively participate in their collective struggle for emancipation, justice and their rights (Blackpast, 2009).Touré (1959) accounts for the depersonalization of an African through his/her embodiment of the colonial system and teachings, and ultimately extols the need for African artistic, cultural, and traditional expressions to preserve an authenticity—an authenticity in how Africans think and act to solve their problems (Blackpast, 2009).

Similarly to Touré's (1959) strong influences in cultural and intellectual fields, Leopold Senghor articulated his version of the "African Personality," through the concept of *négritude*. Senghor and Aimé Cesaire, Francophone and Martinican poet, Afro-Cuban author and politician from La Martinique, coined the term, "négritude", a self-affirmative tool that was designed as a liberating weapon to signify the unique expressions of an African from a cultural and psychological perspective. As a humanist principle, négritude is not a racial term, but instead, "the sum of the cultural values of the black world, that is, a certain active presence in the world, or better, in the universe" (Gbadegesin, 1991, p. 37; Senghor, 1970, p. 180), an active presence in the world that was to be experienced by, and in contact with, other cultures and groups in the world.

This aggregate sum of cultural values, threaded by a socialist movement and heralded by economic and political emancipation from colonial rule, was ultimately to be achieved through Kwame Nkrumah's *pan-African ideology*. In addition to many sub-Saharan African leaders, pan-Africanism was also promoted by Gamut Abdul Nasser of Egypt and Muammad Quaddafi of Libya, who had also linked pan-Africanism with pan-Arabism.

More recent scholarship on the African Personality sheds more light on how newer generations approach the concept in terms of Africa's development. In his study on *African Identity in Pan-Africanism in Globalization*, Thiong'o (2004) addressed the debate of a singular African language, in reference to Frantz Fanon, as means of creating a unified, borderless continent. Thiong'o (2004) addressed the shared, communal similarities that already exist between neighboring countries and encourages an all-African common market, comprised of a voluntary, people-driven process of economic and communications integration. Thiong'o (2004) also proposes an authentically African democratic tradition of participatory and representative practices that actively involve all members of society, including the youth and council members.

Similarly to Thiong'o, Chinwe (2012) also implores that Africans respond to globalization's effect with frameworks that do not mirror Western ideologies, but through political means that address culture.

Similarly to some of the aforementioned African political thought leaders, Dukor (2010) has also considered additional characteristics, including an African mind or African group consciousness that unifies Africans of diverse cultural beliefs, languages, and traditions in Africa and connects them to a common experience or goal, as well as skin color—the Black race—as elements of African identification (Ndubuisi, 2013; Dukor, 2010).

But central to the observation of these various interpretations of the African Personality is Tembo's (2016) observation that different leaders' emphases on the Black race or on cultural imperialism were reflective of the historical context. Hence, I echo Tembo's (2016) observation that we grapple with defining an African Personality or African identity that is reflective of the postcolonial society of our 21st century. Is the African Personality that these leaders conceptualized relevant to our transnational realities? Or if it is relevant, then how can it be applicable?

Sulayman Nyang, former deputy ambassador and head of chancery of the Gambia Embassy in Jeddah, Saudi Arabia; former professor and chairman of the African studies department at Howard University; and one of my former mentors, observed a challenge of African identity within the context of defining African political thought, itself. In a 2012 class lecture, Nyang observes that

> The weakness of African political thought is that people are prisoners of colonial languages and forms of social communications. So long as the language spoken by a nation's people is that of the colonial language, then political thought is held captive within that of the colonists' thoughts. The stronger your cultural identity, the stronger one's political thought and consciousness—as pertinent to the thoughts, worldview and culture of the nation.
>
> (lecture notes, Fall 2012)

Nyang's (2012) observation brings us back to our starting point, as we seek to address the strength of African diasporic identities vis-à-vis the strength of their political thoughts and consciousness of their African home nation. It also introduces the perspectives I raise in the following fourth conceptual orientation that also links to the first conceptual orientation about upholding cultural values.

Representing issues that affect all people of the African continent

Tembo (2016) acknowledged that this particular orientation reflected on issues occurring in one part of the continent that became representative as affecting all people on the African continent. Surely, the vast, diverse African continent reflects various development challenges across regions that should not represent the entire continent. However, engaging the topic of African Personality or African identity affects the entire continent when the brain drain phenomenon illustrates an issue that occurs in all parts of the continent. This phenomenon impacts the whole continent and also results in the reconfiguration of diasporic identities. Hence, I explore arguments, perspectives, and viewpoints to raise questions about the issue of development and if it serves the African diaspora to adopt indigenous viewpoints to engage in African-centric discourse for development-related matters.

Agbakoba (2004) notes that traditionalist viewpoints are those that seek to highlight an irrefutable African idéntity, secured by an African philosophy. In so doing, these viewpoints respond to Western and foreign criticisms that Africans lack a unique history and culture, given their colonial history. Sekou Touré emphasized the necessity for Africans to equip themselves with environmental and cultural influences of African tradition, otherwise "they will be of no value to the revolutionary action which the African populations have undertaken to liberate themselves from colonialism, they will be outcasts and strangers in their own country" (Blackpast, 2009, para. 51).

But Agbakoba (2004) argues against the validity of certain traditionalist viewpoints as a significant source is benefitting a modern Africa; it only serves the foreigner's needs by equipping him or her with deeper understanding about "alternative thought patterns" (para. 4), including African culture, political and socioeconomic structures, and policies that can be applied toward issues of development.

However, what happens if the "foreigner" is the transcultural individual of African descent who is separated from his/her cultural and ancestral homeland and resides overseas? In light of Sekou Touré's reference to outcasts and strangers, some African diaspora are already perceived, at times, to be outcasts or strangers in their African country! An African of hybrid identities who may reside in another African country, or on another continent, for an extensive period of time could also arguably be regarded as a "foreigner" in his/her particular African homeland.

Many transcultural individuals of African descent harbor thought patterns that mirror ideologies of the cultures of their host countries. It is also important to consider the hegemony of Westernization that has influenced education systems, further prompting transcultural individuals of African descent to adopt the "official" Western languages of their host countries, along with mindsets and worldviews that may further distance him/her from ancestral, indigenous teachings, communication patterns, thought patterns, epistemological frameworks, and paradigms of the African homeland. So if this diasporic, transcultural hybrid African is no longer the indigenous one, but the foreigner in his/her own African home, wouldn't a traditionalist or indigenous viewpoint help to educate and benefit the transcultural African in learning more about his or her culture's ideologies and thought patterns, which are important for development?

So perhaps, the "alternative thought patterns" that exist for such a Western-influenced diasporic individual, particularly one born or raised outside of their African homeland, are those that are African. This individual would benefit from an adoption of and exposure to indigenous, traditional Africans' thought patterns, which would familiarize him/her with and re-acclimate him or her to local, regional, and national issues in his/her country's homeland. This is not to say that the transcultural individual should automatically reject one in exchange for another set of worldviews at every turn, but should develop a critical approach that recognizes the value of incorporating other cultural viewpoints (indigenous African worldviews that are contextualized to the particular homeland). Collectively, these viewpoints would culminate in a unique approach and new optimal development paradigms that incorporate indigenous perspectives and practices that make development meaningful to the communities of their African homeland.

In light of this, for instance, the African diaspora would consider how the African ontological significance of the "we-existence" that is opposed to the Western ontology of the "I-existence" may inform communal welfare and practices within the context of a healthcare campaign in a rural community in South Africa or a digital STEM (science, technology, engineering, math) app program in a university in Benin, for instance.

Some scholars argue that traditionalist thought and ideology keep Africans static and incapable of effectively engaging in critical dialogue to transform and develop Africa. Similarly, critics may further argue that one does not need to rely on a cultural identity to support or mobilize efforts in rebuilding a country. After all, many non-Africans are development practitioners and have joined and/or created nongovernmental organizations and associations to connect with and pioneer human-rights causes or support the development of industrial sectors in African countries. By investing their financial and/or human resources in African countries—beyond the borders of their own political or national identity—they have served as instrumental conduits of social, economic, and political change. Therefore, it is not far-fetched for an African diaspora of hybrid cultural identities to similarly invest in or contribute toward the development of their African home countries.

However, it is through an understanding and knowledge of history that one can understand one's relationship to others and find meaning in contemporary dynamics, especially since modernity is an extension of history. Ali Mazuri (1986) also insisted that one refer to cultural influences in legislation and government as a means of reform and progress in Africa, balanced with reference to other global perspectives. Mazuri's (1986) perspective of progress in the 20th century still remains relevant in the 21st century. But Agbakoba (2004) argues against the traditionalist extolment of African history to strengthen African identity, as it is always in a state of influx and hence becomes difficult to use as a justification in collectively rebuilding the continent.

Still, other critics may also argue that engaging in traditionalist or indigenous viewpoints fails to equip the diaspora with indigenous knowledge. In modernity, even an indigenous African does not represent a pure state of cultural identity. Shome and Hegde (2002) reference Radhakrishan, who asserted that "every local-native-indigenous reality has been touched by the morphology of modernism and the dominance of nationalism and the nation-state, [making] it imperative for postcoloniality to participate on more than one level and in more than one location" (Shome & Hegde, 2002, p. 262). Hence, the ability of any African—diaspora or citizen-resident—to approach a traditionalist or indigenous viewpoint that is "authentically African" becomes a challenge.

Yet, it is this challenge that inspires the global, collective body of scholars, philosophers, and African political thought leaders to develop or build upon emerging frameworks and ideologies, including Africanity, Afrocentricity, pan-Africanism, and more. Many African political thought leaders in the 20th century also recognized this challenge and articulated several philosophies or ideologies that illustrated their own definition of the "African Personality" as a revolutionary means to African independence. Many operationalized their vision of the African Personality through a pan-African ideology of liberation from colonial rule. Synergizing their perspectives with accounts from various present-day African scholars raises critical questions about the relevance of the African Personality in the 21st century, as well as its impact on the global, collective community in building African nations and developing a thriving African continent.

Exploring a human development paradigm in Africa

Economists like Dr. Wilfred David, professor of development economics of Africa and the Caribbean at Howard University, assert that meaningful and authentic development in Africa requires forms of critical theory and praxis that are grounded in ideologies that present alternative development paradigms to support Africa's development agenda, such as the *humanitarian development paradigm* (lecture notes, Fall 2012).

Over several decades, various human development paradigms and frameworks have evolved to prioritize the significance of the human dimension in development. Whereas previous models focused on economic impacts to rationalize "development," newer models evolved to present metrics of social equity, political freedoms, gender equality, community empowerment, and other components reflecting a human development approach. However, a singular universally agreed human development approach remains a source of debate and rich discussion, given numerous challenges, including "refining conceptual underpinnings of the human development approach, developing better measurement tools, and above all making the approach useful for policy purposes" (Fakuda-Parr, 2003, pg. 315).

I would like to explore some of the factors of David's (2012) humanitarian development paradigm and draw relevance from how key principles he articulates may be contextualized to center communities in Africa and African diaspora directly in the development process, based on the book's discussions. According to Dr. Wilfred David, meaningful, authentic development in a community should be achieved through six primary tenets of a *humanitarian development paradigm*: humanism, people-centrism, collective welfare, simultaneous legitimacy, grassroots empowerment, and glocalization. Wilfred's (2012) vision of a human development paradigm accentuates a shift toward the manifestation of the emancipatory potential that focuses on people-centered liberation and human well-being.

According to David (2012), *humanism* reinforces the right and opportunity for all community members to shape a wholesome economy and society that challenges all of its community members. *People-centrism* refers to an organization and thinking that is shaped by the input of all community members. *Collective welfare* highlights that development benefits all community members and is supported by *simultaneous legitimacy*, which emphasizes the interconnectedness, wholeness, and relatedness of community members. *Grassroots empowerment* decentralizes development and does not seek to marginalize or disenfranchise members of the community. Lastly, *glocalization* addresses the localization of needs and resources that ultimately enable all community members to participate in the global economy.

David's (2012) discussion of the tenets of the humanitarian development paradigm involves characteristics of human agency, inclusiveness, social co-operation, sustainability, and cultural centrism that can be applicable to various contexts of development. The humanitarian development paradigm clearly reinforces human agency as the primary source and beneficiary of development—a departure from previous development paradigms that emphasized economics, social sciences, and laws of supply and demand as forces of consumption that illustrated development. With a primary focus on human agency, David's paradigm emphasizes that humans are fully engaged participants who are in control of their development. They are not passive audiences on whom development is being conducted; instead, Africans (on the ground and in the diaspora) can contribute to their development as leaders and change agents of their progress. They are invested in their success as humans with an essential role to play in the global economy.

The inclusiveness of the model, including its reinforcement of social co-operation, is evident in its quest to include all forms of capital—social, physical, financial, and human capital. Focusing solely on one form of capital at the expense of another weakens the potential for the diaspora and their community to utilize all the available resources at their disposal. Hence, such an inclusive paradigm fosters a necessary dependency on mutual relationships between the diaspora, local citizens and NGOs (nongovernmental organizations) on the ground, and government officials who can partner and collaborate as mutually interdependent stakeholders. Their partnership ultimately transforms into a network that blends and thrives on an exchange of different resources, information, and tools that contribute toward the building of a vital African country.

The advent of the Internet and social media has allowed virtual networks to serve as optimal sites that governments have used to motivate their diaspora to contribute to their nations' development. Brinkerhoff (2009), Sall (2006), Raunet (2006), Bobeva (2006), and Milio et al. (2012) have demonstrated how the diaspora members have used e-government opportunities to engage in feedback exchange ideas, build relationships, support diaspora incentives and local initiatives, enhance cultural ties, and seek opportunities to adjust economic frameworks. Tyler (2011) praises the effects of bridging social capital, as opposed to bonding social capital, as a source of maximizing diversity from different sources of human capital to avail of optimal approaches to problem-solving. Such a communitarian movement also results in an "economy of affection"—again, emphasizing the significance of human agency.

The sustainability component of the humanitarian development model highlights its intertemporal focus, reinforcing the responsibility that is placed on the current generation to provide resources that will sustain future generations. This is emphasized in efforts to position Africa through forces of its own production, as opposed to those of consumption. By focusing on its own productive ability, generated through its own resources, Africa's development relies less on others that determine the laws of supply and demand, and more on its own ability to grow, manage, and prepare for its future on its own terms.

Lastly, the humanitarian development paradigm is cultural-centric and cultural-specific. Its success depends on the ability of the model to blend and cater to the unique, indigenous needs of the community. David (2012) reinforces that cultures serve as sources of stability and order in communities. Arguably, the unique, cultural hybrid identities of the diaspora—and their cultural allegiance to their communities, therefore—enable the diaspora to code-switch from Anglo-Saxon, "individualized-capitalistic" intercultural transients to those of African-centric subscribers to "Ubuntu" and "Harambee," African ideologies that center around collective welfare through the notions of "I am because we are" and "self-help," respectively. By resonating with these African traditional values that directly involve community members in the development process and prioritize communities' collective welfare, the diaspora can represent and connect with citizen-residents to shape development through their own prisms.

Sattherwaite (2001) and Andrews (2009) emphasized the importance of emphasizing proximity of development with the community. In *Adaptive Reuse and Cultural Heritage* (2011), the writers highlight that it pays to include culture in development. Prominent figures such as Dr Wangari Maathai, a Kenyan social, environmental, and political activist and, in 2004, the first African woman to win the Nobel Peace Prize Laureate, noted that community members learned quickly and successfully how to plant trees in the community and teach others to do so—more effectively than when she had brought some Europeans to demonstrate the tree-planting process through statistical, environmental, and more complicated techniques. Ultimately, the tree-planting tradition created a space to develop other didactic opportunities, resulting in increased political participation as Kenyan residents recognized the integration between socioeconomic development and democratic governance.

Through their roles in articulating, embodying, and implementing the humanitarian development paradigm, the diaspora, consequently, address the concepts of chaord, fragmegration, frenemy, and glocalization that David's (2012) paradigm also acknowledges. *Chaord* refers to states of chaos and order that have resulted in Africa due to displacements and misidentifications of culture and identity. *Fragmegration* highlights the centrifugal aspects of globalization's fragmentation and the centripetal aspects of globalization's integration. According to David (2012), "Africa's ability to distinguish its 'friends,' or allies, from its 'enemies,' or foes (*frenemy*) has been weakened, in attempts to reconcile partnerships of capitalism" (lecture notes, Fall 2012) that may betray the ideological framework of Africa's authentic development paradigms. Lastly, *glocalization* highlights the localizing of Africa's resources and needs and its participation in the global economy.

Ultimately, Africa's authentic development requires renewed alternative paradigms, accentuated through an overview of key issues articulated through David's (2012) humanitarian development paradigm and concrete action policies and action plans that strengthen its economic engine and regional economic integration, as well as positive, valuable international political and social relations. Critical knowledge and praxis, articulated through postcolonial theory, contextualize African development within the emancipatory potential of the diaspora, whose hybrid identities position them to "straddle cultural borders" between their host countries and African homelands. In addition to sending financial remittances to their homelands, the diaspora also transfer various skills, knowledge, abilities and other aptitudes to their countries and support opportunities for meaningful development with local communities. The advent of technology has enhanced the opportunities for the diaspora to strengthen their networks with citizen-residents in Africa, with governments, and with other relevant stakeholders.

Hence, whether it is through influencing political leadership and governance, contributing to the private sector to encourage socioeconomic development, sending remittances, advocating against human-rights violations, supporting healthcare initiatives, and launching education scholarships, to name but a few, the diaspora are positioned to contribute actively and significantly to the transformation of Africa, as we will see in subsequent chapters. Africa's richness (development)—both in terms of human quality or human welfare and GDP—requires a synergy between the continent's diaspora, local residents, the government, and an international body of key stakeholders that share a common perspective on what it means to have Africa's best interests at heart. Attaining such synergy in an interdependent relationship, however, is confronted with challenges that must be addressed transparently, rapidly, and with shared values if sustainable, meaningful, authentic development is to occur.

Conclusion

Defining the African Personality and struggling to extract the pure, untouched, African identity is an arduous task—and one that, if ever successfully conceptualized, would not receive unanimous agreement. However, articulating the authentic African spirit and linking it to an African traditional, ontological philosophy is one step toward inviting an approach toward viewing, questioning, and engaging in critical dialogue in addressing African-centric matters.

In the era of globalization that reinforces dynamic, interconnected relationships between porous boundaries to facilitate exchange of ideas and materials, the African continent is certainly not alone in its role as a participant in the global economy. However, the impacts of globalization have, arguably, left Africa as a continent that struggles in the face of industrialization and capitalistic gain—despite its abundance of resources. One of these resources is Africa's human resources—many of whom self-identify as diasporic Africans, residing as migrants outside of the continent. By forging a connection to unique culture, tradition, values, moral orders, ethics, and, ultimately, an "African way of being and doing things," one strives to inspire the African diaspora to (i) explore indigenous viewpoints as additional resources to consider when engaging in African-centric discourse and development paradigms; (ii) engage in alternative thought patterns, including African thought-consciousness; (iii) acknowledge the significance of African ontology in African personhood and community; and (iv) engage in African political thought and development communication.

It is important that transcultural individuals of African descent expand their knowledge bank and explore additional knowledge frameworks, systems and ideologies, history, and the African political thought of leaders and scholars to gain significant context that helps to orient action and formulate critical thought in their development approach toward Africa.

Nyang (2012) defined political communication as "the process by which the state controllers aggregate and articulate what they perceive to be the collective interest of all members of society" (lecture notes). The African state faces a challenge in identifying the collective interests of its national, resident citizens that are members of society. These challenges are further accentuated for their migrants who struggle to engage in their home countries and fully participate as members of those societies as well. Engaging in processes that synergize political and development communication empowers the African diaspora and citizen-residents in Africa to collaborate in their contributions toward sustainable development in Africa.

The vision of past African leaders should not be lost on the present generation. While there are opportunities to develop an alternative paradigm that incorporates the hybridity of the diaspora in development, there is some value in revisiting history to identify what may still be relevant in the present. Although it is important to respond to contextual variables of development that are relevant and timely, the past could inform us of valuable lessons learned and best practices to leverage for the road ahead.

Chapter summary

Key concepts

African ontology	fragmegration	I-existence
African Personality	frenemy	négritude
African political thought	glocalization	Pan-African ideology
chaord	grassroots empowerment	People-centrism
collective welfare	Harambee	Simultaneous legitimacy
Consciencism	Humanitarian development paradigm	Ubuntu

Discussion questions

1) Is it possible to articulate an "African Personality" in the 21st century? Why or why not? What key factors would be relevant to consider?
2) Various African political thought leaders were identified in the chapter who presented their perspectives about the African Personality. Present a case study on an African political thought leader from the 20th century and another thought leader from the 21st century. Compare and contrast their perspectives and approach in conceptualizing the African

Personality. What key factors may account for their similar perspectives? What factors may account for their different viewpoints? Do you agree or disagree with any of their perspectives? Why or why not?

References

Agbakoba, J. (2004). Dr J. C. Achike Agbakoba—Traditional African political thought and the crisis of governance in contemporary African societies. J. C. Achike Agbakoba. http://www.jsri.ro/old/html%20version/index/no_7/achikeagbakoba-articol.htm

Andrews, N. (2009). Foreign aid and development in Africa: What the literature says and what the reality is. *Journal of African Studies and Development*, *1*(1), 8–15. http://www.academia.edu/202805/Foreign_aid_and_development_in_Africa_What_the_literature_says_and_what_the_reality_is

Blackpast. (2009, August 10). *(1959) Sekou Touré, "The political leader considered as the representative of a culture"*. https://www.blackpast.org/global-african-history/1959-sekou-toure-political-leader-considered-representative-culture/

Bobeva, D. (2006). Turning remittances into investments. In: *OECD. Migration, Remittances and Development* (pp. 297–312). OECD Publishing. doi:10.1787/9789264013896-22-en

Brinkerhoff, J. (2009). *Digital Diasporas: Identity and Transnational Engagement*. Cambridge: Cambridge University Press. doi:10.1017/CBO9780511805158

Culture in Peril. (2011, April 10). *Adaptive Reuse and Cultural Heritage*. Culture in Development. http://www.cultureindevelopment.nl/News/Discussing_Culture_and_Development/892/Adaptive_Reuse_and_Cultural_Heritage_

Chinwe, F. (2012). Africa and the challenges of globalization: A critical appraisal of the relevance of pan-Africanism. Nordic Africa Institute. Retrieved from http://www.nai.uu.se/ecas-4/panels/21-40/panel-30/Asogwa-Felix-Chinwe-Full-paper.pdf

Dukor, M. (2010a). *African freedom of philosophy* (pp. 155–180). Germany: LAP LAMBERT Publications.

Fukuda-Parr, S. (2003). The human development paradigm: Operationalizing Sen's ideas on capabilities. *Feminist Economics*, *9*(2–3), 301–317. https://citeseerx.ist.psu.edu/viewdoc/download?doi=10.1.1.579.7446&rep=rep1&type=pdf

Fanon, F. (1952). *Black Skin, White Masks*. New York: Grove Press.

Gbadegesin, O. (1991). Negritude and its contribution to the civilization of the universal: Leopold Senghor and the question of ultimate reality and meaning. UTP Journals Press. https://www.utpjournals.press/doi/pdf/10.3138/uram.14.1.30

Mamdani, M. (2019, November 7). What is a tribe? *London Review of Books*. https://www.lrb.co.uk/the-paper/v34/n17/mahmood-mamdani/what-is-a-tribe

Martin, G. (2012). African political thought. *African Political Thought*, 1–9. https://www.macmillanihe.com/resources/sample-chapters/9781403966339_sample.pdf

Mazrui, A. A. A. (1986). *The Africans: A Triple Heritage*. London: BBC Publications.

Milio, S., Lattanzi, R., Casadio, F., & Crosta, N. (2012). Brain drain, brain exchange and brain circulation. The case of Italy viewed from a global perspective. Aspen Institute Italia Institutional. http://riccardolattanzi.com/website/wp-content/uploads/PDFs/Reports/BrainDrain(English).pdf

Nduibuisi, F. (2013). The philosophical paradigm of African identity and development. *Open Journal of Philosophy*, *3*(1), 222–230. https://www.scirp.org/pdf/OJPP_2013022614262155.pdf

Ngangah, I. (2019). Vital force, personhood, and community in African philosophy: An ontological study. *The International Journal of Humanities & Social Studies*, 7(10), 48–55. doi:10.24940/theijhss/2019/v7/i10/hs1910-023

Nkrumah, K. (1964). Consciencism: Philosophy and ideology for decolonization and development with particular reference to the African revolution. https://eclass.aegean.gr/modules/document/file.php/SA200/Nkrumah%202008%20%5B1964%5D.pdf

Raunet, M. (2006). Motivating migrants for social and economic development in Mali and Senegal. In: OECD. *Migration, Remittances and Development* (pp. 315–345). OECD Publishing. doi:10.1787/9789264013896-23-en

Reese, L. J. (1992). *Ecocultural factors influencing the academic success of young Latino students.* Unpublished doctoral dissertation, University of California Los Angeles.

Sall, B. (2006). Migration, remittances and economic initiatives in sub-Saharan Africa. In: *OECD. Migration, Remittances and Development* (pp. 265–278). OECD Publishing. doi:10.1787/9789264013896-19-en

Satterthwaite, D. (2001). Environmental governance: A comparative analysis of nine city case studies. *Journal of International Development, 13*(7), 1009–1014. doi: 10.1002/jid.824

Shome, R., & Hegde, R. (2002). Postcolonial approaches to communication: Charting the terrain, engaging the intersections. *Communication Theory, 12*(3), (249–270). ISSN 1050-3293.

Senghor, L. (1970). '*Negritude: A humanism of the twentieth century.*' *The African reader: Independent Africa.* W. Cartey and M. Kilson (Eds.). New York: Random House, pp. 179–199.

Tembo, J. (2016, December). *African Identity: A Question of Conceptual and Theoretical Purchase* (Master's dissertation). University of Pretoria. https://repository.up.ac.za/bitstream/handle/2263/60425/Tembo_African_2017.pdf?sequence=1&isAllowed=y

Tempels, P. (1959). *Bantu philosophy.* Translated by Rubbens, A. Paris: Presence Africaine.

Thiong'o, N. (2004). African identities: Pan-Africanism in the era of globalization and capitalist fundamentalism. *Macalester International, 14*(9), 21–42. https://digitalcommons.macalester.edu/cgi/viewcontent.cgi?referer=https://www.google.com/&httpsredir=1&article=1377&context=macintl

3 The African Diaspora Community Cultural Wealth Model (ADCCW)

A proposal to leverage the cultural capital of the African diaspora in development

The connection between one's cultural and national identity is important in the context of national development, as illustrated in previous chapters. In this chapter, we recognize some of the different forms of cultural capital that the African diaspora have acquired over time that shape the African diaspora's identity as a result of their different interactions and habitus in diverse global contexts. For some African diaspora, residents in their home countries or host countries have problematized their forms of cultural capital that they perceive as not being valuable in certain locales, especially within the context of development in their African home countries. This perspective mirrors Pierre Bourdieu's (1986) earlier argument that one acquires one's forms of cultural capital from the background (economic class) that leads to one's social mobility or success.

But it is not the various forms of cultural capital that the African diaspora have acquired over time that are problematic. Instead, what is problematic is if such a perspective results in oppressive systems or missed opportunities to effectively leverage the diaspora's forms of cultural capital and transform them into vital resources for a nation's development.

This chapter addresses the misconception that, by virtue of their hybrid identities, the African diaspora may inherently suffer cultural deficiencies that result in their limited ability to contribute toward their African countries' development agenda. As a result, some organizations may exclude African diaspora from decision-making opportunities that may benefit from their input, or they may fail to effectively leverage their competencies as vital input in community or national development agendas in the host or African home countries. Therefore, I adapt Yosso's (2005) concept of community cultural wealth, originally coined by Daniel G. Solórzano, and introduce the African Diaspora Community Cultural Wealth framework (ADCCW). This framework targets policymakers, government agencies, embassies, research institutions, and private sectors in host and African home countries to leverage the various forms of cultural capital that the African diaspora already possess and effectively implement them within Africa's development agenda.

DOI: 10.4324/9781351031660-4

Evolving Pierre Bourdieu's concept of "cultural capital" to Yosso's (2005) concept of "community cultural wealth" (CCW)

Pierre Bourdieu's (1986) observations of cultural capital hold important implications in the context of critical theory and are relevant to consider within the context of community development. Specifically, *cultural capital* refers to the knowledge, skills, abilities, and social assets that an individual has accumulated and that promotes their social mobility in a given society. The three states of cultural capital are *embodied*, *objectified*, and *institutionalized*.

Embodied cultural capital includes knowledge, or the intangible dispositions that have been acquired over time. This includes subject-matter expertise in a given topic, i.e., economics, the arts, or fashion. It also includes norms and performative behavior that we have been socialized to display when we travel and interact with others, i.e., language, gestures, traditions, and rituals. *Objectified cultural capital* refers to the physical artifacts and tangible materials that we possess, purchase, and accessorize ourselves with. These could include the clothes, books, cars, houses, tools, equipment, and food we purchase and prepare. Lastly, *institutionalized cultural capital* consists of forms of recognition and ranking, such as academic and professional degrees and certifications, job titles, and offices, as well as social roles that are assumed, including those of spouses and parents.

Bourdieu (1986) asserted that these three forms of cultural capital could be acquired through one's family and/or through formal education, which explained possible interactions between these three states of cultural capital. For instance, an individual develops an embodied cultural capital (competence, knowledge, skills) that would transform into objectified cultural capital (prizes, awards) and present him or her with advantages in securing institutionalized cultural capital. Bourdieu (1986) also acknowledged interactions between cultural, economic, and social capital (Cole, 2019). For instance, economic capital, or the acquisition of financial wealth, could be exchanged for the acquisition of education (embodied cultural capital) that could grant access to social capital (peers, community members, professionals).

Bourdieu's (1986) concept of cultural capital revolved around subcultures within a nation or region, and how class systems allowed the privileged dominant class to gain particular advantages within industries—namely education. Dimensions of cultural capital could be used in the context of power relations to emphasize and reinforce class divisions, hierarchy, and inequalities. In other words, he noted that the cultures of the dominant class that were developed at home mirror those in educational environments and eventually, professional environments, leading to the conclusion that such a habitus (system of dispositions) had been developed and acquired over time. According to Bourdieu (1986), those that were in marginalized, less-privileged classes suffered distinct disadvantages compared to students of the dominant class and did not, therefore, benefit from the advantageous interactions and dynamics of the educational system. He further asserted that the less privileged clashed with those of higher privilege as a result of their cultural dynamics at home—thus resulting in considerably less accumulated wealth, less capital, and less success, due to inadequate performance. Furthermore, limited access to acquiring and learning strategies and resources were restricted to the dominant groups, who maintained their power by using these forms of capital for social mobility (Yosso, 2005, p. 76).

Scholars, including Goldthorpe (2007), challenged Bourdieu's theory and refuted his claim that educational systems reproduce the class differentials in society when individuals from poverty lines enter school systems and achieve upward mobility. These scholars argue that such class differentials do not remain static, as Bourdieu (1986) implies. Individuals are able to adapt to their educational environments, which may differ from their cultural structures and systems at home. Furthermore, in the 21st century, the advent of digital communication and e-learning have further contributed to the mobility of class differentials. They have also contributed to the adoption of various forms of cultural capital from different social classes across the globe.

Yosso (2005) particularly challenged Bourdieu's argument that the knowledge of those in the upper and middle classes was considered to represent more valuable cultural capital than that of lower classes, who should, therefore, access such knowledge through formal education systems. Yosso (2005) argued that contemporary educational systems, particularly in the United States, used this perspective to rationalize that people of color lacked the social and cultural capital needed for social mobility. Yosso (2005) also challenged the rationale that this resulted in their significantly lower academic and social outcomes than those of White people. "As a result, schools most often work from this assumption in structuring ways to help 'disadvantaged' students whose race and class background has left them lacking necessary knowledge, social skills, abilities and cultural capital (see Valenzuela, 1999)" (Yosso, 2005, p. 70).

To address the misconception that communities of color suffer cultural deficiencies that attribute to limitations on their social mobility or success, Yosso (2005) built on previous scholars' works to further develop the concept of *community cultural wealth* (CCW). Yosso's (2005) concept of cultural wealth supports critical race theory (CRT), a framework and tool that confronts race and racial power as constructs of law and culture, and analyzes how their overt and covert manifestations and expressions in dominant cultural modes, "ideologies, structures, and institutions create and maintain racial inequality" (Price, 2016, para. 1). Critical race theory also pursues racial justice, as it examines and analyzes "illegitimate hierarchies that need to be changed" (The Bridge, n.d.).

As a critical race theory, community cultural wealth challenges the traditional view of cultural capital. It asserts that communities of color possess various forms of valuable cultural capital to "survive and resist macro and micro-forms of oppression" (Yosso, 2005, p. 77). Within the context of academia, community cultural wealth exposes racially oppressive social systems and structures of education that reinforce the educational disadvantages of students from marginalized groups. CCW also positions schools to strive toward equality and justice and to address their students' needs by leveraging the cultural capital that students of color already possess and bring into the classrooms.

Yosso (2005) proposed six forms of cultural capital that accumulate into community cultural wealth, which schools in the United States can acknowledge in their students of color and incorporate in their educational frameworks to strive toward social and racial justice: *aspirational*, *linguistic*, *familial*, *social*, *navigational*, and *resistant capital*.

Other scholars have adapted these forms of cultural capital in their works to analyze specific communities' cultural wealth in their school systems. However, community cultural wealth is a concept that can be applied to other systems and expands beyond an analysis of race, especially since critical race theory intersects with other identities and categorizations. The CCW concept can be applied through international lens in other critical cultural theoretical frameworks, including postcolonial theory, to address various oppressive structures and systems that marginalized communities face, and whose forms of cultural capital are underserved in their education, in their workplace, or in their broader, larger global communities.

I use this opportunity to expand on the community cultural wealth model in the context of international development, international diplomacy, or international relations, and I introduce my adapted model, the African Diaspora Community Cultural Wealth (ADCCW) model, which positions the African diaspora similarly to Yosso's (2005) communities of color, but contextualizes it to their unique dynamics (See Figure 3.1).

Figure 3.1 The African Diaspora Community Cultural Wealth Wheel. Adapted from Yosso (2005).

Introducing the African Diaspora Community Cultural Wealth concept (ADCCW)

The African Diaspora Community Cultural Wealth concept (ADCCW) acknowledges the various identity complexities and challenges and oppressive systems and structures that the African diaspora may confront as migrants or foreigners in a host country, or as "foreign citizens" in their African home countries. In both cases, others may problematize their diasporic identity as borderless nationals or permanent residents of nations' peripheral outskirts. As a result, the value of the African diaspora's cultural capital may be questioned by those in their home or host country who assume greater privilege and more cultural capital. Proponents of Bourdieu's (1986) theory may argue that the African diaspora—having resided in the periphery, or outside of their African country and as foreign migrants in their host country—possess less valuable cultural capital than the citizen-residents of the African home country. The African diaspora may also be stereotyped by nationals of their new host country and also assumed to offer less valuable cultural capital.

In both instances, the African diaspora may comprise the minority group that are disadvantaged from the majority groups that occupy a "dominant" space and are assumed to have greater privilege and more valuable cultural capital. Hence, Bourdieu's (1986) theory may conclude that the African diaspora would, therefore, accumulate considerably less wealth, less capital, less upward mobility, and ultimately less success than citizen-residents of their host or homelands. These assumptions could result in education systems, professional organizations, and other formal institutions stereotyping the diaspora as foreigners or immigrants who lack the social and cultural capital needed to advance in their communities of residence. As a result, the African diaspora may suffer forms of discrimination, prejudice, and exclusion and forfeit opportunities to be acknowledged with value. In other cases, the diaspora may also be perceived has having forms of valuable capital that some in "dominant social positions" may perceive as threats to their status quo. As a result, the African diaspora may still be excluded from opportunities, resulting in untapped resources and a loss to some communities.

Hence, echoing Yosso's (2005) assertion about communities of color possessing forms of cultural capital to "survive and resist macro and micro-forms of oppression" (p. 77), the ADCCW concept expresses a similar assertion: the diaspora possess various forms of valuable cultural that enable them to resist oppression and position them to be allies, leaders, and useful resources in their global communities. It also exposes culturally oppressive social systems, structures of education, or professional institutions that reinforce the disadvantages of students or professionals from marginalized groups, particularly those of African descent, in their host countries. Lastly, the ADCCW concept also reinforces the inclusivity of the underrepresented target audience. More specifically, the ADCCW concept seeks to include the diaspora's perspectives in meaningful conversations that acknowledge their needs and leverage the forms of capital they already possess to foster their success in the host country and development goals for Africa.

Although the ADCCW concept aims to effectively integrate the African diaspora in their African nations' development agenda, it acknowledges that this goal rests on the premise that the diaspora are able to receive adequate support from resources in the host country from which they reside, and from the African countries they visit, are nationals of, or seek to do business in. Hence, support may stem from various organizations within their host and African countries that have strategic partnerships, affiliations, and alliances across continents. Some of these organizations include the African country embassies; broader African diaspora entities such as the Mayor's Office on African Affairs (in Washington DC); relevant nongovernmental organizations (NGOs), African countries' Ministries of Foreign Affairs, international student services of university departments, the private sector, research institutions or community-based organizations and networks within their host countries.

Therefore, the ADCCW framework aims to fulfill two objectives:

1) Incorporate the voices, perspectives, and personal and professional experiences of the African diaspora within formalized policies, programs, and resources that support the diaspora in investing in or contributing toward their African nation's welfare;
2) Enable African governments, policymakers, and vital stakeholders in the host country and African homelands to (i) acknowledge the cultural capital that the African diaspora already possess; and (ii) refine or develop frameworks, policies, and programs that further leverage the African diaspora's forms of cultural capital to foster success in their efforts to invest in or contribute toward their African nation's welfare.

To fulfill each objective, the ADCCW framework builds from the works of Yosso (2005), Angela Locke, and other scholars and presents two questionnaires—one that targets the African diaspora and the other for the stakeholder organization that seeks to support the diaspora's pursuits in Africa's development agenda.

The questionnaire for the African diaspora requests them to disclose and assess the forms of capital they already possess, as well as to identify the forms of cultural capital in which they request additional support in their host country or African homeland (see Figure 3.2).

The other format is addressed to relevant government agencies, institutions, the private sector, and vital stakeholders who seek to respond to the needs and leverage the capital of their African diaspora to foster their African development goals. The questionnaire prompts them to (i) acknowledge the forms of cultural capital the African diaspora have identified they already possess; (ii) recognize and acknowledge how the forms of cultural capital the African diaspora possess are demonstrated or manifested, based on their own observations and interactions; and (iii) inquire and reflect on how they may support the diaspora to leverage each particular form of cultural capital to foster their success in their host community and fulfill their African development goals (see Figure 3.3).

Stakeholder organizations could also use these questionnaires as pre-engagement and post-engagement tools to help them gauge if their initiatives have effectively responded to the needs of their diaspora audience who indicated areas for additional support.

Given the unique needs of the African diaspora cultural group, the ADCCW concept contextualizes Yosso's (2005) six forms of cultural capital to those of the African diaspora and introduces two new additional forms: psycho-emotional (PsyCap-EK) capital and African-conscious capital. All these forms of capital are not mutually exclusive and support one another, as presented in the following section.

Forms of cultural capital of the African Diaspora Community Cultural Wealth Wheel (ADCCW)

Aspirational: The ability to maintain and pursue hopes, dreams, and future aspirations, and remain resilient amid obstacles and limitations. Yosso (2005) illustrates this through those who aspire to better possibilities and lifestyles for themselves and their children—despite present conditions to the contrary.

ADCCW lens: It is not unusual for African parents, their families, and individuals to have high educational and professional aspirations for their children, each other, and themselves, prompted by a desire to provide their children and future legacy with better opportunities and fewer challenges and trials than they themselves experienced or observed. This is also instilled in their children or in themselves, with expectations to pursue their ambitions and succeed in spite of inequities and discriminations that they may face as international students, or as foreigners seeking a better life for themselves and their families in their host countries. Some may arrive as university students, refugees, or blue-collar job professionals. Some may have also immigrated with doctorate degrees or other professional licenses and certifications, but due to linguistic barriers, education systems that do not convert, visa regulations, or other constraints, they may occupy professions at lower-income levels to support their families or pursue alternative routes to fulfill their goals. Some may also arrive to the country as white-collar professionals and occupy a range of positions across numerous industries and fields.

Relevant questions for policymakers, government agencies, embassies, research institutions, and key stakeholders of Africa's development to consider are the following:

- How are we supporting the dreams and aspirations of our African diaspora who come to host countries as students, as working professionals, or as those seeking better opportunities but who still maintain ties with their African home countries?

- How are we supporting the dreams and aspirations of our African diaspora who re-migrate to their African home countries and seek to invest in and develop their home countries?
- What assumptions do we have about the African diaspora's aspirations and how do they vary among the different demographics that migrate to their host countries?

Linguistic: The intellectual, social, and various communications skills acquired through the ability to speak in multiple languages, including storytelling skills and the ability to communicate through multiple media platforms.

ADCCW lens: African migrants rely heavily on their multilingualism to navigate between different networks and develop relationships between peers and professional networks. They also rely on their abilities to employ various linguistic techniques; code switch; use performative storytelling techniques; and adopt different accents, dialects, slang and vernacular, and language systems acquired from their exposure to or lived experiences in different countries to connect them to local citizen-residents, as well as to other migrants. This strengthens their sense of "familia" with others of different nationalities, particularly with those with whom they culturally or nationally identify. Relevant questions for policymakers, government agencies, embassies, research institutions, and key stakeholders of Africa's development to consider are the following:

- How are we supporting the various language and communication strengths of our African diaspora in their host and home countries to ensure they are effective in their host countries and home countries?
- What kinds of courses, programs and resources can we make available to the diaspora community in host countries to help them learn the official languages of their host countries, as well remain connected with their indigenous languages and mother tongues of their particular African country?
- What communications and media platforms do diaspora individuals leverage, create, and/or develop that connect them to each other in host countries and to their communities in their home countries? How can we further facilitate their access to these platforms or others that best serve their needs?

Familial: This refers to the kinship ties and connections to immediate and extended family—as well as close friends—and a commitment to maintain a community, its resources, communal history, traditions, and cultural knowledge. It also refers to sharing of lessons of caring and providing, which inform our social, emotional, and moral consciousness and are fostered in social settings (Yosso, 2005; Reese, 1992; Auerbach, 2001, 2004; Elenes et al., 2001; Lopez, 2003).

ADCCW lens: Family values are extremely valuable and important in African communities. Serving as the bedrock and core, family is "both an economic and emotional network and provide individuals with a sense of who they are and where they belong" (The Historical Society of Pennsylvania, n.d.). Whether in the diaspora or in their African homeland, many Africans are quick to identify and engage in familial bonds with "cousins," "sisters," "brothers," "Aunties," or Uncles" who may not necessarily be connected by bloodlines, but still represent family.

Relevant questions for policymakers, government agencies, embassies, research institutions, and key stakeholders of Africa's development to consider are the following:

- How do we help the African diaspora connect with their cultural values and their African heritage and give them the knowledge to help them maintain positive experiences in their host countries and remain connected to their home countries?
- How do we foster environments and develop platforms, or annual/seasonal outreach and events with embassies, local cultural organizations, and national government agencies that will encourage the African diaspora to learn or uphold their cultural values and heritage, and help them maintain positive experiences in their host countries, reinforce family interactions, and remain connected to their home countries?
- How do we develop programs within universities and schools that recognize and help foreign students in host countries draw on indigenous knowledge, cultural values, wisdom, and stories from their home communities?
- How do we develop programs for those migrants who are seeking family ties and have been disconnected? How do we develop programs that can integrate migrants with families in the host country who can assist and guide them with resources? How can those migrants be a resource for other migrants so they develop an intimate community of cultural wealth that newcomers can also join and leverage?

Social: This refers to networks and community of resources, friends, colleagues, peers, and contacts that emotionally support and facilitate navigation through social institutions. This also refers to a sense of "giving back" when people of color "use their social capital to attain education, legal justice, employment and health care and in exchange, give the information and resources they gained through these institutions back to their social networks" (Yosso, 2005, p. 80).

ADCCW lens: Like many migrants in foreign countries, members of the African diaspora rely on the social, personal, professional, and peer networks they interact and engage with to develop and strengthen their social capital. Information and referrals to other social capital are valuable resources that are shared and bartered among each other—especially through positive and dynamic relationships in social circles. Many also rely on family and community principles of "giving starts at home" or "paying it forward" to maintain close connections with their different communities in their host and home countries. Many also rely on the value of personal reputation to build, strengthen and leverage social capital to navigate through various social and professional institutions.

Relevant questions for policymakers, government agencies, embassies, research institutions, and key stakeholders of Africa's development to consider are the following:

- What social platforms can we design to engage diaspora with those who have permanently relocated to Africa from their host countries (returnees), or those that travel back and forth between Africa and the host country and that have successfully managed to start businesses or transition to a new careers in their African home countries?
- What events or social opportunities could we plan with local community leaders and established organizations to connect the African diaspora with other communities?
- How can we develop or strengthen networks with individuals who would be pivotal in the diaspora's careers, dreams, and aspirations in their host countries that support development, business, or investment opportunities in their African home countries?

Navigational: The ability to adjust mental scripts, code switch (deploy different linguistic, cultural, behavior codes in different environmental contexts) to maneuver through social institutions, systems and networks, e.g., job market, schools, judicial—particularly those that historically catered to communities of color and harbor institutional constraints. Yosso (2005) further explains that students' navigational capital empowers them to maneuver within unsupportive or hostile environments.

ADWCC lens: The African diaspora generally rely on adopting various coping mechanisms to support their cultural adjustments in their host countries and upon reacculturation in their African homelands. For instance, this may range from converting from French or British educational and knowledge systems to American systems, or switching or adopting different accents between the workplace and home settings. For those in particular with transcultural or transnational upbringings and experiences, their navigational capital enables them to maneuver among different cultural and linguistic networks, well as through diverse social systems that each carry various degrees of "unspoken rules," or formal or informal codes, or "caste level" rankings. The ability to navigate through each of these systems is a requisite for survival and mobility, especially as the labor market becomes increasingly global, mobile, and diverse.

Relevant questions for policymakers, government agencies, embassies, research institutions, and key stakeholders of Africa's development to consider are the following:

- How do we strengthen formal systems and channels for African diaspora individuals in host countries to share their knowledge, skills, abilities, and other aptitudes with newer migrants in their host countries?

- How do we strengthen formal systems and channels for African returnees who have relocated to their home countries to support the African diaspora individuals who want to invest in and develop their African home countries?
- How do we strengthen formal channels and networks with the African diaspora in their host countries and with citizen-residents in African home countries to facilitate information sharing and other exchanges of resources?

Resistant: The ability to assert, oppose, and confront oppressive structures and systems and challenge inequality and injustices. This is achieved through different types of verbal and nonverbal behaviors, and a conscious use of cultural knowledge or recognition of oppressive structures to motivate behaviors that transform oppressive structures (Yosso, 2005; Pizarro, 1998; Villenas & Deyhle, 1999). Students experienced racial and gender microaggressions, as well as culture shock, in college. Through those experiences, they acquired resistant capital, which they came to depend on when facing academic and social obstacles. According to Yosso (2005), the sources of this form of capital are parents, community members, and an historical legacy of engaging in social justice. This historical legacy of resistance leaves students of color particularly well positioned to leverage their higher education training to enter society prepared to solve challenging problems regarding equitable health, educational, and other social outcomes.

ADCCW lens: Some migrants from Africa may experience variations of cultural shock upon their entry into their host countries. Some may confront racism, colorism, prejudice, and other forms of injustice in unique historical and cultural contexts that are dissimilar to the contexts of their home, or of the previous host countries they resided in. Anecdotally, some African diaspora have reported experiencing taunts ranging from their "nappy hair" and accents to being perceived as "dirty" and "sick" because they hail from the stereotypical "Dark Continent" of Africa. Some may also experience covert microaggressions or overt racial behaviors in educational systems or in the workplace. Hence, some African diaspora have acquired forms of resistant capital to fulfill their goals, as they resist bullying or forms of prejudice and discrimination. Some may assume active roles as community advocates for social justice.

Relevant questions for policymakers, government agencies, embassies, research institutions, and key stakeholders of Africa's development to consider are the following:

- What initiatives can we develop to prepare new diaspora migrants in their host countries that will educate and inform them about some of the socioeconomic and historical contexts of their host country? How can we prepare the diaspora to be informed about potential inequalities and injustices they may confront, given the history of immigration, race, or other factors in the host country that may affect the diaspora's aspirational goals?

- What systems, programs, or initiatives could we develop in the African home country to prepare the African diaspora to recognize and navigate hostile, unsupportive, or resistant attitudes and systems they may experience upon relocation to their African home country?
- How do we strengthen and leverage the knowledge, skills, abilities, and other aptitudes that the African diaspora already possess as tools to survive and transform oppressive structures?
- How do we encourage the African diaspora to celebrate their African cultures, traditions, heritage, achievements, global contributions, and history amid hostile environments that are structured to oppress them?

Psycho-emotional capital, or (*PsyCap-EK*): I introduce a new form of cultural capital, psycho-emotional capital, which is a portmanteau of positive psychological capital, or *PsyCap*, and *emotional capital* (EK). I define PsyCap-EK as one's ability to confront challenges and obstacles productively, *while* managing or developing beneficial self-care, positive emotional connections, and sustained relationships with others.

PsyCap is "an individual's positive appraisal of circumstances and probability for success based on motivated effort and perseverance" (Hauth, 2016, para. 2; Luthans, Avolio, et al., 2007, p. 550). In other words, it is the ability to confront challenges and obstacles in a *productive* way (Hauth, 2016). PsyCap is comprised of four dimensions:

- *Self-efficacy*, or the confidence to pursue a task and put in the required effort to successfully accomplish the task;
- *Hope*, or the motivation to pursue goals and ability to redirect paths, as necessary, to persevere toward goals;
- *Optimism*, or making positive attributions about succeeding through "internal, permanent and pervasive events and interpreting negative events through external, temporary and situation-specific" cases (Hauth, 2016, para.3);
- *Resilience*, or the ability to recover from hindrances and adversity to succeed.

Research indicates that PsyCap benefits individuals, teams, and organizations through positive attitudes, including high job satisfaction, increased productivity, and strong performance (Hauth, 2016).

Emotional capital (EK) is "the set of resources (emotional competencies) that inhere to the person, useful for personal, professional and organizational development, and participates to social cohesion, with personal, economic and social returns" (Gendron, 2013, Abstract). Also simply defined as "a currency of leadership influence and relationship wealth," emotional capital is developed over time and leads to stronger, enhanced emotional connections and sustained relationships with others over time.

According to Fannin (2018), emotional capital is a core component of leadership and trust. Leaders with high emotional capital inspire others to invest in their successful opportunities and encourage risk-taking, and they are more easily granted forgiveness or excused for shortcomings (Fannin, 2018).

Fannin (2018) also offers ways to strengthen emotional capital: personalize emotional connections with individuals; identify and leverage commonalities, as well as individual strengths—particularly those that compensate for your challenges; "have consistent and value-add interactions" (para. 20); and reveal your vulnerability.

ADCCW lens: This form of cultural capital is particularly relevant to the African diaspora, and in particular, to TCKs who seek to invest in or develop their home countries. The ability for the diaspora to effectively manage social, psychological, and emotional intelligence is vital for their success and well-being in their host countries and upon re-entry to their home communities.

Given their ever-changing dynamics across countries and cultural zones, it is common for many diaspora to have sharpened survival instincts and strong work ethics, as well as dispositions and mindsets that are required for "success" in leading or collaborating with others, particularly in professional contexts. Many, particularly as immigrants or foreign nationals, rely on such instincts and ethics for survival—especially if their stakes are high because of limited opportunities for success in their home countries. Furthermore, some may have dependents in their home and host countries relying on them financially, which increases pressure to ensure that "failure" is not an option. Hence, these diaspora recognize the importance of relationship-building, as they seek to skillfully manage and develop relationships in the host and home countries that are vital building blocks for success. They also position themselves as professional mentors who understand how to navigate the system, laws and regulations of their environment and could offer guidance for optimal decision-making and ethical, professional conduct.

However, these very strengths generally also result in the diaspora's ability to build resistance in efforts to mitigate stress that stems from challenges they may confront as migrants in foreign countries. Some have built reputations as community leaders to support newer migrants into the foreign community or have fostered social and professional networks within their diaspora communities. They may represent sources of emotional and psychological support for others, including other migrants, families and extended families who are new to their host country.

But while some individuals may represent the face of "success," as they are rewarded for their determination to overcome challenges and accomplish innumerable achievements , it is also common for them to confront, internalize, and normalize challenges, struggle, and hardship that they may validate as part of their collective identity and fight in their new host country. In so doing, some may subconsciously "suffer in silence" with rippling consequences that adversely impact them individually and others in community. Furthermore, they may resist conventional forms of psychological counseling or therapy, which they may culturally associate with a social stigma or judgment—especially if they grew up in a patriarchal society that regards forms of mental or emotional distress as signs of weakness. But as mental health awareness continues to increase in the black community, particularly in the West, the diaspora are also empowered to be pillars of strength in the community and play a vital role to educate and offer support to others who may confront similar challenges.

Therefore, in the context of PsyCap-EK capital, I expand the concepts and notions of "success" and "leadership currency" to reflect tangible or visible accomplishments, *as well as* intangible core values and personal virtues that yield positive internal and external outcomes for the individual and broader collective community.

Hence, the African diaspora who possess strong PsyCap-EK capital reflect (i) personal attributes of perseverance, hope, optimism, and resilience; (ii) the ability to engage in optimal decision-making and ethical conduct in their pursuit of success and (iii) the ability to value and pursue appropriate mechanisms and resources for continuous psychological and emotional support.

Relevant questions for policymakers, government agencies, embassies, research institutions, and key stakeholders of Africa's development to consider are the following:

- How do we help the African diaspora develop qualities to strengthen their influential leadership, trust, and emotional connectivity with key audiences in the host country, across the African diaspora, and in their African home countries who would support their aspirations for development in their African home country?
- What systems, mechanisms, and resources for emotional or psychological support can we provide for the African diaspora to help them navigate and effectively address any mental and emotional challenges they may confront?
- How could we contextualize these systems and resources to address any cultural stigmas associated with therapy and counseling to effectively target the African diaspora and encourage them to use these resources?
- What self-help tools could we develop that empower the African diaspora to strengthen their psycho-emotional capital, or PsyCap-EK, that they may leverage in their host and home countries?

(Pan)African Consciousness: "Shared experiences of social and educational inequity may foster solidarity among Latino/a students, resulting in what Padilla called "ethnic consciousness" (1985, 61) (Kanagala et al., 2020, para. 7), which resulted in students' commitment to, and beneficial investments in, their families and communities. I define (Pan)African-Conscious capital as the ability to foster a shared solidarity among other Africans on the continent and in the diaspora and support initiatives or causes that are relevant to the uplift and development of Africa in general, irrespective of a particular African country that one may not nationally identify with.

ADCCW lens: Depending on their upbringing or on the circumstances, it is very common for members of the African diaspora to identify with a broader community of other Africans in the diaspora, regardless of their particular African nationality of citizenship. At times, they may even identify more with other African diaspora as a pan-African collective who connect through a transcultural or a diasporic identity than they may with specific diaspora members of their particular African home country who also reside in the same host country. The African diaspora's shared experiences and/or observations cater to various issues. For instance, they may express commonalities in terms of similar social, economic, cultural, or political inequities in their African homelands and host countries. They may express commonalities in reacculturation experiences upon entry into their African homelands and cultural differences with their host environments. Additional commonalities of cultural upbringing, unique relationships between community members, and various dynamics that unify their "African" identities further contribute toward a shared solidarity among the African diaspora, resulting in what I call a "(Pan)African-consciousness." Those that are active in a community of diaspora members of their particular African home country may also foster a solidarity that prompts their "African (national)-consciousness."

Furthermore, specific to the diaspora, their shared experiences of struggles, inequity, opportunity, cultural ambivalence, and commitment to invest in imagined or actual communities back in Africa also fosters a solidarity among those who relate to transnational or transcultural identities.

Hence, those with an "African-consciousness" may be committed to contributing to or investing in their families or communities of their national African country, or other African countries in which they do not have any national identity or citizenship ties. As a result, they may also invest in building networks and initiatives in the host country that cater specifically to the needs of a larger, broader, collective African diaspora community.

Relevant questions for policymakers, government agencies, embassies, research institutions, and key stakeholders of Africa's development to consider are the following:

- How can we strengthen a sense of solidarity and build a collective "African" identity among the African diaspora in their host countries in order to leverage their commitment to their African home countries?
- How can we strengthen a sense of solidarity and build a collective identity among allies in their host countries who are active in their efforts to contribute toward Africa?
- How do we promote, invest in, and celebrate the personal and professional achievements of the African diaspora who are contributing to or investing in their African community in both their host and home countries?
- What programs can we develop and support that expose and educate the African diaspora on their African history, African development matters, scholarly material, and current affairs that affect the African diaspora and their fellow citizen-residents across Africa?

Africans in the diaspora possess various forms of ethnic cultural capital that, when utilized effectively, can position them to succeed in their environments.

It is, therefore, critical for migrant Africans to (i) recognize the various forms of cultural capital that they possess; (ii) determine how these forms of capital may be leveraged effectively to serve their communities with whom they exchange knowledge, skills, and resources; and (iii) collaborate with their global and local networks to most effectively address their nations' welfare.

Sample Questionnaire of the African Diaspora Community Cultural Wealth (ADCCW) Framework for the African Diaspora Community

Name of Sponsoring Organization: ____________________ **Date:** ______________

Target Community: ____________________

Goal: The goal of this activity is to support and empower you with various resources to help you achieve your goals, as you contribute towards Africa's burgeoning development agenda! These goals may include your financial investments, entrepreneurialism, leadership or participation in an organization, business or initiative in the Diaspora or in an African country that caters to the needs of global African audiences, and/ or supports Africa's development agenda.

This questionnaire is designed to help you identify the resources that are readily accessible to you at this present time. We also encourage you to identify areas in which our organization may help you achieve your goals. Your insight could guide us to develop initiatives or to partner with relevant organizations in delivering programs, services or resources to better serve your needs.

Resources (Forms of Cultural Capital)	**Describe and Provide Examples of the Resources (Cultural Capital) You Currently Possess**	**Rate your Satisfaction of Having these Resources to Support your Goals on a Scale of 1 to 10 (1- not at all satisfied; 10 - very satisfied)**	**Additional Resources for Support** Please provide examples, e.g., *Need tutors to improve my Portuguese; need access to African professional mixers in the city; need experts on commercial real estate in South Africa*
Goals, dreams and aspirations that motivate you **(Aspirational Capital)**			
Language and any communication skills you have, at any level of proficiency **(Linguistic Capital)**			
Ties/ connections to any immediate and/ or extended family, including close-knit friends, and any resources* they offer for support **(Familial Capital)**			
Networks and community of friends, peers, colleagues, acquaintances, and any resources* they offer for support **(Social Capital)**			
Ability and skills to navigate/ maneuver between different professional or personal circles and networks **(Navigational Capital)**			
Ability to assert and advocate for your needs and interests, or oppose and confront oppressive systems that affect you **(Resistant Capital)**			
Ability to confront challenges and obstacles productively, while managing and developing self-care routines, positive emotional connections and sustained relationships with others **(PsyCap-EK Capital)**			
A sense of shared solidarity amongst other Africans in Africa or the Diaspora, and the ability or desire to support Africa's development agenda, or the communal needs within the African Diaspora community **((Pan) African-Conscious Capital)**			

**resources: refers to any form of support, including financial, emotional, logistical (transport, accommodation, etc.), other*

Figure 3.2 Sample Questionnaire of the African Diaspora Community Cultural Wealth Framework. Adapted from the University of North Texas , n.d.; Angela Locke's summary of Yosso (2005)

Sample Questionnaire of the African Diaspora Community Cultural Wealth Framework (ADCCW) for the Stakeholder Organization

Goal: The goal of this activity is to support and empower you with various resources to:

- acknowledge the resources that the African Diaspora members of your community possess
- provide additional resources they may need to foster success in their host country and contribute towards their African nations' welfare.

Pre-Requisite: Responses to the ADDCW Questionnaire for the African Diaspora Community to note the capital they identify

Resources (Forms of Cultural Capital)	**Report the Resources (Cultural Capital) the African Diaspora Cultural Community Possess (Refer to previous form)**	**Identify Additional Resources (Cultural Capital) *You Recognize/ Observe* that the African Diaspora Cultural Community Possess**	**Considerations for Additional Support (Abbreviated) *Refer to Chapter 13 for original questions***
Goals, dreams and aspirations that motivate you **(Aspirational Capital)**			• How to support dreams & goals of Diaspora who come to host country? • How to support dreams & goals of Diaspora who re-migrate to African country? • Our assumptions about their goals?
Language and any communication skills you have, at any level of proficiency **(Linguistic Capital)**			• How to support language and communication strengths of Diaspora in host country? • Courses or programs to help them learn language of host culture and indigenous language of African country? • Communication and media platforms that Diaspora leverage to connect them to homeland? How to facilitate access to these platforms?
Ties/ connections to any immediate and/ or extended family, including close-knit friends, and any resources* they offer for support **(Familial Capital)**			• How to help Diaspora connect with cultural values and maintain positive ties with African homeland? • How to develop programs with key partner organizations to foster cultural connections with African home country? • How to support new Diaspora migrants in host country re-connect with any disconnected family, and form new connections with host families? • How to support new Diaspora migrants support others new migrants?
Networks and community of friends, peers, colleagues, acquaintances, and any resources* they offer for support **(Social Capital)**			• How to develop social platforms/ networks to connect African Diaspora with returnees in African countries? • How to develop social platforms/ networks with community leaders and established organizations in host countries and African homelands?

Figure 3.3 Sample Questionnaire of the African Diaspora Community Cultural Wealth Framework (ADCCW) for the Stakeholder Organization. Adapted from the University of North Texas, n.d.; Angela Locke's Summary of Yosso (2005).

Resources (Forms of Cultural Capital) (*Cont'd*)	**Report the Resources (Cultural Capital) the African Diaspora Cultural Community Possess (Refer to previous form) (*Cont'd*)**	**Identify Additional Resources (Cultural Capital) *You Recognize/ Observe* that the African Diaspora Cultural Community Possess (*Cont'd*)**	**Considerations for Additional Support (Abbreviated) *Refer to Chapter 13 for original questions for guidance (Cont'd)***
Ability and skills to navigate/ maneuver between different professional or personal circles and networks **(Navigational Capital)**			• How to strengthen formal system and channels between current Diaspora and new Diaspora migrants to support information sharing in host country? • How to strengthen formal system and channels between Diaspora and African returnees to support information sharing in business start-ups or investments in African country? • How to strengthen formal system and channels between Diaspora and citizen-residents in Africa for information-exchange?
Ability to assert and advocate for your needs and interests, or oppose and confront oppressive systems that affect you **(Resistant Capital)**			• How to inform new Diaspora migrants about socio-economic, political and cultural dynamics of host country and prepare them for potential challenges they may confront? • How to strengthen advocacy of Diaspora and help them assert their rights when confronted with opposing structures? • How to build resilience in Diaspora and strengthen their self-identity/ self-worth amidst oppressive, systemic structures and hostile environments?
Ability to confront challenges and obstacles productively, while managing and developing self-care routines, positive emotional connections and sustained relationships with others **(PsyCap-EK Capital)**			• How to help Diaspora strengthen leadership and relationships with key communities in host country? • How to connect Diaspora to psychological/ emotional resources for support? • How to culturally contextualize therapy and counseling services to encourage Diaspora to seek help?
A sense of shared solidarity amongst other Africans in Africa or the Diaspora, and the ability or desire to support Africa's development agenda, or the communal needs within the African Diaspora community **((Pan) African-Conscious Capital)**			• How to strengthen solidarity and build a collective "African" identity amongst the African Diaspora in host country? • How to strengthen solidarity and build a collective "African" identity amongst allies in host country who are active in Africa's development agenda? • How to inform and/ or educate African Diaspora on African history and current African development matters/ affairs that affect them and citizen-residents at across the African continent?

Figure 3.3 Continued

Chapter summary

Key concepts

African Diaspora Community Cultural Wealth framework
aspirational capital
community cultural wealth
critical race theory
embodied cultural capital
familial capital
institutionalized cultural capital
linguistic capital
navigational capital
objectified cultural capital
(Pan)African consciousness
psycho-emotional capital (PsyCap-EK)
resistant capital
social capital

Discussion question

Imagine that you are responsible for developing an initiative that seeks to address the needs of a particular African diaspora community in a host country that also seeks to invest in their African home country. In your proposal, incorporate the African Diaspora Community Cultural Wealth framework (ADCCW). How will your program leverage the various forms of cultural capital of the unique group? Be creative and innovative, and think outside the box!

A) Develop a proposal to an identified embassy or institution about the value of the program that you are proposing for a clearly identified African diaspora group. In your proposal, include the following:
   a. A problem or challenge that this community is confronting and the purpose of the ADCCW tool in addressing the challenge;
   b. A clear description of this particular African diaspora community and the host country they are located in. To narrow the scope, consider their niche community—are they students of a particular university, professionals of the same organization, trade or industry, or another target group?
   c. A description of their host community environment and the relevant context of the experiences that may be unique to this unique diaspora group;
   d. While articulating the value, also clearly also identify any challenges, e.g., stigmas related to religious affiliations or linguistic barriers that characterize the circumstances of this group, and the relevance of your program. In other words, how would you advocate for the types of valuable contributions that this diaspora groups offers their African community?
   e. Refer to other resources, associations, networks, and other entities to support the feasibility and viability of your proposed initiative. Consider strategic partnerships and collaborations (in-person or online) that would be critical to support your program with funding, sponsorships, or any campaign efforts for particular activities.

References

Auerbach, S. (2001) Under co-construction: parent roles in promoting college access for students of color, unpublished doctoral dissertation, University of California, Los Angeles.

Auerbach, S. (2004) From moral supporters to struggling advocates: reconceptualizing parent involvement through the experience of Latino families, paper presented at annual meeting of the American Educational Research Association. San Diego, CA.

Bourdieu, P. (1986). The forms of capital. In: J. Richardson (Ed.), *Handbook of Theory and Research for the Sociology of Education* (pp. 241–258). Westport, CT: Greenwood.

Cole, N. (2019, September 23). *All About Cultural Capital*. ThoughtCo. https://www.thoughtco.com/what-is-cultural-capital-do-i-have-it-3026374

The Bridge (n.d.). *Critical Race Theory*. https://cyber.harvard.edu/bridge/CriticalTheory/critical4.htm

Elenes, C. A., Gonzalez, F., Delgado Bernal, D. & Villenes, S. (2001) Introduction: Chicana/ Mexicana feminist pedagogies: Consejos respeto, y educación, *International Journal of Qualitative Studies in Education*, 14(5), 595–602.

Fannin, K. (2018). The power of emotional capital in building influence and relationships. *Intelivate*. https://www.intelivate.com/team-strategy/emotional-capital-how-to-build-critical-leadership-wealth

Gendron, B. (2013). Emotional capital and education issues. *Journal of Research and Curriculum Development, 2*, 23–52. https://www.researchgate.net/publication/259972434_Emotional_Capital_and_Education_Issues

Goldthorpe, J. H. (2007). "Cultural capital": Some critical observations. *Sociologia, 1*, 0–0. https://www.semanticscholar.org/paper/%22Cultural-Capital%22%3A-Some-Critical-Observations-Goldthorpe/ce57e89f5ab433da7dfc00df2d69c694c13e4bb4

Hauth, T. (2016, July 5). Invest in the psychological capital for your employees. *ScienceForWork*. https://scienceforwork.com/blog/psychological-capital-employees/

Kanagala, V., Rendon, L., & Nora, A. (2016). *A framework for understanding Latino/a cultural wealth*. Association of American Colleges & Universities. https://www.aacu.org/diversitydemocracy/2016/winter/kanagala

Kanagala, V., Rendón, L., & Nora, A. (2020, December 24). *A Framework for Understanding Latino/a Cultural Wealth*. Association of American Colleges & Universities. https://www.aacu.org/diversitydemocracy/2016/winter/kanagala

Lopez, G. (2003) Parental involvement as racialized performance, in: G. Lopez & L. Parker (Eds) *Interrogating racism in qualitative research methodology* (New York, Peter Lang Publishing), 71–95.

Luthans, F., Avolio, B. J., Avey, J. B., & Norman, S. M. (2007). Positive psychological capital: Measurement and relationship with performance and satisfaction. *Personnel psychology*, 60(3), 541–572.

Pizarro, M. (1998) 'Chicano power!' Epistemology and methodology for social justice and empowerment in Chicana/o communities, *International Journal of Qualitative Studies in Education*, 11(1), 57–80.

Price, P. G. (2016, January 4). Critical race theory. *Oxford Research Encyclopedia of Education*. https://oxfordre.com/education/view/10.1093/acrefore/9780190264093.001.0001/acrefore-9780190264093-e-1

University of North Texas (n.d.). Cultural wealth wheel. UNT Digital Library. https://digital.library.unt.edu/ark:/67531/metadc1464202/m2/1/high_res_d/In_The_Emergency_of_the_N_Word,_Make_Sure_to_Use_AAA-Handout.pdf

Valenzuela, A. (1999) *Subtractive schooling: US-Mexican youth and the politics of caring* (New York, SUNY Press).

Villenas, S. & Deyhle, D. (1999) Critical race theory and ethnographies challenging the stereotypes: Latino families, schooling, resilience and resistance, *Curriculum Inquiry*, 29(4), 413–445.

Yosso, T. J. (2005). Whose culture has capital? A critical race theory discussion of community cultural wealth. *Race, Ethnicity and Education*, *8*(1), 69–91. doi:10.1080/1361332052000341006

Unit 2

Globalization in the 21st century transforms the face of Africa and of her people within and outside the continent. The advent of ever-evolving technology, the growth of the private sector, international business opportunities, and entrepreneurialism are some of the reasons Africa is hailed as the one of the fastest growing continents in the world. As of February 2020, the top African countries to invest in as a result of healthy business environments, measured through parameters of market size, market growth, and operating environment quotient, based on the World Bank's operating environment scoring, include Egypt, Morocco, South Africa, Kenya, Rwanda, Ghana, Cote d'Ivoire, Nigeria, Ethiopia, and Tunisia (Ebatemehi, 2020).

Beginning in Chapter 4, this unit introduces the brain circulation phenomenon as one of the newer migration postulates to have evolved from the "brain drain"–"brain gain" dynamic. The brain circulation phenomenon illustrates how the African diaspora maintain socioeconomic, political, and cultural ties with their homelands and contribute to their African nations' development even as they reside in their host countries.

However, some diaspora may be uninformed or less informed about how to contribute to their African nations' welfare, especially if they have not returned home to their home country. Some may also struggle to locate or identify information about some of Africa's growth sectors to inform their decision-making in investments and opportunities about contributing towards nation-building in their African home country. Different resources and literature may provide snippets of some of the top seven sectors driving growth in Africa, whereas others may omit or include additional sectors and produce a brief snapshot of the top five or top ten sectors to consider investing in. Furthermore, some of these profiles provide little context about country cases or the industry, and may omit additional relevant discourse supporting that field.

Hence, this unit seeks to address these challenges and reduce the information deficit. Chapters 5 through 8 attempt to fulfill one of the objectives of this book: to present a one-stop shop or repository that identifies some of the top-performing industries and sectors driving growth across Africa that may guide the African diaspora in exploring their interests. The following chapters introduce each sector or industry with a snapshot of relevant data and current

DOI: 10.4324/9781351031660-5

trends, breakthroughs, and developments that characterize the industry, cited with examples and data from various African countries. The overviews of the sector also interweave critical theories or concepts and offer recommendations as to how the African diaspora may approach contributing towards the industry. Lastly, each sector also outlines how it has been impacted by the Covid-19 pandemic. Viewpoints from entrepreneurs or industry experts are also shared throughout the sections, including those with whom I conducted interviews for the purpose of this book.

It is important to note that the information provided over the next few chapters in this unit are starting points to introduce audiences to some of Africa's fastest-growing sectors and industries. Therefore, readers should approach this unit aiming to explore sectors and industries of interest; further the discourse surrounding the topics; assess some of the recommendations provided; conduct in-depth country-specific analyses of their selected sector or industry of interest; and connect with industry experts for guidance on how to pursue investments or entrepreneurial endeavors or contribute in other practical ways towards Africa's development. Given the chapters' broad overview, additional research would help the African diaspora gain country or regional data on actual performance and specific productivity indicators of each of these sectors or industries.

Below are the top 11 sectors and industries, as of March 2020, driving growth in Africa that the African diaspora could consider investing in or contributing to.

The sectors and industries have been grouped within broader categories to facilitate relevant cross-sectoral analyses:

- Chapter 5: Industrialization
  - Agribusiness and agriculture
  - Food and gastronomy
  - Start-up funding
  - Fintech and telecommunications
- Chapter 6: Infrastructure
  - Economic Infrastructure: Energy, transport, mining, water/sanitation
  - Social infrastructure
    - Education
    - Healthcare and pharmacy
- Chapter 7: Creative and culture economy
  - Film and music
  - Fashion, textile/apparel/retail/luxury
- Chapter 8: Leisure and hospitality
  - Real estate
  - Tourism

4 Migration postulates

Brain drain, brain gain, brain circulation

Stella-Monica N. Mpande

Vivid hope and signs of Africa's economic boom are clear! Africa's current population growth is expected to increase from 1.2 billion to 1.7 billion by 2030, marking its place as the fastest-urbanizing region in the world, given a projected growth of more than 80% of its population to occur in cities over the next few decades (Leke & Signé, 2019). Increased incomes and new business opportunities in the consumer market also project an increase of "annual spending by African consumers and businesses to reach $6.66 trillion by 2030, up from $4 trillion in 2015 … [and market growth in various] sectors where Africans have unmet needs, including food, beverages, pharmaceuticals, financial services, healthcare, and education" (Leke & Signé, 2019, para. 1). Furthermore, as of 2019, "six of the world's 10 fastest-growing economies are in Africa; for the period 2014–2050, PwC projects that Nigeria, South Africa, and Egypt will remain in the top 10" (Signé & Gurib-Fakim, 2019, para. 1).

Yet, in light of these breakthroughs, Africa still faces an imminent crisis that requires urgent attention: a rapid outflux of talent that has resulted in a *brain drain* from the continent.

Job unemployment, war, an unstable political climate, an autocratic regime, starvation, poverty are just a few of the factors that may push one out of one's home country or force families to emigrate from their country, resulting in the loss of talent or intellectual, financial capital—a brain drain—from a country. Attractive and lucrative employment salaries and benefits, the democratic values of a peaceful country, better education opportunities, and improved healthcare options illustrate factors that "pull" individuals and their families to immigrate into a host country. As a result, the receiving country benefits from human, intellectual, and financial resources that add to its *brain gain*. The aggregate influxes and outfluxes of capital affect countries' development across different sectors. Furthermore, the advent of the 2020 Covid-19 pandemic has crippled the productivity of key industries and sectors in Africa, resulting in declining economic growth in many African countries—particularly their informal economy which "accounts for over 70 percent of hours worked in Africa and is a main income source for at least 60 percent of African households and over 80 percent of rural households" (Fox & Signé, 2020, para. 2).

DOI: 10.4324/9781351031660-6

A significant stakeholder that African nations acknowledge as vital to their development agenda are the African diaspora. The United Nations Development Programme (UNDP) defines development as the "expanding the richness of human life, rather than simply the richness of the economy in which human beings live. It is an approach that is focused on creating fair opportunities and choices for all people" (The United Nations Development Programme, 2018, para. 2).

The African diaspora play a critical role in the political, socioeconomic and cultural development of their African home countries. Mpande's (2015) case study of how the Ugandan government can motivate its Ugandan diaspora in the USA to invest in or contribute to Uganda's development revealed a key implication: "nations must ... adhere to the unique psycho-emotional needs related to trust, commitment, control mutuality, satisfaction and feeling needed and valued by the home community" (Mpande, 2015, Abstract).

Evidently, the African diaspora are recognized and valued for sending financial remittances to their home countries, as we will see in this chapter. However, tensions surrounding identity politics, nationhood, and fragile relationships with governments or citizen-residents in their African home countries, ineffective communication strategies and unclear policies, as well as inaccessible information resources, represent some challenges that affect nations' ability to effectively assimilate diaspora investments into the national welfare.

Ultimately, Africa's sustainable development relies on her nations' ability to address these challenges and effectively leverage their relationships with their key stakeholders—and in this context, their diaspora.

The brain drain from Africa: A harrowing overview

The African continent is no exception to the brain drain–brain gain phenomenon. The continent has been severely impacted by the constant migration patterns of its citizen-residents, particularly the brain drain. With an African diaspora of more than 30 million scattered across the globe, the Africa Union estimates that 70,000 skilled professionals emigrate annually from Africa (Mo Ibrahim Foundation, 2018). The World Bank Group estimated a stock of 23.2 million emigrants from sub-Saharan Africa (2.5% of population) in 2013, compared to 18.0 million immigrants (1.9% of population) (World Bank Group, 2016). Whereas 65.6% consisted of intraregional migrations, 26.1% emigrated to high-income OCED countries. Data pertaining to migration patterns of the Middle East and North Africa reveal an estimated stock of 23.9 million emigrants (6.8% of the population) compared to 11.7 million (3.3% of the population) (World Bank Group, 2016). With 30.9% migrations taking place intraregionally, about 37.7% emigrated to high-income OCED countries. In 2016, the IMF's World Economic Outlook estimated an increase in African migrants in OECD countries to 34 million by 2050 (Mo Ibrahim Foundation, 2018).

As of 2014, the top ten sending African countries were Somalia, Burkina Faso, Sudan, the Democratic Republic of Congo, Nigeria, Côte d'Ivoire, Zimbabwe, Mali, South Africa, and South Sudan. In 2013, France, the United Kingdom (UK), and the United States (US) were the top receiving countries of 50% of the total sub-Saharan African diaspora (Mo Ibrahim Report, 2018). The 2018 Mo Ibrahim Foundation also reported that "Africa's Island countries are most impacted by this phenomenon, with almost one-third of Cabo Verde's population and about 10.0% of Mauritius, São Tomé & Príncipe, and Seychelles' population living outside the country" (para. 3).

Impact of the brain drain on industries and sectors in Africa

As of 2011, 33.4% of total sub-Saharan African emigrants in OECD countries are tertiary-educated, with 31.4% of tertiary-educated sub-Saharan women emigrants living in OECD countries (Migration and Remittances Factbook, 2016). For the Middle East and North Africa, 25.9% of total emigrants in OECD countries were tertiary-educated, with 23.8% of tertiary-educated women as a percentage of total women emigrants in OECD countries (World Bank Group, 2016). These statistics reinforce the loss of valuable talent and resources from the African continent that would otherwise aid the continent's development. The adverse impact of Africa's brain drain continues to affect several industries and sectors.

As doctors are incentivized to relocate abroad, the shortage of medical professionals in Africa further decreases. The World Health Organization (WHO) estimates that about 57% of Africans have poor or no access to quality healthcare, which is further aggravated by reduced ratios of doctors to population. This data reinforces adverse impacts when pandemics, including the Ebola crisis, which resurfaced in 2014, affecting Liberia, Sierra Leone, and Guinea, countries where it is estimated that there are about 0.1 physicians per 1,000 people (Christensen & Goldschmidt, 2014). Due to the Ebola crisis, Liberia witnessed a decrease in doctors from 7.76 doctors per 100,000 people in 1973 to 1.34 doctors per 100,000 people in 2008 (Firsing, 2016).

Uganda, with an estimated population of 35 million people, has less than 5,000 doctors and 30,000 nurses, according to WHO (Firsing, 2016). The shortage of in-house medical professionals to treat patients aggravates pandemics and the ravages of disease. Additionally, 30%–40% of Kenya's 600 doctors who graduate annually leave the country after their internship to pursue opportunities abroad—namely, in South Africa—resulting in a negative impact on the country's health sector, according to a qualitative study (Firsing, 2016). While Zimbabwe is estimated to have 0.08 physicians per 1,000 people of the nation's population, Malawi in 2009 had 0.019 doctors per 1,000 people and Mauritania about 0.13, based on World Health Organization data (Soergel, 2016).

The brain drain has also affected other industries. According to former South African president Thabo Mbeki, Africa's outflow of 20,000 academics and 10% of the highly skilled information and technology industry and financial professionals highlights the severity of Africa's brain drain, exacerbated by estimates that the US and UK are home to many African scientists and engineers (Firsing, 2016).

But the brain drain from Africa does not always commence at the point at which an African physically leaves their home country to attend university or take up job opportunities outside of their home country. A combination of various factors—including British, French, or American educational curricula policy and practice and knowledge systems originating from colonial rule, as well as infrastructure challenges affecting the quality of education in some African countries—prime many Africans to embark on paths outside of their African continent. Hence, from early childhood, many Africans generally prepare or aspire to advance their education or attain scholarships, usually in the US, UK, France, or Canada. They perceive a quality education that would also result in well-compensated, sustainable careers.

Brain circulation: A "happy medium" between the brain gain and brain drain postulates?

Brain circulation, coined by Rubin Patterson, or similarly described as the "triangular human talent flow" by Tung (2008), describes the two-way migration flow that connects migrants to both their home and host countries. This newer postulate of globalization and migration flow deviates from the traditional brain drain–brain gain phenomenon (outward–inward flow of capital). As newer terminology, concepts, and definitions of this migration flow emerge to describe its complex phenomena, the emergence of diaspora groups, however, traces back to history. The urgency to understand patterns of behavior that support socioeconomic development increases as the effect of migrations from developing countries have negative impacts on their economies. In the case of Africa, the impact is devasting when a continent that is rich and abundant in natural resources, and whose human resources have the potential to contribute to its development, struggles to properly unleash its potential.

The brain circulation phenomenon, therefore, positions Africa for an optimistic outlook, as the migration pattern is not permanently one-way, but two-way. The African diaspora may leverage various opportunities to invest in and contribute toward their nations' development. Their psycho-emotional connection and ties to their African motherland generally predisposes them to send remittances back to their African countries; represent their countries as cultural or political ambassadors to foreign publics in host and visiting countries; and contribute critical nonfinancial capital that represent valuable assets for their nations' development. However, as we will see in the next chapters, it takes more than just a love for one's country to develop a nation.

Contributions to and investments of the African diaspora in their nations' development

Remittances, in the context of migration, are generally defined as the financial transfers of money and goods that migrants make to their countries of origin. In 2019, the African diaspora collectively sent more than $40 billion in remittances to Africa (Africa.com, 2019). In 2015, the top ten remittance recipients in Africa were Nigeria ($20.8bn), Ghana ($2.0bn), Senegal ($1.6bn), Kenya ($1.6bn), South Africa ($1.0bn), Uganda ($0.9bn), Mali ($0.9bn), Ethiopia ($0.6bn), Liberia ($0.5bn), and Sudan ($0.5bn) (World Bank Group, 2016). In 2019, Zimbabwe was among the top five countries receiving diasporas' remittances, along with Ghana, Kenya, Uganda, and Nigeria—the latter receiving the most. The top sending countries to the sub-Saharan African region include the US, Australia, Canada, Sweden, and UK—the latter sending the most remittances (World Bank Group, 2016).

According to Africa Tech (2019), the role of the African diaspora has been instrumental in the continent's development, with the value of their remittances being at least three times larger than that of official development assistance (ODA) and exceeding the flow of foreign direct investment (FDI) for various African countries. However, these figures represent the *formal remittance sector*, whose data accounts for remittances transferred through formal, official, public banking channels, rather than the private, unrecorded channels of the *informal remittance sector*. Funds may be transferred through informal channels by undocumented workers in the diaspora who cannot access banks without valid identity cards. Monies that are transferred to families through personal networks also contribute to the informal remittance sector. "Calculations in the World Development Report 2007 suggest that the informal remittance sector is at least 50 percent of the official sector (World Bank 2006)" (Endo et al., 2011, p. 9).

The impact of financial remittances on nations' development, or Gross National Product (GNP), remains a controversial topic among economists and analysts. As remittances are generally personal and directed toward families and personal networks within the country, they are perceived as more stable in various economic conditions that rely less on the market economy—in contrast to the "lesser stability" of the foreign investor, who would weigh investment decisions against the market climate.

But counterarguments highlight the "unproductive" impact of remittances that are consumed in domestic households to pay bills and fees and buy groceries, activities that fail to impact a country's GNP. However, Wahba (2006) insists that remittances spent on health and education are investments in children's human capital and in a future generation, reinforcing the argument that remittances may, therefore, be "productive investments," depending on their impact on the development of a home country (Mpande, 2015).

Subsequently, remittances may also refer to nonfinancial transfers of capital. Nonfinancial remittances, or contributions, from the African diaspora have arguably contributed to their nations' development. As the diaspora acquire knowledge, skills, and abilities in various industries in different sectors from the countries they migrate to, many transfer and apply their knowledge in the effort to improve livelihoods in their African home countries. They may innovate solutions or introduce ideas for problem-solving that also open up opportunities for jobs in sciences and technology, entertainment and the arts, healthcare, financial technology (fintech), digital and ICT, fashion and apparel, and other key sectors that add value creation, create job opportunities, and support their nations' welfare.

Through entrepreneurial investments, start-up companies, nonprofit organizations, strategic partnerships, and collaborations with citizen-residents on the ground and key stakeholders, the African diaspora may contribute toward their nations' sectors and overall economy, which have a significant impact on their communities. Financial remittances arguably support their local communities but present questions about their overall impact on their nations' economies. Nonfinancial remittances, particularly through knowledge transfer, are also viable for nations' development and growth.

The following chapters will illustrate opportunities for nonfinancial remittances that the African diaspora may consider in contributing toward their national welfare.

Chapter summary

Key concepts

brain circulation	formal remittances sector
brain drain	informal remittances sector
brain gain	remittances

Discussion questions

1) Do financial remittances hurt or benefit the economy of the *receiving* country? Why or why not? Provide specific examples to illustrate your argument about their impact or effect on nations' economy.
2) Do financial remittances hurt or benefit the economy of the *sending* country? Why or why not? Provide specific examples to illustrate your argument about their impact or effect on nations' economy.

References

Africa.com (2019, December 16). The African diaspora: Beyond remittance. https://africa.com/the-african-diaspora-beyond-remittance/

Christensen, J., & Goldschmidt, D. (2014). "Out of control." How the world reacted as Ebola spread. *CNN*. https://edition.cnn.com/interactive/2014/11/health/ebola-outbreak-timeline/

Ebatamehi, S. (2020, February 27). Top 10 African countries to invest in 2020. *The African Exponent.* https://www.africanexponent.com/post/7176-best-countries-to-invest-in-africa-2020

Endo, I., Namaaji, J., & Kulathunga, A. (2011). *Uganda's Remittance Corridors from United Kingdom, United States, and South Africa.* Washington D.C.: World Bank Group. doi:10.1596/978-0-8213-8430-5

Firsing, S. (2016, January 21). How severe is Africa's brain drain? *Quartz Africa.* https://qz.com/africa/599140/how-severe-is-africas-brain-drain/#:%7E:text=The%20recent%20Ebola%20crisis%20highlighted,to%201.37%20doctors%20in%202008

Fox, L., & Signé, L. (2020, May 27). COVID-19 and the future of work in Africa: How to shore up incomes for informal sector workers. Brookings. https://www.brookings.edu/blog/africa-in-focus/2020/05/26/covid-19-and-the-future-of-work-in-africa-how-to-shore-up-incomes-for-informal-sector-workers/

Leke, A., & Signé, L. (2019, January 11). Spotlighting opportunities for business in Africa and strategies to succeed in the world's next big growth market. Brookings. https://www.brookings.edu/research/spotlighting-opportunities-for-business-in-africa-and-strategies-to-succeed-in-the-worlds-next-big-growth-market/

Mo Ibrahim Foundation (2018). *Brain Drain: A Bane to Africa's Potential.* https://mo.ibrahim.foundation/news/2018/brain-drain-bane-africas-potential

Mpande, S. (2015). *Relationship management of the brain circulation phenomenon: The case of the Ugandan diaspora in the USA* (Publication No. 3718222) [Doctoral dissertation, Howard University]. ProQuest Dissertations and Theses Global.

Signe, L., & Gurib-Fakim, A. (2019, August 2). The high growth promise of an integrated Africa. Brookings. https://www.brookings.edu/opinions/the-high-growth-promise-of-an-integrated-africa/

Soergel, A. (2016). Sub-Saharan Africa bleeds skilled labor as "brain drain" continues. *U.S. News.* https://www.usnews.com/news/best-countries/articles/2016-10-07/sub-saharan-africa-bleeds-skilled-labor-as-brain-drain-continues#:~:text=Malawi%20in%202009%20held%20only,Mauritania's%20concentration%20sat%20at%200.13.&text=For%20comparison's%20sake%2C%20the%20U.S.,per%201%2C000%20people%20in%202011

Tung, R. L. (2008). Brain circulation, diaspora, and international competitiveness. *European Management Journal, 26*(5), 298–304. Retrieved from http://www.cctr.ust.hk/materials/working_papers/WorkingPaper15.pdf

United Nations Development Programme (2018). *About Human Development | Human Development Reports.* http://hdr.undp.org/en/humandev#:%7E:text=Human%20development%20%E2%80%93%20or%20the%20human,and%20their%20opportunities%20and%20choices

Wahba, J. (2006). What is the macroeconomic impact of international remittances on the home country? In OECD. *Migration, remittances and development* (pp. 185–191). OECD Publishing. doi: 10.1787/9789264013896-13-en

World Bank. (2006). *Global economic prospects 2006: Economic implications of remittances and migration.* Washington, D.C.

World Bank Group (2016). *Migration and Remittances Factbook 2016* (3rd ed.) [E-book]. Washington D.C.: World Bank Group. http://hdl.handle.net/10986/23743

5 An overview of growth sectors and industries in Africa

Part I: Exploring industrialization

Industrialization (general)

Industrialization, or the rapid development of a region or country's industries on a large scale, has been recognized as a key driver in strong and sustainable development in Africa. In 2018, African agribusiness was projected to double production to an estimate of $1 trillion by 2030 (African Development Bank, 2018).

In addition, business-to-business (B2B) spending in manufacturing in Africa is estimated to reach $666.3 billion by 2030—an increase of $201.28 billion since 2015, according to Brookings Institution (Signé, 2018). In short, Africa's economy is booming and growing rapidly!

With emphasis placed on manufacturing and processing capabilities, the continent has been positioned to see boosts in economic development. Infrastructure, institutions, human capital, and technology are also expected to drive Africa's manufacturing-led growth, which will build the continent's economic resilience and shift its dependency from natural resource exports (Tanui, 2019). As of 2020, Africa's imports annually were estimated to be $232 billion of manufactured goods, juxtaposed with exports of a net of $174 billion of raw commodities; in spite of annual economic growth of 5.5% per year since 2005, manufacturing remains a fixed share, accounting for 10% of GDP (Abiodun et al., 2020).

Africa's population growth over the upcoming decades is expected to populate cities and suggests that an increase in food, beverages, healthcare, education, pharmaceuticals, and other resources will be required to address the needs of an increasing urban population (Leke & Signé, 2019). This positions major industries and investors in the manufacturing and retail industries to increase business and job opportunities that will meet the needs of these consumers, and potentially promote social and political stability.

One of the drivers for advancing industrialization lies in the digitization and automation of the manufacturing industry that is positioned for "*Industry 4.0*," also known as *4IR* or the "fourth industrial revolution," a term conceptualized by the German government. Economists, analysts, and experts recognize Industry 4.0 as the next level of the digitization and automation of

DOI: 10.4324/9781351031660-7

industrialization that integrates complex algorithms to create new networks of machines, properties, ICT systems, smart machines, smart factories, and individual customers across the entire value chain and full product cycle. By customizing the value chain from customized product design throughout the manufacturing process to meet unique needs of individual customers, companies aim for maximum customer satisfaction levels at final delivery. Such outcomes would position companies uniquely in the competitive global market.

Also summarized as the "internet of things, services, data and people" (Deloitte, 2016, p. 3), Industry 4.0 is poised to revolutionize development through a disruptive approach that will drive business growth for companies. Additional advantages that traditional industrial economies like Germany and the US foresee include "relocating production to low-cost countries and opening of more domestic production locations in Europe and North America" (Deloitte, 2016, p. 9).

But what does 4IR mean for developing countries in Africa that may still be struggling to address the challenges of disproportionate internet access or connectivity in Industry 3.0, or that are fighting to compete with emerging and developed economies that have more advanced digitization and manufacturing capabilities? As of 2019, less than a third of the population across Africa has access to broadband connectivity, and an investment of US$100 billion would be required to achieve "universal, affordable, and good quality internet access by 2030" (Jeremiah & Umeh, 2019, para. 1).

So, is Africa well-equipped and prepared for Industry 4.0? Will Africa benefit from 4IR or would the continent become vulnerable? To what extent can Africa compete in the global market game of 4IR with other "big players," or will she participate from peripheral seats or the proverbial bench outside of the epicenter of activity?

According to research experts in Deloitte, challenges in internet connectivity and internet access account for low current adoption and impact of 4IR in the Africa region. In addition to lagging infrastructure in developing countries, there are risks of personal privacy and human security, including abuses of technology and violations of privacy. "Given that less than half of African states have dedicated computer emergency response teams … African states arguably need to equip themselves to … police global cybersphere more effectively, to mitigate the effects of data breaches on their own citizens" (Allen, 2019, para. 5).

However, experts surmise that countries like South Africa that are not "weighed down by infrastructure legacy issues … may have little difficulty in embracing change" (Deloitte, 2016, p. 15). Other optimistic benefits about the impact of 4IR on Africa and employment are that data analytics and advanced software enterprise systems would enable rural and business owners to make smarter data-driven business and marketing decisions that strategically target customers; foster more collaboration among stakeholders along the value chain; secure digital payments on their smartphones; and apply for bank loans, due to transparency and clear statistical data on financial activity, including revenues and cash flow (Creamer Media Reporter, 2019).

Ultimately, policy experts suggest that although the adoption of 4IR is at a foundation stage, there may be opportunities to adopt advanced analytics and apply them to particular sectors. This suggests that countries would need to determine how they can gain a unique competitive advantage by identifying which sectors would yield greater returns on investment with an application of 4IR. Tarik Darragi, CEO of Grafica Ivoire in Côte d'Ivoire, also notes how African countries can be positioned to lead the global market with avant-garde innovative, digital technologies that respond to the unique needs of their communities; some technologies that work within the unique context of an African country may not mirror or reflect the same use in the West (personal communication, February 5, 2021).

The industrial revolution will also impact consumer spending in Africa, primarily through e-commerce. Relatively new and with potential to boom, e-commerce can respond effectively to Africa's growing consumer spending, which was estimated at $1.4 trillion in 2015 (to which South Africa, Nigeria and Egypt contributed more than half of the total), and is expected to top $2 trillion by 2025 (Hattingh et al., 2017). Trusted e-commerce players like Ebay, Amazon, Etsy, Alibaba and similar platforms have facilitated business-to-consumer (BTC) transactions and arguably could be some of the biggest competitors to numerous retailers globally. Such competition for retailers and brick-and-mortar stores in Africa remain relatively underwhelming, considering that in 2017, the entire continent only had about 21 million online shoppers—"less than 2% of the world's total" (Lewis, 2020, para. 2), according to data from the United Nations. Although this data reveals an industry still in its infancy, e-commerce is growing steadily in Africa. The number of online shoppers in Africa has increased annually by 18% since 2014, according to the United Nations Conference on Trade and Development (UNCTD) (Masekesa, 2020).

Some of Africa's leading e-commerce platforms hail from the three top dominating economies in Africa: Nigeria, with platforms Jumia and Konga; South Africa, with Takealot and BidorBuy; and Kenya with KiliMall. The total value of the e-commerce industry in Africa reached $16.5 billion in 2017 and is projected to rise to $29 billion by 2022, according to data from Statista (Masekesa, 2020). Technological innovations in mobile technology and smartphones benefit retailers and business owners who rely on e-commerce to drive sales and offer promotions to customers through social media, and communities in rural areas with limited options for products.

Spillover effects of increased online shopping through mobile technology have also spiked the demand for smartphones in Africa. The number of smartphones in South Africa rose by 52% in 2016 and 63% in 2017, and by more than 44% and 30% in Kenya and Nigeria, respectively; there was also a twofold increase resulting from an uptake of smartphones reaching more than 226 million across the continent (She Leads Africa, 2020).

All these technological benefits reinforce breakthroughs for Africa's business owners and consumers. However, critical considerations should also be considered to ensure overall sustainable advancements with greater impact.

Technology as a tool for development has undoubtedly transformed societies, reinforcing the global interaction and integration of processes, ideas, products, and people to provide immeasurable benefits, albeit with some challenges and limitations. The implementation of technology as a conduit for "modernizing" societies to further advance and develop in the world market and allow developing countries to emerge out of poverty outlines one of the basic tenets of modernization theory. *Modernization theory*, one of the early theories of development that originated from German sociologist Max Weber and was further developed by Harvard sociologist Talcott Parsons, was a dominant paradigm in the social sciences between the 1950s and 1960s; it reemerged in 1991 and remains controversial. According to Gavrov and Kluykanov (2015),

> Today, the concept of modernization is understood in three different meanings: (1) as the internal development of Western Europe and North America relating to the European New Era; (2) as a process by which countries that do not belong to the first group of countries aim to catch up with them; and (3) as processes of evolutionary development of the most modernized societies (Western Europe and North America), i.e., modernization as a permanent process, carried out through reform and innovation, which today means a transition to a postindustrial society
>
> (p. 707).

Controversial and complex, modernization theory faces criticism from oppositionists who reject the paradigm for displacing traditional values, culture, human will, and emotion to motivate social behavior through rationalization, power redistributions, and other principles that underline world class theory, dependency theory, globalization theory, and other ideologies.

The *critical theory of technology* that Andrew Feenberg (2002) highlights in his works, including *Transforming Technology*, presents technology as a two-pronged concept that either (i) empowers humans as operators of technical action, or (ii) subjugates society to technological power. According to Feenberg (2005), technical codes are the underlying rules, values, and interests under which technologies are realized to achieved desired goals and hence reveal the biases of unequal power distribution in social contexts, resulting in outcomes that favor influential social groups.

In other words, the elite, technocrats, or those who have influence over technologies embed their goals, interests, and values through technical codes along the technology value chain—from conception and design through implementation and management. Feenberg's (2005) *theory of instrumentalization* considers analyses of technology through two levels: a primary level that addresses the technology's functionality, and a secondary level that addresses technology's design and implementation, which also incorporates the social and political values, aesthetics, and meaning that are assigned to technology.

Perhaps the theory of instrumentalization can also be illustrated through the concept of *values-in-design* (VID), or more fully, *human values in the design of information systems and technology*. Led by Helen Nissenbaum, Geoffrey C. Bowker, and Susan Leigh Star, the approach allows policymakers, designers, corporations, and stakeholders to determine specific criteria for judging the quality, accessibility, and value of ICT that align with and resonate with end-users (Evoke, 2020). They recognize that consumers are recipients of coders' algorithms and sequences of human values and decisions that shape the design process and direct consumers' activities—similarly to Feenberg's (2005) view. It would be important to explore how VID may be integrated into technological designs and implementation of industrial revolutions and ICT initiatives in Africa that engage citizen-residents' needs, preferences, and values within innovative technologies that support development activities.

Another issue to explore, therefore, is the impact of 4IR on employment and talent retention. A general assumption is that advanced automation and digitization of job functions would replace human jobs, resulting in unemployment—a valid concern for countries already struggling with high unemployment rates.

Two schools of thought respond to this issue. On one hand, some economists from the McKinsey Group "estimate that between 400 million and 800 million individuals could be displaced by automation and need to find new jobs by 2030 around the world, based on … midpoint and earliest, (that is the most rapid) automation adoption scenarios" (Manyinka et al., 2019, para. 22). However, this also leads to the contrasting school of thought: that the impact of automation and digitization of jobs will lead to job creation and increases in employment, particularly in the long run. Additional questions ensue: Will such "skill-biased" technological change benefit high-skilled workers more than low-skilled workers? Some may propose that high-skilled workers' adaptability to the new technology would increase their value and productivity compared to low-skilled workers. However, opposing arguments may counter that there will also be a high demand for low-skilled jobs that are difficult to automate, so low-skilled workers will benefit. Byron Reese, author of *The Fourth Age: Smart Robots, Conscious Computers, and the Future of Humanity*, proposes a third and more optimistic perspective: all skilled workers will progress in the labor economy, as there would be a reshuffling of automated and non-automated jobs, requiring all workers to elevate their skillsets to meet new job requirements and opportunities (Reese, 2018).

Suggested opportunities and considerations for the African diaspora

Reference to Feenberg's (2005) observation is key: "Values are formulated by the social theorist as technical codes in ideal-typical terms, i.e. as a simple rule or criterion. A prime example in the history of technology is the imperative requirement to deskill labor in the course of industrialization rather than preserving or enhancing skills" (Feenberg, 2005, p. 52). Therefore, governments, the private sector, and key stakeholders should foster an enabling environment for a digital economy through effective relevant policy, legal, and regulatory frameworks and ICT strategies that clearly define actionable criteria that reflect the values, interests, and goals of African communities, aiming to promote equitable and efficient internet access and connectivity; inclusive platforms; reduce costs and barriers to entry; promote network neutrality supporting open, and unrestricted access, particularly for competition and innovation; and provide additional criteria whose outcomes further Africa's social and economic development.

Essential partnerships with the private sector, including the African diaspora, citizen-residents on the ground, and the international development community, should invest in core training programs that prepare the youthful and elder labor force for successful IT and IT-related careers so that no skill level is left behind. These programs should develop workers' hard technical skills, including coding; and their soft skills, including critical thinking, problem solving, project management, communication, and leadership development. Programs that also incorporate entrepreneurship and business management would support workers' short-term and long-term career objectives, particularly in a rapidly evolving technological industry. Such training programs could be structured similarly to the accelerator or incubator programs that are already functioning in different African regions, but culturally and locally contextualized to accommodate the continuum of skills and learning curves of the diverse labor force in order to provide all workers with equal opportunities for job retention.

Another point to consider is how the proliferation of a fourth industrial revolution could also lead to a challenge on the opposite end of the spectrum: a concentration of IT careers that dominate other skills and competencies of those that may be better suited for career paths outside of IT. A challenge that many diaspora communities confronted was the pressure to develop careers as doctors, lawyers, or engineers—irrespective of their talent or desire—to ensure security and survival in the global market. Hence, training programs for the labor force can also be contextualized to suit the local and cultural needs of the community to accommodate skilled workers who are also seeking career options outside of the IT industry, or careers in which the use of IT provides ancillary services or supports the core program.

Exploring alternative pedagogy of IT-centric training curricula that deviates from traditional IT-centric approaches is also key to help manage the effects of *McDonaldization*, a phenomenon described by American sociologist George Ritzer, which became prominent in the 20th century. Recognized as the "rationalization of production, work, and consumption" (Crossman, 2020, para. 1), McDonaldization is a scientific management system that some organizations have adopted to "do business." Through the principles of efficiency, calculability, predictability, and control that outline the fast-food industry,

McDonaldization has reconstructed cultural processes and ideologies throughout society that result in routine, uniform, standardized outputs. However, many organizations are reportedly denouncing the McDonaldization process that de-emphasizes critical thinking and creativity. When applied to industries ranging from education systems to penal systems, the McDonaldization process may result in dehumanizing, harmful, and irrational outcomes.

Hence, referring to VID or Feenberg's (2002) idea of democratizing technology indicates how it is possible for technological advancements to effectively retain elements of the human touch, serve the needs of local communities, and integrate the interests of marginalized populations. One example of such a venture is Envyl, backed by accelerator Y-Combinator, launched in 2015 by a group of four Nigerian software engineers in the diaspora who developed an international peer-to-peer delivery service across continents. More specifically, the service allows individuals to purchase online products from Amazon and have them delivered by home-bound travelers in Nigeria and Ghana for a less exorbitant price than that of a regular international shipping company. Integrating technology with the end consumer's goals, interests, and values and logistical challenges early on in the design process throughout its implementation, the founders of Envyl, formerly known as Shypmate, developed a technological solution that leverages the convenience of e-commerce and addresses the challenges and logistics of transporting goods between the African diaspora and their homes in Africa.

Such innovations represent entrepreneurial opportunities and collaborations between the private sector, the African diaspora, and citizen-residents in Africa to invest in technological innovation that supports development needs. Some of these theoretical concepts, particularly as they relate to technological advancements, can be applied in other subsectors: agriculture and agribusiness, startup funding, and fintech.

Agriculture and agribusiness

Abundant in agricultural resources, Africa accounts for about 60% of the world's uncultivated arable land. More than 60% of Africa's sub-Saharan population are smallholder famers, and agriculture accounts for about 23% of the region's GDP (Goedde, 2019, p.1). In the 2008 World Development Report, agriculture was identified as a vital development tool in sub-Saharan Africa for energizing growth, overcoming poverty, and enhancing food security. By 2009, "three out of every four poor people in developing countries live in rural areas, and most of the rural poor depend directly or indirectly on agriculture for their livelihoods" (The World Bank, 2009, xiii). Agriculture remains a vital tool in 2020, especially because food security is also a concern.

According to the Food and Agriculture Organization (FAO), food security refers to when all people, at all times, have "physical, social and economic access to sufficient, safe and nutritious food that meets their dietary needs and food preferences for an active and healthy life," (Bonuedi et al., 2020, p. 3). According to the FAO, about 239 million people in sub-Saharan Africa, as of 2018, were undernourished as a result of economic shocks and climate change that have affected agricultural production; and armed conflicts that have caused internal displacement of populations and refugees, amid other factors (Ehui, 2020). Several sources, including annual reports of the World Health Organization (WHO, 2020) and the African Development Bank (ADB, 2020), also cite that about 73 million people in Africa are acutely food insecure. Locust outbreaks in 2019 further exacerbated the vulnerability and fragility of the region, potentially causing an estimated "$8.5 billion loss in crop and livestock production, which resulted in severely reduced harvests, and less food in markets" (Ehui, 2020, para. 2).

Some of the development challenges that contribute to food insecurity also include post-harvest loss and food waste. Post-harvest loss (PHL) accounts for a loss of about 30%–50% of food along the food chain in Africa that never makes it to the end consumer, according to the FAO of the United Nations (Aulakh & Regmi, 2013.). Such an amount would otherwise help to eradicate poverty and feed a growing population. In 2011, a joint report by the FAO and World Bank, *Missing Food: The Case of Postharvest Grain Losses in Sub-Saharan Africa,* reported that food waste in Sub-Saharan Africa costs the continent about $4 billion annually, caused by post-harvest food losses that could, otherwise, feed at least 48 million people. *Food waste* refers to the loss of food at later stages of the food supply chain, and results from inefficient processing, inadequate storage, and deficiencies in infrastructure.

Suggested opportunities and considerations for the African diaspora

Digitization and technologies

Investments in technologies and stronger infrastructure can help to unlock the continent's agriculture potential and improve food security, especially during climate change. Such investments position key stakeholders, including those Africans in the diaspora, to collaborate with citizen-residents on the ground to add value along the agriculture value chain and invest in the growing agribusiness sector.

According to Yinusa and Mabaya (2019), "the agribusiness sector is expected to reach $1 trillion by 2030" (para. 2). The diaspora can invest in the digitization of the agribusiness industry, whose environmentally friendly technologies should be contextualized to suit the needs of African farmers and other end-users along the agroprocess value chain. Hence, investing in advanced technology, including rural storage facilities for produce and milk cooling centers, indoor vertical farming, farm and livestock farm automation, modern greenhouses, and other innovations would increase crop yield, efficiently improve productivity capacity, effectively manage livestock, and produce additional positive outcomes. There has been a surge in agriculture technology investment over the past 11 years, with an investment of $6.7 billion in the last 5 years and $1.9 billion in 2018 alone (Ku, 2019).

To reduce food waste, several innovations originating from the continent have already sparked global headlines. Nigerian entrepreneur Affiong Wiliams founded Reelfruit, which processes and converts seasonal fruits that are usually wasted and unconsumed along the value chain into consumable dried-fruit snacks. Ugandan engineering student Lawrence Okettayot invented a food dehydrator that tackles the world's food waste crisis. Other innovations include the conversion of unused raw foods and fruit into natural cosmetic products that have been popular across the globe, including the UK and other parts of Europe.

Research and development

Through additional research and funding opportunities that identify loopholes, gaps, and inefficiencies that exacerbate costs, the diaspora could collaborate with citizen-residents on the ground to invest in manufacturing or importing technologies. These particular investments and strategic partnerships may result in innovations that increase food yields and improve nutritional quality. They may also increase the diversification of agricultural production to boost revenues and sales domestically for farmers.

Critical approaches to technology coding and use

Although technology use highlights numerous breakthroughs to support the agricultural sector, it is important to critically assess *how* one approaches technology as a solution. More specifically, the diaspora should consider how to incorporate the end-users and beneficiaries of technologies as change agents in development.

Feenberg's (2005) notes on *technological imperialism* could be applied within the context of diaspora engagement in Africa's development. Irrationalist implications, political agendas, biases, and various ideologies that develop technical codes shape the technology end-product and influence its use. These power dynamics are reinforced through locales, especially when the firms may be headquartered in the developed world and end-users reside in "the impoverished periphery" (Feenburg, 2005, p. 10).

In this context, such biases may, therefore, manifest when agribusiness firms' operational autonomy disempowers farmers from serving as technical actors in the production of their goods.

Hence, in efforts to empower farmers and end-users of technology, it would be valuable for the diaspora and key stakeholders to be conscious about suspending unconscious biases that may inadvertently represent cases of technological imperialism. It would also be important to be intentional about the values they incorporate when developing technical codes of agribusiness.

The diaspora should also remain open to how technology-users on the ground, e.g., farmers, may innovatively transform or change the original purpose or design of the technological innovation to address their own practical needs. This highlights the concept of *reinvention*, which is illustrated when end-users of technology modify the original purpose or design of a tool or object and repurpose it to fulfill their needs.

Ultimately, efforts in the development agenda should incorporate farmers' local knowledge and develop research strategies that give agency to local farmers and empower them as active leaders and participants across all technical aspects of their production.

Gender inclusion

Another way to ensure the inclusion of beneficiaries in the production process is for the diaspora to identify gaps in the value chain and create jobs for youth and women in the labor economy of the agricultural sector. Abass' (2018) study in Agriculture, Food and Jobs indicates that the food economy accounts for 66% of employment in West Africa. Although "women account for nearly half of the world's smallholder farmers and produce 70% of Africa's food" (Abass, 2018, para. 6), gender gaps, exclusion, and barriers to entry for land ownership reveal that less than 20% of the land is owned by women, who are also further discriminated against when they are denied property rights. Some of these exclusions result from customary laws and legal frameworks that can be traced back to history and patriarchal societies:

> Despite a progressive legal framework, Kenyan women's land rights continue to lag behind those of men. Customary law, which often discriminates against women and limits their land and property rights, governs at least 65% of land in Kenya, and the patriarchal nature of Kenyan society often limits the rights of even those women not living on land governed by custom. Some estimates indicate that as little as 1% of land is titled in the names of women and 5–6% is titled jointly by women and men.
>
> (Gaafar, 2014, p. 2)

As policymakers, the diaspora can collaborate with governments, citizen-residents, and other stakeholders to develop policies, frameworks, and guidelines that promote the inclusion of women and youth throughout the agricultural value chain, including agribusiness entrepreneurial opportunities that target women and youth. This could help to reduce the gender gap, promote employment, and position youth and women as beneficiaries of their labor and their own produce—as illustrated by the business model of Shea Yeleen, a social impact company that is based in Washington DC and develops shea butter creams, balms, soaps, and other natural products derived from the shea nut.

Ghanaian-American Rahama Wright, founder and CEO of Shea Yeleen, observed that "local people who are the closest to the to the product very rarely benefit from the upside of the market because there's so many intermediaries between them and a customer" (personal communication, January 23, 2020). Hence, Wright developed a business model that is intentional about integrating women's labor and small rural villages in northern Ghana into the supply chain process "from seed to shelf" (Wright, personal communication, January 23, 2020). More specifically, the business model

> provides women access to capital, production equipment, production facilities to create a value-added product that we bring to the US market, and then we distribute those products through our retail partnerships with the very specific goal of creating living wages for the women in our cooperatives.
>
> (Wright, personal communication, January 23, 2020)

Wright (2020) observes that many business models still fail to equip women to be financially independent to make their own personal, business, or family decisions—such as decisions about children's education—which they deem as important. Hence, Shea Yeleen equips women with access to financial resources to empower them to make their own choices about their daily lives and future.

Global agro-food trade and policies

The discourse surrounding Africa as a beneficiary of its own agricultural produce also invites further research and exploration for the diaspora to pursue in efforts to contribute to their African nations' agro-economy. One fundamental issue to explore highlights a perplexing phenomenon and paradox: If Africa is abundantly rich in its own raw resources, then why does Africa export many of the raw ingredients that it buys back through more costly, manufactured, imported goods? For instance, Nigeria's role as one of Africa's leading producers of tomatoes raises eyebrows against its million-dollar imports of processed tomato paste from China. Côte d'Ivoire leads the export of cocoa—yet it pays exorbitant prices for imports of refined chocolate. Imported fruit juice concentrates derived from Africa's exports of raw fruits further illustrate the paradox. As a net food importer, Africa incurred costs surpassing $47 billion in 2018 (Blanke, 2020).

Although addressing the question and phenomenon is complex, one factor to consider is the role of international agro-food trade and its impact on food security. Several challenges surround the international trade of food products, including the exclusion and marginalization of African exporters and processors who struggle to compete in the global market:

With "little expertise in equipment and standard-setting at the enforcement stage and border, lack of clearly defined mandates, insufficient testing capacity [and inefficient oversight of technical regulations and processing resulting in] … delays and duplicating costs," as well as minimal understanding of the international rules, regulations, and policies required for food exports, many exporters in African countries struggle to adhere to international food and feed safety standards, resulting in the ban of some of their country's food exports (Verter, 2017, para. 6). For instance, in 2015, the European Union banned some of Nigeria's food exports, including fish products, for incorrect applications of pesticides and certain chemicals that compromised quality and safety standards.

Another factor that affects food insecurity is linked to international trade barriers, which obstruct the transportation of food from food-surplus production locations to consumers in food-deficit locations (Bonuedi et al., 2020; Mukhtar 2017; World Bank, 2012). Some research points toward complexities of international trade, particularly of food products, that account for some of the challenges affecting Africa's development. Other challenges stem from complex protocols and regulations that relate to intracontinental and external food trade, tax policies, and food import bills, and their overall impact on domestic and foreign agricultural and food policies, regulations, protocols, and various bureaucratic red-tape procedures relating to exports and imports.

For instance, Bonuedi et al. (2020) conducted a study on 45 African countries covering a period between 2006 and 2015 that confirmed the adverse impact of nontariff trade barriers on food security in Africa—particularly affecting access to food, followed by adverse impacts on availability and utilization. Some of their policy recommendations emphasized reducing delays at border crossings and timely deliveries of goods. Additional recommendations include streamlining and modernizing documentation requirements to reduce logistics costs and expediting "clearance of time-sensitive, perishable [food] products to improve consistency of food supplies [in Africa], and investing in transport infrastructure to expedite transportation timelines" (Bonuedi et al., 2020, p. 2).

There is general consensus that opening trade borders to improve food security offers numerous benefits, facilitated by agreements and instruments like Power Africa, the African Growth and Opportunity Act, and the African Continental Free Trade Area (AfCFTA) that aims to accelerate intra-African trade, among others. In light of this, Akinwumi Adesina, president of the African Development Bank (AfDB), noted Africa's heavy reliance on world markets for food security. From 2016 to 2018, Africa imported 85% of its food from outside the continent, resulting in an annual food import bill of $35 billion, which is projected to increase to $110 billion by 2025 (Akiwumi, 2020). In response, the African Development Bank has invested in equipping Africa with greater food self-sufficiency and agricultural industrialization by committing $24 billion toward agriculture in the next decade (Shaban, 2017).

To further address self-sufficiency in production, researchers like Verter (2015) concluded in their study on agriculture that sub-Saharan African countries (SSA) should continue to take advantage of their climate and environmental conditions to produce large quantities of goods that the West cannot produce, and hence become self-sufficient in their exports.

> As postulated by Smith, Ricardo, and H-O models, some SSA countries such as Ghana, Ethiopia, Uganda, Ivory Coast and Nigeria have taken

> advantage of their unique and favourable tropical climatic conditions by producing and exporting agricultural commodities (i.e. absolute or comparative advantage) that could not be produced in advanced countries in large quantities despite their technical know-how.
>
> (Verter, 2015, p. 216)

Aliko Dangote, Nigerian billionaire businessman, Africa's richest person, and founder and chairman of Dangote Group, an industrial conglomerate in Africa, notes that, "with about 65 percent of the world's uncultivated arable land, Africa has the potential to ensure its own food sufficiency and be a major supplier in global food markets" (Leke & Signé, 2019, p. 86).

Economists and experts agree that international trade remains complex. International trade theories continuously evolve to explain some of the barriers of entry and trade sanctions and recommend policies, but there still lacks a single neatly designed, universally agreed-upon international trade theory. As a result, an integration of various theories may explain Africa's international agro-food trade dynamics in the global market. Over time, it is possible that additional theories could emerge to further explain the challenges and opportunities that support trade and investment opportunities in improving global food security, including that across Africa.

In light of these challenges and opportunities, the African diaspora may identify various opportunities to collaborate with citizen-residents on the ground, governments, and relevant stakeholders to implement policies that address trade barriers and increase food access; invest in agribusiness digital technology that adds value along the food supply chain; increase agriculture productivity; promote innovative agri-food systems strategies; and support sustainable, resilient agri-food systems that promote self-sufficiency across Africa.

Food and gastronomy

Related to agriculture is the food and gastronomy industry, which is supported by tourism. "Attiéké chaud!" I will never forget the loud clear chant of the street vendor in Abidjan yelling at the top of her lungs that the hot dish of fermented cassava, accompanied by seasoned smoked fish or grilled chicken, and a tomato stew that occasionally drew a queue of people to her stand, was ready. Now, miles away from what was once accessible at my fingertips, my palate still craves the taste. This is a similar experience for those craving South Africa's "Pap en vleis/Shisa nyama," West Africa's "jollof rice" and "thieboudienne" or "chebu jen," East Africa's Swahili donuts, or "Mandaazi," traditional North African "couscous." Fortunately, the growing gastronomy industry has introduced many of Africa's mouthwatering dishes to the international food market.

The growing market for international cuisine, particularly from the African diaspora who invest in "African home food," has led to rapid penetration of African manufactured foods in the global market. Perhaps this may contribute in the long run to a shift in Africa's role as an exporter of manufactured foods.

In this regard, markets in India represent international markets that are home to food exports and agro-based food products from Africa and are keen to invest in in foreign "exotic" foods across the globe. Hence, the expansion of this growing industry positions diaspora and citizen-residents on the ground to partner with local food manufacturers in Africa through private companies and social enterprises to export nonperishable foods through a simplified supply chain that allows local food manufacturers to compete in the global food market.

There are opportunities for the growing organic food market to be influenced by the raw ingredients that Africa exports to consumers. Numerous factors account for the fueling of consumer demand: a growing African population expected to reach 2 billion by 2030 and 2.5 billion by 2050 (cited by United Nations projections), which translates to "1 in 5 consumers globally that will be African" (Yinusa & Mabaya, 2019, para. 2); and "a projected middle-class population to reach 1.1 billion by 2060 which will make up 42% of the population" (Yinusa & Mabaya, 2019, para. 3). More specifically, the affluence and sophistication of this growing middle class influences their nutrition-conscious and food consumption and safety lifestyles, as well as high consumption and concentrated spending powers of the growing, populous megacities of over 10 million inhabitants in Cairo, Lagos, Kinshasa and other urbanized areas (Yinusa & Mabaya, 2019).

As food ambassadors of a growing gastronomy industry—reinforced by gastronomy tourism—there are opportunities for the diaspora to remain connected to their African cultures, which they can also promote through the exchange and business of food. This presents an opportunity, particularly, for investors to support and include women in the value chain of the industry, ranging from production and packaging to the distribution of food. The proliferation of dried foods and spices that are sold in international markets overseas also expand innovative opportunities for the industry to create jobs and create value across the supply chain.

Attending conferences like the African Diaspora Food Forum and other annual conventions would expose the African diaspora to various networks, industry leaders, and market opportunities, and also educate them on ways to transform Africa's potential into a reality of thriving development.

Startup funding

Startup funding draws numerous international stakeholders to Africa, where they can develop innovation hubs or build tech startups to support untapped talent among engineers, programmers, and technology gurus who will drastically transform an ever-evolving global landscape. The 2019 Disrupt Africa Funding Report highlighted Africa's "record-breaking" year in 2019 for African tech startups, during which 311 companies secured US $491.6 million worth of investment, with Kenya and Nigeria attracting the most funding of $149 million and $122 million, respectively, and Egypt also ranking high in securing the most tech startups (B.R., 2020, para. 2). The South African cities of Johannesburg and Cape Town are also major technology hubs in Africa.

In light of such breakthroughs, there have been controversial disputes that raise questions on how discrimination, prejudice, and racism may affect some African entrepreneurs and African-based startups during investment deals for venture capital. Reports have revealed that African startups that were led by foreigners would gain favor and receive higher amounts of venture capital or more frequently than their African counterparts. For instance, according to the African Private Equity and Venture Capital Association, "North America-headquartered investors accounted for 42% of all African venture capital deals in the last five years … Only 20% of venture cash came from Africa-based investors, forcing the continent's entrepreneurs to seek support from westerners" (Madowo, 2020, para. 5). Based on *The Guardian*'s analysis of public data, eight of the top ten African-based startups that received the highest amount of venture capital in Africa were foreigner-led (Madowo, 2020).

In an interview with *The Guardian* published in 2020, a few White American founders of startups—including Matt Flannery of Africa startups Kiva and Branch International and Grant Brooke, co-founder with Peter Njonjo of Twiga Foods, which connects food producers and vendors to markets—also acknowledged how their privilege, underlying biases, and advantages of their upbringing, educational backgrounds, and access to venture capitalists led to "better access to US-dominated funding funnels" (Madowo, 2020, para. 10). Grant Brooke, an Oxford-educated American and co-founder of Twiga Foods, remarks:

> I've seen this in real time. When I talk to a venture capitalist who looks like me and has the same educational background, even when I mess up something, they'll just correct me and write it off as a conversation among colleagues … If a black African founder were to do the same, they would see him as ignorant and judge him differently. I don't even think that's conscious, but they do it.
>
> (Madowo, 2020, para 14)

Some additional factors that affect the gap in startup tech funding include structural issues in Africa, ranging from structural racism and inequalities that have led to the underrepresentation of Blacks and Africans in venture capital firms; structural challenges in how local banks and pension funds "have not embraced venture capital" (Madowo, 2020, para. 26); and an adoption of "a neo-colonialist mentality to the African startup ecosystem [that] exploits naïve first-time entrepreneurs" (Madowo, 2020, para. 19).

Others believe that an emphasis on race has had negative effects on venture capital proposals. According to Iyinolowa Aboyeji, an entrepreneur and co-founder of Flutterwave, race deterred potential investors from banking on "white savior projects" (Madowo, 2020, para. 25). Flutterwave is a fintech company and Andela a global talent network that connects companies with engineering talent to build teams (Madowo, 2020).

Suggested opportunities and considerations for the diaspora

Although Andela released 400 developers in Nigeria, Kenya, and Uganda in September 2019 to focus on hiring senior talent, the decision is projected to yield profitable returns and positive impacts on tech ecosystems in Africa (Kazeem, 2019). Microsoft, the world's largest software company, seeks to invest over $100 million in development centers that will hire about 500 African software engineering talent in Africa by 2023.

In addition to Facebook's CEO and founder, Mark Zuckerburg, visiting the African continent, the world's biggest social media company made significant investments in Africa in 2019. A few include the launch of an 8-week incubation program in Nigeria's NG_Hub to mentor and train future entrepreneurs; support for reduced misinformation, election integrity, and civic engagement across Africa during elections; the second annual launch of its #SheMeansBusiness in Nigeria, in partnership with She Leads Africa, to train female entrepreneurs and students in vital digital skills and an expansion of their third-party fact-checking work across ten African countries—Ethiopia, Zambia, Somalia, Burkina Faso, Uganda, Tanzania, Democratic Republic of Congo, Côte d'Ivoire, Guinea Conakry, and Ghana (Moyo, 2019).

While such opportunities reinforce investments in developing and nurturing talent in Africa, some local talent still pursues opportunities outside of the continent for additional training and development, as well as job opportunities. Sacha Poignonnec, CEO of Jumia, the Africa-focused online retailer, drew criticism and controversy across media platforms after a 2019 interview on CNBC about not hiring Nigerian-based developers and opting to pursue talent outside of Africa:

> Jumia is completely African. We operate exclusively in Africa and we have over 5000 workers in Africa … but the reality is that there is not enough developers in Africa.
>
> (Abubakar, 2019, para. 2)

While this incident ignited debates about the company, it prompted audiences to pose broader questions regarding Africa's development. The diaspora should consider one fundamental question when seeking to leverage talent in their African nations: Is the issue really about whether or not Africa has talent? Africa is a continent whose people are smart, innovative, strong, and resilient, with a bourgeoning youthful population that is already transforming communities and poised to innovatively do more. Instead, the question and focus should be revised to how we can unleash, develop, nurture, and sustain the talent that already exists on the continent and integrate it as viable human capital within the global market.

Lexy Boahene (2021), managing director of LX HR Solutions, an HR consultancy firm, highlights key observations related to talent management, recruitment challenges, and human capital for the African diaspora to note when seeking entrepreneurial or investment opportunities in their African country:

> Finding local talent and expecting them to perform as you're used to may come as a surprise. When hiring people, it is important to be ready to train and retrain and train again. This is mostly because of expectations from the employee and employer. Dealing with people anywhere in the world comes as a challenge. It is also important to note that people who want to move should also consider getting jobs to add value to businesses across the continent.
>
> (personal communication, February 10, 2021)

The diaspora, the private sector, governments, and stakeholders should continue to redirect focus and attention to enabling and empowering talent. To curtail the brain drain, Africa's young technology-savvy talent should be properly incentivized with job and career growth opportunities across Africa. Hence, the diaspora can play a significant role in developing and strengthening networks with citizen-residents on the ground who are already developing innovations and recruiting local talent among their community. It would be important to connect the talent to multinational organizations whose rotational programs foster talent internationally, yet also connect them with their bases in African countries. It would also be critical that favorable incentives support the market for re-entry back to their African countries and markets.

The level of coordination between the African diaspora, citizen-residents on the ground, international stakeholders from the donor community, the government, and the private sector is important for everyone to contribute to. Every contribution holds significant potential in creating a value-add with rippling effects for a nation's economic growth. After all, there are increasingly numbers of opportunities for Africa to benefit from its innovative demographic, young market.

Fintech and telecommunications

Financial technology, or *fintech*, is the use of technology to support, enable, and enhance financial and banking services, and it is one of the most rapidly emerging and highly evolving industries in Africa. According to the Njoroge (2020), about 66% of sub-Saharan Africa's adult population lack access to traditional bank and financial services, as of 2020. Fintech companies seek to bridge this gap by promoting the financial inclusion of this underserved population in the market. As of 2020, Africa has an estimated average of over 395.7 million active mobile money accounts (out of a global total of 866 million) (Njoroge, 2020). Additionally, the continent's mobile traffic data is expected to increase sevenfold by 2022 and foster additional app-based services (Africanexponent .com, 2020). Hence, fintech also addresses the market opportunity by granting access to a population that already own and use phones, yet lack access to financial banking services.

Suggested opportunities and considerations for the diaspora

Michael Akindele—managing partner of Uncharted Ventures, a company that incubates and advises new ventures with a focus on new product strategy, and lead on Digital Transformation at Resilience Capital Ventures, a boutique capital advisory practice—notes a major challenge many entrepreneurs in this industry seek to solve, particularly in African economies: data acquisition of people and how to involve everyone in the formal economy. "Without Social Security numbers and unique identifiers in some countries, initiatives would need to digitize everyone" (Akindele, personal communication, February 1, 2020). Akindele (2020) observes that such digitization would be important to identify consumer spending habits and deliver products and services that address those needs—from education to family necessities. Fintech also is necessary to assist populations in gaining basic access to credit, ensuring that people can pay for their basic lifestyles and have access to be able to transfer their funds and pay bills (Akindele, personal communication, February 1, 2020).

The fintech industry has skyrocketed in Africa since 2015. The continent's fintech companies raised $320 million in funding since January 2015 with a 60% surge in the ecosystem since 2018 (Njoroge, 2020). Furthermore, Africa has also witnessed an increase in fintech firms from 301 in 2017 to 491 in 2019 (Shapshak, 2019).

Nigeria, South Africa, Kenya, Ghana, Ethiopia, and Egypt are among some of Africa's leading markets and stakeholders in the fintech industry. According to Forbes, Nigeria led investments in 2018 with 58 technology startups raising $94.9 million, followed by South Africa with 40 businesses that raised $59.9 million, and thirdly, Kenya (Shapshak, 2019). Regarding fintech investments, South Africa, Nigeria, and Kenya dominated the fintech markets with "141, 101 and 78 active ventures, respectively, accounting for 65.2% of Africa's startups," according to Tom Jackson, co-founder of Disrupt Africa, a media platform for Africa's tech startup and investment ecosystem (Shapshak, 2019).

Kenyan platforms like M-Pesa boasted 218,495 active mobile money transfer agents and 29.7 million subscriptions in September 2019; Sokowatch, hailed as Africa's Alibaba, delivered over 500,000 orders to 10,000 customers through its B2B e-commerce supply chains between Africa's informal economy and multinational corporations like Proctor and Gamble and Unilever (Cleverely, 2020). In addition to significant investments in infrastructure and structural reform, Ethiopia hosted more than 200 financial tech innovators at its Finnovation Ethiopia conference and over 400 stakeholders from over 30 countries for the Fourth African FinTech Summit in 2019 (Cleverely, 2020).

Ghana's history-long advancements in financial technology resulted in numerous breakthroughs, including 1997's Social Security Bank's introduction of the "Sika Card" to replace banknotes and checks and facilitate cashless transactions, as well as the launch of its first interoperable payment system in Africa (Cleverly, 2020). According to Igor Kaparis, CEO of International Fintech, "African startups are fundamentally building from scratch, filling innumerable gaps in the financial system and creating new ways of financial inclusion" (Iwuoha, 2020, commentary section). Furthermore, the rise of mobile communications and innovations support ever-increasing consumer growth and a shift toward online shopping, which, according to Tanui (2019), is estimated to be valued at $75 billion by 2025.

Early investment opportunities in the fintech, digital, and ICT industries are key for the diaspora, private sector, and citizen-residents in Africa. Investors can invest in fintech to drive business and e-commerce; strengthen education, particularly education administration;; improve healthcare; and accelerate other sectors across the African continent.

Overall impact of Covid-19 on industrialization in Africa

The Covid-19 outbreak has transformed economies at a massive rate. Industrialization had been identified as a driver in converting a lot of the continent's raw commodities to manufactured goods that would optimize job creation and growth opportunities for a range of enterprises and expand the healthcare system. However, the pandemic has led to a reassessment of efforts that suggest Africa may struggle in its capability to produce goods at scale (Abiodun et al., 2020). Some of these struggles include substantial increases in food prices, affected by reduced food supplies and disruptions to trade flows and market function; restricted food transport options, which hinder rural farmers' and consumers' access to food inputs, equipment, and staples; and the accumulation of post-harvest losses and unsold rotten food (Blanke, 2020).

Increased attention on the digital ecosystem suggests opportunities to address some of these struggles in light of a "new normal." In the post-Covid era, Eziakonwa and Gabre-Madhin (2020) highlight the significance of startups and encourage platforms that spurn network opportunities, "forge partnerships like Tony Elumeu Foundation UNDP Entrepreneurship and YouthConnekt" (Eziakonwa & Gabre-Madhin, 2020, para. 11), and provide financial opportunities to support African startups. To encourage opportunities for youth-led businesses to grow from startup to scaleup, it is important to foster an environment that dismantles "regulatory, policy and cultural fences" (Eziakonwa & Gabre-Madhin, 2020, para. 11).

The advent of the pandemic has also shifted the value of digitization from an industrial revolution that would be "important to have" to a dire, urgent necessity for survival. The world is witnessing how the digital tech space also opens new market opportunities that Africa can capitalize on. For instance, Jumia experienced a four-fold increase in grocery sales in March 2020 relative to the same period in 2019 (Lewis, 2020). Such demonstrations of heavy reliance on the digital infrastructure and its resulting increased data usage during the pandemic positions this industry for more success than other sectors after the pandemic. More business opportunities, particularly from industries that have converted to digital platforms and newer markets, attract more private investment to this sector to improve operations and further develop innovative solutions across multiple sectors. New online stores have launched or increased services to respond to consumers' need for home deliveries of groceries and products during the quarantine—consumers who would, otherwise, have relied on traveling by foot to buy them in retail and brick-and-mortar stores.

Despite high active mobile phone and internet penetration in Africa, "only 10% of all payments and transactions in Africa are (technology-based)" (Cleverly, 2020). Hence, there is an even more immediate need to build payment solutions, increase mobile money products, and develop mobile apps beyond peer-to-peer transfers (P2P), and ensure that business, socioeconomic, and development needs are met across the continent. This has resulted in the urgent quest to determine how to rapidly bridge digitization gaps across the continent, particularly if mobile and internet penetrations fluctuate and vary across the continent.

Another challenge resulting from the pandemic is the decline of venture capital investments. However, it has also led to the rise of *impact investing*, which aims for measurable environmental and social benefits, e.g., job creation and reduced pollution, alongside a financial return. Given that the pandemic has led to twin crises affecting the health and economic sector, impact investing is expected to address development issues and offer relief in the healthcare and agriculture sectors, which have already demonstrated returns on investment. Healthcare and agriculture-focused startups respond to crises of blood shortages, increase testing capacity, and supply food to communities affected by food shortage and disruptions in the food sector. These firms also appeal to social enterprises and development finance institutions (DFIs) that invest in firms that impact larger communities (Kazeem, 2020).

Whereas some sectors and industries would be more affected than others, many youth startups have needed to pivot, realign their business strategies, and innovatively develop newer products that would functionally serve their customers or clients during the pandemic. For instance, South Africa's Daniel Ndima, CEO of CapeBio Technologies, built upon his applied genomics research company and developed a qPCR Covid-19 test kit that yields results in 65 minutes through a local flora-based reagent; Nigerian Temi Giwa-Tuboson's LifeBank pivoted from transferring blood to hospitals, screening centers, and connecting donors to blood banks to building data platforms to track ventilators and respirators, as well as developing drive-through Covid-19 testing and supplying oxygen to health centers; Jennet Lemma's garment factory produced face masks and protective gear, retaining jobs for her 75 employees (Eziakonwa & Gabre-Madhin, 2020).

However, as in many other priority sectors, African countries have gained support in Covid-19 from the international community. Multilateral organizations, including the African Development Bank, the World Bank Group, bilateral organizations, and other companies, have sent relief packages to support the global community and support economic recovery during the pandemic. As of August 2020, "the World Bank Group will be deploying up to $160 billion" [of financial assistance] to over 100 countries [over the next 15 months] … including up to $50 billion for African countries" (World Bank Group, 2020, para. 3). The African Development Bank has provided financial assistance, including a deployment of about $3.5 billion toward national and subregional projects across Africa; additional funding toward targeted initiatives for electricity development in Egypt and support for refugees and their host countries in central-northwestern Africa; and "$3m to the Togolese agriculture sector for food security … [as well as] a $20 billion support package for member states" (Oxford Business Group, 2020, para. 13).

African countries have also found solutions through self-reliance programs stemming from lessons learned after the Ebola crisis and the food crisis of 2007–2008.

Many have also identified the potential of the AfCFTA as a highly valued initiative to promote economic diversification of their commodity base, support food procurement, promote intra-African trade, strengthen job and food security, and reduce vulnerability. Government leadership would also need to continue identify new market opportunities, prioritize growth in certain sectors, adjust relevant policies and regulations that facilitate trade, provide access to land, and enhance the infrastructure to support industrialization efforts.

SPOTLIGHT: MICHAEL AKINDELE

Managing Partner, Unchartered Ventures

https://uncharteredventures.com
www.michaelakindele.com

Quotes & Insights from Michael Akindele on the Diaspora in Africa's Development

On identifying ways to get involved in Africa's development agenda:

… You should always try to collaborate with people and never just try to operate in silos, meaning just going at it alone and then make expensive mistakes. So, the way for people to get involved is to connect with other people that are already in that space because no man is an island … [Go to] summits, exhibits, conferences. They give you a sense of pulse of what's happened in the market and a lot of times you get to meet really great people who are also doing interesting things!

On finding innovative solutions:

Observe, don't try to be prescriptive. Try to just observe … What people have done is that they try to take solutions that have worked here [in the US] and take them back home [to Africa], but you don't realize that solutions in Africa need to be for Africa and not necessarily imported solutions.

On penetrating new cultural environments:

… You just have to keep your eyes and ears open because people's perception of you varies … So it's not a one-size cookie-cutter approach … You just also have to be very sharp, very clever … and don't be naive. That's just not for Africa. I've been to India, I've been to China—wherever you go—it will be about your wits and smart. Trust is a huge factor … and [be mindful] of the norms. Norms exist not just in the social settings, but also in the business ethics and professional settings.

On inspiring the Diaspora:

Think about aspects that are shaping development going forward … Every single African is an ambassador, right? You know the stories you choose to tell … You, as an individual, are an ambassador whether you want to acknowledge it or not.

Figure 5.1 L-R. Will Smith and Michael Akindele, co-founders of mbue Inc. Photograph provided by Michael Akindele

HIGHLIGHTS OF MICHAEL AKINDELE

- Managing Partner of UnchartedVentures, a company that incubates and advises new ventures, with a focus on new product strategy
- Lead on Digital Transformation at Resilience CapitalVentures, a boutique capital advisory practice, which provides strategic advisory services and mobilizes capital, working in partnership with a network of investment firms and brokers
- Led team to launch the international frozen yogurt brand, Sweetkiwi, in the Washington, D.C. area, available through Whole Foods and Amazon
- Co-founder of mbue Inc., a startup to support mental health and make therapy inclusive, accessible, affordable and convenient for underserved groups
- Named one of top 50 exemplary alumni of George Mason University and recognized by Forbes, amongst others, as an innovative entrepreneur, currently with 14+ years' experience in the US, Africa, and other emerging markets, and skill set and expertise spanning digital transformation, innovation, agile strategy, and design-thinking
- Bachelor of Science (B.S.) degree from the Volgenau School of Engineering at George Mason University, focus on Computer Science and Information Technology, Minor in Business Administration from George Mason's School of Management

Figure 5.2 Michael Akindele. Photograph provided by Michael Akindele

SPOTLIGHT: RAHAMA WRIGHT

CEO and founder, Shea Yeleen
www.sheayeleen.com

Quotes & Insights from Rahama Wright on the Diaspora in Africa's Development

On developing a business model to impact women in Africa:

I think that a lot of models that you even see [are] still not really talking about the real issue, which is living wages ... [So] that's what we do ... Those are the metrics of change. It's basically giving women more choices. We don't tell them what to do. We just give them access to the financial resources so they can do for themselves and that's really important to me.

On empowering women in Africa:

This is about bringing voice and visibility and creating a space in supply chains that have too long taken advantage of the labor of African women ... [African women] are representing themselves—that's how you move the needle and change perception.

On challenging some of the diaspora's perceptions about doing business in Africa:

Have you actually gone there and taken the time to develop the right relationships? How is doing business in Africa [different] from anywhere [else]? It's all about relationships.

Figure 5.3 Rahama Wright with producers. Photograph provided by Rahama Wright

Figure 5.4 Shea Yeleen products. Photograph provided by Rahama Wright.

HIGHLIGHTS OF RAHAMA WRIGHT

- Ghanaian-American Founder and CEO of Shea Yeleen, a social impact company based in Washington D.C that develops shea butter creams, balms, and soaps that create living-wage jobs for women in Ghana
- Secured first round of venture capital investment from Ron Lauder and Dick Parsons; Landed deals with Whole Foods Markets and MGM Resorts International, with products also featured in a variety of media outlets, including *O, The Oprah Magazine*, *The Washington Post*, *The Huffington Post*, *Washington Business Journal*, *MSNBC*, and *CNBC Africa*
- Leading voice on African women's economic and business development with 150+ speeches and panels globally including the United Nations Thematic Debate on Entrepreneurship for Development, the US Secretary of State Global Diaspora Forum, the World Bank Africa Region Growth Dialogue, and the Global Entrepreneurship Summit
- Appointed in 2014 to the Presidential Advisory Council on Doing Business in Africa; currently serving third term on the council
- BA in International Relations from the State University of New York at Geneseo; Trivia: Avid traveler, visited and worked in 36 countries

Figure 5.5 Rahama Wright. Photograph provided by Rahama Wright.

Chapter summary

Key words

brain drain	industrialization
brain gain	Industry 4.0 (4IR)
brain circulation	McDonaldization
concept of reinvention	modernization theory
fintech	technological imperialism
impact investing	

Discussion questions:

1) What does it mean to "democratize" a technological design or technology process? How will the democratization of technology impact communities? Will there be a more significant impact on some communities than others? If so, how? What are some determinants for a democratization of technology? Provide specific examples and refer to relevant country case studies, examples, and illustrations, particularly within the context of an African country.
2) Identify a particular African country to develop a case study on the impact of 4IR on a selected industry or particular company in an African country. Consider some of the following questions as you develop your response:
    a) What are some positive impacts or unique opportunities that can be leveraged from 4IR? What are foreseeable challenges to address? How can these challenges be mitigated? What policies can be implemented to support the opportunities, challenges, and concerns that you outline in your case study? Be sure to refer to specific examples and illustrations and provide relevant context to justify your response.
    b) What impact would 4IR have on talent acquisition, development, and retention in your selected industry or company? What interventions (programs, policies, etc.) would you propose to support their career development?

References

Abass, J. (2018, March 21). *Women grow 70% of Africa's food. But have few rights over the land they tend.* Cologny, Switzerland: World Economic Forum. https://www.weforum.org/agenda/2018/03/women-farmers-food-production-land-rights/

Abiodun, T., Jallow, M., & Said, J. (2020, November 12). *Driving Africa's industrialisation on the back of COVID-19.* OECD. https://oecd-development-matters.org/2020/05/18/driving-africas-industrialisation-on-the-back-of-covid-19/

Abubakar, I. (2019, April 15). Jumia CEO under fire after claiming Africa does not have quality developers. *Technext.* https://technext.ng/2019/04/15/jumia-ceo-under-heavy-fire-claiming-africa-have-quality-developers/

African Development Bank Group (2018). Africa agribusiness, a US$1 trillion business by 2030. https://www.afdb.org/en/news-and-events/africa-agribusiness-a-us-1-trillion-business-by-2030-18678#:~:text=With%20its%20vast%20agricultural%20potential,the%20motor%20of%20inclusive%20growth

Akiwumi, D. (2020, August 11). COVID-19: A threat to food security in Africa | UNCTAD. United Nations Conference on Trade and Development. https://unctad.org/news/covid-19-threat-food-security-africa

Allen, K. (2019, September 16). Africa should not be too quick to embrace the fourth Industrial Revolution. *The Guardian*. https://www.theguardian.com/global-development/2019/sep/16/africa-should-not-be-too-quick-to-embrace-the-fourth-industrial-revolution

Aulakh, J., & Regmi, A. (2013). Post-harvest food losses estimation-development of consistent methodology introduction. https://www.semanticscholar.org/paper/POST-HARVEST-FOOD-LOSSES-ESTIMATION-DEVELOPMENT-OF-Aulakh-Regmi/7a9d5f2bbe997030ec82f343fd0087909950b1c0

Blanke, J. (2020, June 24). Economic impact of COVID-19: Protecting Africa's food systems from farm to fork. Brookings. https://www.brookings.edu/blog/africa-in-focus/2020/06/19/economic-impact-of-covid-19-protecting-africas-food-systems-from-farm-to-fork/

Bonuedi, I., Kamasa, K., & Opoku, E. E. O. (2020). Enabling trade across borders and food security in Africa. *Food Security*, *12*(5), 1121–1140. doi:10.1007/s12571-020-01095-y

B. R. (2020, January 1). African tech startup funding hits $491m in record-breaking 2019—report. *Independent Online*. https://www.iol.co.za/technology/fintech/african-tech-startup-funding-hits-491m-in-record-breaking-2019-report-40924455

Cleverly, C. (2020, March 5). Diving into three of Africa's emerging Fintech economies. *Cointelegraph*. https://cointelegraph.com/news/diving-into-three-of-africas-emerging-fintech-economies

Creamer Media (2019, April 16). The impact of Industry 4.0 on Africa's manufacturing sector. Creamer Media reporter. https://www.engineeringnews.co.za/article/the-impact-of-industry-40-on-africas-manufacturing-sector-2019-04-16/rep_id:4136

Crossman, A. (2020, January 28). McDonaldization and why sociologists are not "Lovin It." *Thought.Co*. https://www.thoughtco.com/mcdonaldization-of-society-3026751

Deloitte (2016, April 14). Industry 4.0 is Africa ready for digital transformation? https://www2.deloitte.com/content/dam/Deloitte/za/Documents/manufacturing/za-Africa-industry-4.0-report-April14.pdf

Ehui, S. (2020, May 14). Protecting food security in Africa during COVID-19. Brookings. https://www.brookings.edu/blog/africa-in-focus/2020/05/14/protecting-food-security-in-africa-during-covid-19/

Evoke (2020, January 30). Values in design—EVOKE lab and studio. https://evoke.ics.uci.edu/about/values-in-design/

Eziakonwa, A., & Gabre-Madhin, E. (2020, June 26). Africa's COVID-19 moment: How youth startups are addressing the pandemic—and what they need to reach the next level. *NextBillion*. https://nextbillion.net/africa-youth-startups-addressing-the-pandemic/

Feenberg, A. (2002). Transforming technology: A critical theory revised. *Transforming Technology: A Critical Theory Revised*, 1–18. https://www.researchgate.net/publication/44828056_Transforming_Technology_A_Critical_Theory_Revised

Feenberg, A. (2005). Critical theory of technology: An overview. *Tailoring Biotechnologies*, *1*, 47–64. https://www.researchgate.net/publication/261709929_Critical_Theory_of_Technology_An_Overview

Gaafar, R. (2014, October). Women's land and property rights in Kenya. *Landesa.* https://www.landesa.org/wp-content/uploads/LandWise-Guide-Womens-land-and-property-rights-in-Kenya.pdf

Gavrov, S., & Klyukanov, I. (2015). Modernization, Sociological Theories of. In: *Encyclopedia of the Social & Behavioral Sciences (Second Edition)* (pp. 707–713). https://doi.org/10.1016/b978-0-08-097086-8.32094-3

Goedde, L., Ooko-Ombaka, A., & Pais, G. (2019, March 20). Winning in Africa's agricultural market. McKinsey & Company. https://www.mckinsey.com/industries/agriculture/our-insights/winning-in-africas-agricultural-market

Hattingh, D., Leke, A., & Russo, B. (2017, October). Lions (still) on the move: Growth in Africa's consumer sector. McKinsey & Company. https://www.mckinsey.com/~/media/McKinsey/Industries/Consumer%20Packaged%20Goods/Our%20Insights/Lions%20still%20on%20the%20move%20Growth%20in%20Africas%20consumer%20sector/Lions-still-on-the-move-Growth-in-Africas-consumer-sector.pdf

Iwuoha, J. (2020, July 6). 11 business opportunities in Africa that made more millionaires in 2019—and will continue in 2020. *Smallstarter Africa.* https://www.smallstarter.com/browse-ideas/top-11-business-opportunities-in-africa-2019/

Jeremiah, U., & Umeh, J. (2019, October 30). Africa: U.S.$100 billion needed for universal, Quality Internet access—World Bank. *AllAfrica.Com.* https://allafrica.com/stories/201910300279.html

Kazeem, Y. (2019, March 19). What makes Jumia an African startup? *Quartz Africa.* https://qz.com/africa/1572318/what-makes-jumia-an-african-startup/

Kazeem, Y. (2020, June 26). *Covid-19: Impact investors eye African agriculture, health startups.* Quartz. https://qz.com/africa/1869334/covid-19-impact-investors-eye-african-agriculture-health-startups/

Ku, L. (2019, May 21). New agriculture technology in modern farming. *Plug and Play Tech Center.* https://www.plugandplaytechcenter.com/resources/new-agriculture-technology-modern-farming/

Leke, A., & Signé, L. (2019, January 11). Spotlighting opportunities for business in Africa and strategies to succeed in the world's next big growth market. Brookings. https://www.brookings.edu/research/spotlighting-opportunities-for-business-in-africa-and-strategies-to-succeed-in-the-worlds-next-big-growth-market/

Lewis, N. (2020, June 18). Africa's coronavirus lockdowns may trigger a turning point in online shopping. *CNN.* https://edition.cnn.com/2020/06/18/tech/africa-ecommerce-covid-spc-intl/index.html

Madowo, L. (2020, August 6). Silicon Valley has deep pockets for African startups—if you're not African. *The Guardian.* https://www.theguardian.com/business/2020/jul/17/african-businesses-black-entrepreneurs-us-investors

Manyinka, J., Lund, S., Chui, M., Bughin, J., Woetzel, J., Batra, P., Ko, R., & Sanghvi, S. (2019, May 11). Jobs lost, jobs gained: What the future of work will mean for jobs, skills, and wages. McKinsey & Company. https://www.mckinsey.com/featured-insights/future-of-work/jobs-lost-jobs-gained-what-the-future-of-work-will-mean-for-jobs-skills-and-wages

Masekesa, F. (2020, February 4). Nigeria, South Africa and Kenya dominate the e-commerce industry in Sub-Saharan Africa. *The Asian Banker.* https://www.theasianbanker.com/updates-and-articles/nigeria,-south-africa-and-kenya-dominate-the-e-commerce-industry-in- Sub-Saharan-africa

Moyo, A. (2019, December 12). What Facebook did for Africa in 2019. *Italianist.* Web. https://www.itweb.co.za/content/wbrpOqgPR1WvDLZn

Mukhtar, A. (2017). Enhancing food security in Africa through implementing the Trade Facilitation Agreement. International Centre for Trade and Sustainable Development (ICTSD). *Bridges Africa 6*(3).

Njoroge, K. (2020, April 27). Coronavirus is triggering deep digital change in African fintech. *The Africa Report.Com*. https://www.theafricareport.com/26934/coronavirus-is-triggering-deep-digital-change-in-african-fintech/

Oxford Business Group (2020, July 29). Development banks and Covid-19: Stepping up in a time of crisis? https://oxfordbusinessgroup.com/news/development-banks-and-covid-19-stepping-time-crisis

Reese, B. (2018, November 6). Artificial Intelligence will be the greatest jobs engine the world has ever seen. *Entrepreneur*. https://www.entrepreneur.com/article/322141

Shaban, A. (2017, April 21). *Why is Africa importing $35bn in food annually? - AfDB boss asks*. Africanews. https://www.africanews.com/2017/04/21/why-is-africa-importing-35bn-in-food-annually-afdb-boss-asks//

Shapshak, T. (2019, July 1). Africa's Fintech ecosystem raised $320m and grew 60% in two years. *Forbes*. https://www.forbes.com/sites/tobyshapshak/2019/06/29/africas-fintech-ecosystem-raised-320m-and-grew-60-in-two-years/?sh=4921158a7226

She leads Africa (2020, August 25). 5 top e-commerce platforms in Africa. https://sheleadsafrica.org/growth-of-ecommerce/

Signé, L. (2018, September). The potential of manufacturing and industrialization in Africa trends, opportunities, and strategies. Https://Www.Brookings.Edu/Wp-Content/Uploads/2018/09/Manufacturing-and-Industrialization-in-Africa-Signe-20180921.Pdf. https://www.brookings.edu/wp-content/uploads/2018/09/Manufacturing-and-Industrialization-in-Africa-Signe-20180921.pdf

Tanui, N. (2019, June 11). Looking to invest in Africa? The 7 sectors driving growth. *The Standard*. https://www.standardmedia.co.ke/business/hustle/article/2001329461/looking-to-invest-in-africa-the-7-sectors-driving-growth

The World Bank (2009). Gender in agriculture sourcebook. https://openknowledge.worldbank.org/bitstream/handle/10986/6603/461620PUB0Box3101OFFICIAL0USE0ONLY1.pdf?sequence=1&isAllowed=y

Verter, N. (2015). The Application of International Trade Theories to Agriculture. *Mediterranean Journal of Social Sciences, 6*(6), 209–219. https://doi.org/10.5901/mjss.2015.v6n6s4p209

Verter, N. (2017, September 13). International trade: The position of Africa in global merchandise trade. *IntechOpen*. https://www.intechopen.com/books/emerging-issues-in-economics-and-development/international-trade-the-position-of-africa-in-global-merchandise-trade

Yinusa, M., & Mabaya, E. (2019, November 5). *Agribusiness: Africa's new investment frontier*. African Development Bank Group. https://www.afdb.org/en/news-and-events/agribusiness-africas-new-investment-frontier-32461

World Bank. (2012). *Africa can feed itself, earn billions, and avoid food crises by unblocking regional food trade*. Washington, DC: World Bank.

World Bank Group (2020, June 2). World Bank's response to COVID-19 (coronavirus) in Africa. https://www.worldbank.org/en/news/factsheet/2020/06/02/world-banks-response-to-covid-19-coronavirus-in-africa

6 An overview of growth sectors and industries in Africa

Part II: Exploring Infrastructure

Economic infrastructure

Energy, transport, water/sanitation, extractive

Infrastructure development in Africa is critical to enable sustainable growth and development. As of 2020, data and statistics in an African Development Bank report reveal: lack of affordable housing, a population of 65% who cannot access electricity, 53% of unpaved roads that are the primary mode of transport for 80% goods and 90% passengers, lack of road safety, outdated infrastructure and limited maintenance of railways, lack of African aviation safety, inefficiencies and poor equipment of ports, unreliable ICT connectivity, and lack of access to improved water sources and sanitation, as some highlight of the infrastructure challenges in Africa. Furthermore, in 2019, the International Energy Agency (IEA) reported that about 600 million people in Africa still lack access to the electricity grid (Tadesse, 2019).

Although Africa is abundant in natural, energy, wind, wave power and solar resources, the continent lacks abundant access to fossil fuels and renewable energy. This shortage has negatively impacted the efficiency of numerous sectors and households, resulting in challenges to economic development. In rural areas, the shortage of renewable energy and its unreliability aggravate small-scale development opportunities in electrification, desalination, water pumping and water purification. In 2016, an estimated 80% of households on the African used firewood and charcoal as alternatives to energy for daily needs (World Bank Group report, 2016). Over-reliance and overconsumption of wood-fuel negatively endanger natural forest resources, which in turn result in a plethora of challenges, including desertification, increased greenhouse gases in the atmosphere, climate change, flooding and a host of complications for communities, as well as organisms that inhabit the environment.

Climate-friendly innovations and investments to access solar and renewable energy remain a much-needed priority and alternative to address these challenges. Akon, Senegalese-American award-winning musical artist, entrepreneur and philanthropist, launched the Akon Lighting Africa project in 2014 with Samba Bathily to provide electricity by solar energy throughout Africa. As of 2015, the project provided electricity to 14 African countries,

DOI: 10.4324/9781351031660-8

employed 5000 people and reached about 1 million households, according to Akon. In conjunction with this initiative, Akon, Bathily and their group also launched the Solar Academy in Bamako, Mali to educate students about solar energy through the use of solar panels to light Africa.

Across Africa, some notable innovations for energy between 2017 and 2019 include: Ghana's Yam Pro Energy's initiative to sell the electricity it generates and equip about 10,000 households with electricity; East Africa's M-Kopa Solar, Off Grid Electric, StemaCo businesses, among others, that are using the low-cost alternative of solar power to provide households with electricity; West Africa's innovative conversions of human waste into odorless and energy-efficient fuel through charcoal for cooking; the $5 billion, 6000-megawatt hydropower plant and Africa's largest dam from Ethiopia, and DR Congo's BBOXX, a solar systems developer to address electricity needs to an estimated 2.5 million citizens—represent some of Africa's innovative responses to the solar power needs.

An estimate of about 450 million Africans—more than 70% of the total rural population—are disconnected from lack of transport infrastructure and systems, straining negative impacts on businesses (Sustainable Mobility for All, 2017). Multinational businesses like Uber, Kenya's Magic Bus mobile phone SMS-based solutions for urban commuters to pre-book bus tickets represent a few transport-initiatives to address Africa's transport challenges (Iwuoha, 2017).

However, continued infrastructure investments in Africa account for over 50% of improved economic growth, according to the African Development Bank. The annual infrastructure investment has doubled to $80 billion annually since the start of the century (Leke & Signé, 2019). This reinforces the continent's commitment to address some of the infrastructure challenges and achieve more economic growth.

Addressing the challenges of infrastructure is also key for driving the growth of the mining industry in Africa, which comprises the extractive industries (EI), along with oil and gas production—major sources of investment and revenue in many African countries that remain dependent on them for economic growth. As of 2019, Africa holds 30% of the world's global mineral reserves, including platinum, gold, diamonds and coal (Bafana, 2019, para. 5); "10 percent of the world's oil reserves and 8 percent of natural gas" (Bafana, 2019, para. 5; African Development Bank).

These minerals are key components of innumerable products infrastructure and technology, including cell phones that are sold globally. As of 2012, "less than 5% of the total global mineral exploration and extraction budget is invested in the continent," (Edel & Webb, 2012, p. 5). Despite the abundance of resources, Africa confronts challenges in translating these revenues into sustainable economic development—a phenomenon commonly referred to as the "*resource curse*," or the "*poverty paradox*," or the "*paradox of plenty*."

Although numerous factors highlighting the challenges accompanying the extractive industry remains complex, a few include: water shortages and energy constraints that affect efficiency in extracting resources; the threat of climate on the exploitation of these resources, as well as the need for regulatory frameworks to support the industry (Edel & Webb, 2012). Furthermore, additional challenges include: unclear, inconsistent or unpredictable African mining codes that govern mineral exploration and development; poor enforcement of these regulations by governments that ultimately fall in the hands of the private sector; inequitable distribution of mineral wealth that does not alleviate poverty of the underserved communities; the use of conflict diamonds (blood diamonds) or conflict minerals to fund insurgents; competing stakeholders' agendas, including clashes between governments (seeking beneficiations and revenue for infrastructure), and local communities (seeking local socio-economic benefits) and mining companies (seeking to meet government and local communities' demands, while trying to meet cost-efficient goals) (Edel & Webb, 2012).

Additional socio-economic challenges related to the extractive industry result in landmark legal suits, as epitomized by the 2019 lawsuit against Apple and Google in Congolese child cobalt mining deaths, as cobalt mining was used for smartphones, laptops and electric cars, (Kelly, 2019). Child labor has been associated heavily with some of the challenges of the extractive industry for communities mired in poverty. Unable to afford tuition fees or secure job employment, many children in impoverished communities resort to *child labor* or *child slavery*, where they are forced to work for no or little minimal wage.

There have been several interventions to address the challenges of this sector. According to the African Development Bank, one of the key factors that have been identified to support extractive industry (EI) EI revenues for development includes improving the quality of EI-related governance—an effort that donors and recipient governments have been emphasizing. The collaboration of governments and international bodies, including the World Bank and the International Finance Corporation, are also developing transparent and investor-focused mining laws that will support Africa's efforts to diversify mineral portfolios and capitalize on the industries (Edel & Webb, 2012).

Suggested opportunities and considerations for the diaspora

Social services

The diaspora are invited to contribute to this sector in various ways, including providing social services that support the needs of local communities affected by mining. Efforts can be reflected through non-profit organizations or social enterprises that are intentional and strategic about creating employment for local residents and empowering them to gain a sustainable livelihood from the extractive industry.

Research and development, training programs, marketing, business management

The diaspora can also pursue some of the following opportunities within the private sector in the extractive industry, particularly in mining, as illustrated by some cases in Zambia, South Africa, Tanzania and Ghana. Through the private sector, the diaspora can: develop research institutions with professionals whose international expertise can provide technical information, mineral assessment and processing services to domestic mining sectors; provide markets for mineral products that are produced by small-scale miners, as in the case of Ghana's Precious Minerals Marketing Company, a state-owned mining company that has offices and agents in small-scale gold and diamond areas in the country and buys, sells and promotes precious minerals and Ghana's jewelry industry; develop educational programs and "facilities to train geologists, economists and engineers" (Extractive Hubs, 2020, para. 14) that would retain specialized local talent in the country, as well as "develop IT and computerized programs that manage mining from "cradle-to-grave"' (Extractive Hubs, 2020, para. 14) and support administrative, legal, operational, and technical processes of the industry and business.

Vendor procurement

The diaspora can also be effective in providing the specialized equipment and vehicles needed to adhere to environmental, social and labor compliances. They can support government institutions with optimal physical tools that are required to fulfill tasks, including those of inspection, particularly if their offices receive less funding from their national capital budget to adequately fund physical infrastructure that is required for these tasks.

Ultimately, it is important for transparent partnerships between governments, industry players and key stakeholders to support extractive communities, while promoting sustainable socio-economic and environmental development solutions. Solutions range from developing educational programs to build competencies, creating jobs along the value chain of the industry and investing in projects that prioritize sustainable, low-carbon emissions and the use of minerals and metals in renewable energy technologies.

The market is ripe for Africans in the diaspora to innovatively explore how to address infrastructure challenges and provide practical solutions that aim to improve urban and regional connectivity for households and businesses and facilitate inclusion of African firms in global markets.

In the words of Aliko Dangote:

> The business potential of the continent is tremendous in various sectors, including energy, infrastructure, agriculture, natural resources, and information and communications, offering opportunities for entrepreneurs. … Similarly, the continent has the world's largest reserves of vanadium, diamonds, manganese, phosphate, platinum-group metals, cobalt, gold, aluminum, and chromium, offering opportunities for entrepreneurs in the mining sector
>
> (Aliko Dangote, 2019, para. 2).

Overall impact of Covid-19 on infrastructure in Africa

The pandemic has affected Africa's infrastructure, resulting in projections of marked economic slowdown. The International Monetary Fund (IMF) and World Bank Group project a decline of GDP growth rates at −3.2% GDP and between −2.1%. and −5.1%, respectively (Amoah-Darkwah & Reboredo, 2020). Given that the African Development Bank reports Africa's current infrastructure deficit to estimate at $130 billion a year, the pandemic is expected to significantly widen fiscal deficits across sectors, including transportation, water, sanitation and energy (Amoah-Darkwah & Reboredo, 2020). Commodity exporting countries affected by lower oil prices, such as Nigeria and Angola, are expected to more severely impacted fiscally (Lawson, 2020).

Different responses from African governments have also contributed to the variation of different countries' responses and resilience to the pandemic. Governments' interventions that have resulted in a variation of curfews and lockdowns, leading to temporary shutdowns of infrastructural projects, or permitting their continuation that may restrict the mobility of people, rather than on goods (Lawson, 2020). Ultimately, the pandemic has required for countries to identify their critical infrastructure that would need to sustain families and essential services during uncertain times. Some projects, particularly those connected to power and renewable energy and hence, recognized as "essential services," have continued to operate as on-site activities, generating revenue and reflecting a resilience (Lawson, 2020).

However, in other cases, construction projects that have been halted by labor and material shortages through lockdowns, cross border checks and preventative measures further exacerbate the challenges of completing infrastructural projects (Amoah-Darkwah & Reboredo, 2020).

Experts and policy makers anticipate that three key drivers of post-Covid-19-recovery in SSA would consist of: acceleration of energy, with particular focus on clean and renewable energy; digitization, a reconfiguration of supply chains, with renewed focus on regional and local supply chains (CMS Law Now, 2020).

Fortunately, commitments, financial assistance and provisional debt relief from numerous multilateral organizations, official bilateral creditors, and other sources from the international community could lessen the impact of the pandemic and support infrastructural projects and activity. African governments have also learned lessons from previous pandemics, including the Ebola outbreak, to institute best practices and strengthen their resilience in economic development recovery plans.

The pandemic has also severely impacted the informal economy. Recognized as the backbone for many African economies, the informal sector "accounts for over 70 percent of hours worked in Africa and is a main source of income for at least 60 percent of African households and over 80 percent of rural households" (Fox & Signé, 2020, para. 2). Hence, the impact of the pandemic has severely impacted informal businesses, particularly of women and children who are predominantly employed in informal sectors. Hence, there is much attention that needs to gravitate toward vulnerable populations, particularly women, youth and those of the disability community that rely on the informal economy and during the pandemic, are positioned to be further economically-disadvantaged.

Social infrastructure

Healthcare and pharmacy

The healthcare industry, generally, affects many countries with numerous challenges that vary along the spectrum. The World Health Organization (WHO) identified six (6) components to describe healthcare systems that are also used as evaluation metrics for assessment: "i) service delivery; ii) healthcare workforce; iii) healthcare information systems; iv) medicines and technologies; v) financing; and vi) leadership/governance" (Oleribe et al., 2019, para. 1). Poor governance; under-funded systems, human resources limitations from the brain drain; financial barriers exacerbated from exorbitant out-of-pocket expenditures, prior to rendering medical attention, and ineffective health insurance programs highlight some of the challenges facing Africa's healthcare systems (Oleribe et al., 2019, para. 1).

The inefficiencies of the healthcare systems contribute further toward *medical tourism*. In Nigeria, for instance, over 5000 people leave the country for better treatment options overseas, costing the country about $1.2 billion annually to medical tourism (Oleribe et al., 2019). The backdrop of doctor to population ratios reflect adverse impacts of the voluminous brain drain and a deficit of resources to serve the needs of the growing population.

Additionally, Africa's tropical climate renders it vulnerable to diseases, ranging from infectious maladies like malaria to non-communicable diseases (NCDs). According to Luccini (2018):

> With the increasing adoption of Western lifestyle in Africa, there has been a paradigm shift in the burden of illness toward non-communicable diseases (NCDs), driving the demand for chronic prescription drugs. Based on World Health Organisation prediction, the proportional contribution of NCDs to the healthcare burden in Africa will rise by 21% through 2030 (Luccini, 2018, para. 3).

On the flip side, Africa's pharmaceutical market has witnessed growth, leaping from a value of $5.5 billion about a decade ago to $28.56 USD billion in 2017, with estimated growth of the market to be worth $56 billion to $70 billion by 2030 (Goldstein Market Intelligence, 2020). The annual growth rate of Africa's pharmaceutical segments between 2017 to 2030 has been forecast for the following: prescription drugs' "growth rate of 6.5%, generics at 10%, over-the-counter medicines at 7.1%, and medical devices at 12.1%" (Goldstein Market Intelligence, 2020, para. 2). The rapid pace of market value of the pharmaceutical industry highlights the potential for pharmaceutical companies to penetrate the market, facilitated through drivers like increased urbanization, healthcare capacity and an enabling environment (Goldstein Market Intelligence, 2020). Increased health care capacity refers to the augment of hospital personnel, including doctors, nurses and hospital beds that averaged to a total of "1,050,000 beds, 498,370 doctors, and 1,250,000 nurses between 2005 and 2012" (Lucini, 2018, para. 2).

The forecast of the NCD burden on Africa's healthcare, therefore, triggers a demand for chronic prescription drugs—which a burning question: Does Africa have the capacity to produce more local pharmaceutical drugs to address some of these ailments?

An overview of the pharmaceutical market is as follows. As of 2019, about 70% to 90% of drugs that are consumed by sub-Saharan Africa are imported drugs—including prescription and over-the-counter drugs— which place additional financial burdens on governments, households and limited foreign exchanges (Conway et al., 2020). Analysts that assessed the promotion of local pharmaceutical production in Africa observed the following: only a few local companies produce drugs for the domestic market; the majority of Africa's estimated 375 drug makers are in North America (to serve a continent populated with about 1.3 billion people), of which those in sub-Saharan Africa are in nine of 46 countries, small in size, and operate below international standards (Conway et al., 2020). This contrasts to China and India that have about 5,000 and 10,500 drug manufacturers, respectively, to serve their populations of 1.4 billion people (Conway et al., 2020).

Additionally, many sub-Saharan African countries are in early stages of pharmaceutical-industry development, ranging from few, if any local manufacturers, to varying degrees of stable manufactures in the market, as well as fluctuating between being heavily reliant on import distribution to having an emerging export base (Conway et al., 2020).

Lastly, local producers play limited roles in the value chain as either drug-product manufacturers who purchase the active pharmaceutical ingredient (APIs) that they formulate into finished drugs, e.g., pills, syrups, capsules, or who package (Conway et al., 2020). Ultimately, pharmaceutical analysts and economists recognize that markets for local production feasibility will vary by each country's unique environment. As of 2019, Kenya, Nigeria and South Africa were the only sub-Saharan African countries to locally produce and export drugs, and that only three manufacturers—two in South Africa and one in Ghana—produce APIs with no significant research and development (R&D) activity (Conway et al., 2020).

Suggested opportunities and considerations for the diaspora

In light of these figures, the value and need for pharmaceutical production and investment in healthcare are significant. The challenges also invite opportunities along the pharmaceutical production value chain for the African diaspora to support through partnerships with local business partners—both in the private and not-for-profit sector, pharmaceutical companies, and the government.

Halima Aliko Dangote, Trustee of Aliko Dangote Foundation, highlighted the value of engaging in public-private partnerships (PPPs) to enrich the healthcare industry:

> Governments from both developed and developing countries are increasingly looking at public-private partnerships (PPPs) as a way to expand access to higher quality health services by leveraging capital, managerial capacity, and know-how from the private sector… it is clear that PPPs can play an important role in mobilizing additional forms of financing and closing the infrastructure gap. We need to look at innovative ways to mobilize private investment and how to embed the SDG targets into PPP projects and operations
>
> (GBC Health, 2019).

Within the pharmaceutical industry, an overview reveals opportunities to strengthen quality and operational efficiencies of existing manufacturing companies, expand the roles drug manufacturers that go beyond purchasing APIs and packaging.

Research & development

The diaspora can pursue opportunities in research and development to generate and circulates more knowledge of the industry to prompt how Africans can effectively and efficiently harness their abundance of raw materials and process them for local drug manufacturing and distribution. Positive spill-over effects would produce health and economic impacts that reduce the importation of drugs that would be more cost-effective to produce locally, alleviate import tariffs, and increase job creation. There are also opportunities for wholesale and retail distribution of locally-manufactured drugs, technologies, vaccines, medicines, refurbished and new medical technologies and devices both within and outside of African. Furthermore, research opportunities would indicate where and how to identify more markets, drive competition and support growth of the industry through additional marketing communications and advertising efforts. These opportunities, however, would need to be carefully assessed through wide-scale, in-depth, thorough research opportunities and assessments of the healthcare and pharmaceutical market. Recommendations would need to be contextualized to ensure an efficient allocation of resources that address the communities' needs and respond to diverse consumer preferences of the drug or healthcare market.

Education & training

Additionally, the diaspora can also sponsor education and training programs in the medical and healthcare field to build talent pipelines in the industry, and support related job creation in the medical industry. These opportunities offer avenues to support new professionals in the labor market and retain skills and talent in the healthcare industry within local communities. For instance, Johnson & Johnson's partnership with the South African government resulted in an "education program for maternal, newborn, and child health that operates via mobile-phone messaging" (Africa Business Pages, n.d., para. 13).

Social health insurance programs

Other initiatives that have been implemented include social health insurance programs in Nigeria, Ghana, Tanzania, Kenya, Rwanda and Ethiopia to help alleviate financial burdens that displace those who are disenfranchised. Other countries can refer to their frameworks to similarly develop and contextualize appropriate social health insurance programs. Additionally, some African governments' increased spending on healthcare to meet United Nations' Millennium Development Goals and newer technologies support continuous efforts to transform the healthcare industry across the continent.

IP and regulations

Various African governments have also been collaborating with numerous private health sector federations and organizations, including the West Africa Private Healthcare Federation and the East Africa Healthcare Federation, to encourage investments in facilities, protect trademarks and innovations, and draft laws and regulations that attract investors' interests in healthcare projects.

IT innovations

The digitization of products and services across Africa have also led to developments in healthcare technologies like medical drones, e-medical services through mobile apps and telemedicine initiatives. This has been illustrated through numerous entrepreneurial efforts by Africans on the ground and in the diaspora. For instance, Uganda's Brian Turyabagye and his team developed a biomedical kit to diagnose and treat pneumonia—a disease, which, according to UNICEF—kills about 500,000 infants in sub-Saharan Africa annually, as well as Nigeria's Redbank to rapidly identify safe blood supplies for hospitals and patients highlight a few examples (Iwouha, 2016). Such technologies expand Africa's healthcare opportunities for investors and entrepreneurs to further develop this industry and serve communities. Ultimately, such technologies illustrate tenets of the *critical theory of technology,* which enables those on the ground to be a part of the manufacturing process of lab and medical technologies that will address their communities' needs.

Furthermore, investments in healthcare rely on partnerships of various stakeholders, including governments, the private sector and local community residents who can contribute to relevant policy dialogues, national health planning and public-awareness campaigns. The diaspora can also form partnerships with governments to provide health screenings, healthcare equipment and the strategic and efficient use of funds and resources that can build and sustain health systems.

Overall impact of Covid-19 on healthcare in Africa

As of August 2020, Africa accounts for 5% of confirmed cases of the global total, of which South Africa harbors the highest number of recorded cases and deaths and ranks fifth in the highest number globally (Mwai & Giles, 2020). Additionally, compared to its global counterparts, Africa's reported death rate per capital has also been low (Mwai & Giles, 2020). Various hypotheses to account for these factors include issues related to testing and data, as reported by the International Rescue Committee, and that the majority of Africa's youthful population (over 60% are under 25 years old) would be less affected by Covid-19 that primarily affects the elderly, and that health problems like obesity and type 2 diabetes that are less common in Africa are more prevalent among richer countries (Mwai & Giles, 2020).

Given the challenges of an already vulnerable healthcare system, this outlook may surprise some. What is not surprising, however, is the spill-over effects that the pandemic has had on vulnerable groups indirectly, particularly on women and girls in Africa. Throughout Africa, "women account for around 40% of COVID-19 cases, this ranges from 35% in some countries to over 55% in South Africa" (World Health Organization, 2020, para. 2). The lockdowns have resulted in: reduced access to healthcare services, including those for sexual and reproductive health; increased gender and domestic violence, and psychological tensions in resulting from stress (World Health Organization, 2020). According to research conducted by the World Health Organization, preliminary data in Zimbabwe revealed a decrease of caesarean sections between January and April 2020 to 42%, as compared to the same period in 2019; decrease of live births by 21% and new clients on birth control pills by 90%, and a drop of births with skilled attendants from 30,826 in April 2019 to 4,749 in April 2020 (World Health Organization, 2020).

The pandemic has also invited increased attention toward the global health industry and the conceptualization "*global health*." It is critical that scholars, researchers, policymakers and practitioners assess the relevance of normative principles underlying global health in the context of the pandemic. A healthcare professional from the Sudan who works for a leading global organization expressed frustration at characteristics of some underlying systemic racial inequities that govern some healthcare practices in the 21st century:

> The whole concept of White saviorism also exists where you're at the highest level of planning and at the highest level of decision making there isn't there are a handful of African people that are making decisions for the African people for the Africa people. I actually did my study as a qualitative study because I believe context matters greatly. There is no rule that will

> fit that you can say that we're going to solve the HIV epidemic in Africa by doing one two three and it will work across Africa. There's no way…I know that someone from Sudan is completely different from someone from Somalia who is completely different from someone from Nigeria and then South Africa… Just because we're all in this continent, people seem to equate Africa to a country, [but that] does not necessarily mean that we have anything in common
>
> (participant, personal communication, February 1, 2020).

It would also be important for healthcare industry experts to assess how the allocation of resources, policies and interventionist strategies can shape how medical care can be equitably and effectively delivered and tailored to the diverse local African contexts across the continent.

Education

Arguably, the most valuable resource in any continent is its human resources. Investing in the knowledge, skills, abilities and other aptitudes of human capital is key for any sustainable development. Human beings are the only resource with the ability to reuse, recycle, rebuild, transform, convert, learn, leverage skills and unleash potential to build on external resources to further development. Any community relies on the development of its human base to organize, lead and develop their community. One way to unleash the potential of human talent, therefore, is to invest in the education system.

Unfortunately, Africa's education system has long been characterized as having a "twin deficit" in both access and learning, given low access to education opportunities and little learning that results in illiteracy, also coined as "zero-value added." According to the UNESCO Institute for Statistics, 59 million children of primary school age across the world are out of school, of which 32 million reside in sub-Saharan Africa, which also has the highest school-exclusion rate (UNESCO Institute of Statistics, 2019). The wide distribution of out-of-school children stems characterizes those who dropped out after attendance, may attend in the future or may never attend (UNESCO Institute of Statistics, 2019). Across the world, gender disparities in education reveal that as of 2019:

> 9 million girls of primary school age will never have the opportunity to learn to read and write in primary school, compared to about 3 million boys. Across sub-Saharan Africa, 4 million girls will never attend school compared to 2 million boys
>
> (UNESCO Institute of Statistics, 2019, p. 11).

Several barriers account for the statistics reducing access and learning opportunities. Many children are child laborers who are employed in informal economies to contribute toward their home, forfeiting an education, and engage in various forms of child labor—many of which are physically exhaustive, exploitative and dangerous—such as prostitution, working in mines, agriculture and livestock farming, and various forms of unpaid labor. Additionally, having the right governance and leadership also account for the policies needed to foster a supporting environment. In a 2013 report by *Foresight Africa*, analysts attributed factors to some governments' less public spending on rural disadvantaged populations than those in wealthier populations, reduced investment in teaching and learning materials and training and on implementing national assessment systems that meet national standards. Those who are in school spend years of "zero-value added" education that bear little fruit, including the lack of skills in basic competencies.

Corruption in education over the past few decades to present-day have also further complicated the development of the education sector in Africa, particularly at primary school levels. A 2010 Transparency International report, *Africa Education Watch: Good Governance Lessons for Primary Education*, revealed that lack of parent involvement in their children's education, as well as a sense of disempowerment in their ability to influence decision making of their children's education lessened their abilities to oversee or hold governments accountable. Furthermore, the African Education Watch revealed that illegal collection of registration fees, embezzlement of school funds—evidenced by 64% of schools in Africa that were surveyed that published no financial information—and the abuse of power—including cases of sexual abuse—along with mismanagement of resources and funds, were the top common practices of corruption (Antonowicz et al., 2010). There have since been continuous reforms to strengthen accountability and 'good governance' in education.

However, the twin deficits of access and quality are also pervasive in the higher education sector. Africa has a long history of investing in higher education, given that it produced the world's oldest universities: The University of Al Qarawiyyin in Fez in Morocco, founded in 859 AD, as well as Al-Azhar University in Egypt, founded in 970 AD. By 2016, Africa hailed an estimated 1650 higher education institutions (Mba, 2017), from which the 15 best in the continent hailed from South Africa, Egypt, Morocco, Ghana, Kenya, Nigeria and Uganda, according to a 2016 *Times Higher Education Report* (Daniel et al., 2019). By 2020, some of the best universities in Africa hailed from these countries; globally, universities from Egypt, Nigeria, Uganda and South Africa ranked globally in the top 500 of worldwide university rankings, with Egypt and South Africa featuring "the two best represented African countries…with 21 and 10 universities each" (The Student, 2020, para. 3). Furthermore, South Africa's University of Cape Town and the University of Witwatersrand rank in the top 250 or the worldwide rankings (The Student, 2020).

Despite such rankings, higher education in Africa overall highlights various challenges. "Access to higher education for the relevant age group remains at 5%, the lowest regional average in the world, just one-fifth of the global average of about 25%" (Mba, 2017, para. 4). Furthermore, shortcomings that affect the quality of education include: an accumulation of lack of reforms to make curricula and programs relevant; a brain drain of talented professionals and researchers who leave the continent; disincentives of low salaries; lack of resources and funding for research, equipment, provisions; "poor administrative leadership" and constraints in hiring a critical mass of quality faculty (Mba, 2017). Also, there are still challenges of perception, particularly when some professionals face discrimination or biases in the global workplace, when their university degrees are assumed to reflect less quality experience than their peers and colleagues who may have acquired degrees in Western countries.

Another development challenge links education to Africa's youth unemployment rate, estimated at 60% by the World Bank (Ighobor, 2017), although education is only one of various factors that account for unemployment in Africa. Nevertheless, a frightening reality of the supply and demand of higher education emerges: a lack of correlation between the skills and competencies acquired from the university degree and the demands of the labor market. Some professors and analysts, including Sarah Anyang Agbor, the African Union (AU) Commissioner for Human Resources, Science and Technology, attribute this mismatch to outdated education curricula. Other constraints include challenges of recruiting new faculty and conducting innovative research to revitalize the knowledge economy. According to Mba (2017), "the average percentage of staff with PhD in public higher education institutions in Africa is estimated to be less than 20%" (para. 13; Soucat et al. 2013; *Chronicle of Higher Education* 2013), with departments limited to one or two faculty, with many nearing retirement. Specialists and international development leaders also recognize that more attention and investment in practical skills for the labor market need to be strengthened in STEM—sciences, technology, engineering and mathematics, confirmed also by low percentage of graduates in these fields.

Adekunbi Oyelade, one of Africa's leading experts on education to employment, also noted some of related challenges that contribute to youth unemployment. In addition to old curricula, of which "most of them are not 21st century compliant and some of them are still very old" (Oyelade, personal communication, December 21, 2019), many students lack work experience to prepare for employment. With a lack of internships and apprenticeships, these students are not in a position to build on their soft skills and prepare for the "world of work" (Oyelade, personal communication, December 21, 2019).

Lastly, gender disparities in education—both in the primary and higher education sectors—affect the development agenda in many African countries. As of 2019, "young women in Africa are over 1.5 times less likely than young men to be formally employed or undergoing education or training" (Santos & Rubiano-Matulievich, 2019, para. 1). As of 2018, "in sub-Saharan Africa, 33.3 million girls of primary and lower secondary school age are out of school, [but] rises to 52.2 million, [when also accounting for] girls of upper secondary school age" (CAMFED, n.d.; UIS, 2018). Gender norms that some communities place over education that force young girls to fulfill traditional domestic responsibilities and cultural traditions that value the dowry of child brides are only a few factors that account for the gender disparity in education. "In Sub-Saharan Africa, two-thirds (66 percent) of women with no education became child brides, versus 13 percent of those with secondary or higher education—a rate over five times higher" (Saur, 2017, para. 33).

Data, however, indicates that investing in girls' education yields exponential gains in development in the short-term and long-term. In 2014, UNESCO's Global Education Monitoring Report revealed that generally, increasing female education by one percentage point leads to a 0.3 percentage point increase in gross domestic product (GDP) and a 0.2 percentage point increase of the annual GDP (Bourne, 2014). Former President of Liberia, Ellen Johnson Sirleaf, also noted that "girls who complete primary education are likely to increase earnings by 5 to 15% over their lifetimes" (Sirleaf, 2015, para. 7). Specific to Africa, Former President Sirleaf also remarked that "investing in girls' education could boost sub-Saharan Africa's agricultural output by up to 25%" (Sirleaf, 2015, para. 8). Other benefits of investing in female education include a reduction of child marriages and maternal mortality, reduced HIV and STD rates, increased agency and participation in leadership positions, particularly in politics, and investments in their own children for education opportunities, among many more.

Suggested opportunities and considerations for the diaspora

In light of this, various efforts have been made to address the twin deficit in education and ensure progress in this sector across the continent.

Technology and apps

Mobile apps and advanced technological tools have been transforming the education sector across African countries over the past decade. In 2010, the Kenyan government collaborated with UNIICEF to launch mobile schools that address the needs of nomadic families who travel with teachers and set up temporary schools and tents (She Leads Africa, 2018).

Over the years, more innovative apps continue to shape the market to-date. Other innovations including, Kytaby, a low-cost Android app that allows users to rent textbooks, chapters and learning material through the M-Pesa East African mobile money transfer service, as well as Feenix, a crowdfunding initiative in South Africa to assist students with tuition fees further epitomize technology promoting education.

Solar-powered classrooms that can work 'off-grid,' as those powered by Ambit Technologies, and cheap tablets have already taken over some classrooms in Africa to bridge education gaps through technology. eLimu, headquartered in Nairobi, Kenya, is a highly-featured EdTech company and leading digital educational content provider in East Africa. Through engaging edutainment driven literacy apps in various local languages and online curricula, infused with locally-produced content, including songs, music, games and quizzes, as well as train-the-teacher materials, their pedagogical approaches aims for improved test scores, cognitive thinking, social and life skills and digital literacy.

Ben Nortey, regarded as the Botmaster, has used his skills as a robot builder, entrepreneur and teacher to found the Metro Institute of Innovation and Technology in Ghana to teach children how to code through his course that also promotes science, entrepreneurship programming, game design and other innovations.

Core curricula development

There is also an opportunity for students in Africa and those in the diaspora to collaborate in producing and developing core curricula that support pre-primary and K-12 levels of education, as well as higher levels of learning at the university level. Contributing to the development of academic content, theoretical information, critical forms of scholarship, and skills-based learning material to strengthen the knowledge economy, fortify the academic rigor and prepare students for careers in industries that target development sectors in their countries. Although online and distant learning cannot replace the values of in-person teaching experiences and there is value in hybrid, or blended learning modalities that combine face-to-face and online modules, online learning transfers the costs of travel and lodging from teaching or student exchange programs to more investments in innovative mobile technology and digitization of content to increase access and improve quality of education for students in primary, secondary and higher learning in Africa and outside of the continent.

This is particularly valuable for the diaspora who are distant from their home countries. They can remain connected to literature that educates them on their history and cultures, deriving knowledge directly from the lived experiences expressed by peers, specialists and educators in Africa. Critical scholarship addresses, particularly in development curricula, the one-way information flow from Western sources toward indigenous groups in developing countries. Hence, concepts like *African Diaspora literacy* would be effective to implement in education systems in efforts to educate students, particularly of African descent, of their collective history and cultural ideologies. Boutte et al. (2017) recognize how diaspora literacy "challenges and critiques social and equity issues while building the racial and ethnic uplifting of people who are often on the margins in society" (p. 68; Boutte, 2016; Lynn et al., 2013). Additional theoretical frameworks, including those related to critical theory, are key to generate, promote and circulate knowledge that derives from indigenous Africans and citizen-residents on the ground. Including knowledge, concepts and theories from their lens would further promote diverse and expand inclusive paradigms, viewpoints, perspectives and experiences that will form the basis of curricula. This enriches dialogues, contributes to a high caliber of quality education programs and research, and adequately prepares a generation of skilled and competent critical scholars and pragmatists who can effectively compete in the global labor market, or contribute to the development agenda of their African home countries.

Such early committed interactions and strategic long-term engagements between Africans and the diaspora creates a network that extends throughout their scholastic and career trajectory and educates each group about newer and diverse interests in different fields and sectors that they may have had limited exposure to, otherwise. Childhood development theories in education would guide educators about the quality of content that would shape students' earlier exposures to diverse cultural teachings and enrich their learning and development. By fostering a space for African diaspora literacy, early childhood educators can expose children to hegemonic ideologies that form normative principles and encourage their critical mindset that can challenge "deeply embedded Eurocentric curricula" and empower them to reassert their agency (Boutte et al., 2017, p. 68; Dei, 2012).

Internship and apprenticeship programs

To bridge the gap between school and employment in Nigeria, Adekunbi Oyelade founded SESEWA in 2009 to prepare the youth for jobs and careers through internships and apprenticeship programs. To-date, the programs have also been instrumental in assisting governments address challenges with the youth and support requisites of a 21st century workplace. Such opportunities prepare students to refine both soft skills and the technical, hard skills that are required for progression in the workplace—especially as the workplace culture increasingly reflects diverse staff and clients from different parts of the world.

Cultural exchange educational programs

Earlier in their educational careers, students in Africa and in the larger diaspora may also identify a wide variety of career interests, including those that prepare them for entrepreneurial opportunities to pursue and further develop in Africa. This would be equally beneficial for those who reside or grew up overseas, with little context of on-the-ground realities. Such exposures would allow them to invest strategically in university degrees, or vocational training and develop competencies that prepare them adequately for the labor market upon graduation or completion of their studies.

An added benefit of facilitated online or media-integrated cultural exchanges within the curricula is that Africans on the ground can learn about the unique experiences of their African diaspora who live in Western countries. In particular, tensions that stem from the misunderstandings of African and African-Americans have long been well-documented. Many Africans who migrate to the U.S., particularly in their adult years, note the cultural shock that stems primarily from a lack of familiarity with the history of racism and structural racism in the host country—a set of different socio-economic ills that they may experience in their African home nations. Similarly, some African-Americans may not understand why African immigrants have a different narrative of their experiences as a "Black" person in their host and African home countries.

Hence, such cultural exchange programs inform and prepare both groups about other Black Diasporic experiences.

Additional opportunities for international exchanges through online or on-ground curricula engagements set the foundation for students to embrace their identified cultural heritage and promote diversity and inclusion in their endeavors, as they seek to implement development solutions.

The diaspora can further collaborate with those on the ground to develop content and cultural exchange programs. The pandemic has unleashed job opportunities and innovations for online academic content creators and cultural program facilitators. In parallel, this also creates job opportunities for video producers, video editors, gamers, instructional design and multimedia specialists, as well as technical engineers, among others, to play vital roles in this space. Duties and responsibilities, therefore, include developing and producing training materials, virtual training programs, content management systems and learning management systems and other related functions. Additionally, career paths also emerge in fields related to educational therapy to support mental and emotional challenges for distant online learners and trainers, from primary, secondary and higher education.

Distance learning organizations and private universities

Headquartered in Kenya and Senegal, the African Virtual University, an open and distance learning organization, epitomizes a Pan-African effort to serve Africa and address the twin deficit in education—virtually. Originally funded by the World Bank in 1997, the University became an intergovernmental organization in 2003, funded and led by African governments. The University has faced some controversies and debates from some analysts who suggest that it offers neocolonial curricula, question its caliber of quality education, as well as its impact and reach of students. Nevertheless, the African Virtual University represents an e-learning initiative that is particularly relevant during the Covid-19 pandemic. Opportunities range from investing further in the university's structure and program, or referring to it as a framework and model to build private virtual universities or other educational programs.

Non-formal educational programs

There is also an opportunity to design innovative education programs that deviate from the conventional formal education system. One example would be to leverage further on the tradition of Africa's rich culture of oral, storytelling *griots*. Hailing from the Mande empire of Mali since the 13th century, griots' complex and unique integration of music, entertainment and education aim to preserve and transmit knowledge of genealogies, historical narratives, cultural values, rituals and long-held traditions. Griots offer unique and much-needed insight and perspectives that that will further contextualize knowledge that is disseminated in the classrooms. "Western academia often excluded the complexity of oral tradition by offering false narratives about Africa which drew on loaded colonial clichés" (Stennett, 2019, para. 7). It would be valuable to invest in innovative opportunities that preserve the legacy of griots through their integration in academic curricula and enrich students' learning experiences.

Targeted non-traditional learning programs

Some lessons can be learnt from Develop Africa, the non-profit organization that offers young mothers with children opportunities to attain their education. There are similar non-profits and organizations, including community colleges, that focus on non-traditional students, including mothers and adults who return to school to complete their studies. Investments can prioritize on unconventional education systems, which focus specifically on unique needs of underserved populations, e.g., young mothers, members of the disabled community and those who are traditionally denied access from educational opportunities in their communities.

Ancillary services that support core delivery services

The private sector can also be valuable in investing in ancillary services that support core delivery services of education. These include teacher training, supplementary education, e.g. after-school tutoring and test preparation, investing in educational technology, as well as student and institutional finance systems that support student loan programs and ways to access funds (Caerus International 2017).

Like all investments, however, such initiatives are not independent efforts. Strengthening governance and leadership will ensure the monitoring of strategic decisions and proper allocation of resources, particularly in the public sector of education. It is also important that resources are allocated to support initiatives and coordinate efforts from the private sector that can privatize education systems, incorporate innovative digitized solutions, and further collaborate with international organizations.

In addition to technological breakthroughs to advance education, other innovative solutions to address some challenges in education—particularly in higher education—involve active collaborations between the African diaspora and Africans on the ground to generate knowledge production and dissemination. Dr. Sahar Khamis, Professor at the University of Maryland, College Park, expert on Arab and Muslim media, former Head of the Mass Communication Department at Qatar University and former human rights commissioner, strongly encourages opportunities for the diaspora and citizen-residents to co-author and co-publish academic journals, hosting conventions and other platforms further generate knowledge that could be applied in vast fields to foster development (personal communication, March 7, 2020).

Dr. Khamis also notes that more infrastructure opportunities should also support better resources, transform education systems and support critical intellectual academic thinking (personal communication, March 7, 2020). According to Dr. Khamis, such an investment would also require changing the mindsets of those in supervisory or leadership roles of the educational process and ensuring that the curriculum reflects that mentality and approaches that work ethic (personal communication, March 7, 2020).

Overall impact of Covid-19 on education in Africa

The advent of Covid-19 has disrupted education systems worldwide, affecting about 1.5 billion students and 63 million primary and secondary teachers" (para. 6) and closing schools in 191 countries (UN News, 2020). More specifically, as of June 2020, the pandemic has resulted in "over 250 million primary and secondary children who are out of school in Africa," with fears of prolonged closure resulting in increased permanent drop out rates" (para. 1), a pull into "precarious job markets," and no access to ancillary school services like meals, sanitary pads and immunizations" (Adeniran, 2020). Furthermore, the digital divide pronounces greater disadvantages for those in remote, rural areas. UNESCO (2020) cites that "89% of students in sub-Saharan Africa [lack] access to household computers and that 82% lack internet access," with an "estimated 56 million learners who live in locations not served by mobile networks." This reduces the effectiveness and efficiency of online learning as a global solution during the pandemic.

In light of these drawbacks, heavy reliance on digitization invites the diaspora to invest in coding and technological-driven industries that support culture, learning and infrastructure. Ultimately, there are numerous opportunities to invest in education-related fields that could address unemployment, and also address some of the challenges of the pandemic. These include educational and healthcare core delivery or ancillary programs that would address challenges of child labor, or by developing projects that provide infrastructure that can support various initiatives. The education landscape is transforming rapidly. The pivot into online and distance learning opens the path for many Africans in the diaspora to collaborate with the private sector, public sector, the international development community and many on the ground.

SPOTLIGHT: ADEKUNBI OYELADE

Founder, SESEWA
www.adekunbioyelade.com

Quotes & Insights from Adekunbi Oyelade on the Diaspora in Africa's Development

On ways the Diaspora can support Africa's education and employment sector:

The Diaspora can build that gap between the world of work/ labor market needs—what government needs to do, as well as what students need to be learning. Another thing that the Diaspora can do is also help young people want to start their own businesses, because Africa is in such dire need of more jobs [and] more entrepreneurial opportunities, and there's a lot the Diaspora can do, in that regard, to help government achieve some of these goals and purposes.

On embracing differences:

There's no perfect country. If you come to the U.S., you're going to meet your challenges. If you come to Australia, you're going to meet your challenges. If you live in Nigeria, you're going to meet your challenges. All of them may differ in terms of levels, but there's no perfect society. There is such a beautiful thing about ... diversity and the differences that people bring to the table.

On the Diaspora identifying ways to contribute towards Africa:

There are a lot of ways that you can be of help. One is to understand who is making a difference in those countries, in small places—not the government, not big companies—but people who are making very small differences, small changes. [For example], a person could just decide to help 20 people in a community—maybe [for] girls to go to school. Find out about those people. Understand what the challenges are. Find ways where you, as a person in the Diaspora, can meet that need.

HIGHLIGHTS OF ADEKUNBI OYELADE

- One of Africa's leading experts on education to employment
- Founded one of the continent's (Nigeria's) first Internship placement organization, SESEWA, and created employment pathways for thousands of youth
- Provides wide range of employment support to students, academia, governments, and private businesses
- Harvard University Alum, Mandela Washington Fellow and Ashoka Changemaker
- Recipient of several awards in social innovation and exemplary leadership for her work at SESEWA

Figure 6.1 Adekunbi Oyelade. Photography provided by Adekunbi Oyelade.

SPOTLIGHT: DR. SAHAR KHAMIS

Professor, Media Commentator & Analyst

Quotes & Insights from Dr. Sahar Khamis on the Diaspora in Africa's Development

On educating audiences about the power of social media in gender activism

Now we have opportunities we did not have before ... So many times, the trials and challenges are your greatest opportunities, and they are your greatest blessing. When you think about corrupt regimes, think, 'Ok, these women, they revolted, and they became iconic figures, and they became role models. These women are now rebelling and they're having a role and they are becoming role models.' So, the challenge of corruption and bad regimes in [different parts of the world] gave birth to the opportunity of gendered activism ...

On educating audiences about the power of social media in youth activism

You can use [social media] for social activism, political activism, community engagement, mobilization, networking—even regime change. So, I'm telling young people. Listen, you have all of that stuff at your fingertips—you have to take advantage of technology!

On educating audiences about the significance of interfaith dialogue in community development

This is a very strong message of solidarity, of love of unity...There is the theological part and the personal part, like learning about your identity and enriching your own spiritual experience, but there is also the practical social part, which is where the social activism and community engagement part come in...We have all of these pressing challenges today now...and we cannot face these challenges alone—of Islamophobia, anti-Semitism, hatred, racism, hatred for immigrants...We have to be united, and we have to be in solidarity, and how can we be united when we don't know each other?...Knowledge and getting to know each other is step number one, and then being able to join hands and stand together in solidarity is step number two.

Figure 6.2 Dr. Sahar Khamis delivering a keynote speech in Berlin, Germany. Photography provided by Dr. Sahar Khamis

Figure 6.3 Dr. Sahar Khamis interviewed by TRT Arabic TV. Photography provided by Dr. Sahar Khamis

HIGHLIGHTS OF DR. SAHAR KHAMIS

- Associate Professor in the Department of Communication and an Affiliate Professor in the Department of Women's Studies and the Consortium on Race, Gender and Ethnicity at the University of Maryland, College Park
- Expert on Arab and Muslim media, and the former Head of the Mass Communication Department at Qatar University
- Holds a Ph.D. in Mass Media and Cultural Studies from the University of Manchester in England
- Former Mellon Islamic Studies Initiative Visiting Professor at the University of Chicago
- Scholarly Works: Co-author of the books: *Islam Dot Com: Contemporary Islamic Discourses in Cyberspace* (Palgrave Macmillan, 2009) and *Egyptian Revolution 2.0: Political Blogging, Civic Engagement and Citizen Journalism* (Palgrave Macmillan, 2013); Co-editor of the book: *Arab Women's Activism and Socio-Political Transformation: Unfinished Gendered Revolutions* (Palgrave Macmillan, 2018); Authored and co-authored numerous book chapters, journal articles and conference papers, regionally and internationally, in both English and Arabic
- Recipient of a number of prestigious academic and professional awards and a member of the editorial boards of several journals in the field of communication, in general, and the field of Arab and Muslim media, in particular
- Radio host and former human rights commissioner

Figure 6.4 Dr. Sahar Khamis. Photography provided by Dr. Sahar Khamis

Chapter Summary

Key Concepts

African Diaspora Literacy	global health
child labor	griots
child slavery	"resource curse"/ "poverty paradox"/ "paradox of plenty"
critical theory of technology	

Discussion Questions:

1) Identify an economic or social infrastructure project that addresses the needs of a selected African community. Is this a project that you would invest in, or support in any particular way? Why or why not? In your analysis, be sure to also include the following:
   - Key strengths of this project and how it supports the community and its target audience
   - Key areas, priority actions and recommendations for improvement of this project

- What strategies would you deploy to strengthen productive public engagement from both the citizen-residents in the selected African country and Africans in the diaspora in this project?

2) Compare and contrast two global social health insurance programs, of which one is in a selected African country. In your analysis, consider the following:
   - How effectively does each address program support the needs of the target community? Identify each of the programs' strengths and their opportunities for improvement.
   - Are there best practices of one program that could be adopted or adapted by another?

   Remember to consider the unique environmental contexts (social, economic, political, cultural) and other unique factors that influence each of these programs.
3) Illustrate an example of the "paradox of poverty", in the context of Africa's development. What is the issue and what is the paradox? Present any relevant historical context of the issue. Who are the key actors and targets involved in this paradox? How can this paradox be resolved? Propose a resolution to resolve the paradox and foreseeable limitations.

Bibliography

Africa Business Pages. (n.d.). *The Changing Face Of The Pharmaceuticals Market In Africa - Africa Business Pages*. Retrieved July 7, 2020, from https://news.africa-business.com/post/the-changing-face-of-the-pharmaceuticals-market-in-africa-

Adeniran, A. (2020, June 4). Ensuring learning continuity for every African child in the time of COVID-19. Brookings. https://www.brookings.edu/blog/education-plus-development/2020/06/04/ensuring-learning-continuity-for-every-african-child-in-the-time-of-covid-19/

Amoah-Darkwah, E., & Reboredo, R. (2020, July 2). The impact of the COVID-19 pandemic on infrastructure development in Africa. *The China Africa Project*. https://chinaafricaproject.com/analysis/the-impact-of-the-covid-19-pandemic-on-infrastructure-development-in-africa/

Antonowicz, L., Lesne, F., Stassen, S., & Wood, J. (2010). Africa education watch: Good governance lessons for primary education. Transparency International. http://image.guardian.co.uk/sys-files/Guardian/documents/2010/02/23/AfricaEducationWatch.pdf

Bafana, B. (2019, October 28). Africa's mineral wealth may just have to stay in the ground to protect a changing climate. *Inter Press Service*. http://www.ipsnews.net/2019/10/africas-mineral-wealth-may-just-have-to-stay-in-the-ground-to-protect-a-changing-climate/

Bourne, J. (2014, March 6). Why educating girls makes economic sense. *Global Partnership for Education*. https://www.globalpartnership.org/blog/why-educating-girls-makes-economic-sense

Boutte, G. S. (2016). *Educating African American students. And how are the children?* New York, NY: Routledge.

Boutte, G., Johnson, G., Winter-Hoyte, K., & Uyoata, U. E. (2017). Using African diaspora literacy to heal and restore the souls of young black children. *International Critical Childhood Policy Studies*, *6*(1), 66–79. https://journals.sfu.ca/iccps/index.php/childhoods/article/viewFile/56/pdf

Caerus International (2017). The business of Africa. https://edafricareport.caeruscapital.co/thebusinessofeducationinafrica.pdf?aug_2017

Conway, M., Holt, T., Sabow, A., & Sun, I. Y. (2020, August 7). Should sub-Saharan Africa make its own drugs? McKinsey & Company. https://www.mckinsey.com/industries/public-and-social-sector/our-insights/should-sub-saharan-africa-make-its-own-drugs

C. M. S. Law-Now (2020, June 24). Paving the way for post-COVID-19 recovery: Key considerations for the energy and infrastructure sectors in Sub-Saharan Africa. https://www.cms-lawnow.com/ealerts/2020/06/post-covid-key-considerations-for-the-energy-and-infra-sectors-in-sub-saharan-africa

Dangote, A. (2019, January 31). Doing business in Africa: My experience. Brookings. https://www.brookings.edu/blog/africa-in-focus/2019/02/01/doing-business-in-africa-my-experience/

Daniel, D., Robert, O. B., & Samuel, A. (2019, June 11). A philosophical outlook on Africa's higher education in the twenty-first century: Challenges and prospects. *IntechOpen*. https://www.intechopen.com/books/pedagogy-in-basic-and-higher-education-current-developments-and-challenges/a-philosophical-outlook-on-africa-s-higher-education-in-the-twenty-first-century-challenges-and-pros

Dei, G. S. (2012). Indigenous anti-colonial knowledge as 'heritage knowledge 'for promoting Black/African education in diasporic contexts. *Decolonization: Indigeneity, Education & Society*, *1*(1), 102–119.

Edel, R., & Webb, S. (2012, September 3). Mining in Africa and the Middle East: A legal overview. *DLA Piper*. https://www.dlapiper.com/en/oman/insights/publications/2012/09/mining-in-africa-and-the-middle-east-a-legal-ove__/

Extractive Hubs. (2020). *Issues for Government | Mining Institutions | Extractives Hub*. https://www.extractiveshub.org/topic/view/id/23/chapterId/195

Fox, L., & Signé, L. (2020, May 27). COVID-19 and the future of work in Africa: How to shore up incomes for informal sector workers. Brookings. https://www.brookings.edu/blog/africa-in-focus/2020/05/26/covid-19-and-the-future-of-work-in-africa-how-to-shore-up-incomes-for-informal-sector-workers/

GBC Health. (2019, August). *Healthcare and Economic Growth in Africa: Public-Private Partnerships*. https://www.gbchealth.org/healthcare-and-economic-growth-in-africa-public-private-partnerships/

Giles, C., & Mwai, P. (2020, August 14). Coronavirus – How fast is it spreading in Africa? L. Https://Www.Bbc.Com/News/World-Africa-53181555

Ighobor, K. (2017, May 16). Africa's jobless youth cast a shadow over economic growth. *Africa Renewal*. https://www.un.org/africarenewal/magazine/special-edition-youth-2017/africas-jobless-youth-cast-shadow-over-economic-growth#:%7E:text=Youths%20account%20for%2060%25%20of,and%20South%20Africa%2C%20among%20others

Iwuoha, J., & Iwuoha, J. (2020, July 6). 11 business opportunities in africa that made more Millionaires in 2019 — And will continue in 2020. *Smallstarter Africa*. https://www.smallstarter.com/browse-ideas/top-11-business-opportunities-in-africa-2019/

Kelly, A. (2019, December 16). Apple and Google named in US lawsuit over Congolese child cobalt mining deaths. *The Guardian*. https://www.theguardian.com/global-development/2019/dec/16/apple-and-google-named-in-us-lawsuit-over-congolese-child-cobalt-mining-deaths

KPMG Africa. (2013). *Mining in Africa – Towards 2020 - Welcome to Foresight For Development.* Foresight For Development. http://www.foresightfordevelopment.org/sobipro/55/1289-mining-in-africa-towards-2020

Lawson, O. (2020, August 4). Commentary: The impact of COVID-19 on African infrastructure. *Pensions & Investments.* https://www.pionline.com/industry-voices/commentary-impact-covid-19-african-infrastructure

Leke, A., & Signé, L. (2019, January 11). Spotlighting opportunities for business in Africa and strategies to succeed in the world's next big growth market. Brookings. https://www.brookings.edu/research/spotlighting-opportunities-for-business-in-africa-and-strategies-to-succeed-in-the-worlds-next-big-growth-market/

Lucchini, C. (2018, November 30). African pharmaceutical market. *Pharma World.* https://www.pharmaworldmagazine.com/african-pharmaceutical-market/

Lynn, M., Jennings, M. E. & Hughes, S. (2013). Critical race pedagogy 2.0: Lessons from Derrick Bell. *Race, Ethnicity and Education,* 16(4), 603–628.

Mba, J. C. (2017, May 3). *Challenges and prospects of Africa's higher education.* Global Partnership for Education. https://www.globalpartnership.org/blog/challenges-and-prospects-africas-higher-education

News Control Room (2020, December 15). African Pharmaceutical Market Outlook 2017–2030 by Goldstein Market Intelligence. https://www.newscontrolroom.com/african-pharmaceutical-market-outlook-2017-2030-by-goldstein-market-intelligence/

Njoroge, K. (2020, April 27). Coronavirus is triggering deep digital change in African fintech. *The Africa Report.Com.* https://www.theafricareport.com/26934/coronavirus-is-triggering-deep-digital-change-in-african-fintech/

Oleribe, O., Momoh, J., Uzochukwu, B., Mbofana, F., Adebiyi, A., Barbera, T., Williams, R., & Taylor-Robinson, S. (2019, November 6). Identifying key challenges facing healthcare systems in Africa and potential solutions. PubMed *Central (PMC).* https://www.ncbi.nlm.nih.gov/pmc/articles/PMC6844097/

Santos, I., & Rubiano-Matulevich, E. (2019, August 12). Minding the gender gap in training in Sub-Saharan Africa: Five things to know. World Bank Blogs. https://blogs.worldbank.org/africacan/minding-gender-gap-training-sub-saharan-africa-five-things-know

Saur, T. (2017, February 13). *Top 10 reasons to invest in girls' education.* FAWCO. https://www.fawco.org/global-issues/target-program/target-program-education/education-blog/3616-top-10-reasons-invest-in-girls-education

Shapshak, T. (2019, July 1). Africa's Fintech ecosystem raised $320m and grew 60% in two years. *Forbes.* https://www.forbes.com/sites/tobyshapshak/2019/06/29/africas-fintech-ecosystem-raised-320m-and-grew-60-in-two-years/?sh=127a24927226

She leads Africa (2018, February 5). 5 innovative initiatives transforming education in Africa. https://sheleadsafrica.org/education-in-africa/

Sirleaf, E. J. (2015, August 20). "To tackle poverty, invest in girls". *CNN.* https://edition.cnn.com/2014/06/16/world/africa/africa-rising-invest-girls-johnson-sirleaf/index.html

Soucat, A., Scheffler, R., Adhanom, T. (2013). *The labor market for health workers in Africa. A new look at the crisis.* Washington, D.C.: World Bank.

Stennett, L. (2019, December 17). West Africa's oral history griots tell a more complete story. *Quartz Africa.* https://qz.com/africa/1770108/west-africas-oral-history-griots-tell-a-more-complete-story/

Sustainable mobility for all (2017). *Universal access.* Sum4all. https://www.sum4all.org/priorities/universal-access

Tadesse, A. (2019, June 12). 600 Million Africans go without electricity: IEA chief. *Anadolu Agency*. https://www.aa.com.tr/en/africa/600-million-africans-go-without-electricity-iea-chief/1502097#:%7E:text=Hailu%20%2D%20Anadolu%20Agency%20)-,ADDIS%20ABABA%2C%20Ethiopia.IEA%20statement%20on%20Wednesday

Tanui, N. (2019, June 11). Looking to invest in Africa? The 7 sectors driving growth. *The Standard*. https://www.standardmedia.co.ke/business/hustle/article/2001329461/looking-to-invest-in-africa-the-7-sectors-driving-growth

The African Exponent (2020, March 2). The fastest growing industries in the booming African economy. https://www.africanexponent.com/post/7200-the-fastest-growing-industries-in-the-booming-african-economy

The Student (2020a, October 1). Best universities in Africa. https://www.timeshighereducation.com/student/best-universities/best-universities-africa

The World Bank (2016, October 27). *New report shows how Africa's electricity providers can be profitable and still make electricity affordable*. Washington DC: World Bank. https://www.worldbank.org/en/news/press-release/2016/10/27/how-africas-electricity-providers-can-be-profitable-and-still-make-electricity-affordable

UNESCO Institute for Statistics (2019, September). *New methodology shows that 258 million children, adolescents and youth are out of school*. UNESCO. http://uis.unesco.org/sites/default/files/documents/new-methodology-shows-258-million-children-adolescents-and-youth-are-out-school.pdf

UN News (2020, April 24). Startling disparities in digital learning emerge as COVID-19 spreads. https://news.un.org/en/story/2020/04/1062232

World Bank Group (2016). Public-private partnerships in health : World Bank Group engagement in health PPPs. http://hdl.handle.net/10986/25383

World Health Organization (2021, January 30). *WHO concerned over COVID-19 impact on women, girls in Africa*. WHO. Regional Office for Africa. https://www.afro.who.int/news/who-concerned-over-covid-19-impact-women-girls-africa

7 An overview of growth sectors and industries in Africa

Part III: Exploring the creative and cultural economy

Cultural products representing the diverse continent's rich storytelling power and capturing the riveting history of a people, centered on vibrant music scenes and natural breathtaking landscapes, set the idyll backdrop and foreground for Africa's music, cinematic, and athletic scenes.

So how can the African diaspora contribute toward, or invest in, this space?

Entertainment broadcast media

Music

Africa's largest creative export, Africa's music, continues to influence the global creative musical scene. Africa's rich musical sounds and instruments have influenced numerous genres, styles, and contemporary instruments around the world, pre-dating colonization. For instance, the Akoting, an instrument found across West Africa, is believed to have inspired the modern-day banjo; the Mbira, also known as the agidigbo, kisanji, sanza, and the Caribbean marimbula, recorded as early as the 16th century, has found variants in Siberia; while Zimbabwe's Marimba, known as the "mother of song" and creator of musical instruments (wooden bars arranged like a piano keyboard), was introduced to Central America in 1680, and was declared Guatemala's national instrument in 1821 (Olofintuade, 2017).

In addition to instruments, musicians' crafts and masterpieces also influenced the proliferation of Africa's distinct sounds across the globe: South Africa's Hugh Masakela influenced American jazz, and Miriam Makeba's musical contributions included collaborations with Harry Belafonte in the 1960s; Nigeria's Femi Kuti has been hailed as the King of Afrobeats; Paris-based Cameroonian artist Manu Dibango's Soul Makossa's *Mama-ko, mama-sa, maka-mako-sa* echoed throughout Michael Jackson's and Rihanna's billboard-topping hits, reflecting one of his global influences; Senegal's Youssou N'dour and Touré Kunda and Mali's Salif Keita were also among pioneers in the 1970s and 1980s who introduced their African multilinguistic, multicultural, eclectic, and musical influences to international audiences. Reflecting on the musical innovations of the 1970s and 1980s, Touré Kunda notes that "it was the first time that African people living in France had seen African people play in their own language

DOI: 10.4324/9781351031660-9

in the country of Victor Hugo" (Good Governance Africa, 2018, para. 13). These artists' contributions further elicited the birthname of the genre, "world music," a term that has been criticized for generalizing all non-Western music, yet also hailed for encompassing strength in its vagueness and longevity (Good Governance Africa, 2018, para. 13).

Fast-forward to 2020, and Nigeria's Burna Boy, Egypt's Amr Diab, and South Africa's Kabza De Small are among the top five most-streamed African artists in Africa (Further Africa, 2020), reflecting the dramatic transformation of the international music industry as more breakthroughs illuminate beyond the continent. Other top artists, including Angelique Kidjo, Wizkid and Davido, also top international charts and collaborate with various artists across the globe.

Suggested opportunities and considerations for the diaspora

The African diaspora that are interested in investing in the music industry could take a closer look at the impact of the digital service industry, the Internet, and streaming services that support the distribution channels of music. Hailed as one of the biggest in Africa, Nigeria's music industry generated a revenue of \$39 million in 2016—a 9% increase from 2015—with an expected annual growth rate of 13.4% to reach \$73 million in 2021 (Further Africa, 2020). In Kenya, music revenue was expected to rise from US\$19 million to US\$29 million in 2020 (In-house East Africa, 2016).

The forecast of smartphone growth in Africa suggests innovative opportunities, including the first virtual concert that was hosted by Idris Elba, the English actor, writer, producer, rapper, singer, songwriter, and DJ, who has ethnic origins in Sierra Leone. Local companies support the music industry indirectly, evident through MTN Nigeria, for instance, whose "17 million subscribers, and Safaricom, with 10 million subscribers, have helped build a sizeable ring back tone market" (Further Africa, 2020, para. 10). Local companies also forge relationships with Nigeria international record companies that range from aggregators to publishing societies and independent labels (Further Africa, 2020, para. 10). Such partnerships represent innovative opportunities for one to contribute to the music industry. Through streaming services, concerts, and innovative distribution channels, Africa draws investment opportunities that can contribute to the continent's local economies.

Many music industry professionals have noted that the music industry remains a complex industry to navigate and, hence, invest in. However, there are various ways one may still support the industry. Given their experiences, several music artists have also strengthened their business acumen to become investors in other artists or in other areas of the industry. They are knowledgeable of the nuances and can identify with the challenges that many artists also confront. For instance, in 2020, award-winning Nigerian artist Mr. Eazi launched the Africa Music Fund, a \$20 million fund to financially support African artists to expand their catalog and offer them access to larger audiences and distribution channels for their music. Mr. Eazi's other ventures for African artists, such as Cinch Distro, a music distribution platform for new artists, is a partnership between his parent company emPawa Africa and music technology company Vydia. The collaboration seeks to provide artists with access to data that will inform them of revenue derived from their content and empower them to own their intellectual property.

Therefore, those who are not performers, yet have a penchant for the business, may follow the lead of these artists-turned-investors to support their vision, invest in their programs, or develop similar models that address the broader needs of the other artists. It remains a balancing act to maintain and nurture creativity, as well as targeting goals of the bottom line in the world of "show business."

TV/film

Similarly, Africa has developed, or served as the inspiration for, many of the thought-provoking, emotionally riveting, socially conscious, slapstick comedies or sensually captivating dramas, musicals, comedies, or action films that have dominated award seasons at the Oscars, Emmys, and Grammys, or at internationally renowned festivals like the African Film Festival, pan-African Festivals, Cannes Film Festival and more. Films, documentaries, musicals, and television programs over previous decades, ranging from *Sankofa*, the *Shaka Zulu* mini-series, the *Battle of Algiers*, *Sarafina*, *Blood Diamonds*, *Amistad*, and *Hotel Rwanda* to *The Black Panther*, are examples of a few high-profile, blockbuster films that captured international attention.

However, Tambay Obenson (2019), founder of *Shadow and Act*, an online multimedia platform dedicated to cinema, television, and web content from Africa and its global diaspora, notes the complex history of African cinema that remains greatly intertwined with a colonial legacy, evident in how the majority of African films that compete on the international stage receive financial backing from and are under the control of European companies.

In light of this, Obenson (2019) also praises initiatives like the African Film Heritage Project, a partnership in 2019 between the Pan African Federation of Filmmakers and Martin Scorsese's World Cinema Project to locate, restore, and make available 50 African cinema classics to the world. Such milestone works could educate and inspire younger generations of filmmakers who reference cultural products to learn more about classic technical aspects of filmmaking, as well as the content and material presented in the films.

This observation hints at the classic debate of the conceptualization and evolution of "African cinema" and presents more nuances. But what exactly is "African cinema"? Is African cinema defined as a product of African filmmakers? Can African cinema refer to film productions that are produced in geographical locales that center on African-themed concepts that exist outside of their geographical terrains? What does this mean for African diaspora who produce films narrated from their viewpoints that are influenced from the transculturation of Western, Eastern, and African influences? Does transculturation oppose the authenticity of African cinema or does it hegemonically reproduce Eurocentric and non-African ideologies that reinforce a dominant gaze? Scholars have challenged and debated the authenticity of African cinema. This authenticity is complicated as we account for the diversity of African cinema across the continent. For instance, the history of North African filmmaking has long been aligned with France and European politics; contemporary South African cinema emerged from the "cinema of apartheid" and, like much African cinema, has been "closely aligned with the narratological patterns of Hollywood and European cinemas" (Ukadike, 2017, Introduction). Although conceptualizing "African cinema" goes beyond the scope of this discussion, the topic opens discussions about identity and representation in media, or the agency that filmmakers and talent across Africa and the diaspora have in the narratives they write, produce, and perform.

Over the past few decades, an increasing emergence of African filmmakers and African female filmmakers as storytellers, producers, or leading talent position them as agents of the content they disseminate in their own styles. The increasing demand and market for African-centric content shifts the "dominant gaze" to that of the "other." Implementing *postcolonial gaze theory* or *feminist gaze theory* as frameworks in filmmaking, for instance, positions filmmakers to reject and counteract normative social, political constructs and barriers that skewed their viewpoints. Some filmmakers may challenge the value of gaze, and assert that ultimately, they seek to critically assert their rights, liberally express their views, adopt their own approach to storytelling, and challenge the subject positions. Ultimately, this permits African storytellers on the ground and in the diaspora to challenge various normative paradigms of storytelling, as well as subject-matter that may stereotypically or culturally be considered "taboo." They may expand dimensions of filmmaking techniques to assert their unique experiences, realities, and truths.

The South African and Nigerian film industries epitomize cultural sites for critical analyses on colonial, postcolonial, contemporary influences on filmmaking in Africa, while asserting their own resistance through a commitment to indigenous expression and tradition. Arguably, audiences witness newer similar filmmaking genres from the West that influence film techniques and aesthetics to drive the narratives. On the other hand, their cinema has also maintained authentic homage to culture and storytelling, reinforced by indigenous language, dialects, cultural values and tradition, and unique creative aesthetics. For instance, storylines that increasingly appeal to the realities of younger generations on the continent and many in the diaspora are evident in plots surrounding negotiations of Western and African culture and tradition within marriage, or dichotomies between a diasporic identity and an indigenous "authentic" identity, for instance. The multi-arc melodramatic storylines, indigenous combinations of English, French, Arabic, or Portuguese with pidgin, creole, Zulu, Wolof, Twi, Luganda, Swahili, and other languages, highlight familiar cultural values that appeal to the nostalgia of innumerable fans, particularly the African diaspora, seeking to reconnect with their homeland.

Ironically, the challenge of defining "African cinema" has also influenced award categories. For instance, the Nigerian-produced and cast film of *Lionheart*, featuring Nigerian actress and producer Genevieve Nnaji, was disqualified from the International Feature category of the Oscars Academy because most of the dialogue in the film was in English. This observation begs numerous critical questions: What amount of indigenous language use or representation qualifies as sufficient for a film to be considered "international" or "African?" Furthermore, how would any formerly colonized country represent an authenticity that is completely void of any Western influence—especially if postcolonial ties continue to infiltrate political, socioeconomic, cultural spaces that reflect the history between colonizers and their colonized, and if the official business languages of most African countries are European languages?

Whether the appeal is to promote and assert narratives from Africa or to profit from a billion-dollar market industry—or both—the African film industry invites investors seeking to contribute to Africa's cultural sector. In 2018, Nigerian's film industry, popularly known as "Nollywood", was valued at about $50 billion annually (Eye Witness News, 2018). As of 2020, Nollywood is ranked as the second largest film industry in the world, after India's Bollywood film industry in terms of output, and it produces about 2,500 films annually—more than Hollywood (Maio, 2019).

Loyal consumers who bought films, cassettes, and DVDs in the later 1990s and throughout the 2000s now pay monthly or annual subscriptions to digital streaming platforms, including Nigeria's iROKOtv (the "Netflix of Africa"), which are rapidly transforming Africa's film industry. iROKOtv is home to about 35 African countries, South Africa's Multichoice (which formed from the subscriber-management branch of the M-Net Terrestrial Pay TV company) and other Pay TV platforms consistently beam new content across the continent. In Africa, Pay TV subscriptions are expected to increase. According to RapidTV news, new consumers would increase the base by "54% between 2019 and 2025 to 47.26 million"—a 17 million gain of pay-TV subscribers by the end quarter of 2019 (O'Halloran, 2020, para. 1).

Enter another breakthrough for Africa's film industry: Netflix, a gamechanger to date for live streaming of African film and TV products. In 2019, 28 million subscribers joined Netflix, which added 26 million paid new subscribers in the first two quarters of 2020 (Alexander, 2020). Global audiences have been introduced to some of Nollywood's internationally renowned talents and breakthrough films, including Adesua Etomi-Wellington, Banky Wellington, and Joke Silva in blockbuster Nigerian hits like *The Wedding Party 1* (one of the highest grossing African movies of all time, raking in over 400 million Nigerian Naira, or just over $1 million, in less than 60 days after release) and its sequel, *The Wedding Party 2*; Genevieve Nnaji's *Road to Yesterday* and *Lionheart* (the first Nigerian movie to be acquired by an American film streaming company); and other well-praised films like *Chief Daddy*. Furthermore, Netflix also inked a deal with Mo Abudu, Nigerian filmmaker and owner of EbonyLife TV, to create Netflix-branded films and two original series showcasing content from Nigeria. Netflix has also introduced its first original African series, *Queen Sono* from South Africa; South Africa's *Blood and Water*, a teen series; and *Mama K's Team 4*, its first African animated series from Zimbabwe, and it continues to inspire African cinema and storytelling from the continent.

Ultimately, the future for Netflix and streaming in Africa appears bright. Netflix aspires to gain 5 million subscribers from Africa by 2025, and analysts predict that "the market for streaming in sub-Saharan Africa will surpass $1 billion by 2024" (Kimeria, 2020, para. 9). In light of this, the high cost of mobile data, exorbitant pricing for video streaming services for the majority of demographics, and competition from local African providers are some of the challenges that Netflix faces (Cascius, 2020).

Regardless, the future for Africa and African media is transforming and highlights immense potential for growth. As of 2019, Netflix invested an annual $14 billion annual budget in the development of original content (Statt, 2019). Such competition motivates and challenges filmmakers to use increased funding to produce African films at a technical caliber of filmmaking that attracts a wide array of diverse audiences, yet resists the dominant narratological patterns by placing African cultural content and narratives of underrepresented African storytellers at the forefront.

The link between African cinema, entertainment, and the arts and its contributions to African nations' economic development has generally been obscured to some. Arguably, the arts have been perceived as "too soft" and "impractical," and it could be said that many would not support communities' investment in the arts, or that parents would rather their offspring invest in "hard core," "technical" industries that would support a steady income: medicine, law, business, or engineering.

However, recent numbers narrate a different story. In 2016, the Nigerian film industry contributed about 2.3% (NGN239biliion) to Nigeria's Gross Domestic Product (GDP) (PricewaterhouseCoopers, 2017). As of 2019, the Nigerian film industry employed over 1 million people—a source of Nigeria's largest employers after agriculture, and in the first quarter, it raked in approximately N87 billion, accounting for 0.27% of the nation's GDP (Guardian, 2019). The filmmaking industry also has spillover effects in countless industries that create numerous job opportunities for many other talents, offering career opportunities that respond to unemployment deficits. Those with different skillsets, irrespective of advanced formal education, can find opportunities within the film industry. As a result, investing in this young, fertile industry provides numerous opportunities for investors and talent to contribute toward its growth and impact in developing Africa. After all, there are multiple parts and roles behind the scenes that one can play that directly or indirectly affect film production, and the entry points to contribute toward this industry and Africa's development remain numerous—many that I can also attest to through my own career and experiences as a professional actress, playwright, and filmmaker.

Suggested opportunities and considerations for the diaspora

Behind-the-scenes creative production

Several African actors, whose training overseas specialized in film and arts schools, broadcast journalism programs, or degrees in communications, for instance, have returned to their African continent and transferred these skills into the media industry. Several have joined the pool of talent among their citizen-residents in their African home countries and collaborate as on-air talent on media platforms that hail from their African country. They may also collaborate behind the scenes as producers, writers, content creators, fashion designers, make-up artists, hair stylists, musicians, film editors, photographers, and more. A rarely discussed yet critical opportunity for investment and employment is set and design construction—a source of employment and job creation for many in the local community.

Providing rental equipment for technical productions, catering services on the set, and market and research databases for films and actors are other opportunities to explore. Such opportunities reinforce the exponential impact that additional funding in one sector of the film industry can produce in other sectors of the industry, resulting in a net overall positive impact on an entire industry and economy.

How many companies in Africa focus on such sources of short-term or long-term use of film, music, and theater projects of a growing, yet niche, market?

Legal, finance, and accounting

Other important roles in the industry also include financing film and music productions to ensure quality deliverables, protecting ownership, copyright, and intellectual property rights. These are critical to reduce piracy or exploitation, developing media production houses and digital distribution platforms. For instance, piracy remains a rampant issue that costs Nollywood about $2 billion annually (The Africa Report, 2020). Hence, specialists with business, legal, marketing, finance, and accounting backgrounds hold critical roles in supporting the African entertainment and media industry and its professionals. For instance, in 2012, entrepreneur Kene Mkparu created The Filmhouse Limited, also known simply as Filmhouse, to build a series of cinemas in Nigeria, and in 2015, launched Filmhouse IMAX, the first IMAX theater in West Africa. Also, the last decade has witnessed over $60 million worth of investments in developing new cinemas, resulting in box office increases, reduced piracy, and increased profitability for film producers (Iwuoha, 2020). Silverbird Cinemas, the largest cinema chain in West Africa, first launched in 2014 in Victoria Island, Lagos, Nigeria and eventually rolled out ten cinemas and 50 screens throughout Nigeria and Ghana—strategically also mitigating piracy and supporting the caliber of well-made films in the industry (Okpamen, 2014). These theaters also create jobs for those employed by these companies. Arguably, local smaller cinema complexes and other digital distribution channels could be explored as other entry points to invest in the film industry.

Mobolaji Adeoye, founder/CIO of Consonance Investment Managers, an Africa-focused early stage and growth investing platform, offers three ways that investors can invest in the creative sector: 1) understand the value chain complexities and how one step may interact or pose risk for other steps or the entire production; 2) spread risk and strategically adopt insurance products, such as completion bonds, that are issued to film producers to ensure the timely production and completion of a film on budget, protecting guarantors from unforeseen losses that the film producer must legally pay through insurance premiums or payouts if the film goes over budget; and 3) innovating in international distributions, including streaming services that cater to the international market (Adeoye, 2020).

Networks and associations for distribution

Other initiatives with rippling effects include pan-African cinematic networks on the continent and in the diaspora, which further strengthen collaboration ties for film and television productions. Filmmakers hailing from Senegal, Burkina Faso, Sierra Leone, Kenya, Uganda, Algeria, Morocco, South Africa, Somalia, and other parts of the continent are visibly making strides ahead. Positive outcomes can result from increased distribution of financial and human resources, innovations of distributing film products and benefits of aggregated economies of scale. Distribution continues to be a challenge for many independent filmmakers. Strategically-designed networks and associations could support filmmakers in developing distribution platforms, alongside Netflix, that enable them to penetrate untapped, diverse markets, reach wider target audiences and increase revenue.

Such pan-African and diasporic collaborations have been more visibly recognized in the music industry, particularly through collaborations that fuse Afrobeats, international reggae, rhythm and blues (R&B), and rap among famous Nigerian superstar music artists like Davido, WizKid, and Burna Boy; Beninese-American Angelique Kidjo; the United States' Usher, Drake, Chris Brown, and Beyonce. Beyonce's visual album *Black Is King* made headlines as it drew inspiration from numerous African cultures and represents a collaboration among some notable directors, including Blitz the Ambassador (born Samuel Bazawule), a Ghanaian hip-hop artist, filmmaker, and visual artist.

Training and business development hubs for talent and creatives

Also, less discussed but highly critical is the opportunity for the diaspora to collaborate with professionals on the continent to develop professional training and business hubs to hone and nurture creative talent in Africa. The entertainment industry undeniably projects fame, glitz and glamour on silver screens, laptops, magazine covers, and billboards, which may appeal to an impressionable audience—particularly a gullible youth. However, many remain uninformed about the business realities and challenges of "show business." Several talents have been exploited or misinformed because they lack the business or legal acumen to protect their creative or intellectual property. They may also mismanage their unique brand or fail to build a resilient, diverse investment portfolio and tragically end their careers prematurely as they incur massive debt. Furthermore, the culture and approach of the filmmaking or music industry varies among different local environments, let alone across geographical terrains in Africa, Europe or the United States, which may further challenge those who struggle to successfully cross over into different markets.

As the African entertainment industry competes even further on a global scale, it is important that creatives and artists in the diaspora and on the ground share their unique insight, experiences, and best practices about how to effectively navigate the nuances and realities of the filmmaking or music-making business. In an industry that relies on informal connections and relationship-building—arguably even more so than on merit, skills, and talent, at times—it would be essential to develop strong networks and formal programs that connect and mentor professionals on how to manage their careers and position themselves for career longevity in the industry—or for an alternative, more sustainable career path outside the fickle entertainment industry.

The creative industry is a major economic development engine that impacts a nation's and region's infrastructure, including electricity, sanitation, transport, mobile, energy, and connectivity. It would be of value to invest in cultural development programs that also positively affect Africa's regional and national economies. There is also great value for business management and creative professionals to gain understanding of loopholes and challenges that are unique to the creative industry. Their insight may inspire innovative opportunities that support their community's needs.

Overall impact of Covid-19 on entertainment industry in Africa

The pandemic has also led to the halt of productions and unemployment for many actors and crew as a result of maintaining precautions and safety of talent and crew and curtailing the spread of the virus. Film and music festivals that were opportune sites for networking and exhibition of films and concerts also halted, with distributors eventually converting to digital platforms to distribute and exhibit film and music projects through live streaming platforms. Similarly, box office hits at theaters have also been curtailed, given similar strategies to mitigate risk. Lastly, the outbreak in Wuhan, China, home to the world's largest producer of optical fiber and cable technology, which is an essential source for high-speed broadband and fourth industrial revolution technology infrastructure, also affects the supply chain for products in Africa's telecommunications industry (Baker Mckenzie, 2020). It remains to be seen how the industry will emerge from the pandemic.

Fashion, apparel, retail, and luxury

Brightly colored Ankara gowns, hand-woven cotton shawls with wooden beads, golden accessories, African headwraps, busutus, lemlem terefs—the fashion scene of Africa's diverse tapestry of clothing illuminates the runways of Fashion Week in Milan, Paris, London, New York, Dakar, Nairobi, Johannesburg, Washington, D.C.,and all the way to the silver screens of blockbuster films, including Wakanda, the fictitious country of the 2018 Blockbuster film *The Black Panther*.

The merchandise of African print and apparel and the revolution of African fashion invites tailors, seamstresses, fashion designers, e-commerce players, and various entrepreneurs in the fashion value chain to contribute to and benefit from Africa's fashion industry. The African Development Bank estimates the African fashion industry to be worth $15.5 billion over the next 5 years. In 2019, the global fashion industry was worth $2.4 trillion, of which Africa owns merely a little portion (Iwuoha, 2020). Globally, it has been estimated that the textile and fashion industry will double in value over the next 10 years and generate US $5 trillion annually (Gregorio, 2019). The purchase of 19 billion garments worth US$284 billion by the United States alone highlights various opportunities for Africa to maximize various levels of the value chain that lead to job creation and value creation along each step, ranging from design to production and marketing and from smallholder farmers to retail stores (Gregorio, 2019).

Supporting the growth of the fashion industry is the apparel industry, which, combined with the footwear market in sub-Saharan Africa, is worth an estimated US$31 billion (Gregorio, 2019). The African Growth and Opportunity Act (AGOA) supports the textile and apparel industries, which many African countries recognize as a major source of tax revenue and employment in the export sector. Evidently, major African cities like Johannesburg, Lagos, Nairobi, Casablanca, and, more recently, Dakar, pioneer and represent cornerstones of Africa's fashion scene. Cities in Ethiopia and Mauritius are also growing their potential market on the continent, while Lesotho, Kenya, and Mauritius lead the textile and apparel exports on the continent (Gregorio, 2019). Mauritius, Ethiopia, and Ghana are some of the continent's top production hubs, with Mauritius accounting for 66% of the African textile and clothing imports to South Africa; Mozambique, Angola, and Ethiopia are witnessing growth in African textile factories—and Ethiopia attracted US $1.2 billion foreign direct investments (half in the textile and clothing sector) in the first six months of the 2016–2017 fiscal year (Gregorio, 2019).

Despite opportunities illustrating a booming industry with innumerable potential, there exist some challenges and critical debates within the African fashion, textile, and apparel industry that potentially have a larger, significant impact on Africa's development. It would be of value for those seeking to invest in or contribute to this sector to be mindful of a few factors:

(i) *Weak enabling environment*

Gregorio (2020) attributes African countries' challenges to weak business environments and a shortage of skilled and unskilled workers; high production costs and low production capacity; unclear national policies on textile and apparel; unclear strategies to promote local designers' entry in domestic, regional, and international markets; and insufficient data and market and analytical research to define evidence-based policy making and establish clear roles and responsibilities for governments, local private sectors, development partners, and foreign investors.

Jacqueline Shaw, consultant and director of the Africa Fashion Guide, also notes the challenge of a supply chain in Africa that pales in comparison to the dynamic supply chain in Asia (Bii, 2020). The Africa Fashion Guide is a business that connects African designers, craftspeople, manufacturers, and textile designers with UK and EU fashion design companies and consumer markets. Shaw highlights that Africa requires investments in supply-chain machinery and processing of raw materials to support the processing system of the fashion industry in Africa (Bii, 2020).

(ii) *Cultural appropriation*

Some of the common challenges that face the African creative industry include the exploitation of talent or workers in the industry and the appropriation of African culture in the interests of commercialization. As an objective definition, *cultural appropriation* refers to the adoption of an element or elements of one culture or identity by members of another identity. The term, however, carries loaded meaning when it connotes *cultural exploitation*, unacknowledged and inappropriate adoption of the customs, elements, objects, and practices of members of a disadvantaged or minority group by members typically of dominant cultural groups.

The argument against cultural appropriation is that dominant groups take from marginalized groups and commercialize cultural representations without understanding the meaning or significance of the cultural element. Some argue that cultural products of inherent, authentic, and intangible value are "reduced" and "devalued" to mere commercial products. However, those that believe that cultural appropriation harbors no real social harm assert to not be "gatekeepers of culture." They argue that one should not ban others from adopting styles, fashions, or artifacts of different cultures, especially since cultural exchange promotes the dissemination of knowledge and ideas that are required for communities to thrive.

Whereas both perspectives present valid arguments, it is important to be clear about the distinction between cases of cultural appropriation and those of cultural exchange. Because cultural exchange generally connotes a mutual, fair exchange of ideas and practices between groups, its practices are generally accepted and encouraged. However, the generally accepted term "cultural exchange" should not be not confounded with or used as a cover-up to falsely justify or validate practices of cultural exploitation or *cultural dominance* that adversely affect groups that may not have the resources to assert their ownership or their intellectual or creative property rights.

In the context of fashion, there have been numerous accounts of the use of African fashion styles that represent indigenous African heritage or cultural themes being displayed on models—except Black or African models. For instance, the international fashion magazine *Numero* raised eyebrows when it published images of a white model in *blackface* to portray an African Queen, resulting in controversial remarks from other outlets with the highly referenced quote, "Why hire a black model when you could just paint a white one!" (Zhang, 2013, para. 2) However, the relevant question here should be "But why not just hire a Black model rather than go to the length and cost of painting a white one?" Natural questions one may pose: Why would one go to the farthest, more expensive, and more immoral lengths as to paint White models in black when there are African and other models of Black descent that can be hired to do the job? Is the notion of actual Black representation so distasteful that one would resort to blackface as an alternative?

Similarly, there have been cases of African fashion designers that remain uncredited for being the inspiration behind styles that only gain commercial attention through European or American platforms. The present-day misrepresentation, underrepresentation, or exclusion of Black and African-descent individuals in fashion magazines, mainstream media platforms that cater to Eurocentric standards of beauty, and cosmetic ideals trace their origins to a colonial and cultural imperialistic history with ripple effects in the present day.

Hence, the issue may not so much be about banning other cultural groups from adopting fashion and wearing styles and accessories from other cultural groups. Borrowing and exchanging cultural ideas or fusing new styles into avant-garde fashion could be celebrated, and even encouraged, as a means of diplomacy and building positive relations across the globe. However, it is important to give credit where credit is due. If a style originated from a cultural group in Mali, for instance, then the origins should be accredited as Malian. How can Africa be acknowledged for her immense and vast contributions to societies or showcase her rich history if dominant systems, policies, and media platforms dismiss, erase, diminish, exclude, or rewrite Africa's role in global development? Furthermore, it also appears ironic and hypocritical when the same dominant systems that adopt Africa's cultural resources to suit their commercial purposes also perpetuate the narrative that Africa has little to offer or contribute to global communities.

Ultimately, Africa should be publicly acknowledged for the vast, immense contributions she offers globally, along with the rest of the world.

(iii) *False advertising and counterfeit production of African print:*

Other related challenges are the misrepresentation and false advertising of African print and fashion. The fashion industry has seen a rapid rise of computer-generated counterfeit African designs, print, and materials that are falsely marketed as "African styles" yet are sold from some online warehouses, including some that are based in China and other countries outside of Africa. According to Nico Kang, cultural curator and actor, such counterfeit production jeopardizes the welfare, business, and livelihood of the local independent manufacturer and seller in Africa (personal communication, February 1, 2020). Local laborers in Africa whose traditional, manual, handcrafted approach and unique technique and specialized craftsmanship struggle to compete with rapid rates of advanced technological manufacturing and mass production in an era that seeks rapid and instant customer delivery and gratification. Kang (2020) also notes that such counterfeit productions deter the pass-down of teaching culture and tradition, especially when local manufacturers in Africa opt for alternative means to compete with a market model:

> People don't realize that when you buy from that lady [back home in Africa], you are supporting not only the business, but you are helping to keep the culture going so that it can be handed over and handed down to other generations—whom that lady has to teach. If she realizes she is not making money from that, her kids are not going to want to learn that"
> (personal communication, February 1, 2020)

Such counterfeit and false advertising may also deter online customers from purchasing authentic traditional clothing and garments from other online stores owned by craftspeople in African countries seeking customers for their traditional merchandise.

Ultimately, borrowing and adopting from different cultures, learning from different groups and respectfully celebrating and embracing new systems, ideologies, and styles or resources is a key driver for innovation. In the era of globalization and technology, it is arguably a requisite. However, given the fragile history related to cultural imperialism and its postcolonial effects in the modern day, it is important to carefully distinguish and critically assess cases of cultural exchange from those of cultural exploitation or cultural dominance.

Opportunities for honest, mutual cultural exchange that uphold ethical business integrity and honorably acknowledge the cultural property of its community members should be encouraged for further advancement of communal development.

Suggested opportunities and considerations for the diaspora

Ultimately, the rise of African talent in the creative space invites partnerships and collaborations between African diaspora, local creatives on the ground, and international governments to create value across the complex and elaborate value chain. Recognizing the challenges that exist from idea and inception, production, distribution, innovative marketing, and market research, as well as e-commerce and digital innovative opportunities, are some of the areas that the diaspora can explore to support the fashion, textile, and apparel industry.

The diaspora that seek to contribute to this space can play active roles along the value chain. Whether it is through leadership roles in fashion corporate houses to advocate for fair, accurate, and balanced cultural representation of

African and African-descent communities, or as creatives that compose new narratives of Africa across media platforms, the avenues to contribute or invest in the fashion, apparel, retail, and luxury industry in Africa are vast.

Marketing/branding

The topic of cultural appropriation of African print and fashion leads to a perplexing yet important question—particularly for those seeking to penetrate the African fashion, apparel, and textile industry through brand marketing, advertising, and promotions business sectors: What exactly is the "African brand"? In other words, what distinguishes an African brand from a non-African brand and how can its intangible nature be leveraged effectively in the global market? Attempts to define an "African brand" also characterize the dichotomy of reasserting cultural identity and perpetuating cultural stereotypes. On one hand, we champion the pronouncement of an "African brand" to reassert the unique, cultural identity that strengthens communal ties of a collective people. On the flip side, however, we teeter on the edge of countenancing stereotypes that have ill-characterized a dark Africa.

Although the feat of defining an African brand is beyond the scope of this book—and extremely complicated—it opens discussion for marketing and branding professionals in the fashion industry who are interesting in contributing to this sector. Perhaps one approach in promoting "African" fashion brands is connected to preserving unique, traditionally passed-down principles through storytelling, ideologies, techniques, and knowledge that are central to the particular community. For instance, different ethnic groups across the African continent use unique cultural garments and clothes to commemorate milestones that range from weddings to baptisms and burials. To maintain their consecration or to preserve tradition, some of these styles, garments, and cultural elements may not be promoted on a runway. Other styles, however, incorporate a hybrid of various cultures that are promoted during African Fashion International Week and fashion product placements in films, music videos, and other media platforms. Hence, the diaspora can explore how to effectively market and promote particular brands effectively and reinforce relevant messaging that articulates their unique brand identity and personality through appropriate traditional and innovative digital strategies and channels.

Influencing distribution and export through flow and diffusion

As exporters of goods and fashion, the diaspora can contribute to the distribution channel of the value chain. Whereas an option is to invest in building supply-chain houses to distribute goods, other forces can explain the fashion distribution of Africa. The increase in the boom and interest in African brands and African styles can be leveraged to support global attention.

Proponents of the *trickle-down* theory, the oldest theory of distribution, described by Veblen in 1899, acknowledge the trickle-down movement of a style that is offered, adopted, or approved by those of the top strata before it is accepted by those on the lowest rungs of society's ladder (DeLong, 2020). Hence, applying fashion distribution theories within a global context, one can refer to trickle-down theory to illustrate how Westernization and Eurocentric ideologies of styles have dominated global commercial markets. As discussed earlier, fashion, couture, styles, and trends from the West have been upheld as "international" standards of beauty and popular culture and have trickled down and been hegemonically adopted and commercialized by non-Western communities.

However, the resurgence of African-print, African-themed and indigenous styles by African artisans—marketed by African and global celebrities in commercial media—suggest the relevance of the *trickle-up theory* of African fashion that is dominating the global market.

> The trickle-up theory is based on the movement of fashions from lower income families, blue-collar workers, and street styles. In trickle up theory these subcultures are the base of where these fashions are originated, and then they trickle up to the higher-class subcultures.
>
> (Futris, 2012, para. 1)

Through a global lens, Africa's historical depiction as a "dark, ill-stricken continent" has long represented a subcultural base of a marginalized, oppressed group of people who have been excluded from, or restricted to the peripheries and outskirts of, the global mainstream fashion industry. However, the 21st century highlights the movement of African fashion, garments, and accessories from local communities in African countries that now trickle up to "higher-class subcultures" within the country and continent or across continents. It now becomes cool and hip, trendy or hot to wear African authentic style or accents of African couture from the African homelands and dramatically display them unapologetically in mainstream circles. This is a departure from the disdain and shame that once dogged "Made in Africa" products, resulting in taunts of "African booty scratcher" and similar derogatory remarks that rejected the representation of Africa and perpetuated stereotypes of a rejected continent. Now, however, African fashion concepts more boldly appeal to the elite of the "higher" subcultures. These elites are comprised of diverse influencers, celebrities, or fashion gurus outside of Africa who embrace, adopt, and globally promote these fashion concepts.

Ironically, the trickle-down theory also becomes relevant once these higher-class subcultures influence the rest of mainstream populations in their local and global communities to adopt African couture, styles, and garments that they see have been accepted into the community.

The *trickle-across model* also accurately describes the diffusion of African fashion. The trickle-across model describes how styles migrate across social, contiguous groups on similar levels with little lag time. By assuming multiple roles as manufacturers, models, retailers, fashion leaders, and influencers of African fashion within Africa *and* overseas, the African diaspora simultaneously straddle borderlines of "higher" class subcultures *and* "lower" class subcultures—both within local African and across global contexts. Their social mobility and adoption of numerous roles in the fashion industry contribute to the rapid distribution of fashion and trending styles within and outside the continent.

Launching international brands

Evidently, once perceived as holding a place only on the periphery and outskirts of the global fashion industry, much of Africa's fashion scene continues to influence mainstream avenues through its flow and diffusion across the globe. One such creative agent influencing the globe with Africa's fashion on international platforms is Adama Ndiaye, Senegalese fashion designer, organizer of Dakar Fashion Week, and innovator of numerous international events for African Fashion Week. Ndiaye actively leads the space for the city and across Africa, while exhibiting local talent on an international scale. Such attention has been garnered in *The New York Times* and other publications to reflect Dakar's status as one of top places in the world to visit with highly revered innovative fashion and fashion creations.

Other creatives hailing from Africa and in the diaspora are actively shaping the global runway and launching brands to showcase cultural influences from their African upbringings, or defying stereotypes across African and gender communities include designers like Ivory Coast–born menswear designer Laurence Chauvin Buthau; Ugandan designer Sarah Nakisanze and her brand, Easy Afric Designs; South African knitwear designer Laduma Ngxokolo of the MaXhosa Africa brand; and Nigerian designer Adebayo Oke-Lawal, who founded the Orange Culture Brand, to only highlight a few. As faces and models on magazine covers and runways, Somali model Iman, South Sudanese model Alek Wek, South Sudanese-Australian model Adut Akech Bior, and Nigerian model Oluchi Onweagba-Orlandi are a few of the supermodels whose breakthroughs in the industry have pioneered conversations and opened doors to create paradigm shifts in the fashion industry by redefining standards of representation and beauty in the global community and colorism within African and the broader Black sub-communities.

In addition to penetrating the industry as fashion designers and models that position them for entrepreneurial and business opportunities, other opportunities for the diaspora to explore along the value chain include retail companies, supported by e-commerce and innovative technologies that can support various levels of the value chain. Cheaper labor costs in Africa have led to the development of companies in African countries and the relocation of garment factories from Asia to Africa. Companies like H&M, Primark, and Huajan (one of China's largest shoe manufacturers) have expanded into East Africa, including Ethiopia, and apparel producers of uniforms, safety vests, and military kits that have set up shop in Rwanda export these goods to Europe and the United States (Iwuoha, 2020). Numerous African fashion designers have also opened up their own African stores. Moving away from brick-and-mortar options, designer Kelechi Anyadiegwu founded her own online clothing store, Zuvaa, which grew from her $500 investment into what resulted in approximately $2 million in 2016 (Iwuoha, 2020).

The skills and knowledge to create fashion and accessorize styles with local materials, as well as access to raw materials for garments, accessories, and hair braiding are deeply infused within indigenous cultures, positioning local Africans to own their crafts and craftsmanship and dominate a space in the global fashion market. But it requires effort from local and regional stakeholders, including the diaspora and citizen-residents and governments, to support an enabling environment that permits local creative fashion designers in Africa to launch successful careers in the fashion, textile, and apparel industries, as well as reap the sustainable socioeconomic and environmental rewards that create jobs and promote African regional integration.

Estifanos Berta-Samuel, creative director, fashion model, and CEO of Established Fashion and Lifestyle (EST), a personal brand committed to fashion business education, luxury lifestyle, and spiritual empowerment, notes similarities between Ethiopia and other African markets and many emerging fashion and entertainment markets in the West (personal communication, November 20, 2020). According to Berta-Samuel (2020), only a marginal percentage of those in the industry have skillsets to operate their own businesses, yet they may lack the vision or acumen to invest in larger economic structures that serve a broader base:

> I've noted in the South African market the propensity to be noted as a very potent force or epicenter of fashion and entertainment, deported into the world. However, there is the dichotomy of the "haves and the have nots." Plus, many are not employing all the available resources to strategically build and place their brands. I really would love to see the import–export sector employed more and the use of retail buyer programs designed to present and make readily available African art, fashion and entertainment to the global markets.
>
> (Berta-Samuel, personal communication, November 20, 2020)

Building funds and apprenticeships

Recognizing similar gaps in the industry as Berta-Samuel, some organizations and business leaders have initiated funds and apprenticeships to address these challenges and maximize Africa's potential in the fashion, textile, and apparel industry. Many designers struggle to control the value chain from "an idea to the ethical sourcing of materials to production to retail in order to make a profitable fashion brand in Africa. And of course, to produce a line, you need money" (McCormick, 2019, para. 3). Enter Roberta Annan, award-winning businesswoman and owner of Annan Capital Partners, an investment company in sub-Saharan Africa, and of RACP, a portfolio of assets in sustainable hospitality, agribusiness, and sustainable luxury in Africa. Annan launched the

African Fashion Fund in 2014 to empower African designers to gain access to global apprenticeships and the global fashion industry and markets, as well as increase their ability to finance their creative businesses in Africa (McCormick, 2019). Annan is also the co-founder of Impact Fund For African Creatives, which invests in creative businesses across Africa in partnership with UN-ITC Ethical Fashion Initiative.

For designers seeking to gain entry into the program and fuel capital in their business, Annan seeks three criteria at the idea stage: originality, which reflects the designer's unique perspective; commitment, which marks an entrepreneur's determination to overcome challenges; and adaptability or malleability, which reflects a designer's ability to adapt their business model to suit investors' interests and collaborate with them (McCormick, 2019). For designers beyond the idea stage that already own their business, Annan seeks adaptability to markets both within intra-Africa and also in overseas locations like London and Milan; scalability, based on the assumption that they already have manufacturing processes and a strong capable team; and a commitment to a bigger vision (McCormick, 2019).

The industry reinforces the value of preserving rich African cultures, traditions, and providing opportunities for youth and women in particular, who are generally considered to be the driving force for socioeconomic development and innovation in our societies, yet are often left vulnerable and are more severely affected by high unemployment and underemployment rates. The creative and cultural space offers job opportunities for many artisans who already possess expertise in their craftsmanship and innovative skills that have been passed down to them since childhood, e.g., hair braiding, sewing and weaving, and other crafts. However, many lack access to the required resources, capital, and infrastructure to support sustainable employment. Hence, it would be important to ensure that Africa's rich resources, innovations, and cultural heritage that influence pop culture in mainstream audiences and support fashion industries globally also financially benefit its own people on the continent.

One way to achieve this is for industries to intentionally uphold concepts like ethical fashion, as illustrated by Congolese designer Kahindo Mateene. Mateene defines "ethical fashion" as the deployment of ethical practices—producing garments in a safe environment, fair and equal wages for women with access to adequate healthcare, and eliminating children or slave labor (Moosa, 2019). For instance, the Ethical Fashion Initiative is a program of the International Trade Center, a co-secretariat of The United Nations Alliance for Sustainable Fashion formed in 2018, which connects marginalized artisan communities in fragile and remote locations with global lifestyle brands and international markets (ITC EFI website).

Policymaking and governing structures

Berta-Samuel stresses the importance of African creatives owning their narratives, which can be protected through the important roles of governing bodies that (i) outline and enforce bylaws of daily operations, and (ii) adhere to fair and ethical practices across all job functions (personal communication, November 20, 2020). The African diaspora could ensure that accountable standard-setting policies and mechanisms are institutionalized in operations through think tanks and organizations "whose sole purpose is to forward the agenda of all markets and economies operating per the same standards which are observed without geographic restriction" (Berta-Samuel, personal communication, November 20, 2020).

Luxury brands

Also connected to the fashion industry is the growing African luxury-brands market, which is increasingly ethical and socially conscious. Comprised of luxury jewelry and luxury fashion, the top five African markets for this industry appeal to the growing expanding affluent class and target high net worth individuals (HNWIs) worth over $1 million, excluding their primary residences: "South Africa, with 39,200, followed by Egypt (16,700), Nigeria (9,900), Morocco (4,600) and Kenya (8,600)" (Collins, 2020, para. 8). According to the "Luxury & Retail Trends in sub-Saharan Africa, In Capsule by Ifop" 2019 study conducted for luxury customers, the top five promising luxury markets, albeit at different maturity levels, include South Africa (gateway to Africa's luxury market, supported by increased international exposure and massive shopping culture); Kenya (gateway to East Africa's market and one of sub-Saharan's advanced economies); Nigeria (Africa's largest population GDP, biggest economic power and enormous market size); Angola (Africa's popular investment destination and high-end emerging market) and Ivory Coast (Africa's fastest growing economy, state of prosperity and secure positioning in international markets) (CPP-Luxury, 2019).

As of 2019, the appeal to younger consumers who are focused on quality, the experience and storytelling behind brands, and adaptability to local palettes support drivers for these brands' success. However, challenges that African designers and luxury producers face include

> building a loyal customer base; competing against a "buy abroad," culture where local African consumers prefer foreign brands that are more heavily marketed than their own locally produced brands; stiff competition against international brands whose economy of scales can maximize production at lower prices that markets find more affordable and accessible; black markets selling counterfeit productions; and Africa's poor manufacturing capacity, which results in local factories struggling to "produce top quality goods, meaning many local designers must outsource their craftmanship if they want to produce at a larger scale" (Collins, 2020, para. 36). Other challenges include European and North American access to global supply chains and international markets that are facilitated through preferential bilateral and multilateral trade agreements and low tariffs (Collins, 2020, para. 37).

Despite these challenges, many luxury goods innovators remain optimistic about the reality of Africa's ability to assume leadership roles and success as both producers and consumers of luxury products that are made in and sold in Africa.

Overall impact of Covid-19 on fashion industry in Africa

Similar to the music, film, and other entertainment industries, the fashion industry continues to pivot their business products and events online like Fashion Week to support business objectives. In June 2020, the African Development Bank hosted Fashionomics Africa with about 100 African fashion creatives and digital innovators to "create jobs and drive growth for the local fashion industry, worth $31 billion" to help designers pivot their businesses (Owoh, 2020, para. 2).

According to Kestenbaum (2020), luxury retailers and innovators acknowledge that the Covid-19 pandemic has caused many in the industry to reposition how they expand and prioritize sustainability and environmentally conscious values within their products and brands.

Sports

Sports have been recognized for their increased significance in national development as they continue to become more globalized through media, multinational corporate ownership, and management of sports brands and teams and the internationalization of job creation and mobility of athletes. Sports have also been active in representing both divisive and unifying cultural and political realities on the field. On one hand, sports have been

> a vehicle of: resistance and protest (e.g. in pre-independent Zanzibar and more recently, in Egypt's "Arab Spring" uprising); racial division and disharmony (like in Apartheid South Africa); and political antipathy and coercion (e.g. the ban of Apartheid South Africa from the Olympic Games in 1960 and countless cases of event boycotts).
>
> (Onyebueke, 2020, para. 5)

They have also been recognized as vehicles of national cohesion and conflict resolution.

Perhaps another one of the biggest exports from Africa's entertainment sector is the sport of football—or *soccer*, as it is referred to in the United States and a few other parts of the world. Recognized as the most "accessible" and popular sport in the world, soccer gained "an estimated four billion fans and 260 million players around the world" (Mohamed, 2018, para. 4). In addition to furthering political activism and conflict resolution, as illustrated by Didier Drogba's plea, along with his team, to unite Côte d'Ivoire during civil unrest (see Chapter 11), soccer continues to connect and unify the African diaspora with a pan-African identity:

> Whether you're a Ghanaian rooting for Nigeria, or an African-American representing in your Senegal jersey, there are no longer borders that separate us—we're all African … (para. 13) … We are all tied to an originating

> lineage in Africa that you see throughout the world and in our art, culture, music and foods (para. 17).
>
> (Mohamed, 2018)

But the question of identity and representation continues to attract debate and controversy, particularly surrounding the question the identity of players of African descent and if they identify as Europeans or Africans, resulting in what some nickname as the "foot drain" in sports.

Interestingly, unconventional sports in Africa have also garnered global attention, serving as another source of nation building, representation, identity formation, and connectivity between the African diaspora and citizen-residents in their African homelands. First established in 2016 by Seun Adigun, bobsled team leader and driver for a two-person team, three American women, born to Nigerian parents, made Olympic history. In 2017, Seun Adigun, Ngozi Onwumere, and Akuoma Omeoga became the first Nigerians to qualify at the 2018 Winter Olympics and the first Africans in bobsled at the Winter Olympics. The team has been recognized for representing their culture and, in particular, for advancing strides for women in this particular sport.

Award-winning Dutch-Ghanaian runner and bobsledder Akwasi Frimpong also made history as the first skeleton athlete from Ghana and the second Winter Olympian from Ghana in 2018, who also qualified for the Winter Olympics in 2022. Inspired by being the first African to win a medal at the Winter Olympics, Frimpong established Hope of a Billion to encourage anyone with a dream to persevere and work hard. According to Frimpong (2020)

> That is part of my story of my non-profit, Hope of a Billion. I want to show kids all over the world, with focus in Africa, the way we want to become is possible—if you want to become doctor, lawyer, nurse, in Olympics—the sky is the limit.
>
> (personal communication, August 30, 2020)

The future of sports continues to play a powerful role in diplomacy, international relations, and international development. The African diaspora have represented their homelands and drawn issues close to home through their public platform—facilitated even further through the rise of social and digital media (see Chapter 11).

Overall impact of Covid-19 on sports industry in Africa

Given the contact nature of sports and the social settings that reinforce the experience, sports games, events, and competitions have been postponed in the wake of the pandemic. It remains to be seen how adjustments and accommodations made in the pandemic may result in the "new normal" of the sports industry.

SPOTLIGHT: ESTIFANOS BERTA-SAMUEL

CEO, Established Fashion and Lifestyle (EST)
https://estifanosberta-samuel.com

Quotes & Insights from Estifanos Berta-Samuel on the Diaspora in Africa's Development

On finding inspiration to create a brand:

Countless Africans, especially Ethiopians, approached me via social media asking for direction regarding breaking into the Fashion and Entertainment sectors. They said, in so many words, "Estifanos, when are you going to do something in Ethiopia for us? Everyone leaves the country and never returns to invest in or develop the arts sector." Others stated: "Can't you take me under your wing as my mentor and teach me everything you know about the industry? The only Black people that succeed here are those that go to the West and return with their education and work experiences. This is my own backyard and I don't how to properly tap in." ... Determined to do something about the burden I felt, I used the culmination of all my knowledge and experiences, along with the skill of a brand developer, to create a personal brand, "Established Fashion and Lifestyle," focusing on skills transfer, development and workforce placement, luxury lifestyle, and spirituality.

On addressing a key challenge in Africa:

We must engage in constant, open dialogue of the issues plaguing all of us. The first major challenge is obviously ownership. If we [Africans] operate as the proverbial gatekeepers of our own truths; narratives, art, fashion, history, entertainment, and cultures, then that positions us to have the world approach us directly for what they desire.

On the collective way forward in Africa:

We [Africans] are "our own" salvation and possess everything we need to heal and prosper ourselves. We simply need to remain open, receptive, and pliable enough to transmute everything we have to offer into that which serves the collective best ... We have a responsibility—of epic proportion—to the bloodlines, ethnic pools, and nations that we are born to—inclusive of the whole of Africa.

Figure 7.1 Estifanos Berta-Samuel. Courtesy: estifanosberta-samuel.com

Figure 7.2 Estifanos Berta-Samuel. Courtesy: Fashion Week, South Africa

HIGHLIGHTS OF ESTIFANOS BERTA-SAMUEL

- Multitalented artist, ecstatic about empowerment and inspiring everyone through fashion and entertainment
- Published author, creative director, fashion model, and founder of Global African Fashion Incubator
- CEO of Established Fashion and Lifestyle, a personal brand committed to fashion business education, luxury lifestyle, and spiritual empowerment
- Work has been featured in campaigns such as Absolute Vodka, Los Angeles and South Africa Fashion Weeks, Cartoon Network's *Dance Club*, and *So You Think You Can Dance*
- Graduate of Howard University and currently splits his time between Atlanta, Georgia (USA) and Johannesburg, South Africa

Figure 7.3 Estifanos Berta-Samuel. Photo Credit: Lope Navo, New York

SPOTLIGHT: RAFIYA

International artist
https://rafiyaonline.com

Quotes & Insights from RAFIYA on the Diaspora in Africa's Development

On embracing cultural connections:

I tend to gravitate to gravitate toward songs celebrating my African Heritage, but I also have songs that are about relationships. Still, in the music and in the instrumentation, there are always the African elements—there is always some African touch.

On maintaining integrity through cultural identity:

One of the challenges I have noticed in the industry is learning how to maintain your cultural identity, yet also being part of the global trends. For example, I'm Congolese. For me to express my culture, for people to know my culture, I have to stay [true to me as] Congolese, and I am proud to be me. I will sometimes sing in Lingala, so I had made it a point to learn Lingala. Everybody should embrace their own unique cultures and share their cultures. That's what makes diversity beautiful, otherwise, everybody just sounds the same ... [Try to avoid the pressure] to just be "whatever is working."

On the future of media in Africa:

We need more ownership of our own big media companies. On our continent, we still rely heavily on a lot of foreign channels. We don't have a lot of our own formal structures or large music companies, or media companies, in general ...

Figure 7.4 RAFIYA. Photography provided by RAFIYA

HIGHLIGHTS OF RAFIYA

- First gained international attention in 2010 upon the release of her "Amazing" debut album which gained traction in France, Mozambique, Côte d'Ivoire, and the Democratic Republic of Congo
- Performed in legendary venues around the world, including the Apollo and SOBs in New York, The Kennedy Center in DC, and le Bataclan in Paris, headlining shows, but also collaborating and sharing the stage with artists like Youssou N'Dour, Yemi Alade, Fally Ipupa, Burna Boy, Estelle, Dadju, and more
- Mission is to uplift and to promote African pride and solidarity; Her singles, "Where I'm From" and "Bana Africa" are true anthems that celebrate her African heritage
- RAFIYA's sound is a unique fusion of pop music and African sounds, influenced by her expansive exposure to various cultures

Figure 7.5 RAFIYA. Photography provided by RAFIYA

SPOTLIGHT: AKWASI FRIMPONG

Olympic Athlete
https://frimpong.com

Quotes & Insights from Akwasi Frimpong on the Diaspora in Africa's Development

On the enigma of a winter Olympic sport as an African:

The whole thing was about: What can I do to inspire kids in my country to come out of comfort zone? To show them I'm using my winter sport as a way to help them become whatever they want to become ... To start a winter sport in Ghana—in Africa—is to get them out of their comfort zone, to let them know that they can become anything they want, so they don't just become the soccer player that everybody wants to become. They have so many talents that they can use in different things that they might have never thought about they are capable of doing.

***On instilling hope through his campaign,* Hope of a Billion:**

When you start believing in yourself, you get rid of self-doubt. You realize things that you never thought you could do that you could do. That gives people perspective. You can become more than the stereotypical thing that they know. So, *Hope of a Billion* is to inspire the youth in Ghana, to instill that belief and that attitude of possibilities—that potential.

On being 'successful':

We have a lot in Africa that we can use that is in our benefit. I always try to teach people back in Africa that I'm not just successful because I live in America, but I'm successful became I'm African and I can use my African story, my African resilience to [accomplish] a lot of things.

HIGHLIGHTS OF AKWASI FRIMPONG

- Made history in 2018 when he became the first skeleton athlete from Ghana and just the second Winter Olympian from Ghana
- Born and raised in Ghana and moved to the Netherlands when he was eight years old
- In 2020, Akwasi became the first African athlete to win an elite sliding event
- Refused to allow life's challenges to derail an athletic career that includes more than a dozen medals in international events
- Has successfully represented his country in several local and international sports events, including the 2011 Universiade in Shenzhen, China
- Hopes to change sporting history for his birthplace, Ghana, by competing in the 2022 Winter Olympic Games in Beijing, China
- Personal story of courage and triumph in the face of adversity

Figure 7.6 Akwasi Frimpong. Photo Credit: Mandy Jonen

SPOTLIGHT: CHRISS PORTELLA

Founder, Chriss Consulting

Quotes & Insights from Chriss Portella on the Diaspora in Africa's Development

On strengthening liaisons between African citizen-residents and the African diaspora:

For the two to become one, we have to understand each other, not take each other for granted, and when we talk and try to do some work together, to just do the right thing with respect. I believe this is the only way that we can really become great partners between the Diaspora and the Africans on the ground.

On leadership and motivating Africans to develop their country:

You have to change the culture. You have to change the mentality ... We are Africans. We're not destined to be poor. It's not a fatality to be African. We have great countries ...We want people to respect us. Like me, for example, I'm from Congo. I want people to be like, "Oh, I've been to Congo it's great country. You guys are working hard, you guys are honest people. I love it. I want to do more. I want to have more people to come and invest. I want to share the word, my testimony with other business leaders in the U.S." I think when you give that good image of your population, you create a momentum where more foreigners and people in your population are doing something good for their country. Then it becomes easier to have a great leader who is going to know how to capitalize on this and make it even better.

Figure 7.7 Chriss Portella. Photography provided by Chriss Portella

HIGHLIGHTS OF CHRISS PORTELLA

- Born and raised in Paris, France, *Chriss Portella* is an entrepreneur and philanthropist
- After completing high school in Abidjan, Côte d'Ivoire, Chriss arrived in the United States in 1999, where he studied International Business at the University of Maryland
- Upon completion of his studies, Chriss Portella joined the restaurant industry and became a director of the most famous French restaurant in Georgetown, Washington DC, where many notable people would dine and entertain themselves
- In 2013, he created Chriss Consulting, a non-profit consulting firm, representing African organizations in the United States, including at the United Nations
- Today, Chriss Consulting is a well-trusted entity in the industry, representing major organizations

Figure 7.8 Chriss Portella. Photography provided by Chriss Portella

Chapter summary

Key concepts

African cinema	cultural exchange	trickle-up theory
blackface	cultural exploitation	
"cinema of apartheid"	postcolonial gaze theory	
cultural appropriation	trickle-across model	
cultural dominance	trickle-down theory	

Discussion questions:

Develop a proposal to develop an artist safety-net program, creative social enterprise, or creative business model in a local community in a selected African country. In the proposal, consider and discuss the following:

- Identify the goals and objectives of the initiative.
- What opportunities and challenges do the targeted creatives face?
- How would your initiative empower the creatives? How would your initiative address the challenges you outlined? Identify some criteria of critical factors of success and barriers that would impact the initiative.
- How would you engage support from the local community, the diaspora community, and other key stakeholders in the broader global community? Be sure to specify the kind of support that you are requesting from each group of identified stakeholders. What strategies would you deploy to communicate with each identified group of key stakeholders? How would these stakeholders also benefit from this initiative?

References

Adeoye, M. (2020, January 27). Three ways investors can grow Africa's creative industries. *The Africa Report.Com*. https://www.theafricareport.com/22577/three-ways-investors-can-grow-africas-creative-industries/

African Studies Center Leiden (2020, June 18). Sport in Africa. https://www.ascleiden.nl/content/webdossiers/sport-africa

Alexander, J. (2020, July 16). Netflix adds another whopping 10 million subscribers, but warns growth may slow. *The Verge*. https://www.theverge.com/2020/7/16/21326434/netflix-second-quarter-earnings-tv-shows-movies-originals-subscribers-adds-ted-sarandos

Baker, McKenzie. (2020, March 10). *The Impact of COVID-19 on Key African Sectors*. https://www.bakermckenzie.com/en/insight/publications/2020/03/the-impact-of-covid19-on-key-african-sectors

Bii, T.N. (2020, February 14). Jacqueline Shaw (African Fashion Guide): "The industry 4.0 is the opportunity for Africa." *The MDS*. https://www.themds.com/markets/jacqueline-shaw-african-fashion-guide-the-industry-40-is-the-opportunity-for-africa.html

Cascius, A. (2020, February 26). *Netflix: Will first African series launch a new chapter in African filmmaking?* DW.COM. https://www.dw.com/en/netflix-will-first-african-series-launch-a-new-chapter-in-african-filmmaking/a-52528867

Collins, T. (2020, January 29). Big spenders: Africa's luxury goods market. *African Business*. https://african.business/2020/01/economy/big-spenders-africas-luxury-goods-market/

CPP Luxury (2019, January 17). *Africa: The luxury market of the future?* London: CPP Luxury. https://cpp-luxury.com/africa-the-luxury-market-of-the-future/

DeLong, M. (n.d.). *Theories of Fashion*. LoveToKnow. Retrieved Jan. 8, 2020, from https://fashion-history.lovetoknow.com/fashion-history-eras/theories-fashion

Eye Witness News (2018, August 23). [LISTEN] Nollywood worth $50bn & has become Nigeria's second largest employer. https://ewn.co.za/2018/08/23/listen-nollywood-has-become-nigeria-s-second-largest-employer

Further Africa (2020, May 24). African music industry can spark billions worth of investments. https://furtherafrica.com/2020/05/24/african-music-industry-can-spark-billions-worth-of-investments/

Futris, K. (2012, March 2). Trickle up fashion in the 21st century. *Katie Futris*. https://katiefutris.wordpress.com/2012/03/02/trickle-up-fashion-in-the-21st-century/

Good Governance Africa (2018, November 9). Lagos archives—Page 3 of 4. https://gga.org/tag/lagos/page/3/

Gregorio, E. (2019, January 31). Building Africa's manufacturing strength in the textile and clothing sector. *Agoa.info*—African Growth and Opportunity Act. https://agoa.info/news/article/15566-building-africa-s-manufacturing-strength-in-the-textile-and-clothing-sector.html

Guardian Nigeria (2019, December 2). The Nigerian film industry. *The Guardian Nigeria News*. https://guardian.ng/life/the-nigerian-film-industry/

In-house East Africa. (2016, September 27). Magazine. *Music In Africa*. https://www.musicinafrica.net/magazine/mobile-music-boost-ke%20nyas-music-revenue-29-million-2020

Iwuoha, J. (2020, July 6). 11 business opportunities in Africa that made more millionaires in 2019—And will continue in 2020. *Smallstarter Africa*. https://www.smallstarter.com/browse-ideas/top-11-business-opportunities-in-africa-2019/

Kestenbaum, R. (2020, November 3). *The Future Of Luxury, Post-Coronavirus*. Forbes. https://www.forbes.com/sites/richardkestenbaum/2020/11/02/the-future-of-luxury-post-coronavirus/?sh=55adeaff33ef

Kimeria, C. (2020, April 29). *Netflix renews African TV series Queen Sono for Season 2*. Quartz. https://qz.com/africa/1847687/netflix-debut-african-tv-series-queen-sono-renewed-for-season-2/

Maio, A. (2019, December 5). What is Nollywood and how did it become the 2nd largest film industry? *StudioBinder*. https://www.studiobinder.com/blog/what-is-nollywood/

McCormick, M. (2019, January 31). Fashion entrepreneurs must display these 3 traits to attract investors. *Forbes*. https://www.forbes.com/sites/meghanmccormick/2019/01/31/fashion-entrepreneurs-must-display-these-3-traits-to-attract-investors/

Mohamed, M. (2018, June 28). How the World Cup inspires and unites the African diaspora like no other sport. *ABC News*. https://abcnews.go.com/International/world-cup-inspires-unites-african-diaspora-sport/story?id=56213619

Moosa, F. (2019, October 18). Kahindo Mateene: "The African fashion industry needs more investment." *The Daily Vox*. https://www.thedailyvox.co.za/kahindo-mateene-african-fashion-industry-needs-more-investment/

Obenson, T. (2019, October 12). *Africa Has More Oscar Submissions Than Ever, but When Will They Be Nominated?* IndieWire. https://www.indiewire.com/2019/10/oscars-africa-1202180640/

Okpamen, E. (2014, June 15). Over $61.4m Invested in Nigeria's big screen business. *Ventures Africa*. http://venturesafrica.com/over-61-4m-invested-in-nigerias-big-screen-business/

O'Halloran, J. (2020, March 23). Asia-Pac pay-TV to add 45MN subs by 2025. *Rapid TV News*. https://www.rapidtvnews.com/2020032358237/asia-pac-pay-tv-to-add-45mn-subs-by-2025.html#axzz6lGfLWK8q

Olofintuade, A. (2017, July 7). 10 instruments you didn't know were from Africa. *Culture Trip*. https://theculturetrip.com/africa/nigeria/articles/10-instruments-you-didnt-know-were-from-africa/

Onyebueke, V. (2020, June 18). *Sport in Africa*. African Studies Centre Leiden. https://www.ascleiden.nl/content/webdossiers/sport-africa

Owoh, U. (2020, July 24). The future of African fashion, post-Covid-19. *Vogue Business*. https://www.voguebusiness.com/fashion/the-future-of-african-fashion-post-covid-19

PricewaterhouseCoopers (2017, July). Spotlight—The Nigerian film industry. https://www.pwc.com/ng/en/publications/spotlight-the-nigerian-film-industry.html#:%7E:text=The%20Nigerian%20Film%20Industry%20(Nollywood,Product%20(GDP)%20in%202016

Statt, N. (2019, August 20). Apple reportedly ups TV spending by $5 billion to compete with Amazon and Netflix. *The Verge*. https://www.theverge.com/2019/8/19/20813005/apple-tv-plus-original-video-spending-6-billion-the-morning-show-amazon-netflix-streaming-wars

Ukadike, F. (2017, April 28). *African Cinema*. Oxford Bibliographies. https://www.oxfordbibliographies.com/view/document/obo-9780199791286/obo-9780199791286-0073.xml

Zhang, M. (2013, February 26). Fashion mag uses photos of White model to illustrate "African Queen" editorial. *PetaPixel*. https://petapixel.com/2013/02/26/fashion-mag-uses-photos-of-white-model-to-illustrate-african-queen-editorial/

8 An overview of growth sectors and industries in Africa

Part IV: Exploring leisure and hospitality

Tourism

Diverse cultural sights, archeological sites, rare and exotic minerals and animal and plant species, painted against a tapestry of rich historical landmarks, music, art, and dance traditions and rituals highlight some of the attractions that draw millions of tourists to Africa. It is, therefore, not a surprise that tourism in Africa ranks as the "second-fastest growing tourism region in the world" (Hospitality Net, 2019, para. 1), after the Asia Pacific region. International travel generated $38 billion in Africa in 2018, according to the United World Tourism Organization (UNWTO) (Salaudeen, 2020). According to the World Travel and Tourism Council (WTTC), figures boasted a growth rate of 5.6% in 2018 against an annual growth rate of 3.9%. In terms of increases of tourists in Africa, there were 58 million arrivals in 2016, 63 million in 2017, and 67 million in 2018, with an annual 10–11 million arrivals in top tourist spots, including Morocco and South Africa (Africa Business Online, 2019).

In 2018, 33 of 48 Sub-Saharan African countries focused their investments in their tourism sector—unlike in other economic sectors—through incentivized investments, attractive financial opportunities, and less restrictive travel policies (Signé & Johnson, 2018). Countries have also highlighted tourism destinations in films, music videos, and other avenues for marketing or in service and product placement opportunities. Kenya, Rwanda, and South Africa have implemented other types of tourism development strategies that pull in international business through meetings, incentives, conferences, and exhibitions or MICE (Africa Business, 2019). Such business-centric initiatives now make up 29% of tourism spending and 71% of leisure spending, resulting in a new niche target audience of "blesiure" travelers who maximize the leisure opportunities from their business-purpose travels (Kimeria, 2019).

But there has been debate on the impact of the tourism sector on economic growth, outlining the risks and opportunities of *sustainable tourism development.* According to Sharpley (2000), sustainable tourism development is generally defined as an economic activity, or as a component of sustainable development

DOI: 10.4324/9781351031660-10

policies. The World Tourism Organization defines sustainable tourism as tourism development that

> meets the needs of present tourists and host regions while protecting and enhancing opportunities for the future … leading to management of all resources in such a way that economic, social, and aesthetic needs can be fulfilled while maintaining cultural integrity, essential ecological processes, biological diversity, and life support systems.
>
> (Berno & Bricker, 2001, p. 9; WTO, 1998, p. 21)

Theorists and practitioners face challenges operationalizing this concept, questioning how tourism can be sustainable and struggling to identify what is being sustained.

One school of thought acknowledges the potential destruction of tourism, which creates numerous challenges posed by this global phenomenon. Some regard sustainable tourism as a myth and assert that promoting tourism while simultaneously maintaining the quality of the environment are impossible to achieve (Berno & Bricker, 2001; Niles, 1991). They argue that the principles of sustainable development are inapplicable to the nature of tourism, given the complexity of the tourism industry and product and the fragmented nature of how tourism is organized (Berno & Bricker, 2001). Over the years, some have illustrated the validity of these arguments by emphasizing the volatility of short-term investments from foreign visitors who rely on political or health stability; the risks of cultural appropriation and environmental degradation, which fail to benefit local communities; as well as an influx of diseases, prostitution, and other factors that are debilitating to a sustainable economy (Signé & Johnson, 2018).

Within the context of tourism in Africa, various economic and environmental risks pose some challenges for and limitations to Africa's tourism industry. According to a 2018 study by the Brookings Institution, Africa's tourism industry faces economic risks in terms of exorbitant airfare costs. Additional challenges of tourism are its reliance on imported goods, weakened infrastructure, the underfunding of ministries of tourism in some African governments, low standards of customer service, poor management, and lack of training in the restaurant and hotel sector for local staff. Additional challenges include nations' political instability; reduced environmental sustainability stemming from deforestation, exploitation, and poaching; and stringent visa policies that restrict movement between countries (Signé & Johnson, 2018).

However, the opposing school of thought paints a more positive impact of the tourism sector on economic growth. Proponents, including scholars and policy makers, highlight the flexibility and opportunities for specialization within the tourism industry that different countries can leverage (Signé & Johnson, 2018). In 2018, the two African airlines that made the top ten most profitable air routes in Africa were Angola Airlines and South Africa Airways (Africa Business Online, 2019). Resulting outcomes of profitable gain would contribute to these nations' economic growth. Furthermore, tourism also opens doors for employment opportunities. Nations' economies can gain traction for directly employing their citizens across a range of sectors, including automation, manufacturing, mining, chemical manufacturing, and communications—as has also been the case of South Africa and several African countries that have invested heavily in their tourism sector.

Additional macroeconomic benefits include "increased foreign exchange earnings, state revenues and domestic consumption" (Signé & Johnson, 2018, p. 6). For instance, Ethiopia's tourist industry witnessed a 48.6% increase in 2018 that totaled $7.4 billion, the result of less stringent visa rules and improved transport infrastructure (Africa Business Online, 2019).

Furthermore, the hotel and leisure industry provide employment opportunities for women, who are generally unemployed in the formal economy in developing countries. According to a study by the U.N. World Tourism Organization, women generally outnumber men and receive equal pay in the global hotel and restaurant industry (Signé & Johnson, 2018). As of 2019, more women: held leadership roles in tourism and hospitality boards, and a significant proportion were in various parts of the tourism industry; for example, 30% of employees in Ethiopian Airlines are women; at Botswana's Chobe Game Lodge there is a 14-member all-female safari guide group known as Chobe Angeles; and the Black Mambas Anti-Poaching Unit is the only majority female anti-poaching unit in Africa that protects the environment and has been lauded with awards, including the United Nations' Champion of the Earth Award (Temblador, 2019).

Nonetheless, the growing phenomenon of tourism as an activity or development tool impacts nations' economies and is poised to forge ahead. Hence, sustainable tourism planning should focus on economic effectiveness, or the economy's capacity to be competitive and resilient to mono-cultivation phenomena that would, otherwise, weaken economic systems; social justice, which improves societal welfare distribution and provides adequate employment; and environmental conservation, which preserves the ecosystem's capacity to fulfill human survival necessities and maintain quality of life (Spinalis et al., 2013).

Hence, it is important to recognize the different elements that play a critical role in sustainable development and how they may be integrated in a meaningful way in sustainable tourism. The organizational structure of tourism development is comprised of decision-making bodies at the local, regional, national, and international levels. Non-governmental organizations (NGOs), professional and industry organizations and tourists approach sustainable tourism with a range of conflicting and diverse interests, agendas, motivations, attitudes, and values. Therefore, it is important to ensure that collaboration between these different stakeholders results in sustainable tourism development that has a positive social, cultural, environmental, and economic impact on communities.

Suggested opportunities and considerations for the diaspora

These challenges invite the African diaspora to invest in and contribute to the tourism sector and ultimately, nations' economic growth with a critical lens that promotes equity, social justice, and environmental conservation in their African country.

Digitization of products and services

The diaspora can invest in different sectors that support the tourism sector, including the digitization of products and services. Hotel bookings and online travel bookings, especially through third parties, are opportunities for investments. As of 2018, about 15% of hotel room bookings are made via mobile phone, which further reduces costs and opens up domestic travel (Signé & Johnson, 2018). The adoption of technology and focus on innovation and digital transformation to expand the tourism sector is also a goal for other organizations, including the UNWTO.

Exploring the tourism value chain

There are different aspects of the value chain of the tourism industry that could be applied to both leisure tourism—defined as tourism intended for recreation (excluding travel visits to family and friends)—and business tourism, defined as travel intended for professional reasons, including client visits, potential investment opportunities, and for conferences (Daly & Gereffi, 2018). The diaspora seeking to contribute toward this sector can explore the roles of the different actors (consumers or end markets), distribution intermediaries, and service providers and the different distribution channels: the direct booking distribution channel, whereby consumers book directly with service providers, resulting in direct money flow from the consumer to transport and accommodation businesses; the online package distribution channel (industry's most dynamic growth over the last decade), characterized by online portals, including Expedia and Priceline; and the package booking distribution channel, which consists of a network of travel agents, global and inbound tour operators, and Destination Management Companies (DMCs) that further serve as resource providers for consumers by assisting with visa applications and wildlife and park permits (Daly & Gereffi, 2018).

Daly and Gereffi (2018) identified the following five key characteristics of the African tourism value chain:

1) The traditional package booking channel is more durable in Africa than elsewhere, due to myriad factors, including more appeal for wildlife and parks and challenges associated with logistics and organizing domestic travel;
2) Global lead firms have high positionality, resulting from the low domestic demand for African tourism;
3) "The pre-eminence of global lead firms influences the linkages vs. leakages dynamics observed in Africa";

4) "Business tourism constitutes a greater share of overall tourism receipts in Africa than in other locations";
5) "Government policy encourages bottlenecks among critical service providers that impair African tourism" (p.11).

Additional analyses in Daly and Gereffi's (2018) study led to further recommendations, including (i) increasing access to consumers by facilitating product upgrades in outreach to African travelers and targeted marketing campaigns and travel and trade shows among African-focused travel agents; (ii) skills training, supported by government-sponsored funding and scholarship sources or hospitality programs that provide certifications to increase competencies of distribution intermediaries and service providers in areas of management, organization, communication, and IT; (iii) concession, investment, and management policies that provide adequate regulation for investments and penetration of domestic service providers in value chains; (iv) improving infrastructure to support tourism; and (v) institutionalization of tourism ministries and the creation and maintenance of databases, investment departments, or boards to support the construction of projects and networks that assist foreign investors (Daly & Gereffi, 2018).

Strategic partnerships

The diaspora can also collaborate with government agencies to address gaps that the public sector may neglect or require additional support, including advertising and marketing promotion strategies, as well as innovative technological databases and operational management systems to improve efficiency in the industry and increase national or regional tourism revenue.

In addition to identifying opportunities to contribute to these recommended actions through the private sector or collaborations with the government, the diaspora can also formalize mechanisms and initiatives through micro-enterprises and firms to create local linkages within the overall tourism development strategy. By creating more linkages between local capital and the resources of the local economy and the tourism sector, such integration can support and spill over into other sectors that create value and jobs. The diaspora can also seek to create linkages between the informal economy and the tourism sector that particularly target youth and women to contribute toward poverty reduction and alleviation and job creation.

Owning a tourism business

There are various approaches the diaspora could adopt to participate in the tourism industry, including owning a tourism business. Fess (2019) offers a few guidelines for this endeavor, including the importance of determining the particular tourism sector to focus on, including transportation services (providing transportation to and from tourist destinations); travel agencies (one-stop shops for all components related to tourist locations or visits);

tour operators (provides holiday sessions by combining tour and travel components through itineraries); destination management companies (offering expertise and resources for logistics, events, transportation); accommodation (hotels, guesthouses, lodges, bed-and-breakfasts) guided tours and tourist guides (offering informative and entertaining tours through local attractions); and hospitality (food and beverage establishments for tourists). Additional guidance includes paying careful attention to location and the competition, and following local business regulations that are required for operation.

It is important for the diaspora to also be conscious about creating opportunities for inclusion of marginalized and vulnerable groups in an approach toward sustainable tourism development. The diaspora could collaborate with international organizations and other institutional efforts on the ground, or create networks that guide policy making and address structural inequalities to promote gender-inclusive practices and those of marginalized groups in business operations.

Furthermore, specializing in subsectors of tourism that leverage a country's unique value propositions would effectively shape their marketing and promotion strategies to domestic or international audiences. For instance, some countries may benefit more from branding their tourism opportunities through *eco-tourism*, or tourism that focuses on learning about and preserving the ecosystem. Others may focus on *voluntourism*, which promotes tourism activities in conjunction with volunteer work.

But, perhaps, in 2019, none other than Ghana best illustrated the power of *diaspora tourism, cultural tourism, and ancestry tourism*, also known as *genealogy tourism* or *roots tourism*, in Africa. Through its notable year-long campaign the Year of the Return in 2019, Ghana invited its target diaspora audience to identify their ancestral roots, commemorating the 400 years since Africans' first arrival in Jamestown, Virginia, as slaves in the transatlantic slave trade. The campaign relied on coordination and cooperation between public, nongovernmental, and private stakeholders, and the integration of infrastructure, finance, education, transport, and commercial industries across multiple sectors, all of which are requisites for effective tourism businesses and promoting strategies. The Year of the Return represents a model of tourism planning that theorists, practitioners, and stakeholders can assess and analyze when considering future tourism development opportunities.

Below are some key recommendations and strategies for the promotion of tourism that can be applied to African countries, based on my research from different studies and interviews. The Year of the Return campaign will epitomize the application of these strategies, as it leveraged on the mobilization of international and diaspora goodwill for tourism and investment branding purposes.

Visa regulations:

The Brookings Institution noted that African countries generally restrict visa-free travel to other African countries, in contrast to other regions that are more open. The African Union Agenda 2063 seeks to remove visa requirement travel restrictions for Africans traveling intra-continent and to adopt "visa on arrival" policies for Africans. For the Year of the Return, certain citizens were granted visa-free travel to Ghana for up to 90 days, including citizens of ECOWAS and Egypt, Guyana, Jamaica, Kenya, Lesotho, Malawi, Mauritius, Namibya, Rwanda, the Seychelles, Singapore, Tanzania, Trinidad, Tobago, Uganda, and Zimbabwe (Circumspecte, 2019). Although this may not have been specific to the Year of the Return campaign, it was an effort that was promoted for diaspora from these nations to travel to Ghana. A specific effort was also the reduction of the visa arrival fees from $150 to $75 to encourage the diaspora to participate in the activities. Individuals that were issued Ghanaian citizenship from other government initiatives outside of the scope of the Year of the Return also benefitted from the opportunity to travel to the country.

Integrated marketing communications and public relations:

Research highlights the importance of creative marketing strategies to access target audiences through reduced costs of travel and online logistics. According to an organizer of the Year of the Return campaign, the series of events relied heavily on social media to connect with audiences, international media houses like CNN and BBC Africa, and word-of-mouth marketing from international celebrities like Boris Kodjoe to draw public attention (Owusu-Boahene, personal communication, September 26, 2020). Facebook, Twitter, Instagram, and various platforms held groups that relied on networking strategies to inform others of their experiences and create opportunities for groups to travel together, promote Ghana's diverse culture, and celebrate their cultural identity as diaspora of Ghana.

It would also be important for communication strategies to be directed from leaders to local citizen-residents and to explain some of the initiatives, ceremonies, and traditional rituals that will take place in efforts to extend the experience to visitors. This will help to mitigate any potential misunderstandings from those that do not understand why some foreigners may be exposed to practices that are considered sacred or generally reserved for family members.

Environmental and cultural preservations:

Investing in a country's unique natural and cultural resources is vital to preserve the sustainability of tourism and requires collaboration between public and private sectors (Signé & Johnson, 2018). In addition to promoting Ghana's rich natural resources, the Year of the Return promoted the cultural sites that reinforced the historical significance of the commemoration. The Elmina Castle, the Door of No Return, and other guided tour cultural heritage sites on trips across the country also reinforced emotional and cultural heritage ties. Guided trips permitted members to connect with their ancestral roots and forge communal bonds with each other as they relived history and visited slave dungeons—of which an estimated 75% were in Ghana—from which millions of people were taken and transported (Busari & Siaw, 2019).

Fostering tourism local experience through effective partnerships:

Engaging the local community for support in tourism activities is essential for visitors to feel welcome and experience authenticity (Signé & Johnson, 2018). Some of the highlights of the Year of the Return included traditional ceremonies that featured traditional rituals and rites of passage to reclaim cultural identity and heritage, reinforced through traditional attire, artifacts, dance, and food. Some diaspora community members were also introduced to communities they traced their lineage to as newly adopted family members, with names and titles that symbolized their roles in their adopted families.

Investing in local communities:

In addition to engaging effectively with the local industry to support the tourism experience, it is important for the tourism industry to facilitate opportunities for tourists to support the local community for employment—artisans, small business owners—or to volunteer in projects. The Year of the Return featured opportunities for tourists to volunteer in various projects, including farms and other natural ecosystems, as well as in small schools. This contributed to the increasing rise of the "voluntourism" sector, where tourists participate in volunteer or community activities during their visits.

Additional opportunities to support the local community were also evident in supporting local employment opportunities. According to a participant of my study who helped to organize and attended the Year of the Return initiative, smaller performance groups and local artists who were featured as part of the entertainment scene were marketed, promoted, and supported (Owusu-Boahene, personal communication, September 26, 2020). Spillover effects of the different activities impacted local food and beverage, leisure and hospitality, and entertainment industries, resulting in employment opportunities (Owusu-Boahene, personal communication, September 26, 2020).

Capitalizing on significant landmark events:

The Year of the Return in 2019 marked the 400-year anniversary of the first slave arrival in Virginia, the United States, from Africa. The campaign appropriately leveraged the historical significance that held deep monumental global significance for the diaspora and citizen-residents in the continent. The month of December 2019 marked a celebration climax of the Year of the Return campaign, which neared its end during the holiday season, heightened with festivities in a hot, sunny climate that appealed to those visiting from colder climate zones.

Another research participant from Ghana, who resides in the United States, participated in the Year of the Return, and asserted that the annual campaign represented more than a revisit of the history of slavery. The Year of the Return focused on moving beyond that history, reconnecting with different people, rediscovering genetic roots that connected them to specific countries in Africa and mobilizing toward a movement that encouraged opportunities of economic development.

Tarik Darragi (2021), serial entrepreneur from Côte d'Ivoire, also implores the global African community to take pride in their cultures and natural ecosystems—particularly those that are endangered and risk losing financial preservation and funding (personal communication, February 4, 2021). Darragi (2021) also acknowledges the potential and beneficial socioeconomic impacts that occur when the African community invest in opportunities that heighten African tourism to levels that compare to the Carnaval and other global attractive events. In particular, the impact serves the economy in greater ways than many realize (personal communication, February 4, 2021).

Ultimately, the vision for tourism requires the collaboration of numerous stakeholders and collaborative strategies. Suggestions have included calling on governments to invest in long-term plans to foster resource mobilization to construct better facilities and building an investment product that targets the diaspora to create a hotel chain in every country.

Overall impact of Covid-19 on tourism industry in Africa

Prior to Covid-19, various statistics projected increases and boosts in African tourism from 2018. A 2018 study from the Brookings Institution predicted that African tourism would witness 85 million arrivals by 2020 and 134 million by 2030. Increases in demand for travel and relaxed visa processes would increase international arrivals to Africa by 3%–5%, according to UNWTO (Salaudeen, 2020).

However, the shutting down of airports and the cancellation and rescheduling of air travel, meetings, conferences, and hotels bookings have led to massive revenue loss for the industry—a loss that the United Nations estimates to be between $30 billion and $50 billion. Additional sectors adversely impacted include the food and beverage industry, as well as employment for those in the services industry.

A regional director for Africa at UNWTO revealed a decline in international travel to minus 47%, of which South Africa suffered the most severe loss, as cases of 45,000 infected by the virus hindered the industry (Euronews, 2020).

It remains to be seen how the tourism industry will pivot from the pandemic, although it appears that many activities that rely on air travel and the hospitality industries will resume in 2021.

Real estate

The real-estate sector in Africa reflects sharp growth from over 20 years ago and remains a space that many investors are keen to explore. As of 2019, the top five African cities to invest in real estate are Lagos, Nigeria; Accra, Ghana; Kigali, Rwanda; Nairobi, Kenya, and Luanda, Angola (Akua, 2020).

Africa's changing demography and landscape are some of the primary key drivers for this space. In 2019, about 60% of Africa's population was under the age of 25—making it the world's youngest continent (Mo Ibrahim Report, 2019). The World Bank Group reported that "Africa's median age was 19.7 years in 2012, and … is expected to increase to 25.4 years in 2050, making Africa the continent with the youngest population". The United Nations estimates Africa's youth population, aged between 15 and 24 years old, to have been 226 million in 2015, and projects this figure to double by 2045. Additionally, the United Nations also estimates an increase in Africa's urban population to 56% in 2060—which would make it the "most rapidly urbanising region in the world". In other data, the United Nations projects that Africa's population will have reached an estimated 4 billion people by 2100, of which 1 billion will reside in Nigeria (Givens, 2020).

Hence, such a rapidly growing young population in a rapidly urbanizing region requires close attention in housing development markets and the real-estate sector. Additional key drivers of the real-estate sector include the increasing wealth and growth of the middle-class population; business tourism; retail and commercial development of malls and hotels; and continuous industrialization and rising innovation in the digitized space. According to the Africa Report 2020/2021, the expected increase of the middle-class population in Africa from 355 million people in 2010 to 1.1 billion in 2050 is expected to drive demand for goods and services, for which the "African Development Bank forecasts a combined business and consumer expenditure of US$6.7 trillion by 2030" (Knight Frank, 2020, p. 4). Furthermore, statistics forecast a rise in inhabitants of Africa's town and cities from 42% in 2015 to 62% in 2050 (Givens, 2020); the highest urbanization rates of 80% by 2050 in Nigeria, Angola, and Ghana; and that Africa "will be home to at least six of the world's 43 megacities by 2030" (Knight Frank, 2020, p. 4)—all of which highlight the urgency required to invest in and contribute toward the growth of this sector.

Kfir Ruffin, host of the tenth annual Africa Property Investment (API) Summit in 2019, noted that the entire African continent, including South Africa, is "witnessing sophisticated deal structuring in affordable housing, hospitality, logistics, office space, and mixed use, across countries and regions" (Abuya, 2019, para. 6). Some of these observations are illustrated in several multi-million dollar top deals in real estate in 2019: Actis and Shapoorji launched the affordable housing Joint Venture in Kenya, with a deal size of $120M; and Shelter Afrique established the Affordable Housing Deal with Habitat International with a deal size of $100M (Africa News, APO Group, 2019). Other globally recognized brands also penetrated the real-estate sector in Africa, including WeWork, which established the first of numerous African office locations in Johannesburg, South Africa (undisclosed deal size).

Landmark Group, a real-estate investment firm, developed and promoted Landmark Village, a new island city of 38,000 m^2 that is bordered by the

Atlantic Ocean and by Upper Victoria Island in Lagos, Nigeria. Hailed as the number one destination in West Africa, Landmark Village boasts a state-of-the-art development that will also include five nine-story towers to fulfill its vision as a one-stop site for business, leisure, and lifestyle.

Projections of rising costs of urban real-estate and its effect in terms of reduced affordability and greater urban density, and smaller apartments that lead to much-needed innovative design and construction of real estate through fast, cheap, and eco-friendly techniques and materials represent additional key drivers for the sector. These also present investment opportunities from diaspora and residents on the continent, which create jobs that can contribute to economic development.

There is also an opportunity for the diaspora and invested stakeholders to support knowledge hubs that educate and increase the awareness of communities, particularly the youth, about property investment. Vuyiswa Mutshekwane, CEO of the South African Institute of Black Property Practitioners (SAIBPP), reinforces the importance for African people to increase awareness of property ownership, particularly for those that inherited township homes and may not recognize that they possess a financial asset (Property Wheel, 2020). Increasing financial literacy about financial banks, other financial instruments, asset accumulation, value creation, property investments, portfolio diversification for wealth building, and related concepts would support (younger) generations of Africans seeking employment, wealth creation, and financial empowerment.

According to several resources, diaspora members who seek to invest in the industry can learn more about the growing market to gain further insight into some of the opportunities and challenges that have long characterized this sector. Several real-estate developers across Africa and from the diaspora reinforce the need for research and to not rely on media images of Africa that falsely represent the opportunities to invest in real-estate on the continent.

One research participant, Sobe*, in this study highlights the top five common hang-ups that discourage many African diaspora from investing in real estate and offers the following guidelines, based on personal experience and observation (personal communication, December 28, 2020):

1) *Ascertain land ownership:*

   First and foremost, ascertain the status of the land. Some countries disallow some individuals from privately owning land, as land is public and government-owned. As the government is the owner of that land, one would need to engage with the relevant government agency to secure a lease. Understanding the dynamics of land ownership is very important, as many people have lost investments due to dubious land-ownership rights. Hence, it is key that the diaspora ascertain who owns the land and from whom they will lease it.
2) *Know the laws of the country and that are pertinent to external investors, including taxation:*

   Some countries heavily tax external investors. As a result, most investors seek to partner with local citizen-residents who would not be heavily taxed. It is important for government to be clear about their rules and policies, and for the diaspora to ask pertinent questions so that if they are going to do business on a large scale, they are knowledgeable of the schedule of taxation.

3) *Know if there are restrictions on repatriations on profits from investments:*

   Know the laws governing foreign exchange and repatriation of profits to determine if one is able, or legally allowed, to even transfer money and profits from their investments into their other (host or home) country.

4) *Know the input base of the industry:*

   If one is going to build houses, then one must know the source and location of all input material and laborers. For instance, if one is using building materials, are the building materials locally available, or do they have to be imported? Are laborers who are able to fulfill the task within accessible geographical reach? Are they locally available, and is their access sustainable? Many begin the building phase and only learn afterward that certain materials or specialized labor skills may not be readily available or are inaccessible, resulting in delays and exorbitant costs.

5) *Know the scale of corruption:*

   Unfortunately, some government agencies seek underhanded ways to request a cut or a percentage for their own personal profits when issuing licenses to invest in real estate or property. It is crucial that one is aware of such corruptive practices and finds ways to mitigate these instances.

Overall impact of Covid-19 on real estate industry in Africa

The effect of the pandemic has affected real estate globally, both in the short term and the long term. Short-term effects for investors and executives include pressures of preserving property value, liquidity, and ensuring the safety of their tenants. Tenants face challenges of deferring or ceasing mortgages, rents, and leases. In addition to tenant liquidity capacity, office tenants confront similar challenges with immediate impacts; subcontractors and those in numerous industries, including hospitality, also are affected by workers and employees along the supply chain.

It remains to be seen how adjustments and accommodations made in the pandemic may result in the "new normal" of the real-estate industry.

SPOTLIGHT: LEXY OWUSU-BOAHENE

Human Resources and Recruitment Consultant, LX HR Solutions
www.lxhrsolutions.com
@LexyBoahene

Reflecting on preparations for the Year of the Return in Ghana in 2019, and on investing in, or contributing toward tourism:

If you want to invest, it is important that you think about perhaps taking equity out of any investments you have abroad and using that as capital for your next investment on the continent, as loans on the continent have high interest rates and one may not qualify. Tourism is a big industry here; carve your niche and be consistent. Before you come, make sure you're ready; you will have to unlearn some behaviors, understand local context, keep an open mind, and get ready to take some risks.

On entrepreneurial opportunities upon re-entry to an African country:

As an entrepreneur, you need to keep your eyes open! There are opportunities everywhere, from the time you wake up to the time you go to bed. Don't stick to industries or businesses that you're used to. Get ready to think outside the box and to create magic. This will not only add value, but real change!

HIGHLIGHTS OF LEXY OWUSU-BOAHENE

- British-born Ghanaian human resources professional and managing director of the ever growing, innovative, and solution-focused international human resource consultancy LX HR Solutions, which works with CEOs, directors, managers, and stakeholders of educational institutions and professional organizations, to engage, develop, and retain employees for business growth through the provision of optimal services in recruitment, HR strategy, training, and development
- Started LX HR Solutions shortly after earning her Masters in HR Development and Consultancy at Birkbeck University of London
- Her annual project Diaspora Drive: (i) provides a networking platform to connect international and local employers with potential employees; (ii) and to help diaspora returnees settle and connect them with local logistics and opportunities, and (iii) features prominent politicians, government officials, and CEOs as regular guest speakers at the events
- Founded a women's networking society, Divas on Demand, to unite and support

Figure 8.1 Lexy Owusu-Boahene
Photography provided by Lexy Owusu-Boahene

professional, like-minded women with career development, resulting in collaborations with leading UK-based professional organizations, including O2 Think BiG, Museum of London, Channel 4, Barclays, The British Council, ITV, Black Youth Achievements, Birkbeck University, and Queen Mary University

- Gained notable recognition for various works: Aries Emerging African Business of the Year in Lagos, Nigeria (2015); nominated for awards such as the Women4Africa Awards (Young Entrepreneur) and the GUBA Awards for charity work; Featured in: *The Voice Newspaper*; *TNBT Magazine*; *OnInLondon* online magazine and many other publications, and on BEN TV, and is a regular guest on BBC Africa, discussing an array of women's issues
- Listed as one of the Top 50 CEOs in Ghana and given a certification of recognition in Dubai, UAE
- Recently opened a café, Café Accra, in East Legon, Ghana

Chapter summary

Key concepts

ancestry tourism	genealogy tourism
cultural tourism	roots tourism
eco-tourism	sustainable tourism development
diaspora tourism	voluntourism

Discussion questions

1) Do you believe that sustainable tourism development can be achieved? Why or why not? What are some determinants for sustainable tourism development? Refer to specific country-contexts and other specific examples to justify your argument.
2) Develop a funding proposal for a new cultural tourism program you are developing or investing in within a specified African country. Be sure to specify the target audience. In your proposal, be sure to answer the following questions:
   - What is the justification for this proposal and why is it relevant for the nation's development agenda?
   - How does this program address current risks of cultural extinction or cultural loss in the community, if applicable? What are the implications of these risks on the specified community? Or would it enhance opportunities that need to be leveraged?
   - What forms of sustainable tourism development does your program support, including any socioeconomic, cultural, political, or national impacts of the program?

- What sustainable tourism development guidelines and management practices will you establish?
- What strategies in marketing, promotions, and funding for different key stakeholders would support the sustainable tourism development alternatives of your program? Who are these key stakeholders and how would they benefit your program? How would this program benefit them?

References

Abuya, S. (2019, August 16). Africa's real estate sector registering impressive growth. *Africa Global News*. https://africaglobalnews.com/africas-real-estate-sector-registering-impressive-growth/

African Business (2019, September 24). Across Africa tourism is booming. https://african.business/2019/09/economy/across-africa-tourism-is-booming/

AfricaNews (2019, August 7). Billions poised for Africa's real estate sector. https://www.africanews.com/2019/08/07/billions-poised-for-africas-real-estate-sector/

Akua, L. (2020, September 14). Top 5 cities for real estate investment in Africa. *Lux Afrique*. https://luxafrique.net/top-5-cities-invest-real-estate-africa/

Berno, T., & Bricker, K. (2001). Sustainable tourism development: The long road from theory to practice. *International Journal of Economic Development*, *3*, 1–18. https://www.researchgate.net/publication/266499417_Sustainable_tourism_development_The_long_road_from_theory_to_practice

Busari, S., & Siaw, L. (2019, February 7). *Ghana is being heralded as the next big tourist destination. Here's why*. CNN. https://edition.cnn.com/travel/article/ghana-year-of-return-tourism-intl/index.html

Circumspecte (2019, August 30). Year of Return: What you need to know to plan your Ghana travel. *Circumspecte*. https://circumspecte.com/2019/08/year-of-return-ghana-travel-planning-visa-tips/

Daly, J., & Gereffi, G. (2018). Tourism Global Value Chains and Africa. In R. Newfarmer, J. Page, & F. Tarp (Eds.), *Industries without Smokestacks: Industrialization in Africa Reconsidered* (pp. 1–28). Oxford Scholarship Online. https://doi.org/10.1093/oso/9780198821885.001.0001

Euronews (2020, July 28). COVID-19 a "disaster" for Africa's growing tourism industry: Can it recover? https://www.euronews.com/2020/07/21/africa-s-tourism-industry-ready-for-recovery-euronews-debate

Fess, C. (2019, February 11). Beginners guide to starting a tourism business. *Tourism Tattler*. https://www.tourismtattler.com/articles/business-and-finance/beginners-guide-to-starting-a-tourism-business/

Givens, D. (2020, April 6). Thinking of moving to Africa? Here's how to invest in real estate on the continent. *Black Enterprise*. https://www.blackenterprise.com/how-to-invest-in-real-estate-in-africa/

Hospitality Net (2019, September 24). Africa, 2nd fastest growing tourism region in the world. https://www.hospitalitynet.org/news/4095186.html

Kimeria, C. (2019, September 28). Africa's tourism industry is second fastest growing in world. *Quartz Africa*. https://qz.com/africa/1717902/africas-tourism-industry-is-second-fastest-growing-in-world/

Knight Frank (2020). The Africa Report, 2020/1. https://view.digital-hub.global/the-africa-report-2020/p/4

Mo Ibrahim Foundation (2019, July 10). Africa's first challenge: The youth bulge stuck in "Waithood". https://mo.ibrahim.foundation/news/2019/africas-first-challenge-youth-bulge-stuck-waithood#:%7E:text=Almost%2060%25%20of%20Africa's%20population, to%20be%2019.8%20in%202020

Niles, E. (1991). Sustainable tourism development-A myth or reality? In *Focus*, 1, 3-4

PropertyWheel_G, B (2020, August 11). Unlocking the concept of wealth creation through property investment—Property Wheel. *Property Wheel*. https://propertywheel.co.za/2020/08/unlocking-the-concept-of-wealth-creation-through-property-investment/

Salaudeen, A. C. (2020, June 1). Africa's tourism industry is preparing for a post-coronavirus era. *CNN*. https://edition.cnn.com/2020/06/01/africa/africa-tourism-coronavirus/index.html

Sharpley, R. (2000). Tourism and sustainable development: Exploring the theoretical divide. *Journal of Sustainable Development, 8*(1), 1–19.

Signé, L., & Johnson, C. (2018, December). Africa's tourism potential: Trends, drivers, opportunities, and strategies. Brookings. https://www.brookings.edu/wp-content/uploads/2018/12/Africas-tourism-potential_LandrySigne1.pdf

Spilanis, I., Vayanni, H., & Glyptou, K. (2013). Evaluating the tourism activity in a destination: The case of Samos Island. *Études Caribéennes, 23*(23), 1–13. doi:10.4000/etudescaribeennes.6257

Temblador, A. (2019, April 1). How women are playing a pivotal role in the African travel industry. *Travelpulse*. https://www.travelpulse.com/news/destinations/how-women-are-playing-a-pivotal-role-in-the-african-travel-industry.html

Unit 3

The African diaspora confront several challenges that may affect their desire or ability to effectively contribute to their nations' development. In Chapter 9, we explore the "double-edged sword" of the diaspora's hybrid identities, which result in cultural clashes with citizen-residents in their African homeland. In Chapter 10, we explore the role of Western media in perpetuating the narrative of Africa as a "Dark Continent" and its potential effects in dissuading the diaspora from investing in their African home countries. In Chapter 11, we present the fragile dynamics that characterize the African diaspora's relationship with their African nation governments, which may challenge opportunities for nation-building.

DOI: 10.4324/9781351031660-11

9 Managing cultural conundra 101

Cultural shifts, cultural contracts, cultural clash!

Pending their sense of allegiance and psycho-emotional connections of national identity, citizenry, and the quality of maintenance of ties to their African home land, the African diaspora may be motivated to invest in their country. But how does the African diaspora effectively manage cultural shifts and coping mechanisms in their re-acculturation processes when they migrate between their African countries and host lands, upon entry and re-entry? Their ability to manage cultural conflicts in pursuit of national development is also challenged upon entry into their African homeland. On one hand, the diaspora possess various forms of cultural capital that may account for their ascent in global markets and laissez-passer in social circles. However, at times, their perceived "Whiteness" results in opposition from some citizen-residents in their African home country who challenge their authenticity and intentions as their fellow "Africans." As a result, the diaspora may assume the unofficial status of "foreigners" in their African homelands. Ironically, the diaspora also experience resistance from some citizen-residents upon return to their African home country when they promote indigenous-owned and locally produced products and challenge some of the Eurocentric hegemonic ideals or biases of foreign privilege, which reflect colonial legacies in their African communities. Amidst the conundra, the value of diaspora contributions to their African homes is challenged, their intentions questioned.

This chapter introduces some of the cultural negotiations and experiences that some African diaspora confront and make upon entry or contact with their African homeland communities. The ability of the African diaspora to effectively manage cultural dynamics in the diverse cultural contexts of their environment depends also on their different cultural identity shifts, cultural contract types, and coping mechanisms, especially when experiencing cultural clashes with those in their African home communities. Recognizing the role of culture is a vital tool for development for citizen-residents and the African diaspora who need to ensure an appropriate degree of cultural fit to collaborate effectively on their nations' development.

During an interview I conducted with Estifanos Berta-Samuel, CEO of Established Fashion and Lifestyle, he amusingly observes

DOI: 10.4324/9781351031660-12

> One that hits home for me is the stereotype that I am Black on the outside, but a White man inwardly because I was partly educated in the West, travel the world, and—oh I speak with a European accent. I mean, have you any idea how said experiences have shaped my paradigm for life and the awareness of my African identity in a world that views me as a Black Man and treats me "accordingly"? I am constantly reminded of who I am and what I look like, rather directly or indirectly, the moment I leave my front door … I'd love to address the misconception of others when being in the West and called too African to be Western, yet when I'm in Africa, I'm too Western to be completely African. I ask the question, "Where do I belong then?" and just as well decide that if you're looking for me, I'll be in the "Expat" section of town!
>
> (Estifanos Berta-Samuel, personal communication, December 27, 2019).

The roles of cultural identity shifts and cultural contracts in the diaspora's re-acculturation experiences

Sussman's (2002) *cultural identity model* (CIM) has been developed and used to explain the different identity shifts and outcomes that sojourners, or those who reside in temporary places before relocating again, experience upon remigration to their homelands from their host country. The outcomes of the model specifically predict the level of adaptation to the host country and level of repatriation distress that one experiences in the homeland. This is important in determining how the diaspora may effectively adjust to, and maintain ties with, their African home country in their efforts to contribute to their nation's development agenda after residing in the host country.

The four *identity shifts* with corresponding predictive outcomes from the CIM are affirmative, subtractive, additive, and global (Tambyah & Chng, 2006):

- The *affirmative identity shift* refers to those who harbor positive feelings with their identified homelands and sense strong connectivity with their compatriots. Hence, those with an affirmative identity shift would have low adaptation to the host country (less comfort in their host land) and low repatriation distress in their remigration to the homeland because they are eager and appreciative of their return home.
- The *subtractive identity shift* and the *additive identity shift* both refer to sojourners who adapt to the host country to a great extent and are highly distressed in their remigration to their homeland. However, the reasons for their elevated levels of distress between these two shifts vary. Subtractive identifiers experience a heightened discomfort, an increased sense of being

a foreigner, and a feeling of being alienated in a home culture they no longer identify with—an identity loss (subtractive identity)—upon their return to the homeland.

- The high repatriation distress for the *additive identifiers*, however, stems from a significant shift in cultural identity. More specifically, these sojourners experience an overwhelming sensation after immersing themselves deeply and extensively in numerous cultural aspects of the host land (additive identity).
- Sojourners of a *global identity shift* adapt to the host land to a great extent and experience low repatriation distress, given their multiple international experiences, frequent acculturation to different cultures geographically, and strong identification with a global community, resulting in a favorable repatriation experience.

Exploring these particular cultural identity shifts and their impact on the African diaspora offers a unique opportunity in explaining and predicting levels of potential stress and adaptation in their host lands and repatriation distress upon re-entry to their home countries. Those with strong affirmative identity shifts, for instance, may be better positioned to invest in their home countries and may even consider migrating permanently after living abroad for a short time. If governments are seeking to attract their African diaspora to invest in and contribute to their homelands' development, they can benefit from a thorough understanding of these cultural identity shifts. Government agencies that are focused on diaspora affairs, for instance, may tailor specific communications strategies to attract affirmative identifiers to invest back home differently from those who are subtractive identifiers, as the latter are more likely to be severely stressed, and perhaps resistant, upon remigration to their African homeland. Governments can also tap into the sources of distress to develop specific policies that address the psychological, safety, economic, and political needs of their different target audiences.

Representing both the Western and African worlds means that the African diaspora are positioned to build rapports with local communities, in which they are trusted and identified as community members. Their ability to effectively interact with community members in their African countries may best be explained through identity effects and the cultural contract theoretical framework that various scholars have presented in literature surrounding cultural identity.

Applying concepts like *mindfulness*, *intercultural personhood*, and identity shifting of the cultural identity model suggest that through their mindfulness, the diaspora are open to and aware of their circumstances and environment and are willing to be changed through their interactions and negotiated meanings of "reality" with their community. Such negotiated meanings and redefined relationships would further allow the diaspora to embody an intercultural competence in which they eradicate all assumptions that they are completely different or completely similar from their African community members. With *intercultural personhood*, the transcultural person "competently traverses cultural borders" (Onwumechili et al., 2003, p. 52) and can persevere due to their ability to withstand long periods of identity stress and to adjust during different cultural transitions (Onwumechili et al., 2003; Kim, 2001). Ultimately, such an effect further suggests that the diaspora may also engage in valuable interactions that may result in "community-building," which Chen and Starosta (98) highlight is an additional attribute of the cultural identity model. "Community-building," similar to Fred Casmir's (93) "third-culture building," refers to the co-constructed relationships and negotiated "realities" that the diaspora develop in their acculturation or re-acculturation processes upon entry or re-entry to a "new" environment. This particular concept is interesting to consider. It suggests that the diaspora may be less prejudiced and stereotypical because they possess the specific resources and forms of capital that they may have acquired from the West, but are able to leverage them along with resources they possess from their African communities and disseminate them strategically as sources of meaningful development in Africa.

However, the *cultural contracts theory* holds more appeal to studies related to re-acculturation, as explored further by Onwumechili et al. (2003) in their exploration of identity issues of intercultural transients and their multiple re-acculturation processes and cultural readjustment experiences. Their (2003) study conceptualized "intercultural transients" as those that "straddle cultural borders," as they migrate and (re)-migrate frequently between their homelands and host countries in pursuit socioeconomic/political development or service employment—whether on a short-term or long-term basis. They illustrated the multiple re-acculturation through transients' repeated cyclical curves, which represent various valleys of the cultural identity negotiation process. Their portrayal of multiple re-acculturation is most apt in our reference to the brain circulation phenomenon, which characterizes the diaspora's short-term, circulatory migration patterns between their host and home countries in their pursuit to maintain ties with their communities in Africa and contribute to their national welfare.

Onwumechili et al. (2003) refer to cultural contract types to represent ways that intercultural transients may negotiate their cultural identity upon multiple re-acculturations. These cultural contract types could also be applied to the African diaspora upon their multiple re-acculturations to their African homelands:

- the *ready-to-sign* cultural contract, which reinforces the transients' pre-negotiated disposition upon entry with that culture, barring any additional negation or any opportunities for collaboration or relationship-building, as they strictly maintain their own worldview and cultural identity and refuse to learn those of the hosts;
- *quasi-completed*, or partial, negotiations with another culture, with any cultural shift taking place at varying degrees, pending their purpose to fulfill

professional or social goals, resulting in merely some openness to other worldviews, with little motivation to co-create another culture;
- a *co-created contract* that reflects the individual's full negotiation and acceptance of other worldviews and cultural identity that completely embraces mindfulness and intercultural personhood.

As illustrated by Onwumechili et al. (2003), there are potential negative outcomes that accompany each contract type. These outcomes could also be applicable to the African diaspora upon their re-entry into their African homeland, or "new" host countries. Transients that choose to adopt a ready-to-sign contract may risk encountering stress, shock, and relational conflict as a result of being closed-minded (Onwumechili et al., 2003). In our context, the African diaspora may refuse to learn or adopt the cultural views of their "new host land"—their Africa homeland communities—and hence limit opportunities for collaboration and relationship-building with citizen-residents to develop their nations.

Transients who "sign" quasi-completed contracts are in "limbo," so they must remain true to their core self, otherwise they may risk self-protection if they choose to ignore their instinct, or may come across as inauthentic, particularly if "the familiar other may wonder why that individual is not acting like him or herself—that self that is indigenous to the home the familiar other knows you are a part of" (Onwumechili et al., 2003, p. 58). Therefore, it would be increasingly important that the African diaspora accept and embrace the multiple cultural synergies that comprise the whole individual, instead of exaggerating ways to validate or "downplay" the other cultural self that is also part of the individual. It would also be important for the African diaspora to be honest with themselves and respond organically to the natural inclinations toward their cultural experiences at that period in time. Such authenticity is critical for the diaspora to ensure that they are clear, transparent, and honest about the partnership agreements, development goals, and development agenda that they pursue with other citizen-residents and key stakeholders in their pursuit to develop their African nations' agenda.

Those who adopt a co-created contract risk being perceived as disloyal, especially as Onwumechili et al. (2003) note that the transient is the one who would adjust more than the individual in the host country. Hence, the African diaspora would need to be aware of others' potential misperceptions, as well as intentional about building trust and maintaining their integrity with the citizen-residents and key stakeholders with whom they collaborate.

To negotiate these contract types and adjust to their new cultural environments, many migrants adopt coping mechanisms. Perhaps one of the most popular mechanisms is the ability to *code switch*, which Cross and Strauss (1998) define as an adaptive function that involves intercultural transients' relearning of and adhering to the codes of the cultural ingroup, which relieves them from experiencing judgment or criticism of their cultural competency (Onwumechili et al., 2003). For the African diaspora, this could involve alternating between different languages, linguistic patterns, and diction to accommodate their work environment. More specifically, this includes adopting and "turning on" or "turning off" European, American, or African accents and diction unique to their country of residence; adapting to certain slang or urban vernacular as necessary; modifying physical appearance; and developing certain mannerisms and work styles to meet the criteria and qualifications for success in a particular environment. Other forms of coping mechanisms that are included in Cross and Strauss' (1998) daily functions of cultural identity shifting are *buffering*, or protecting and creating a division or wall between one's self and the other to mitigate or avoid potential identity threats; *bonding*, or strengthening personal connections, enhancing closeness, and re-establishing friendship networks with those upon re-entry; and *bridging*, which enables one to empathize with another's cultural worldview by remaining informed by current updates of the greater collective community and individual relationships and learning codes of the ingroup (Onwumechili et al., 2003).

Ultimately, it is important that Africans in the diaspora who seek to invest in or contribute toward their African nations are prepared to examine their own resistance, critically re-assess their own unconscious biases, and be mindful of the cultural contract types they may sign upon entry into their African home communities. It is also important that the African diaspora maintain their integrity as they adjust their coping mechanisms within the new cultural contexts of their communities.

Exploring divergent indigenous and Western perspectives: The clash of cultural capital!

The traits and attributes of dominant groups tend to be most valued in society. These groups have the power and privilege of setting norms in their society that others are expected to follow. These norms set the standards and policies in institutions, in groups, and individually. Anything or anyone that deviates from these norms is considered an outlier or a minority and could be marginalized from the dominant accepted group. On a global scale—particularly in Africa—Eurocentric or Westernized traits, attributes, and sources of cultural capital have been valued as dominant standards for the rest of the world to adhere to, both during and post colonialism, in various contexts. This has been reflected through different forms of linguistic capital, where the official languages for trade and business in most African and Asian countries are English, French, or Portuguese. Most education standards from elementary through high school across the world follow American, British, or French curricula, which require most students to migrate to North America or Europe to pursue higher education and build careers. Essentially, this has been the framework for the brain drain in most developing countries.

However, some of these forms of cultural capital that have been valued in the West have also posed challenges upon migrants' re-entry into their African communities. On micro levels, some individuals who have returned to their

African homelands in pursuit of work may have experienced cultural clashes and rejection from locals who criticize them for "being White" and showcasing a Westernized approach, mentality, and attitude toward issues pertinent to their African home environment. On the flip side, African returnees may have similarly experienced frustration upon their re-entry to their African home country, the systems and policies of which they perceive to be more ineffective and inefficient than those they have been accustomed to in their Western host countries. At the macro level, there is continued and significant debate on the extent to which "Whiteness" and Westernized principles reflecting colonial strongholds "disrupt" African cultures, traditions, and value systems. Some migrants who return to their African homelands have been accused of introducing Western practices that defy tradition; others are hailed for being "progressive" and for advocating a "moral standard" for equality, egality, and human rights.

Let's explore a few illustrations through some debates that contextualize some cultural clashes between the African diaspora and citizen-residents in Africa, particularly within the context of some development issues.

- *"Let's talk about sex, baby" (or not): Confronting (sexual) liberation in Africa*

Discourse and media platforms dedicated to topics surrounding sexuality, sexual health, and forms of sexual behavior are generally discussed openly and promoted casually, and generate conversation between parents and children, adults and youth … predominantly in Western societies. For many African communities, such conversations about sex—let alone media that reflect any sexually explicit content—are generally avoided at all costs between youth and adults, particularly parents and their children. Hence, it is not uncommon for some African diaspora to encounter challenges upon re-entry into their home country, confronting the dichotomy of sexuality as a form of modesty and its contrast: overt display.

In many African societies, sexuality is generally concealed and treated with modesty, and public displays of affection are minimal (Ugwu, 2015, para. 1). Some researchers and scholars argue that religion—traditional African religions, Christianity, and Islam—has influenced the thoughts, attitudes, and approaches to the modest discreet approach of sexuality (Ugwu, 2015, para. 1). Traditionally, sexual dances and rituals have generally been reserved for "coming of age" ceremonies or symbolic gestures to mark maturity of reproduction or significant marital milestones. Ultimately, an open dialogue, overt expression and candid, perhaps even casual, discussion of sexuality in mainstream public spheres is treated and perceived as a topic of taboo within some African cultures.

However, the last two decades have witnessed African film, music, accompanying music videos, advertising, and various pop-culture products continuously push the envelope with more sexually explicit content—arguably, a mimicry of the liberalization of sexuality in Western public spheres and media platforms. This has been met with worldwide criticism, particularly from those who "denounce objectification in advertising and blame media imperialism for disseminating overt, Westernized sexuality" (Nelson & Paek, 2005, p. 371).

However, such overt sexuality and pop culture invite both praise and criticism from the global community, prompting questions about the effect of transposing sexually explicit content or discourse from a private space of taboo into the public sphere. Does pop culture revolutionize what some hail as "female empowerment" or the "women's liberation movement"? Proponents argue that pop-culture media sites have become recognized platforms for women to increasingly claim their own sexual liberation. "Acceptance of female sexuality, for example, has reached the point that women are, in principle, as free to claim and express their sexual side as men. A large part of the credit for this shift must go to pop culture and its influence" (Trew, 2015, para. 2).

Some diaspora who are proponents of sexual liberation applaud the outcome. By desensitizing the topic of sexuality through its increasingly overt display to mass audiences, more women—particularly from patriarchal societies—are positioned to question the status quo governing their bodies and rise up as agents of their own sexuality. Sexuality is no longer restricted to a male privilege; women are more empowered to own and control their bodies, challenge traditional or societal norms and the codes and cues of the mating game, and vocally articulate the conditionalities and permissibility of their own sexual preferences on their own terms—starting, perhaps, as simply with a "yes" or "no."

However, other critics paint a grim, daunting outcome. So long as the media market model for the pop-culture industry underscores the adage that "sex sells," then African media products that strive to compete with the market model in domestic and global markets will remain committed to "selling sex" to its target audience and primary base: teenagers. Exposing young demographics to sexually explicit content may result in unhealthy perceptions of self-image and promote underage sexual activity among immature adolescents, misogyny, deviant or irresponsible sexual behavior, and, on a broader community scale, fuel the spread of sexually transmitted infections (STIs). Although unhealthy sexual behavior carries greater risks and costs for all global communities, the cost is even greater for vulnerable communities in Africa that already struggle with compromised health infrastructure, inefficient healthcare systems, and reduced access to healthcare resources and medical intervention in response to STIs. The cost is further exacerbated for a community whose culture generally treats overt sexuality as a taboo, and then stigmatizes its members who become infected with STIs. As a result, those infected with STIs become marginalized in their communities and, ultimately, suffer in silence.

Hence, upon return to their motherland, some diaspora are forewarned or advised to re-assess how they present themselves publicly to mitigate the risk of being perceived as promiscuous, "loose," or sexually deviant—or to address topics related to sex and sexuality carefully. Others push the envelope as they advocate for a liberal movement and challenge traditional and cultural norms.

- *LGBTQIAPK+ Rights*

Some diaspora Africans who accommodate the lesbian-gay-bisexual-transgender-queer-intersex-asexual-pansexual-kink (LGBTQIAPK+) community or advocate for their rights have been accused of appropriating Western ideologies by some African communities, who reject the movement's association with their cultural values. Mikael Owunna, who resides in the United States and identifies as gay, explored the ways in which LGBTQIAPK+ African immigrants "navigate and explore how to overcome the challenges between their LGBTQIAPK+ and African identities" through *Limit(less)*, a photo art gallery of different portraits of LGBTQIAPK+ Africans in the diaspora.

However, the attitude toward homosexuality is not homogeneous among all members of the African diaspora who have resided in the West. Whereas some diaspora Africans advocate for LGBTQIAPK+ rights as human rights, there are some who reject homosexuality for spiritual, traditional, and other reasons.

Criticisms that "the White man brought homosexuality to Africa," or that "being gay is not African" have been common headlines in literature, dialogues, and campaigns to disconfirm and reject homosexuality in most African communities. Homosexuality in many African traditions has been viewed as a taboo, and its unacceptance has resulted in incarcerations, brutal attacks, and death among those who have identified or been accused as being members of the LGBTQIAPK+ community.

In Kenya, Uganda, and several other African countries, homosexual acts are illegal. In Kenya, "surveys show nine in 10 people find them unacceptable" (Smith, 2017, para. 2), and in 2019, the High Court upheld the criminalization of homosexual acts between consenting adults (Kushner, 2019). Uganda's Anti-Homosexuality Act, which was introduced to Parliament in 2009 and signed into law in 2014 by President Yoweri Museveni, gained global attention and notoriety. The "Kill the Gays" bill resulted in backlash from several prominent African leaders, including Nobel Peace Prize Laureate Reverend Desmond Tutu; the World Bank Group's suspension of a $90 million healthcare loan to Uganda; and other foreign aid cuts from the United States, Denmark, the Netherlands, Norway, and Sweden (Thapa, 2015). In January 2014, Nigerian President Goodluck Jonathan passed a law that carried a prison sentence of 14 years for same-sex marital couples and up to 10 years for those who were members of or promoted gay groups (Smith, 2017).

When US President Barack Obama visited Kenya in 2015, he challenged the country's treatment of its gay population. In response to President Obama's criticisms, Irungu Kang'ata, an MP in Kenyatta's governing party, was quoted in *The Guardian*:

> They are in bad taste … It's a breach of the principle of sovereignty and equality of states. What if Kenyatta goes to America and says it should abolish the death penalty? Or for example it is like Obama goes to London

> or Madrid or The Hague or even Japan and says your monarchy is oppressive and a waste of money and should be done away with. In the same manner he can't come to Kenya to tell us things that are unacceptable.
>
> (Smith, 2017, para. 12)

Opposing the notion that Westernization introduced homosexuality to Africa, Alimi (2015) asserts that homosexuality was not introduced to Africa by colonialism. In Nigeria, specific terms describe homosexuality or same-sexualities: in Yoruba, the term *adofuro* translates specifically to "anal sex" and is a nonderogatory term that simply means "homosexuality," while in Hausa, *yan daudu* describes the effeminate look and behavior of men who are considered as wives to men (Alimi, 2015). Hence, the fact that these terms exist in the language systems suggests that they have been used to describe a behavior that existed prior to colonialism. Other references to homosexuality in Africa include King Mwanga II of the Buganda kingdom in Uganda who has also been identified as openly gay; boy to adulthood rites of passage in some African communities that have involved same-sex activities; and Bushman artwork that illustrates men engaging in homosexual activity (Alimi, 2015). Alimi (2015) suggests that the rise in the HIV epidemic and the pressures of the Christian religion contribute toward the intense scrutiny and criticism of homosexuality in Africa. He also notes that the intolerance of homosexuality has been used by African politicians to garner votes among their constituencies.

References to homosexuality have also dated to biblical times—further suggesting that this was a practice that had long existed prior to colonialism. Hence, the arguments that homosexuality is not African, or that it was introduced by Westernization, remain contested. Some further argue that heightened negative attention and homophobia toward homosexuality are tactics that political leaders use to divert attention from their economic shortcomings and other issues that they would be judged heavily for, particularly during peak times of their election campaign. Hence, some suggest that political leaders may employ anti-homosexual propaganda to appeal to the emotional sensibilities and consensus of the popular vote among constituents. As a result, some audiences question the legitimacy of some politicians' stance against homosexuality.

- *Traditional rituals and practices (female genital mutilation)*

Traditional rituals like female genital mutilation (FGM) that are practiced in Africa and Asia are controversial. Female genital mutilation, also referred to as *female genital cutting* (FGC), refers to the cutting of a woman's clitoris or labia as part of a ceremonial ritual to mark a young girl's maturity at puberty. Organizations such as the World Health Organization (WHO) and the United Nations (UN) have campaigned to abolish the practice and have cited health concerns, human rights violations, and social pressures to ban the ritual. Some people regard FMG to be a practice that victimizes young girls who undergo unclean procedures and suffer in silence.

Despite this popular outlook, research also has countered some misconceptions about FMG. In some communities, women visit dispensaries and receive antibiotics and anti-tetanus injections, garner support and care from the elderly women who lead the ceremony, and eagerly celebrate their rite of passage into adult womanhood after a successful procedure. This contradicts some narratives that depict young women as helpless victims of a deadly procedure, led by men, and who suffer a myriad of health and societal consequences. Alternatively, ritual and traditional practices of adulthood, like male circumcision, in the Western hemisphere could be equally controversial and misunderstood in the context of indigenous populations in African or Asian countries where FGM is practiced.

A health professional I interviewed for this book reflected on her experiences as a Sudanese national who grew up in Sudan and has also lived in different European countries outside of the Sudan, including the United States:

> With issues like FGM, you have to realize that you have culture and you have religion and you have the Western world and they are all mixed together. FGM is believed to be about religion, but it is not. Some people at home [in the Sudan] believe it should be done because it is part of Islam, which is not the case, but that's what they push for. But at the same time, you have that conversation knowing that you are arguing with people here [in the United States] that men should be circumcised because that is our religion. And so, you're having two different conversations about the same thing in two different worlds. My sister sees this differently, so let alone someone else who grew up in different environments.
>
> (Aliyah*, personal communication, February 1, 2020)

As illustrated, these practices are also debated within communities and households, so their controversy is not limited to dynamics between indigenous or diasporic groups.

- *Eurocentric hegemonic ideals of beauty and favoritism within African communities*

As we have seen in the previous examples, the diaspora's (subconscious) adoption of a Western or Eurocentric mentality to address issues in their African home country may result in cultural clashes and forms of resistance from their African home communities. However, the reverse is also true: some African diaspora may also encounter resistance when they challenge

Eurocentric ideals that they perceive are still maintained and reinforced within their own home African communities. Some diaspora report experiencing shock, and at times confusion or frustration, upon their return to their African home countries where some citizen-residents or businesses still uphold ideologies that may prioritize the needs of Caucasians before African citizen-residents, or favor "foreign brands" more than their own locally produced, indigenous-owned brands—even if the products may be identical or bear minimal differences.

To understand the complexity and controversy surrounding the appeal of Eurocentric brands in some local African communities is to acknowledge the significant role of colonial history and the effects of cultural imperialism or cultural colonialism. Colonialism in Africa marked an era of Eurocentric cultural dominance that imposed Eurocentric economic and cultural values, ideologies, and practices on African state colonies. Present-day effects of cultural hegemony subtly reverberate through structural and systemic forces that normalize behaviors and manifest our realities through policy, assumptions of "common sense," and generally accepted standards of "that's how it's always been done." As a result, dominant standards of appeal and acceptance reflecting Eurocentrism have been evident across a range of industries, and are evident more visibly in beauty and grooming industries globally.

For instance, lighter and fairer complexions and features that reflect Caucasian traits or "Whiteness" have been acknowledged as "acceptable" and used as a source of preferential treatment, favoritism, or bias. This has been evident in media images and representations of beauty—including beauty products with skin bleaching agents to lighten dark skin complexions. As of 2019, the skin-bleaching epidemic steadily rose in developing countries like Jamaica, the Philippines, China, South Korea, and Nigeria, with Nigeria having a skin-bleaching product use rate of 77% (Lebsack, 2019). The rapidly growing industry of skin bleaching is estimated to be valued at $24 billion, and remains highly controversial for placing individuals' lives and health at risk of organ failure and poisoning, as the pills and creams are usually unregulated or untested, as well as for promoting discrimination through colorism and shadism (Lebsack, 2019). "By perpetuating the idea that a lighter complexion will make you more desirable, Western beauty standards continue to feed a global market that profits off women's insecurities" (Lebsack, 2019, para. 5).

It becomes a challenge to inform and even educate those who may not perceive or agree that skin bleaching is a reinforcement of Eurocentric hegemony that has normalized Whiteness as an international beauty standard. Some African diaspora may experience more frustration when they observe new institutionalized legislations that seek to confront racial biases in their host countries, but witness little response to mitigating racism from their own African home countries. For instance, Black professionals in the United States who wear hair braids, twists, locs, and natural hair textures have reported cases of workplace harassment or suffered repercussions for violating policies in the workplace because their hair was considered "unkempt," "unprofessional," or inappropriate. In response to such discriminatory practices, some states, including California, New York, and New Jersey, passed laws banning hair discrimination as of January 2020, and other states are proposing similar legislation to protect employees. "The California Legislature admits that enforcing a 'Eurocentric image of professionalism' through grooming policies that 'disparately impact black' people is inequitable" (MWH Staff, 2020, para. 2). Such laws and policies, including the Crown Act, that are designed to reinforce the acceptability, equity, and equitability of indigenous cultural traits reflect an attitude that challenges Eurocentrism as the dominant standard of cultural identity and acceptability.

Some diaspora also experience frustration upon re-entry into their African country when they witness cases where their home communities adhere to Eurocentric ideals and are prejudiced against their own Africans. One participant in my study, Gregory* (personal communication, October 13, 2020), recalls an incident where many years ago, while on a business trip, he witnessed an African female receptionist, working in a hotel that was located in Kenya checking in hotel guests, who would skip over Africans in the queue to favor a European couple. She defended her actions by claiming that the Europeans were "guests" and that those she perceived as Africans were dismissed because they were "one of them" or "her people." Although she was admonished and received administrative sanctions, this individual case illustrates a larger, more pervasive issue in the present day.

These epitomes shine a bright light on the intricacy of challenges that are rooted in the complex layers of culture and tradition, religion, political, social and economic disparities, nestled with Eurocentric ideologies that are entrenched in historical legacies of colonialism. Therefore, it is critical for Africans in the diaspora to recognize the forms of resistance that they may encounter. On one hand, some members of their African homeland community may regard them as foreign ambassadors of Westernization who seek to displace and uproot their customs. On the other hand, some Africans in the diaspora betray the hegemonic norms of their African homelands when they challenge Eurocentric biases.

Such cultural clashes that exist in the 21st century reflect some of the negotiations and challenges that the diaspora may confront in efforts to assert a cultural identity and "fit" between cultural spaces that are diametrically opposed. Arguably, African migrants who reside in the West may have adopted Eurocentric ideologies and acquired Eurocentric standards of cultural capital that have fostered their social mobility and positioned them for social mobility, career development, and professional success in their host lands. However, these forms of cultural capital may also present stress, frustration, and tension for the African diaspora who seek (re)-entry in their African home communities, if not properly managed. Some of these cultural clashes may bring opposing viewpoints about development issues to the forefront, raise ethical questions about whether "morality" and "human rights" reflect Western or African nations' indigenous ideologies, and pose potential conflict in collaborations between the African diaspora and their fellow citizen-residents in pursuit of their African nation's welfare. Hence, the African diaspora's coping mechanisms in response to the cultural shifts they experience and how they resolve potential risks of cultural contract types would impact their effectiveness in contributing toward their African nation's development agenda. Both citizen-residents and African diaspora need to ensure an appropriate degree of cultural fit in their relationship toward Africa's development.

Chapter summary

Key concepts

additive identifiers	code switch	mindfulness
affirmative identity shift	community-building	ready-to-sign
bonding	cultural contracts theory	subtractive identity shift
bridging	cultural identity model	
buffering	global identity shift	
co-created contract	intercultural personhood	

Discussion questions

Identify a traditional practice, ritual, or societal issue within a selected African country that may be considered as controversial. It could be a topic identified in the chapter, including sexualization, female genital mutilation (FGM), homosexuality, or any other topic of interest.

Include the following in your case study:

- Describe the ritual or controversial issue, whom it impacts, and controversial arguments surrounding this issue from different opposing groups;
- Outline any relevant context—historical, cultural, or underlying motivating factors from each of the opposing groups—that may explain the root causes of the controversy and its impact on communities in the present day;
- Describe community local or global interventions that have been implemented to address this practice or the controversial arguments;
- Say whether you believe these interventions are an assertion of cultural-centric ideologies (Eurocentric, African-centric, other), or a pursuit of a human freedom that defies any cultural ideology, and explain why or why not.

References

Alimi, B. (2015, September 9). *If you say being gay is not African, you don't know your history.* The Guardian. https://www.theguardian.com/commentisfree/2015/sep/09/being-gay-african-history-homosexuality-christianity

Cross, W., & Strauss, L. (1998). The everyday functions of African American identity. In J. Swim, & C. Stangor (Eds.), *Prejudice: The target's perspective*. New York: Academic Press.

Kim, Y. Y. (2001). *Becoming intercultural: An integrative theory of communication and cross-cultural adaptation* (pp. 3–43). Newbury Park, CA: Sage.

Kushner, J. (2019, June 18). Kenya's Supreme Court upholds a colonial-era Anti-LGBTQ law. *The Atlantic*. https://www.theatlantic.com/international/archive/2019/05/kenya-supreme-court-lgbtq/590014/

Lebsack, L. (2019, May 28). Skin bleaching is poisoning women—but business is booming. *Refinery29*. https://www.refinery29.com/en-us/2019/05/233409/skin-bleaching-lightening-products-safety-controversy

Staff, M. W. H. (2020, May 29). Hair discrimination in the workplace. *MWH Law Group LLP*. https://mwhlawgroup.com/hair-discrimination-workplace/

Sussman, N. M. (2002). Testing the cultural identity model of the cultural transition cycle: sojourners return home. *International Journal of Intercultural Relations*, *26*(4), 391–408. https://doi.org/10.1016/s0147-1767(02)00013-5

Nelson, M., & Paek, H. (2005). Cross-cultural differences in sexual advertising content in a transnational women's magazine. *Sex Roles*, *53*(5–6), 371–383. doi:10.1007/s11199-005-6760-5

Onwumechili, C., Nwosu, P., Jackson, R., & James-Hughes, J. (2003). In the deep valley with mountains to climb: Exploring identity and multiple reacculturation. *International Journal of Intercultural Relations*, *27*(1), 41–62. doi:10.1016/s0147-1767(02)00063-9

Smith, D. (2017, December 2). Barack Obama tells African states to abandon anti-gay discrimination. *The Guardian*. https://www.theguardian.com/us-news/2015/jul/25/barack-obama-african-states-abandon-anti-gay-discrimination

Tambyah, S., & Chng, R. (2006). Revisiting the Cultural Identity Model: Sojourners' Negotiations of Identity and Consumption Experience. In C. Pechmann & L. Price (Eds.), *NA - Advances in Consumer Research* (Vol. 33, pp. 464–465). Duluth, MN: Association for Consumer Research. https://www.acrwebsite.org/volumes/12385/volumes/v33/NA-33

Thapa, S. (2015, September). LGBT Uganda today: Continuing danger despite nullification of Anti-Homosexuality Act. Human Rights Campaign. https://assets2.hrc.org/files/assets/resources/Global_Spotlight_Uganda__designed_version__September_25__2015.pdf

Trew, G. (2015, June 18). Pop culture and sexuality. *The Missing Slate*. http://journal.themissingslate.com/article/pop-culture-sexuality/

Ugwu, C. (2015, August 27). Sexuality and culture in postcolonial Africa | *H*-Announce | *H*-Net. Https://Networks.h-Net.Org/Node/73374/Announcements/79780/Sexuality-and-Culture-Postcolonial-Africa. https://networks.h-net.org/node/73374/announcements/79780/sexuality-and-culture-postcolonial-africa

10 The miseducation of the African diaspora by Western media

I remember vividly in 2002, I was in Côte d'Ivoire, West Africa, during a civil rebellion. The government had finally lifted the state of emergency and families were freed after a period of house arrest and curfews. However, what we had known of the crisis that we lived during the week we were confined to our homes we got from television news. My family was glued to the repetitive harrowing images of the news still vibrant in my mind, "Live from CNN," featuring two military men in army trucks, boldly firing shots in the air in the middle of a deserted street near my neighborhood, laughing at each other. In spite of the severity of our life-threatening danger that CNN was describing, a family guest randomly surprised us with an unexpected visit one day. After some moments of hesitation before letting him into our home, he enthusiastically refuted our concerns for his safety. He kept reiterating to us that we were safe and that what we were seeing on the news was not reflective of the reality outside our gates. Shortly thereafter, my family and I were addressing the same concerns expressed by friends overseas who called us frequently to inquire about our safety, as well as of the security of their investments in the country, based on their knowledge of the situation from the news.

Fast forward to December 2010, during a period where there was some political unrest in Côte d'Ivoire. At this point, I was living in the United States, and like many of my transcultural friends who lived overseas, I relied on television and online news reports about this African country. A close friend of mine traveled back to the country over the Christmas holidays and, in what felt like a déjà-vu, I reprimanded him for his disregard for his own safety and assumed that the nation's security had been weakened—based on what I had seen in the media. However, his accounts of his visit described a relatively calmer and more stable country than those featured in Western news platforms.

Then came my own newsflash: I sounded no different from those in the Western world and foreigners who had stereotyped me and my culture because they based their knowledge of Africa on its portrayal in Western media. The only difference was that I was born in Uganda, East Africa; raised in Côte d'Ivoire, West Africa; and resided in the United States. Should I have been inquiring about my own African homelands as though I didn't know better? What became apparent to me was that I was viewing African-centric content through the cultural prisms of a foreigner, as though I had never set foot in the continent. Congratulations, Stella-Monica: The media had successfully framed "insecurity," "unsafety," and "dejection" of my "home" in Africa—and sadly, in three seconds, I bought into it …

DOI: 10.4324/9781351031660-13

So, in my search for "truth" about one of the countries that I identified as "home," three questions burned:

1) Why did news coverage about Africa consistently paint in bleak images that only those who inhabited the continent were in the position to refute or support?
2) Why was so little information about Africa reported in the mainstream media, and, if it was, was it so rarely reported from the perspectives of Africans and those with a vested interest in the well-being of Africa?
3) More critically, if news coverage on our African homelands remains inaccurate, how will this it affect the decisions of those of us of the African diaspora to invest in our "home," especially if we live overseas and rely on mainstream news coverage to connect to our home countries?

The critical questions triggered by my personal experiences led me to re-examine and problematize the evolution of what has been named "the global media debate" (MacBride & Roach, 1993), pertaining to the news flow from the developed, Western world (Global North) into the developing nations (Global South), and its relationship to the news flow today.

History of the global media debate

The history of what Gerbner, Mowlana, and Nordenstreng (1993) refer to as the "global media debate" dates to the early 1950s, when nonaligned nations that perceived themselves as "victims of 'cultural colonialism'" convened at a summit in Algiers in 1973 to establish what would eventually became known as the "new world information and communication order [NWICO]" (MacBride & Roach, 1993, p. 3–4).

The debate regarding information flow emerged from three main problems affecting the developing countries vis-à-vis developed countries:

a) the distribution gap in the means of communication "[whereby] in 1970 there were 32 newspapers and 9 TV sets for 1000 people in developing countries, while for countries in the developed world 314 newspapers and 237 TV sets were available, which means a disparity of 1:10 concerning newspaper and 1:25 as to TV sets" (Kleinwachter, 1993, p. 14);
b) the imbalance of information flow, whereby there was more information and news from the Global North to the Global South than from the Global South to the Global North;
c) the distortion of news coverage and sensationalism of media content that "manipulated the image of the developing countries in the world public opinion and produced political, economic, and cultural consequences" (Kleinwachter, 1993, p. 14).

In addition to the imbalance in the flow of entertainment and advertising, the inception of the debate centered on the imbalanced news flow of information that stemmed from the Western world and infiltrated into the Third World. "The major Western international news services—AP and UPI of the United States, the French Agence France-Presse, and Reuters of the United Kingdom—were consistently described as having monopoly control over the flow of news from developing countries, and exercising it from a limited perspective reflecting the economic and cultural interests of the industrialized nations" (MacBride & Roach, 1993, p. 6).

Several resolutions, reports, and documents attempted to redress the balance of this "'new order' in international information structures and policies" of the international flow (MacBride & Roach, 1993, p. 3). MacBride and Roach (1993) cite the UNESCO General Conference of Nairobi in 1973 as a critical turning point in the debate between developed nations that supported a "free flow of information" (MacBride & Roach, 1993, p. 4), which the developing nations viewed as unregulated, dominating, and a threat to their liberties, and instead proposed a "free flow and balance of information" (MacBride & Roach, 1993, p. 4).

MacBride and Roach (1993) also refer to the 1978 UNESCO Declaration on the Mass Media, which nonaligned nations "regarded [as] the first international instrument referring directly to moral, social, and professional responsibilities of mass media in the context of 'the universally recognized principles of freedom of expression, information, and opinion'" (MacBride & Roach, 1993, p. 7). The principles of the Declaration were further reinforced in the MacBride Report of 1980, headed by Sean MacBride and published under the title "Many Voices, One World." The Report presented policies and regulations that supported the freedom of the press and of journalists and the elimination of obstacles that infringed upon the ability of developing nations to control their own communication media (MacBride & Roach, 1993, p. 5). The Report also called for the promotion of diversity and plurality of perspectives and collaborative efforts between developed and developing nations (MacBride & Roach, 1993, p. 5).

In efforts to assess and balance the role of technology in the socioeconomic development of a nation, the MacBride Commission Report urged for the involvement of "wide public participation and discussion" in communication frameworks (MacBride & Roach, 1993, p. 9). The commission recognized the complexities of a dynamic, global world and reinforced the need for responsibility in the management of communication. An emphasis of the "democratization of communication" permitted "everyone [to] be both 'producer and consumer of communication'" (MacBride & Roach, 1993, p. 10) and exercise their fundamental right to self-expression.

Kleinwachter (1993) also compares the role of the United Nations to that of the International Programme for the Development of Communication, which supported the works of the Declaration and also "[initiated] and [promoted] communication projects in developing nations" (Kleinwachter, 1993, p.15). By the 1980s, the New World Information and Communication Order (NWICO) concept had resurfaced as an engine that promoted the development, concepts, and roles of mass media and national communications in developing nations and on an international scale (Kleinwachter, 1993, p.15).

Kleinwachter (1993) refers to the Talloires Declaration (1981) as a response of "right-wing groups that identified NWICO as an attempt to restrict the freedom of the press," as supported by President Reagan and his administration (Kleinwachter, 1993, p.16). The ongoing debate related to NWICO presented a new conflict between developed and developing nations over the use of information as a commercial good or a social good with public interests (Kleinwachter, 1993, p. 19).

White (1993) characterizes NWICO as "a dialectical historical process involving a mixture of sociopolitical forces" (White, 1993, p. 22). The Third World regards NWICO as a symbol of unity and solidarity whose movement "has deep roots in an historic sociopolitical and cultural process" (White, 1993, p. 25). In addition to articulating equitable communication policies and encouraging public participation, the movement also responds to concerns of "cultural imperialism" (White, 1993, p, 27), or the dominance of one culture as a stronger entity over another as a weaker entity.

Scholars and practitioners continue to question and assess the domination of US and Western media, including international news agencies, in developing countries. We should direct our focus more toward the implications of Western domination in the media for developing countries and their development agenda.

Relevance of the debate for present-day Africa and for migrants

The relevance of the global media debate in the 21st century raise the issue of whether *media imperialism* continues to exist today. Media imperialism, a subcategory of cultural imperialism, has been viewed as an instrument by which more developed countries, particularly of the Western world, would impose their media programs, systems, and content on lesser developed countries and subjugate them to their agenda, cultures, values, and ideology.

Other studies have examined and analyzed international media flow over the years, focusing on different aspects of the media debate. In Kunihira's (2007) study on African news covered by American media, data revealed consistent crisis themes of ethnic war, violence, war, and disease, as well as noncrisis themes of women's empowerment and humanitarian assistance—whereby Africa sought more assistance from non-Africans and donors. According to Kunihara's (2007) data analysis, "The results clearly show that American media has not changed its coverage of the African news for the last eighteen years. There is a persistence of stereotypical images that continue to impact the self-esteem of African people and people of African ancestry... The data reveals little about Africans helping Africans, giving the impression that Africans are powerless and dependent entirely on the Western countries, thus giving Westerners a continued sense of superiority" (Kunihara, 2007, p. 10).

Himelboim, Chang, and McCreery (2010) examined patterns of information flow in online news media through theories of preferential attachment, the world system, and that of the triadic world. Results from their quantitative analyses of 223 websites in 73 countries revealed a reproduction of world hierarchies "perpetuating existing order among nations," and that the possible elitism of foreign correspondents accounts for the "the relatively low coverage of developing countries" (Himelboim, Chang & McCreery, 2010, p. 297). Ultimately, "[from] the developing world's perspective, the struggle to gain world exposure for their domestic and international concerns continues" (Himelboim, Chang & McCreery, 2010, p. 310).

Furthermore, additional research into international media flow also shows that about 6%–9% of the total amount of internationally focused Westerns news outlets is African content, and this figure drops down to 2%–3% in Japanese news media; overall, less than 2% of coverage in a Western newspaper is about Africa (Hawkins, 2018).

Such 21st-century illustrations of the global media debate and NWICO contextualize the relevance of this critical, interdisciplinary study of identity and socioeconomic development in Africa. This discussion is more critical when exploring how media plays a significant role in informing, educating, and persuading migrant-investors about socioeconomic political "on-the-ground" realities that would influence their decisions to invest in and/or return to their home countries.

Relationship of migrants to nations of origin through media and migration flows

Extensive research that delves into the relationship between media and communities or media and identity construction of the diaspora focus generally on the psychological aspect of the media-cultural relationship; few sources of literature discuss the direct economic effects of biased information on a country.

Diasporic media that focuses on connecting the diaspora to their homeland feature messages and perspectives directly from the homeland so that the diaspora receive nonmediated messages directly from their homeland's source. Kim and Olonade (2012) report the effect of such media as changing the views of diasporic female Nigerians about their country and continent; instead of a battlefield of massacres, they saw it instead as a "global village" with development and more positive images and representation. In addressing whether "the effects of connectivity [experienced by the Nigerian female Diaspora members] would make them want to return to their home country," Kim and Olonade (2012) refer to Lazarsfeld and Merton (1948), who highlight three conditions for media messages to have a strong effect (e.g., returning to the homeland): *monopolization*, *canalization*, and *supplementation* (p. 13).

Referring to the effects of returning to one's homeland, monopolization means the "absence of a counter voice or counter propaganda" (Kim & Olonade, 2012; Lazarsfeld & Merton, 1948), and hence a reinforcement of positive messages about development and progress (p. 13). Canalization refers to the targeting of pre-existing attitudes and values of the individual that would be merely reinforced by the positive or supportive messages of media (Kim & Olonade, 2012; Lazarsfeld & Merton, 1948). Lastly, supplementation refers to a two-step communication flow of face-to-face communication, which Kim and Olonade (2012) suggest would involve direct communication between the Nigerian female diaspora and those in the country who encourage their return by also reinforcing the value of their return for the country's progress.

Ultimately, media messages, particularly from the news, affect diaspora members, migrants, and expatriates in how they learn about and connect with their nations of origin. In the following section, we will identify the potential impacts of unjust news flow on the diaspora's decisions to invest in or contribute toward their home countries.

Potential impacts of news on the diaspora's decisions to invest in their nations of origin

"Africa-less"-ness and misconstrued self-identity development

Martin's (2008) study identifies that African-Americans may experience "stereotype threat" as a possible consequence of viewing negative portrayals of their race in the media. "Stereotype threat" refers to individuals' fear of confirming existing stereotypes with the group s/he identifies with, which ultimately leads to the manifestation of these fears as a result of self-fulfilling prophecies (Martin, 2008, p. 340). These social psychological discomforts and fears lead to hindered performances and depression. As a result of the devaluation of culture and identity, Martin (2008) refers to Arroyo and Zigler's (1995) concept of "racelessness" to describe how some African-Americans respond to this struggle and aim to portray a "raceless" persona to navigate their worlds and fulfill the demands of their own culture in the Black community and those of the majority culture in the Caucasian American community (Martin, 2008, p. 340). Martin (2008) further addresses racial identity development to address the application of Cross et al. (1991) description of a person's racial identity development that is incrementally organized into four stages: pre-encounter,

encounter, immersion-emersion, and internalization. Of significance, the pre-encounter stage highlights that where "individuals … consciously or unconsciously devalue their own sense of blackness and concurrently value majority ways and values" of where their self-worth stems from a White prism and influences their desire to acculturate and identify in White society" (Martin, 2008, p. 341). This is epitomized in a 1998 study in which the majority of 1,200 American children who were interviewed on how they perceive the portrayals of their race on television associated White characters with positive traits of financial and academic excellence, leadership, and intelligence, whereby minority characters were associated with illegal activities, financial struggles, unintelligible behavior, and poor work ethics (Burr, 2013).

Martin (2008) also states that "the negative images and devaluation of Blacks as seen in the media (news, cinema, or TV) can contribute to this stage as well as prevent a person from moving past it if the only sense of self he or she has derived is from negative depictions, creating a sense of self-hatred" (p. 341).

Similarly, the African diaspora—particularly those unfamiliar with their African homelands—may experience an "African-lessness" in their struggle to disassociate themselves from negative African stereotypes in the news. Such an experience enables them to forcibly navigate in a non-African world, and perhaps to position themselves even more strongly within their host country to feel culturally accepted. A self-denial and rejection of their African identity further weakens their cultural ties and connections to their African countries of origin. Their perceived lack of a sense of a belonging potentially results in their failure to connect with and identify with others that, unbeknownst to them, share more commonalities with them. Resulting isolations from cultural groups would result in failures to develop significant relationships with other African communities that they may otherwise have identified with.

Furthermore, by adopting another cultural lens other than that of their homeland when observing or engaging with their African homeland, the diaspora in a state of "African-lessness" or "African nation-lessness" adopts cultural and ideological biases that assert their separation of identity from their community or network of African citizen-residents. Hence, by displacing the cultural identity model and reducing opportunities for citizen-residents to accept them as community members, their relationship mirrors that of an African citizen-resident and a non-African foreign investor. After all, in this context, the diaspora neither self-identifies nor can be recognized or treated as a fellow community member in their African community.

The concept of African-lessness also threatens relationships with the African diaspora and their network in their host country. One may compare the disassociation of African-lessness from home communities with the projections of the "model minority" myth. A model minority member is a member of a minority group in a given community whose attainment of higher education, career advancements, high levels of income, and other highly distinguished societal traits mark them as more successful than other members of their population group. More widely applied in US cultural contexts, this concept reinforces stereotypes that historically pit Asian-Americans as finer examples of minorities against Hispanic-Americans and African-Americans who have been depicted as the less successful, violent, derogatory minority groups. The concept of the model minorities myth, however, has expanded to be applied more broadly to any particular group to whom it applies within a given context. However, the perpetuation of the model minority myth is dangerous as it proliferates stereotypes. Some may use it to justify and validate disparate, racial, or unjust treatment of different minority groups. In this context, some African diaspora members who embody an "African-lessness" and are accused of projecting themselves as "model minorities" may disassociate themselves from other Africans or nationals in their host community. This disassociation may reinforce negative stereotypes and mistreatment of the broader African diaspora in a host country and complicates their African nation-building efforts with key stakeholders in Africa's development, including other African diaspora groups.

Reinforced ignorance of developmental and informational resources

"Communication is a symbolic process whereby reality is produced, maintained, repaired, and transformed" (Carey, 1988, p. 23). "Similarly, communication, through language and other symbolic forms, comprises the ambience of human existence" (Carey, 1988, p. 24). The role of language and symbolism further contribute to the community that connects individuals to each other. Media messages and images that have been strategically framed, packaged, and produced as news coverage contribute toward "social constructions of reality" (Croteau et al., 2012b, p. 8). The diaspora are a particularly sensitive target audience of broadcast media, given that their own sociological identity is greatly influenced by the cultural dimension of communication.

Language in news coverage that continues to underrepresent and distort the image of Africa can dangerously misinform and miseducate the Africa diaspora about their homelands, cultures, and legacy. By disassociating themselves from African communities in host countries as a result of African-lessness, or simply by remaining ignorant of accurate "on-the-ground" realities, the diaspora potentially limit informational resources that would address and develop specific cultural and developmental needs within their hybrid cultural makeup. They also continue to remain misinformed about specific development opportunities they could otherwise learn about to invest in or contribute toward their African homelands.

Various organizations serve as information hubs or provide annual platforms, including annual African Business Conferences that are hosted in the United States, the United Kingdom, and other countries to inform audiences about business, investment, and entrepreneurial opportunities in Africa.

The rapid rise of social media and virtual platforms has resulted in more authorial control of individuals becoming storytellers and content creators. Individuals can assume journalistic control of the messages and media they create, produce, and disseminate on YouTube, Instagram, Pinterest, Facebook, blogs, personal websites, and various other platforms with little to no restrictions imposed by third-party sources. In so doing, marginalized groups that mainstream media systems have oppressed are increasingly empowered to bypass bureaucratic red tape, challenge the status quo by narrating their own truths and experiences, disseminating valuable informational resources through their own unfiltered lenses in their own voices.

Complacency and "Hopeless Africa" within the diaspora

Croteau and Hoynes (2006a) cite Susan Moeller, who

> argues that the nature of the news media's coverage of international events—focusing on pestilence, famine, death, and war—have helped to produce "compassion fatigue" among American citizens. The source of compassion fatigue, according to Moeller, is the news media's formulaic, sensationalistic, and image-driven coverage, which "helps us to feel overstimulated and bored all at once … The result is a growing sense that there is nothing that we can do about these faraway crises, which seem to disappear from the news media's radar screen as quickly as they appear. More generally, the news media's tendency to highlight dramatic problems with little context can discourage participation in public life and engagement with current affairs.
>
> (Croteau & Hoynes, 2006a, p. 218)

Such "compassion fatigue" is precisely the source of the complacency and dejection that have long characterized responses to Africa's "Dark Continent" depiction. This depiction is especially problematic for those of African descent who inherently desire to invest in their countries, but may be dissuaded by the perceived lack of economic and political instability, which Wahba (2006) and Bobeva (2006) argue are fundamental factors necessary to attract and encourage expatriates or migrants to invest in the country.

Arguably, such unstable conditions may not affect migrants from sending remittances—and may even heighten the urgency to send money and relieve the financial burdens of family members. However, collaborations between key stakeholders and investment decisions depend more on long-term development models than on short-term panaceas and emergency remedies provided by sporadic financial remittances. Hence, long-term development models require a trust in the nation's formal monetary channels, reliable infrastructure, and effective communication pathways that are not hindered by conflicting media messages of civil unrest, wars, and coup d'états—political or economic instability that would, otherwise, negate the effectiveness of some development opportunities.

Perpetual cycle of global hegemonic media production and distribution

Michira (2002) attributes negative portrayals of Africa in the media to "the commercialization of the media especially the entertainment and news industries in the West—which have perfected biased subjective presentation of inaccurate, fallacious images of propaganda about Africa, which are meant to suit the business interests of the media corporation" (Michira, 2002, p.2).

The *dual market model* of media organizations values the interests of advertisers and financiers. "With a profit orientation, it mattered less what the media content was, as long as it translated into profits" (Croteau & Hoynes, 2006a, p. 50). By centering on the basics of economic supply and demand, news media and information become a basic commodity of which media owners seek private, unregulated control and ownership (Croteau & Hoynes, 2006b, p. 17). In their pursuit of profit-maximizing opportunities to serve consumer interests, media owners seek innovative models to produce newer goods and services in the competitive marketplace at relatively lower costs (Croteau & Hoynes, 2006b, p. 17). The dual market of the market model signifies the role that advertising plays in the commercialization of the media. Consequently, when broadcast news media organizations seek to attract consumers to their news content, they are also selling these consumers to the advertisers who finance their media organization (Croteau & Hoynes, 2006c, p. 50).

Such commercialization of journalism accounts for a reduction in the standard of professionalism, which bears negative impacts on public audiences worldwide. Furthermore, in addition to less investment on investigative or international journalism (McChesney, 2004, p. 85), "[commercialism] also pushes journalists to make content directed at demographics considered desirable by media owners and big ticket advertisers" (McChesney, 2004, p. 87). McChesney (2004) further describes the racial and class bias and states that "African-American and Latinos are invisible or misrepresented in the news partly because they are not considered economically attractive to advertisers" (McChesney, 2004, p. 87). Vincent (2013) internationally contextualizes McChesney's (2004) study when he examines the potential impact of the Information Super Highway as an international initiative that links social policy with economic objectives to address issues of inequity. Vincent (2013) argues that those in developing countries may not benefit from such Western-driven initiatives, whose "ideological assumptions conflate the interests of communications corporations with the interest of citizens" (p. 16). Consequently, there is a growing challenge to represent a "new," more accurate identity for Africa when her doomsday images and supporting texts have branded the continent as "the dark continent" (Michira, 2002).

So long as journalism follows a capitalistic market model that thrives on profit margins and views African representation as economically unattractive to advertisers, the imbalance and distorted portrayals in the media may continue to reverberate. This will also perpetuate the cycle of hegemonic media products that articulate the relevance of the global media–NWICO debate of the 1950s in the 21st century.

Recruitment challenges for African companies

Media audiences from diverse cultural backgrounds, particularly those of hybrid identities or multinational African backgrounds, would, therefore continue to learn of their "home" as a site of terror and hopelessness. Consequently, such mediated exposure to the continent does not serve to educate or mobilize them to actively participate in and invest in the development of the continent.

A challenge for organizations in Africa to market their companies to employers and attract competitive talent.

Recruitment companies across Africa have reported challenges in recruiting Africans from the Diaspora whose perceptions are tainted by portrayals of Africa in the media, including the misconceptions that they would gain less salaries compared to the West, or that companies in Africa would not want them, but would prefer an expatriate.

In Forbes, Dr Menghis Bairu, founder and CEO of Serenus Biotherapeutics, notes the importance of communicating and marketing a narrative that will impact Africa's economy:

> And it's not just a matter of attracting African expatriates home. We need to share the story of world class opportunities that are available for world class talent. That includes not only drawing Africa's best and brightest across borders to build our collective economy, but also attract talented professionals from developed nations who have a passion for the continent and find rewards in being challenged to build, contribute and grow.
>
> (Bairu, 2015, para. 12)

Faye Tillery, a travel blogger and entrepreneur who advises potential investors in foreign real estate, notes that inaccurate media coverage leads to distorted impressions of African real estate, including the misconception that it is cheap (Givens, 2020).

Therefore, the necessity of fair and balanced news flow is not only a professional requirement of ethical journalism. Marginalized groups need more accurate representation in media and through storytelling platforms to gain information that will shape the decisions that affect their welfare. The ability to make informed key decisions will equip them with vital tools, information, and the critical resources required to develop key sectors of their countries and apply their knowledge, skillsets, and other competencies toward job creation, value-generating opportunities, and long-term sustainable development.

Necessity for alternative, African-Centric media

Avle (2011) critically examines the role of globalization and media's impact on cultural communities and democracies in the Global South. She examines factors of "[a] vibrant media ecology … [that] have led to the liberalization of the broadcast industry, reconstitution of the public sphere and creation of a new 'cultural elite' in Ghana" (Avle, 2011, p.1). The highly skilled natives of Ghana who were educated in Europe and the United States "were most vocal about their ideologies and could influence the socio-political climate in the country" (Avle, 2011, p. 20). The "cultural elites" represent mobile publics who, with "brain circulation of talent," and "networked publics" (Avle, 2011, p. 20), serve as sources of intervention to redeem cultural and political opportunities in developing countries.

It is critical, therefore, that Africans invest in developing their own media platforms so that they are in a position to narrate their stories and inform global target audiences about their own agendas, as articulated by former prime minister of India, Indira Ghandi:

> We want to hear Africans on events in Africa. You should similarly be able to get an Indian explanation of events in India. It is astonishing that we know so little about leading poets, novelists, historians, and editors of various Asian, African, and Latin American countries while we are familiar with minor authors and columnists of Europe and America.
>
> (MacBride & Roach, 1993, p, 6)

In the attempt to enable Africans to make informed decisions about their role in Africa's future, the African Business Reporting Awards, organized by Africa Practice, focused reporting on more balanced African stories that are "less skewed towards political unrest and disasters … which are vital to create an enabling environment for businesses to succeed in Africa—which would lead to less need for handouts" (Ethical Consumer, 2009). The organization has experienced positive results in African investments as a consequence of more balanced reporting. More balanced reporting from African-centered media organizations would generate more similar, optimal results for Africa's development.

Ultimately, the illustrations of media's impact on investment decisions underscores the relevance of the *magic bullet theory*, or *hypodermic needle theory*, in communications fields. Both theories, introduced in the late 1930s, implied that mass media had a direct, powerful impact on the minds of a passive audience and controlled their behavior. The media was represented either as a magic gun that fired the message into the audience's minds, unbeknownst to them, or a needle that injected the message into audiences' heads.

The hypodermic needle theory gained significance after audiences who had tuned into the "War of the Worlds" radio program about Martians landing in New Jersey and attacking people mistakenly believed that they, too, would be attacked. Reacting in panic, they bought emergency supplies—birthing the idea of "the panic broadcast" (Wroblewski, 2018). These theories were addressed by the *two-step flow of communication model*—originally introduced by sociologist Paul Lazarsfeld et al. in 1944 and further elaborated upon by Elihu Katz and Lazarsfeld in1955.

This model introduces an intermediary step between mass media and the audience: opinion leaders. Opinion leaders are those who interpret the media, form their opinion, and share it with wider audiences whom they influence. Opinion leaders are increasingly recognized as influencers on social media, whose content creation and endorsement of news posts rapidly reach large audiences with calls-to-action to support or fund a cause, charity, business, or investment proposal—or criticize, boycott, or "cancel" unfavorable issues or celebrities.

Indeed, the advent of digitization and virtual communication—primarily through innovative social media platforms—facilitates a flow of news and information that is critical for decision-making. The uses of social media and technology have further increased participation in national development among the diaspora. Wetherell (2013) notes in *TechPresident* that "social media has connected and mobilized Africans watching developments in their home countries from abroad, and they're working to counter narratives of incapability and dependence espoused by NGOs and the international media" (para. 2). Ruge, a Ugandan social media strategist who, in 2013, reported in *The Guardian Professional* that "Twitter, Facebook and other forms of social media are bringing African voices and new, varied narratives to the forefront ... These tools are also being used to replace staid development paradigms, by organising and developing African-driven institutions" (Wetherell, 2013, para.2).

Hence, by relying less on international media to report on Africa and more on its own resources, Africa becomes increasingly self-sustaining in solving some of its own problems. Asante (2013) observes the importance of contextualizing crises within European colonial political and ethnic reconfigurations and interpreting the news through the lens of African philosophical values and concepts.

It is important that the media showcases some of the works and stories that hail from Africa by Africans and her diaspora. More media platforms can educate the world about Africa to change the narrative that has depicted Africa as a "Dark Continent." The consistent stereotypes of flies swarming around orphaned children or naked clansmen, juxtaposed near on-screen texts soliciting donations, cannot continue to be the sole depictions of the diverse, rich African continent, which also boasts skyscrapers, luxury vehicles, state-of-the-art buildings and homes, and a fast-growing population of middle-class and high-net worth individuals—who are rarely portrayed in media. Increased efforts by nonprofit organizations; more alternative media outlets, including Nalugwa Productions, Inc.; African-based for-profit news outlets; the proliferation of social media platforms; and increased content from Nigerian, South African, and other original African content producers distributed through platforms like iroKo, Netflix, and M-Net streaming services demonstrate an increased global and Pan-African collective commitment toward promoting African products.

Critical theory requires an emancipatory potential that challenges the status quo of society and seeks to liberate the oppressed from their oppressors. The relationships between the oppressed and their oppressors have manifested differently over generations, and these power dynamics are reflected in media portrayals and representations of racial and ethnic "minority" groups. In addition to physical forms of capital that Marxian scholars refer to as primary sources of power, intellectual capital is a vital source of wealth and power in society that those in dominant positions also seek to control. The perpetual imbalance and distortion in news coverage in the 21st century adversely impacts global audiences and the African diaspora, whose interpretation of news coverage and misleading information may negatively affect their perception of actual development opportunities in Africa. While I do not deny atrocities that certainly occur across the African continent—as they also occur elsewhere—I argue for more balanced and fair representation of content about Africa that also privileges voices of Africans who have been historically excluded, underrepresented and misrepresented from media platforms.

Understanding the potential impacts of such unjust news flow reinforces the urgency in investing in African-centric news and media production. Audiences are encouraged to seek or create alternative media platforms that empower them and others as informed key stakeholders and pivotal actors in their African nations' development.

Chapter summary

Key concepts

canalization	magic bullet theory or hypodermic needle theory
compassion fatigue	media imperialism
cultural imperialism	monopolization
dual market model	New World Information and Communication Order (NWICO)
global media debate	supplementation
	two-step flow of communication model

Discussion questions:

1) Describe a specific occasion when the media portrayal of an event or cultural group contrasted with your lived reality. What underlying factors do you believe influenced these media portrayals?

2) Do you believe that the media industry has evolved in its representation of African-centric content? Why or why not? In your analysis, be sure to cite specific examples as they relate to policies, industry trends, and other factors to support your analysis.
3) Identify a media program or platform (print or digital media) that caters to the representation of Africans across the globe. Describe the platform and its objectives. What are some of the strengths of this program? What are its various impacts on some of its diverse audiences? Identify areas for improvement and recommendations to address some of the challenges that you have presented.

Bibliography

Arroyo, C. G., & Zigler, E. (1995). Racial identity, academic achievement, and the psychological well-being of economically disadvantaged adolescents. *Journal of Personality and Social Psychology, 69*(5), 903–914. https://doi.org/10.1037/0022-3514.69.5.903

Asante, M. K. (2013). The Western media and the falsification of Africa: Complications of value and evaluation. *China Media Research, 9*(2), 64–70.

Avle, S. (2011). Global flows, media and developing democracies: The Ghanaian case. *Journal of African Media Studies, 3*(1), 7–23. doi:10.1386/jams.3.1.7_1

Bairu, M. (2015, April 14). In *Africa, Moving From A Brain Drain To A Brain Gain*. Forbes. https://www.forbes.com/sites/realspin/2015/04/14/in-africa-moving-from-a-brain-drain-to-a-brain-gain/?sh=7201a7ba330e

Besova, A. A., & Cooley, S. C. (2009). Foreign news and public opinion: Attribute agenda-setting theory revisited. *Ecquid Novi: African Journalism Studies, 30*(2), 219–242. doi:10.3368/ajs.30.2.219

Birch, S. (2009). Africa in the media. *Ethical Consumer, 118*. http://www.ethicalconsumer.org/commentanalysis/ethicalsceptic/isafricaalwaysbadnews.aspx

Bobeva, D. (2006). Turning remittances into investments. In OECD. *Migration, remittances and development* (pp. 297–312). In OECD Publishing. doi: 10.1787/9789264013896-22-en

Burr, S. (2013). Television and societal effects: An analysis of media images of African-Americans in historical context. *Journal of Gender, Race and Justice, 4*, 1–3.

Carey, J. (1988). A cultural approach to communication. In: D. Thornborn (Ed.), *Communication as Culture* (pp. 13–36). New York: Unwin Hyman.

Cross, W. E., Jr., Parham, T. A., & Helms, J. E. (1991). The stages of Black identity development: Nigrescence models. In R. L. Jones (Ed.), *Black psychology* (pp. 319–338). Cobb & Henry Publishers.

Croteau, D., & Hoynes, W. (2006a). How the media business influences society. In: *The business of media—corporate media and the public interest* (pp. 191–221). Thousand Oaks, CA: Pine Forge Press.

Croteau, D., & Hoynes, W. (2006b). Media, markets, and the public sphere. *The business of media—corporate media and the public interest* (pp.17–23). Thousand Oaks, CA: Pine Forge Press.

Croteau, D., & Hoynes, W. (2006c). The rise and (de) regulation of the media industry. *The business of media—corporate media and the public interest* (pp.50–65). Thousand Oaks, CA: Pine Forge Press.

Croteau, D., Hoynes, W., & Milan, S. (2012a). Content: Media representations of the social world. In: *Media and society* (pp. 151–185). Los Angeles, CA: Sage Publications.

Croteau, D., Hoynes, W., & Milan, S. (2012b). Media and the social world. In: *Media and society* (pp. 3–28). Los Angeles, CA: Sage Publications.

Croteau, D., Hoynes, W., & Milan, S. (2012c). Production: The media industry and the social world. In: *Media and society* (pp. 29–113). Los Angeles, CA: Sage Publications.

Gerbner, G., Mowlana, H., & Nordenstreng, K. (Eds.). (1993). *The global media debate: Its rise, fall and renewal (communication and information science series).* Norwood, NJ: Ablex Publishing Corporation.

Givens, D. (2020, April 6). Thinking of moving to Africa? Here's how to invest in real estate on the continent. *Black Enterprise.* https://www.blackenterprise.com/how-to-invest-in-real-estate-in-africa/

Hawkins, V. (2018, January 16). *"Shithole" Countries? The Media's Portrayal of Africa Reconsidered.* Fair Observer. https://www.fairobserver.com/region/africa/donald-trump-shithole-countries-media-africa-coverage-news-headlines-87600/

Himelboim, I., Chang, T. K., & McCreery, S. (2010). International Network of Foreign News Coverage: Old Global Hierarchies in a New Online World. *Journalism & Mass Communication Quarterly,* *87*(2), 297–314. https://doi.org/10.1177/107769901008700205

Kim, J., & Oyelade, A. (2012). *"Diasporas in virtual homeland: The role of the Internet in the lives of female Nigerians."* Intercultural Communication Association, Phoenix, Arizona.

Kleinwachter, W. (1993). Three waves of the debate. In: G. Gerbner, H. Mowlana, & K. Nordenstreng (Eds.), *The Global Media Debate—Its Rise, Fall, and Renewal* (pp. 13–20). Norwood, NJ: Ablex Publishing Corporation.

Kothari, A. (2010). The framing of the Darfur conflict in the New York Times: 2003–2006. *Journalism Studies, 11*(2), 209–224. doi:10.1080/14616700903481978

Kunihara, S. (2007). Africa in American media: A content analysis of *Newsweek* magazine's portrayal of Africa, 1988–2006. https://www.saintmarys.edu/files/Stella%20Maris%20Pap.doc

Lazarsfeld, P.F. and Merton, R.K. (1948). Mass communication, popular taste and organized social action. In Bryson, L. (ed.) *The Communication of Ideas,* New York: Harper and Brothers, pp. 95–118.

MacBride, S., & Roach, C. (1993). The new international information order. In: G. Gerbner, H. Mowlana, & K. Nordenstreng (Eds.), *The Global Media Debate—Its Rise, Fall, and Renewal* (pp. 3–11). Norwood, NJ: Ablex Publishing Corporation.

Martin, A. C. (2008). Television media as a potential negative factor in the racial identity development of African American youth. *Academic Psychiatry* , *32*(4), 338–342.

McChesney, R. (2004). Understanding U.S. journalism I: Corporate control and professionalism. In *The Problem of the Media* (pp. 85–89). New York : Monthly Review Press.

Michira, J. (2002, December 23). *Images of Africa in the Western Media.* Minnesota State University: Moorhead. http://web.mnstate.edu/robertsb/313/images_of_africa_michira.pdf

Vincent, R. (2013). The New World Information and Communication Order (NWICO) in the context of the information super-highway. Retrieved from http://www.academia.edu/4041289/THE_NEW_WORLD_INFORMATION_AND_COMMUNICATION_ORDER_NWICO_IN_THE_CONTEXT_OF_THE_INFORMATION_SUPER-HIGHWAY

Wahba, J. (2006). What is the macroeconomic impact of international remittances on the home country? In OECD. *Migration, remittances and development* (pp. 185–191). OECD Publishing. doi: 10.1787/9789264013896-13-en

Wetherell, J. (2013, February 8). On social media, the African diaspora redirects the conversation on international aid. *TechPresident*. http://techpresident.com/news/wegov/23476/african-diaspora-leveraging-social-media-redirect-conversation-international-aid

White, R. (1993). The new order and the Third World. In: G. Gerbner, H. Mowlana, & K. Nordenstreng (Eds.), *The Global Media Debate—Its Rise, Fall, and Renewal* (pp. 3–11). Norwood, NJ: Ablex Publishing Corporation.

Wroblewski, M. T. (2018, January 21). *What is the Magic Bullet Theory of Mass Media?* Small Business - Chron.Com. https://smallbusiness.chron.com/magic-bullet-theory-mass-media-3346.html

11 It's not just politics … or is it?

Engaging the African diaspora in Africa's political affairs

Even from afar, many diaspora Africans seek various ways to be politically engaged with or to participate in the political affairs of their African home countries. Through their roles as policy makers, educators, media professionals, social influencers, grassroots leaders, and engaged stakeholders, the diaspora have served as unofficial or official ambassadors and engaged with their home countries.

However, the diaspora face various challenges in their efforts to be politically engaged with their home nations. Some desire to be more politically involved or engaged with the affairs of their African home nations, but for various reasons, choose to be disengaged or limit their participation. They may believe that voting is the sole way to lend their voices to critical issues, and if they are ineligible or unable to vote, then they disengage from other political options. Others fear for their safety and will refrain from any political activity to avoid risking their lives or those of their families, especially if the political climate in their home country is fragile. Regardless of the reason, most will agree that participating in the political affairs of one's country is fundamentally important and shapes the development of a nation. And some simply believe that the diaspora are uninformed about the realities of their home nations and should disengage from or limit their engagement in their homelands' political affairs.

This chapter will introduce a common complexity that many nation-states face with regards to their diaspora populations in the context of political engagement. The chapter will also present complex state–diaspora relationships that are not particularly unique to the African diaspora, yet are still significant in the context of national development. The chapter will also illustrate various forms of political participation and engagement to showcase ways that African diaspora members contribute to the political spheres of their African nations, engage with citizens in their homelands, and can identify ways to make a difference in the political landscape of their African nations.

Overview of complex state–diaspora relationships

There remains a push-and-pull dynamic and dance between many nations' governments and their diaspora citizens—African state–diaspora relationships are no exception. The ability of the African diaspora to play active roles in their nations'

DOI: 10.4324/9781351031660-14

political affairs is not straightforward or easy. While the role of the African diaspora in shaping Africa's political agenda may be arguably understood to be significant, the degree to which the diaspora can be politically involved is debatable, particularly regarding voting rights. This debate highlights the conundrum in state–diaspora relationships, as articulated by Østergaard-Nielsen (2003):

> While sending countries are quick to call for their expatriate population's economic and political contribution to development in the country of origin, it is clear that most expatriates and their representative organizations expect this to be a two-way deal … Migrant and diaspora groups demand more transparency and good governance in order to feel that their remittances and foreign direct investment is spent in the best possible way. [Acting as ambassadors of their countries of origin overseas], they would often like some influence on the policies that they are expected to represent.
>
> (Vertovek, 2004, p. 36)

In light of this fragile relationship, governments and African diasporic communities around the world have launched various initiatives and engaged in different approaches to promote political participation in their country.

Expanding the concept of political engagement: Manifest versus civil political participation

There are various ways to engage in the political affairs of a nation so as to contribute toward its development. Some argue that manifest activities, or those that are more explicit—like voting—carry the most impact in shaping the political agenda of a nation. *Manifest political participation* refers to goal-oriented or rational, observable, and measurable actions that explicitly influence political outcomes or public affairs (Ekman & Amna, 2012). Some individual activities that are manifest may more easily be recognized through their formal and conventional nature, such as electoral participation, contact, or party activity (Ekman & Amna, 2012; Teorell et al., 2007).

However, other political activities that are less explicit may be falsely presumed to have little influence on political participation. Also categorized as "civil participation," these latent, less obvious forms of political participation may not be readily identifiable as being "political" or influential in transforming the landscape. Ekman and Amna (2012) subdivide this category into two groups: *social involvement*, characterized by attentiveness; and *civic engagement,* characterized by action.

Collective civic engagement highlights active involvement through affiliations with organizations, e.g., faith-based charity work or volunteering through an organization. Civil participation, also referred to as *support activities*, can also lead to active political engagement. Individuals who attend events, concerts or other activities that are designed to raise awareness of an issue may seek ways to learn more about that topic and eventually become more politically involved in those issues. Hence, although voting is a critical component of civic responsibility in influencing the political landscape, other forms of political participation that may be more subtle are equally important.

Recognizing the value in manifest and civil forms of political participation, particularly across different cultural and geographical contexts, expands a global view of how the African diaspora could contribute toward their nations' political development. Some individuals may dismiss, disregard, or forgo pursuing certain activities that they consider "unconventional." Such an attitude or behavior, however, could result in unintentional or uninformed decisions to be apolitical or nonpolitical. This may be unfortunate if a person desires to contribute to the political affairs of one's home nation but self-censors due to a false perception that their contributions would have little to no impact on their nation's development. But regardless of manifest or latent forms of political engagement—conducted individually or collectively with other community members in the diaspora or in Africa—the African diaspora can help shape the political landscape of their home country and serve as vital ambassadors to their host countries, if they choose to do so.

Let us explore some examples of how the African diaspora and some African governments have engaged in or have fostered various manifest and civil forms of participation to shape their nations' political agenda:

Voting

There remains great debate surrounding the diaspora's participation in their electoral process, particularly regarding voting rights. Many may agree that participating in the political affairs of one's country is fundamentally important and critical in shaping a nation's development. Advocates for diaspora voting rights, therefore, argue that their ability to vote in their home country is a citizenship birthright that should not be revoked. They assert that voting integrates all citizens—including the diaspora—into the public affairs and decision-making spaces of their home nation. Ultimately, voting reaffirms and reclaims their political identity and citizenship and allows them to fulfil their civic duties and responsibilities. Furthermore, as the diaspora's remittances and contributions tend to be the largest source of foreign aid that impact their nations' economy, many consider it exploitative when they are denied voting rights. Some countries have offered dual citizenship to their diaspora but have denied them voting rights in their home country, the cause of some of the tensions between some diasporic groups and their home countries.

Arguments opposing diaspora voting rights emphasize the diaspora's separation from their home country; question the assertion of their national identity; criticize their lack of understanding of issues on the ground and of candidates; and reinforce that the diaspora's short-term presence in the country makes them "blindsided" or that they lack understanding of the on-the-ground realities of day-to-day life. All these reasons underscore the following concern: the diaspora would be positioned to greatly influence the livelihood of citizen-residents who remain on the ground to bear the consequences of decisions made by those who reside outside of the country.

There are also views—though perhaps expressed less overtly—that some governments may resist granting voting rights to their diaspora because they seek to curtail the level of influence the diaspora may have on their leadership; fear that the diaspora's influence on local communities may empower, lead, or mobilize some citizen-residents to uprise with opposition parties; and fear that the diaspora could re-assert dominant ethnic majority votes that would (i) lead to their losing elections, (ii) increase the decision-making power of rivalry dominant ethnic groups, and (iii) transform their socioeconomic and political agenda.

However, several governments have also recognized the value of including the diaspora in their electoral processes. Politicians have incorporated perspectives and insights from the diaspora within their campaigns to address their lived experiences and realities abroad. As of 2015, 23 African nations granted voting rights to their diasporas in their host communities, including those originating from Algeria, Mozambique, Benin, Algeria, Mali, and Namibia. In 2013, Guinea Conakry granted voting rights to its diaspora, resulting in about 123,000 voters registered in 18 different embassies and consulates that participated in the legislative election in late September 2013 (Laloupo, 2014, p. 24). Electoral processes, campaigns, and communications have been designed to be inclusive of the plurality of voices from both home and host countries. Such universal suffrage positions nations to identify the diverse political and ideological perspectives across the wide spectrum of their different African communities across the globe (Laloupo, 2014, p. 23).

Perhaps Laloupo's (2014) observation articulates the positionality of the African diaspora vis-à-vis their quest to remain engaged politically through voting:

> The purpose of the right to vote is not to turn all Africans living abroad into political actors, but to strengthen citizens' awareness and their feeling of belonging to a collective destiny … While the influence of the "opinion of the diaspora" remains relative, it is not secondary. It imperceptibly influences political situations and decisions. Their opinion is not intended to be essential, but it is a contribution, confined as it is within its objective limits.
>
> (Laloupo, 2014, p. 25)

Although voting clearly illustrates how the diaspora may remain politically engaged in their home countries and thereby contribute toward their home nations' development, it remains unclear and debatable that voting rights would naturally lead to a nation's democratization or achievement of its sustainable development goals. This reinforces the importance of identifying other forms of political engagement, as we will see.

Shaping policies and "good" governance

The African diaspora could also concentrate their efforts on developing policy initiatives that support priority areas of development. For instance, in 2019, *The African Governance Report*, published by the Mo Ibrahim Foundation, revealed data that indicates the progress that the Africa Union and the UN are making toward their Agenda 2063 and Sustainable Development Goals (SDGs), respectively. As per the 2019 report, some of the following priority areas to address through the following recommendations are (i) quality of education, with emphasis on aligning education with market needs of job requirements, which could be achieved through stronger partnerships between governments, relevant actors, and the private sector; (ii) healthcare and food security, including improving the quality, affordability, and availability of healthcare; and (iii) increasing prosperity and economic opportunities by diversifying economies and continuing to invest in the effectiveness and efficiency of infrastructure, ICT, the rural sector, and regional integration. Ultimately, these findings reinforce the importance of developing policies, systems, and frameworks that support their implementation, contextualized to each African country. Enhancing effective governance would also allow for equitable provisions of these goods and services throughout the country and lead to positive spill-over effects in other sectors that shape development.

This also leads to another platform: the African Diaspora could also contribute to their nations' sustainable development by helping to shape policies that support governance. The Mo Ibrahim Foundation (MIF), an African foundation developed by Mo Ibrahim in 2006, is one of the key institutions established to support governance and leadership in Africa. The MIF defines *governance* as the "provision of the political, social and economic public goods and services that every citizen has the right to expect from their state, and that a state has the responsibility to deliver to its citizens" (Mo Ibrahim Foundation website). The MIF developed several initiatives to define, assess, and enhance governance and leadership in Africa. One initiative is the Ibrahim Index of African Governance (IIAG), a statistical assessment tool that measures and monitors African countries' governance performance across four key components: Safety & Rule of Law, Participation & Human Rights, Sustainable Economic Opportunity, and Human Development. The IIAG focuses on assessing the outputs and outcomes of policy to inform and support policy solutions.

However, various historical accounts and contemporary analyses have lamented that Africa has a failed democracy or a failing democratization process that complicates opportunities to promote good governance. This perspective is reinforced through some African nations' ad hoc violent protests and demonstrations; underrepresented groups and ethnicities who are denied voting rights or are minimally represented in government; or opponents of political parties who have been jailed or attacked for expressing their contrary viewpoints, citing corruption. "The rigging of elections, amendments to constitutions to enable ruling parties to remain in power indefinitely, and electoral violence" reinforce these concerns (Tutlam et al., 2019, p. 32; Adejumobi, 2000). Tutlam et al. (2019) also note that "the use of violence to silence people from exercising their fundamental freedoms such as the right to free expression (Southern African Litigation Centre 2015) and association (International Service for Human Rights 2016) has become frequent occurrences across the continent" (p. 32).

Although democracy does not necessarily lead directly to sustainable development, there is an inextricable link between the two. Democracy has been associated with governance, which various international aid and development organizations use as a policy instrument to promote sustainable development in developing countries. With a keen focus on development, the diaspora can aim to reform policies, systems, procedures, and structural frameworks that enhance leadership effectiveness that will set the moral tone of the country; strengthen accountability mechanisms to address corruption, ensure equity, and preserve universal human rights; strengthen frameworks to improve education that supports citizens' literacy, activism, entrepreneurialism, or professional marketability in various socioeconomic and political affairs in their countries; and mobilize innovation and increase investments in healthcare, infrastructure, and rural sectors across regions. Such cross-cutting solutions would help to create an enabling environment that promotes growth, prosperity, and sustainable development that addresses the needs of the African country.

The Brookings Institution also acknowledges that Africa's road to political and economic transformation lies in the interconnectedness of "good governance, democracy, respect for human rights, justice and the rule of law," as articulated in the Africa Union's (AU) 50-year development and transformation program, listed in Agenda 2063 (Mbaku, 2020, p. 23).

But what exactly is "good" governance, and how can the diaspora help to implement "good" governance in their African home nations? Various scholars' and theorists' models of governance conclude that a universal model of "good" governance is still in development. There remains no universal or single answer of what "good" governance is (Asaaduzzaman & Virtanen 2018, p. 6; Human Development Report, 2002). However, institutions like the World Bank Group, the United Nations Development Programme (UNDP), and the Organization for Economic Co-operation and Development (OECD) refer to similar, overlapping sets of criteria that they view as preconditions for "good" governance to support their work in aid-receiving countries: political accountability; freedom of association and participation; promotion of the rule of law and independence of the judiciary; bureaucratic accountability; freedom of information; a sound administrative system; equal participation of all citizens in decision-making; transparent, accountable, and equitable systems; power decentralization; responsiveness; consensus orientation; effectiveness and efficiency and strategic vision (Asaaduzzaman & Virtanen 2018). The African Development Bank accredits effective states, mobilized civil societies, and an efficient private sector as preconditions for good governance that similarly reflect accountability citizen participation; transparency, ,combating corruption, and an enabling legal/judicial framework (Mbaku, 2020).

In efforts toward developing policies, systems, and development models, the African Diaspora and other stakeholders should also consider the subjectivity and agency of "good" governance:

(i) First, the term "good" bears normative assumptions of value that are subjective. Who determines what is "good" or "bad," and whose normative values justify this? What may be considered "good" or "bad" would vary by context.
(ii) Second, determining if governance is "good" or "bad" should be reflective of the quality of outcomes that impact the people and health of a nation's political, social, and cultural economy; the quality of governance should not be reflective of the instrument or policy itself. Consequently, it is critical that the beneficiaries of aid and citizens of the country are given authority in determining the quality of governance.
(iii) Third, global and regional influences exert more influence in developing countries than in developed countries (Asaaduzzaman & Virtanen 2018; Farazmand, 2013). Farazmand (2013) therefore, proposed that "sound governance" replace "good governance" to emphasize the inclusiveness, participation, and interaction of various actors and stakeholders in the complex, dynamic, and diverse national and global environment (Asaaduzzaman & Virtanen 2018). These actors and stakeholders include "the state as an enabling institution, the constitutional framework, the civil society, the private sector, the engaged citizens, and the international/global institutional structure within limits" (Asaaduzzaman & Virtanen 2018, p. 7).

Integrating cultural dynamics within already complex political, socioeconomic models is vital to developing a model that is adaptive to the dynamic needs of the local and global environment, yet also resilient in managing conflict peacefully and promoting community cohesion after crises.

It would also be key for diaspora and citizen-residents to acknowledge and effectively manage cultural biases in their engagements. These biases may perpetuate rivalry and factionalism that could adversely affect their activism and political activities. According to some analysts, various cases of factionalism have influenced activism by African diasporas hailing from Nigeria, Cameroon, and Kenya, to name, but a few countries; in the United Kingdom, diverse political opinions held by the Zimbabwean diaspora community, for instance, have also perpetuated factionalism and affected their activism. Some countries' internal conflicts also originate from decade-long ethnic divisions or historical tensions between religious groups, including Muslim and Christian groups. Hence, it could be helpful to consider which frameworks could incorporate cross-cultural conflict resolution strategies and accommodate conditions for public diplomatic efforts that restore relationships between opposing groups.

The diaspora could also strengthen engagements in their various networks and stakeholder organizations within their host countries to help refine democratization processes in their homelands through more formal and structured frameworks. The diaspora residing in host countries may have more localized context of their home countries to help them understand some of the historical, cultural, and socioeconomic complexities involved, compared to some of the external actors.

The African diaspora can play an important role in further shaping this discourse through feasible interventions and realizable actions. Some of these interventions and actions include implementing public policies and conflict-resolution and peacebuilding instruments; creating migration and development funds to support political and economic priorities; and developing systems and practices that support "good" governance, human rights, rule of law, and sustainable economic opportunity and human development. In the words of former United Nations Secretary-General Kofi Annan, "Good governance is perhaps the single most important factor in eradicating poverty and promoting development" (Mbaku, 2020, p. 23).

As we will see in the next section of this chapter, some interventions to support "good" governance" and the development agenda have required coordination between the diaspora and citizen-residents in Africa—facilitated by social and digital media technological breakthroughs. The result: significant global milestones that are rapidly and drastically redefining Africa's political landscape and transforming development.

The role of social and digital media in political activism

Exploring theories related to social movement in the social media era

Among the various ways that the African diaspora have remained engaged in their home countries' political affairs is by supporting the *protest behavior* of citizen residents on the ground. Protests, demonstrations, marches, boycotts, and strikes are examples of protest behavior that range from silent and peaceful to violent and destructive forms of rebellion. They could also be classified as *collective behavior*, or forms of activities that people voluntarily engage in, or as parts of a *social movement*—"purposeful, organized groups striving to work toward a common goal" (Little, 2014, para. 4). Regardless of their classification, social movements have played critical roles in triggering social change.

The rise of ICT and social media have also played a critical role in the development and effectiveness of social movements. There have also been studies and debates about how the prominence of digital technology refutes or supports some of the traditional theories related to social movements. In our context, there is value in understanding how these different theories can help to predict or explain the types of protest behavior and collective interactions between the African diaspora and stakeholders in their host and home nations to support their homeland.

Let us begin our exploration with the classical *collective theorists of social movements*, including Neil Smelser, Ralph Turner and Lewis Killian. These theorists viewed social movements as irrational, disorganized behavior that stemmed from structural strains, pressures, and changes in norms and values that conflict with societal values or leaders in authoritative positions. Values from different groups, such as minorities, immigrants, and the youth, that are in conflict with those of the established groups often contribute to these strains. These earlier theories emphasized that conditions rooted in individual factors, including psychological states of alienation, isolation, deprivation, discontent, and frustration, as well as sociological factors like poverty and suffering—supported by the paradoxical notion of the hope of alleviating such conditions—formed the basis of these sudden social movements, which were disruptions to social order.

However, in the 1960s and 1970s, theorists like John D. McCarthy and Mayor N. Zald opposed these classical theories' assertions that social movements were irrational, sudden, social disruptions that stemmed from alienated and disgruntled protesters. Departing from this paradigm, their works outlined fundamental principles of *resource mobilization theory*, which posits that social movements stem from rational, organized, planned strategies that rely on resources to be effective. Sociologists of this theory categorized five resource groups needed to fuel social movements: (i) *material resources*, or tangible resources like money and financial capital, physical supplies, location; (ii) *human resources* or labor capital, e.g., paid or unpaid volunteers, staff, or professionals in a particular field or industry related to the cause; (iii) *social-organizational resources*, or resources that build social-movement organizations' networks, e.g., mailing lists, strategies, recruitment policies; (iv) *cultural resources*, including the knowledge, skillsets, and aptitudes or media products that can facilitate the cause; and (v) *moral resources*, or sources that legitimize the movement's cause, strengthen its credibility, and further its goals.

We can see how the relevance of these theories—particularly of resource mobilization theory—is evident in coordinated efforts between the diaspora and their counterparts in their homelands during political unrest. The diaspora and citizen-residents on the ground will organize networks to funnel critical information to each other through websites, social media, and other communicative platforms; coordinate money transfers to victims in hospital; fund resources that support activists on the frontline; develop online petitions to manage desired calls-to-action; or engage in meetings with political lobbyists. Such efforts require the mobilization of resource groups to effectively fuel the social movement.

Framing theory addresses the gaps in resource mobilization theory to explain why supporters would align with a cause at any given time, especially if there were a lack of resources to adequately plan a social movement, or a lack of individual and social factors to prompt sudden disruption to a social order. By presenting or framing issues in a way that resonates with the values, attitudes, and commonly held beliefs of supporters, social movements can appeal to supporters who readily identify and understand the issues and can follow their accompanying norms in any given situation.

Another principle theory that is relevant to discourse about social movements is the *political processes* or *political opportunity theory*. Political processes theory acknowledges the restrictions of formal organizations that overlook dynamics of networks in classical collective social movement theories, and unlike resource mobilization theory, which focuses on internal dynamics, it presents factors external to the movement that affect social movements (Hara & Huang, 2010; Tarrow, 1998). These factors consist of four conditions of a political climate, or political context, that affect the opportunity or potential for social movement activity: "(i) relative openness or closure of an institutionalized political system, or access to political decision-making power; (ii) stability or instability in the alignment of ruling elites; (iii) access to elite allies, and (v) the state's capacity and propensity for repression" (Hara & Huang, 2010, p. 6; McAdam, 1996, p. 27; Meyer, 2004).

Lastly, the *new social movement theory* (NST) that emerged in western Europe in the 1980s rebelled against the traditional theories of social movements. The new social movement theory emphasized its appeal to protesters on issues central to identity, values, and cultural dimensions of "race, ethnicity, youth, sexuality, countercultures, environmentalism, pacifism, human rights, and the like" (Buechler, 1995, abstract).

In the contemporary digitally driven global era, online movements have challenged or supported the relevance of these theories. The internet makes it easier for activists to share rapid, real-time news and receive responses and engagement from followers and supporters to the cause. Although this does not devalue traditional and conventional media, online activity makes news faster and more accessible and covers larger populations. Nowadays, news in shorter soundbites appeals more to consumers who are invited and triggered to specific calls-to-action.

Individuals and groups can also access alternative frames that pluralize the diversity of information that consumers can have access to. Activists can make more informed decisions. Traditional media outlets also rely on digital sources of news for their content. Lastly, the advent of social media and the digital platform allows consumers to gain close proximity to those in their networks and direct access to influencers on whom they rely as information leaders in the cause.

The online platform offers the diaspora and those on the home ground an opportunity to form a collective social network that supports the functionality of facilitating an exchange of resources for organized, strategic collective action to fulfill desired goals. The online network offers a platform to extend its reach to numerous members across the globe. Some of these members may have citizenship ties to the nation; others may have close, familial ties with the country they grew up in as transcultural individuals without any particular citizenship. Hence, an online network offers a platform for like-minded supporters who share significant commonalities, as prescribed by the group, and can convene and advocate for a cause. Similarly, they can convene to rebel against an issue when their values are in conflict with established order, or when they perceive their ideals to be threatened.

Another dominant strength of innovative media as a vital engine in social movements lies in its power to frame issues in ways that appeal to the cognitive or psycho-emotional values of supporters. The diaspora who have familial, emotional ties to their homeland or to the issues that resonate with them may be strongly affected by the audio-visual representations of terrorism, war, or crisis that are framed in the media. Influenced by the media exposure to the issues, the diaspora may feel compelled to respond and engage in manifest or civil activities in that contribute toward the political development of their home nation. Innovative media is particularly effective in pulling the diaspora away from the periphery outskirts of an issue and drawing them into the epicenter of action.

However, media framing may also misinform audiences about the lifecycle of issues and provide limited, inaccurate context. Imagery and messages of certain groups inciting violence, protests, mob activity, riots, and other forms of civil or political unrest may give the false impression that these disruptions erupted suddenly, unprovoked. Furthermore, contemporary video and camera capabilities enable almost anyone to upload pictures, video, and media content they have produced to social media. Some are quick to upload media content with shock value to gain clicks to their post or draw massive numbers of followers to their profile page, but without providing enough context to inform audiences of the full narrative surrounding the circumstances. Hence, audiences viewing these 30-second soundbites or hour-long videos may be quick to stereotype those portrayed in the video, characterize them as "troublemakers," and further marginalize them in society. However, these audiences may be unaware that these "sudden disruptions" actually reflect tipping points of a frustration, deeply rooted in a long history of oppression, injustice, and power imbalance for some groups.

But on the positive side, media framing of these issues may stir curiosity from new audiences. These audiences may be prompted to educate themselves more about the topic through other colleagues, networks, and accessible online sources. Hence, media framing also has the power to introduce and contextualize some of these historical issues for newer generations of the diaspora and citizen-residents in the homeland. These new audiences may seek ways to get involved in these issues and pursue manifest or civil forms of participation that they find meaningful within their present-day context of locale, time, and space. In the 21st century, digital media undeniably brings political participation closer to one's fingertips, one swipe at a time.

The Jasmine Revolution and Arab Spring have been analyzed by numerous scholars and professionals of various disciplines. In our context, this discussion will briefly illustrate how media—particularly social media—contributed toward the activism and collaboration between citizen-residents across northern Africa and globally dispersed diaspora groups. Although in-depth analyses about the Arab Spring go beyond the scope of this book, the broader topic introduces relevant questions about the digital evolution of information and its overall impact on global power and societal change.

Case in point: It is difficult to erase the harrowing visual of a man dousing himself with fuel, and then striking his body with a match that will consume him in violent flames of fire. But this is the well-known story of Tarek el-Tayeb Mohamed Bouazizi, a Tunisian street vendor who set his body on fire on December 17, 2010, as an act of *self-immolation* to express frustration at local police officers for allegedly mistreating him, confiscating his wheelbarrow of produce, and extorting money from him and others through bribes over the years. Subsequent eruptions of public anger and violence led the then Tunisian president, Zine El Abidine Be Ali, to resign on January 14, 2011, after 23 years in power.

Some who learnt of Bouazizi's story through social media and other platforms may have identified this incident as "isolated." However, tensions and unrest had begun before Bouazizi's protest, which merely marked the tipping point of a climate that frustrated many like Bouazizi and catalyzed the Jasmine Revolution. The Jasmine Revolution, also known as the Tunisian Revolution, was one of the first of revolts that occurred in 2011 that eventually culminated into what the world refers to as the "Arab Spring." The Arab Spring described a series of revolutions and generated various forms of activism that spread across Libya, Egypt, Syria, and other Middle Eastern and Arab countries to oppose their political regimes and deeply rooted history-long conflicts.

Sahar Khamis, a professor at the University of Maryland and expert on Arab and Muslim media, former Head of the Mass Communication Department at Qatar University, and former human rights commissioner, notes various forms of activism that also emerged from the Arab Spring, including gender and youth activism. According to Khamis (2020), the Arab Spring events of 2011 were

> an eye-opener and a game-changer for a lot of people because people saw women, Arab women, Muslim women, you know in the case of Egyptians and Tunisians and Libyans—African women … going out and shaking the power structures and power dynamics in their own society and shifting and switching things around.
>
> (personal communication, February 27, 2020)

Khamis (2020) acknowledges that these women who had "triple invisible identities" in three spheres—socioeconomic, media, and academia—now represented role models for other women, as well as for men who sought to emulate the women's courage, power, and strength which they acknowledged and admired (personal communication, February 27, 2020). In their co-edited book *Arab Women's Activism and Socio-Political Transformation: Unfinished*

Gendered Revolutions, Khamis and Mili (2018) recognizes the simultaneous dynamics surrounding Arab women's activism during that time. Many women took the front lines of resistance, resulting in deaths, harassments, rape, and new statuses as refugees in new host countries. However, there was also a growing wave of women's empowerment:

> But then you see … a woman like Tawakkul Karman, who is the first Arab woman to win the Nobel Peace Prize … She was called the "Mother of the Revolution" in Yemen … and she became a model and an icon in her own right … You can think of other young women who became also icons and became faces of this new phase of revolt and revolution by shaking the power structures in their own societies.
>
> (personal communication, February 27, 2020)

The shifts in power dynamics, structures of control, authority, and power also resulted in various opportunities for people to work in different areas of activism, including women's activism and political activism and youth activism (Khamis, personal communication, February 27, 2020). The younger generation have started revolutions, shaken regimes, ousted dictators out of office, and shaken the political and social structures in their own country using social media (Khamis, personal communication, February 27, 2020).

Although there may be controversy and debate about the degree of influence that social media had on the protests, what may be more clear are some of the critical roles played by social media in organizing, mobilizing, and fostering an online network, in conjunction with the Al Jazeera network, among other traditional media platforms. First, as per some analysts, "[it was] as if Tunisians had "found their political voice online and [had] held their meeting virtually" (Graziano, 2012, p. 9; Howard et al., 2011, p. 5), "before taking to the streets and reaching a transnational audience with an immediacy inconceivable some decades ago" (Graziano, 2012, p. 9). Second, the momentum also generated online accompanied offline protest behavior and reinforced collaborations between the Tunisian diaspora and their citizen residents on the homeland. Diverse groups across citizen-residents and the diaspora that shared common views intersected across "barriers" in newer ways to fight for causes that they resonated with.

Third, Khamis' (2020) observations also note that in addition to increasing the visibility of formerly marginalized groups, these protests—catalyzed by social media—played a role in shifting paradigms regarding gender and cultural stereotypes.

Diasporic mobilizations also prompted political engagements through ad hoc developments by nongovernmental organizations (NGOs) and rallies, as illustrated with the Egyptian diaspora in Europe during the Arab Spring. Newly formed collective identities, including "the Egyptians in France," reflected new relationships to strengthen ties among those that had been scattered in widespread Egyptian migrant communities (Beaugrand & Geisser, 2016). The global mobilization of Arab-descent communities also resulted in financial and logistical provisions to support the revolutions and those in their homelands and equip diaspora groups in host communities with information and tangible resources to support efforts in the homeland.

As illustrated, this brief overview of the Arab Spring also underscores that explaining, understanding, or predicting the effectiveness of social movements cannot rely solely on one particular theory. The dynamic nature of online social movements is best explained through a combination of different social movement theories. One may effectively illustrate the relevance and interactions of resource mobilization theory, framing theory, political opportunity theory, or the new social movement theory in a deeper analysis of the Arab Spring, or for any of the following country-specific case studies that depict diaspora and citizen-residents' collaborations in the political sphere to develop their home nation.

Prompted to pursue a call-to-action, both citizen-residents in the homeland and the diaspora have collaborated to create fundraisers and online petitions to advocate for a cause, provide aid, and contribute additional resources to support the efforts of citizen-residents in their home country. The advent of digital platforms enables the diaspora to reassert their national identity within cultural networks, which further validate their efforts and contributions toward developing their African home country.

The intersectionality of these various social movement theories, ICT, interpersonal interactions between the African diaspora and citizen-residents, and their audience interactions with media present opportunities for additional studies of the phenomenon.

The diaspora's role during the elections process through social media

The advent of social and digital media fuels the energy, rapid transmission, coordination, and cooperation of diverse actors to mobilize transformation in a community. As of March 2020, several sources, including Lefor (2020), estimated that 526 million of Africa's 1.3 billion inhabitants are Internet users, and, according to Semaya (2020), an estimated 212 million are users of Facebook.

Although social media originated as a media platform to strengthen ties within informal social networks, its importance as a primary engine in official political spaces revolutionized its relationship-building channels that presidents can leverage with their constituents and foreign audiences. Twitter and Facebook are primary platforms that many global leaders rely on to communicate their actions with their publics.

As of January 2019, Sub-Saharan Africa's most followed leader on social media, with nearly 3.5 million followers, was Kenyan President Uhuru Kenyatta (@UKenyatta), followed by Nigeria's Muhammadu Buhari (@

MBuhari) with 1.8 million followers, and Rwandan leader Paul Kagame (@PaulKagame) with 1.3 million followers. Other Sub-Saharan African leaders include Cyril Ramaphosa (@CyrilRamaphosa), who joined the platform in 2015 and gained 385,000 followers; and Zimbabwe's Emmerson Mnangagwa (@edmnangagwa), who joined in late 2011 and garnered 288,000 followers. This list of African politicians who use social media platforms to engage with their followers increases especially during pivotal moments like elections. The then incumbent president of Nigeria, Goodluck Jonathan, announced his candidacy on Facebook on September 15, 2010, to about 217,000 of his Facebook followers, a number that increased to over 500,000 by the end of election day on April 16, 2011. This earned him the CNN-dubbed nickname "The Facebook President."

The shift of politics toward more digital and social media platforms afforded the African diaspora more opportunities to participate in political affairs and influence elections. Between 2017 and 2018, 54% of key influencers in contesting polls of African elections were from the African diaspora, hailing predominantly from the United States, the United Kingdom, and France, according to *How Africa Tweets*, a study released by Portland Communications, a UK-based consultancy. The study reviewed the role of Twitter in election polls, and how they were shaped by diaspora influencers, between June 2017 and May 2018 in Angola, Kenya, Egypt, Liberia, Equatorial Guinea, Senegal, Lesotho, Rwanda, and the Republic of Somaliland.

The Twitter platform hosted debates and discussions, showed political trends, and influenced electorates' decisions through tweets and top hashtags in different countries that directly referenced politicians or political parties, e.g., #umaangolaparatodos (Angola), #Kagame (Rwanda), and #Weah (surname of Liberia's president). In 2018, the *How Africa Tweets* study also revealed that the evolution of social media and the emergence of closed networks like Facebook messenger, WhatsApp, and Telegram competed greatly with the influence of Twitter as a news source channel.

Diaspora influencers—particularly from the United States—held greater influence in the overall election process in Liberia and Equatorial Guinea. Generally, a number of these influencers were journalists and bloggers who would share opinions, contribute perspectives, and use their own platforms to add to the discourse. The study also revealed that Rwanda proved the exception, with the highest number of influential politicians and governmental organizations at 31%, compared to the other countries.

Protests, marches, boycotts, and strikes

Cyberactivism

The advent of social media results daily in new platforms that rapidly create, disseminate, and exchange information to supplement, fuel, or counteract mainstream media that promote *cyberactivism*, also known as *webactivism*, or the use of social media communications and Internet communication and technological processes to organize and mobilize activism or change. Nowadays, cyberactivism is a common precursor for supporting in-person forms of protest behavior. The democratic nature of social media and digital ICT spaces invites marginalized, underrepresented, or misrepresented minority groups to gain access to credible information through diverse sources, exchange differing perspectives, and educate each other on content-creators and information providers through the uninhibited political conversations they can conduct online.

For instance, in Tunisia, some members of the diaspora community were cyberactivists and spearheaded blogs and online platforms such as *Takriz*, which evolved in an e-magazine, although the platform was subsequently blocked for provocative content about sex, religion, and political issues. The influential website *Nawaat*, founded in 2004, and *GlobalVoices*, a global nonprofit organization formed by a blogging community, sought to promote dialogue and raise awareness of issues that were neglected in mainstream media (Graziano, 2012). *500 Words Magazine*, an online magazine that focuses on Sudan, was founded by Ola Diab, based in Doha, Qatar, and gained attention for incorporating voices from Sudanese individuals who were experiencing the country's revolts first-hand as soon as they erupted in December 2018.

These initiatives also epitomize *participatory models of journalism*, which play a significant role in influencing political and social change globally, including across Africa. Whether public journalism, citizen journalism, independent journalism, participatory journalism, or grassroots journalism, these different types of journalism offer collaborative platforms between citizens and journalists in news and content creation—albeit with varying degrees of involvement. The digitization and fuel rapid diffusion of ideas radically transform communities in ways that were not possible decades ago (*Definition of Terms*, 2011). They also permit a democratic space that allows online communities to project *cyberdissident* voices that oppose dominant political ideas and stir more activism.

Cyberactivism and participatory journalism pluralize diverse ideas that transcend digital borders and rapidly connect diaspora communities to those residing in other host communities and citizen residents within their homelands. Generally, an inclusive online environment reflects democratic principles that promote free speech and encourage healthy dissent among expansive networks. These inclusive environments have also allowed citizen-residents and diaspora members to more effectively serve as "watchdogs" in attempts to hold government officials, community, and organization leaders accountable and to mobilize their efforts to foster change in their communities. The diaspora tend to reside in Western host countries with more politically stable climates that permit them certain privileges and freedoms that their citizen-residents in their home nations may lack access to.

However, these democratic appeals of the social media environment may also be perceived to threaten the values of some regimes. Government and state authorities may block certain social media platforms and mobile phones, shut down the Internet entirely, restrict access to certain digital content, blogs, forums, and censor any online activity to curtail any radical liberalization of ideas online that oppose their ideologies. Ultimately, these authorities assume the role of "watchdog" to surveil their own citizens. Through surveillance, repression, and other restrictive measures, including tracking online activities, some state authorities may issue cyberthreats to social media influencers with a large following and manipulate activists' agenda with their own counter-rhetoric. "Shadow banning," also known as "ghost banning," is an act of blocking or partially blocking a user or their online content without alerting the user that their content has been concealed. Such online interactions may move offline when authorities identify and arrest individuals for their controversial blogs or content.

Peaceful demonstrations, protests and rallies in host countries

Some African diaspora recognize that their host countries' political climates permit them more freedom of expression and the right to peacefully protest, unlike in their home countries. Hence, in a spirit of solidarity, some diaspora use their resources and liberties in the host country to advocate for pertinent issues occurring in their home nations on behalf of citizen-residents on the ground. The diaspora will use legislations and amendments in their host country that advocate the right of free speech and to hold peaceful protests or gain signatures in their host countries to mobilize other diasporic communities, including nonnational allies who share common viewpoints. This has been epitomized in various ways.

In 2019, the Sudanese diaspora in the United Kingdom protested in front of the British embassy, in Trafalgar Square, and in front of the British parliament to put pressure on the British government to not support the regime of then president Omar al-Bashir.

In 2020, the EndSars protests against police brutality in Nigeria reflected the mobilization of citizen-residents and their diaspora across North America, Europe and other parts of the world to pressurize the Nigerian government to disband the controversial police unit. Online platforms offered live and "current" updates occurring on the ground in Lekki and other cities around Nigeria to inform global audiences of realities. Some diaspora and citizen-residents on the ground in Nigeria actively collaborated in efforts to support victims and families and offer resources to activists. Some also sought to engage with officials in efforts to reach peaceful resolutions.

Sponsorship of campaigns

The Gambian diaspora played an active role in 2016 elections by allegedly sponsoring mass protests for electoral reforms, and sponsoring youth and women's participation in national elections through the NotTooYoungToRun and GamWomenInParliament campaigns (Jaw, 2017). In 2016, the Gambian diaspora also contributed funds through the Gambia Democracy Fund (GMF) to financially support opposition political parties and the families of victims affected by political violence.

Funding medical interventions and logistics in homelands

About 5 million Sudanese live overseas—the majority reside between the middle East, Europe, North America, and Australia. Various sources reported how many were active in the anti-Bashir protests and led efforts in various ways. Some raised tens of thousand dollars for urgent medical assistance, supported by the University of Khartoum Alumni Association based in Philadelphia (Kushkush, 2019). Organizations like the Sudanese Physician Association, a subgroup of the Sudanese Professionals Association (SPA), offered on-the-ground assistance, as did the US-established Sudanese-American Physician Association (SAPA), which provided medical aid in the country. Meanwhile, the Sudanese Doctors Central Committee provided data on the protests' fatalities and injuries (Kushkush, 2019).

Creating art as sites of political resistance and conduits for development

Music, drawings, theatre, pop culture, and other creative platforms have long been channels for creative expressionists to depict resistance against a country's political status quo, advocate for political reform, or inform audiences of rarely disseminated footage and narratives.

In the Netherlands, Nigerian-British Ikenna Azuike, lauded in 2014 by *New African* magazine as one of the "100 Most Influential Africans," created, hosts, and presents the BBC World News satirical and pop-culture show "What's Up, Africa," a YouTube vlog that covers African news and political satire, and the "Planet Nigeria" TV series, in which he discovers more about his Nigerian roots.

Renowned Romanian-born Sudanese political cartoonist and artist Khalid Albaih, who resides in Doha, Qatar, gained worldwide attention for witty cartoons that address daily and political issues in the Arab world that are generally underrepresented in mainstream media. In 2019, the artist was granted the inaugural Freedom residency in Manhattan, New York, which was organized by the Artists at Risk Connection (ARC), a project of PEN America and ArtX to support "at-risk artists." Khalid Albaih also launched FADAA, a digital platform that aims to connect artists and provide them with accessible platforms, build an artistic community, promote solidarity, and work toward a better future.

World-famous South African musicians Miriam Makeba and Hugh Masekela famously used their music as sites of resistance against apartheid to place pressure against the South African government. Similarly, Nigeria's Fela Kuti, a world-renowned musician, multi-instrumentalist, pioneer of Afrobeats music, and human-rights activist, wrote and performed politically charged songs that appealed to the marginalized, the unemployed, and oppressed groups. Subsequently, these songs also prompted consistent jail raids of his performances in clubs by the Nigerian police. Côte d'Ivoire's world-renowned singer and international recording artist Alpha Blondy, born Seydou Koné, introduced reggae to his country as a platform for political and social activism as well as religious unification, gaining massive followings in Europe and globally.

Some hip-hop and rap artists in the diaspora have also long used these genres to address political and social issues that affect their daily lives or their communities. In the United States, Chuck D of the American rap group Public Enemy famously said, "Rap is our invisible network. It's the CNN black Americans never had" (Quoteresearch, 2014, para. 7; Gold, 1989, p. 16). Hip-hop artists Nas Jota in Washington DC, Walid Abdulhamid in Canada, and Ayman Mao in Dallas are among the many African diaspora artists who have composed solidarity songs.

Numerous debates and critics have analyzed whether hip hop and rap create cultural change and their impact on political transformation. Book review critics like Robert Beck challenge the role of hip hop "as revolutionary politics, hip-hop as a vaguely defined 'movement' (toward what?), hip-hop as a generational struggle, and even hip-hop as a theory of justice" (Beck, 2014, p. 3). Furthermore, like most music in a revenue-generating industry, different groups have accused each other of misappropriating the genres of hip hop and rap to promote sex, misogyny, and material wealth. Some critics have also cautioned against generalizing hip hop and rap as an identifier for Black people to avoid synonymizing these genres with "trouble," "problems," and plights that are associated with Black people (Beck, 2014). Hence, recognizing hip hop or rap music as a conduit for political and social consciousness and social change has different connotations across the globe.

Still others argue that some artists have used rap and hip hop for self-expression and self-identity and to promote social and political consciousness, also referred to in American pop cultures as being "woke." "Woke" is a political term coined in the United States in the 1940s that originally derived from the African-American vernacular English expression of "staying woke," emphasizing an "alertness" or a perceived "heightened awareness" of social and racial justice issues and a movement against injustice prejudice and discrimination.

As modern-day griots, hip-hop and rap artists in the diaspora and in their home nations portray these justice issues artistically through lyrics, edgy rhythms, and raw and catchy beats, complemented by graphic or abstract imagery in their music videos, which may reflect impoverished realities of the "have nots." The artists may humanize stories of marginalized and socially disenfranchised populations who are denied access to resources; live in poverty, amidst substandard quality in healthcare, education, housing, and living conditions; face unemployment; and may desperately resort to illegal activities to financially provide for their families. Mainstream media, however, may statistically analyze these social ills that stereotype these oppressed group's as society's "misfits" or "delinquents." Specific to African countries, similar societal challenges may illustrate the spill-over effects of rural-to-urban migration in search of employment opportunities, which lead to urban overcrowding, lack of employment, and the resort to a reliance on an informal economy or illegal lifestyles.

Fanbases may resonate with these lyrics and with the accompanying videos of art that may graphically imitate their life. When artists' subject matter traces poverty and injustices to flawed political leadership, corrupt government regimes, and unsuccessful economic policies that fail to address societal and sustainable development needs, artists' music crosses over into political territory. When fans and audiences who are introduced to or connect with the music's subject matter are prompted by calls to action, artists' music crosses over into political activism. Fans may be prompted to conduct research and become more literate about that topic. Within their individual capacity of civil participation, they may actively contact influencers, donate to charities, or jumpstart their own collective movements. Hence, in this manner, hip hop also lives up to its role as a "lifestyle brand," as it inspires and influences audiences to express their own unique perspectives on an issue; promote a collective identity of similar "political or societal focus"; acquire representative artifacts; showcase identifiable paraphernalia; and pursue other forms of social engagement to build solidarity, raise consciousness, and make community change in their collective civic engagement.

Soft power, celebrity diplomacy, and sports (football) diplomacy

In the interconnected global economy of the 21st century, nations must rely on "smart power," or a combination of *soft power* and *hard power* mechanisms to remain vibrant, strong, and competitive. Joseph Nye, cofounder of the international relations theory of neoliberalism, pioneered and conceptualized the theory of soft power as the ability to attract and persuade others to want what one wants or one has through positive images, without coercion or payment—unlike hard power, which relies on the latter. The three intangible sources of attraction include a nation's culture (as perceived attractively by others); political values (which are identified with domestically and overseas); and foreign policies (when perceived to be legitimate and of a strong moral compass) (Zhang, 2010, p. 385; Nye, 2006).

Nye (2004) also noted that sports are organic soft-power tools that significantly communicate a nation's values—leveraged through its international media exposure, cultural focus, and the promotion of peaceful, constructive values (Abdi et al., 2019). The international exposure and the focus on culture and peaceful values, therefore, present sports as a natural soft-power device for countries (Nye 2004). "Sports diplomacy falls under public diplomacy, which is used to improve intermediate and long-term relations between states by influencing the public abroad to accomplish foreign policy goals" (Trunkos & Heere, 2018, p. 1; Gilboa, 2008). "Sports diplomacy is gaining more attention in diplomatic circles due to sports' ability to promote constructive values, mitigate tension and conflict, and bring about the development of exchanges and dialogs among individuals and nations" (Abdi et al., 2019, p. 147; Deos, 2014).

Football diplomacy, in particular, refers to the use of football (also known as *soccer*) as a particular sports tool to improve states' relations and accomplish foreign policy goals. Arguably the most popular sport in the world—and a unifier—football has been used to mitigate conflict. Notably, Didier Drogba, a retired Ivorian professional football player, epitomizes his leverage of celebrity and football diplomacy in addressing international conflict and political relations. Drogba famously used his leadership and support from his teammates in their qualification of the World Cup in 2006 to face the cameras and visibly appeal for an to end the bloody civil war and surrender of weapons and violence that ravaged their homeland. The diverse team reasserted their collective national identity to demonstrate their inclusiveness and solidarity of the various ethnic groups and religious factions that had resulted in violence and political deadlocks in the country. This gesture led to a road toward mutual reconciliation and peace—and a surrender of tensions, resulting in the end of the war after a week. Subway stations throughout New York mounted billboards with images of the Ivorian flag and football, along with FIFA and World Cup related logos, with messages, "A Country Divided Now United." Echoing the words of Nelson Mandela, former president of South Africa, "Sports personalities—especially footballers—are more important than politicians, because people look up to them" (*Football Diplomacy: A New Form of Soft Power*, 2014, para. 1).

In addition to the African diaspora representing their nations as ambassadors of soft power, as significant nonpolitical state actors, some could effectively use their celebrity status to effect necessary change. Nico Kang, an actor and curator of AYOO Africa, also notes that it would also be important that influential media figures and celebrities who tour across Africa and the West use their media tours, their influential status, and their platforms to encourage people to invest in Africa (Kang, personal communication, February 1, 2020).

The use of celebrities to attract attention to causes and international issues has positioned many to serve as global ambassadors supporting development organizations to advocate causes. Many have positioned themselves to bridge the gap between foreign policy and international development. Among these famous people are Bono, Angelina Jolie, and Brad Pitt, whose celebrity power as international artists has also transcended boundaries of media and entertainment, public affairs, and international foreign relations—and they have also secured levels of credibility and professionalism in their knowledge of various topics. Although the phenomenon of "celebrity diplomacy" requires additional research, Andrew Cooper, author of the book *Celebrity Diplomacy*, encourages more exploration of the impact of celebrity on foreign diplomacy. Cooper underscores three criteria to explore the potential role of celebrities in diplomacy: "global reach, interaction with high-level state actors, and a sense of purpose" (Wilson Center, 2007, para. 3). Many celebrities rely on their celebrity status, accentuated by international fame and media attention, as well as their access to political officials to draw global attention to international causes, especially those that have garnered little or no media attention.

The rapid evolution and advent of social and digital media have also birthed a range of celebrity-affiliated public figures. The rise of digital media has opened the door for Tik Tok or "overnight" celebrities, ranging from the now-famous "Vietnamese cow-herding YouTube number-singer" to thought leaders, scholars, community leaders, and professional practitioners—all of whom have been catapulted to varying levels of celebrity status through social media. Their massive digital followings and access to political and other celebrity figures position them favorably—or notoriously—in the eyes of their audiences. However, such sensationalism and massive attention presents both opportunities and drawbacks.

The advantage is that those who recognize their own celebrity status may feel a responsibility to educate themselves more fully on issues that resonate with them. By learning more about certain topics, collaborating with subject-matter experts, and identifying opportunities to be more informed about issues on the ground, these individuals can form alliances with already-established networks or develop initiatives to support specific issues in their homelands. They may eventually gain credibility as subject-matter experts in particular topics, which they can introduce to audiences through the media. They may also gain access to political figures to access power, build powerful relationships, and leverage resources to effectively address issues that impact their local or global communities.

However, it is also important to differentiate celebrity diplomacy from "glamorous enthusiasts," who use their celebrity status to advocate for certain causes on "ad hoc bases" (Wilson Center, 2007, para. 6). Some "overnight" celebrities may appear to be more invested in strengthening their social media presence than in leveraging their influential statuses for community engagement and development. Those seeking to use their platforms for public service could encourage others to click on posts or to "swipe right" or "swipe left," as they direct audiences toward resources, knowledge hubs, and specific initiatives that seek to curb poverty, improve healthcare and education, or shape policy making on relevant issues affecting Africa's development. Educating themselves in issues affecting Africa's development allows them to build their credibility as spokespersons and thought leaders on topics in which they are knowledgeable. This is important to mitigate the risk of advocating for issues that go beyond their scope and depth of understanding and comfort level. Otherwise, they risk damaging relationships with and the reputations of relevant stakeholders and losing credibility.

Politics are a contestable subject that reflect history-long complex dynamics of international relations, agreements, power, leadership, and diverse agendas to serve diverse needs. Africa's development rests on the ability of the African diaspora, citizen-residents, nation and state officials, and other relevant stakeholders to reach mutual understandings, foster cooperation, and devise peacebuilding strategies that support national development goals. The will and desire for the diaspora to be politically active in their African homeland; the level of interconnectedness, quality of relationships, and strength of networks between citizen-residents, other Diasporic groups, and stakeholders; access to information, resources, and rapid transmission of ideas; and the effectiveness and organization of coordinated efforts between citizen-residents and the diaspora—all of these factors position the diaspora in their host countries to collaborate with others and play integral roles in international diplomacy and politically support their nations.

Chapter summary

Key words:

celebrity diplomacy	human resources	self-immolation
civil participation	Ibrahim Index of African Governance (IIAG)	shadow banning/ghost banning
collective behavior	manifest political participation	smart power
collective theorists of social movements	material resources	social movement
cultural resources	moral resources	social-organizational resources
cyberactivism/webactivism	new social movement theory (NST)	soft power
cyberdissident	participatory models of journalism	sports diplomacy
football diplomacy	political opportunity theory	watchdogs
framing theory	protest behavior	woke
governance	resource mobilization theory	

Discussion questions:

1) Is "democracy" feasible in Africa or an ideal that is not feasible for African countries? What would an ideal democratic model in a selected African country look like? Consider external and internal variables; unique dynamics between various groups and cultures; and any historical factors that would influence your design of the model.
2) How have the three eras of precolonial Africa, colonial Africa, and the era of independence influenced Africa's self-governance, economic, and political liberation to date? Select an African country to present your case study.
3) How has the shift of some African countries' one-party to multiparty political systems shaped their democratization process and influenced their development agenda? Select an African country to focus on in your case study.
4) Given that the African diaspora do not reside in their African country, to what degree do you think they should contribute politically toward their African home country? Why or why not?
5) Describe a protest activity that occurred in an African home country that involved the coordination of its diaspora, citizen-residents, and other stakeholders. If you also participated in this activity, explain your role and personal observations. In your case study, be sure to also discuss the following:
   - Manifest and civil forms of political participation that various stakeholders conducted;
   - Media strategies (including any social media) to influence social change;
   - Theoretical frameworks that may explain the types of protest behavior and collective interactions between the diaspora, citizen-residents, and stakeholders in their host and home nations to address the issue in the African homeland;
   - Your personal assessment of the coordinated efforts between the different stakeholders.
6) A) In your opinion, what are some limitations and challenges that may hinder efforts between the African diaspora and citizen-residents in their efforts to mobilize for social or political change in their African home country? What may be some of the opportunities from either group to consider that may impact strategic efforts? Select an African country for your analysis. Be sure to identify factors that may influence their collaboration, including external and internal country variables, cultural dynamics, and the historical context between the groups.

   B) What recommendations could strengthen the collaboration and mobilization between key stakeholders of a selected African country toward a specific national development goal? Please note that the stakeholders include the diaspora, citizen-residents, governments, and international bodies. Are your recommendations feasible? Be sure to indicate any foreseeable challenges and opportunities that may affect the feasibility of your recommendations.

7) A) Some analysts argue that models for African media may not be sustainable enough to provide journalists in African countries with freedom and independence. Why do you agree or disagree? Be sure to cite specific examples, including country-specific contexts, in your response.

   B) Propose an alternative model of the media that would provide journalists with freedom and independence. What factors would need to be set in place for it to be feasible and implemented? Be sure to cite specific examples, including country-specific contexts, in your response.

References

Abdi, K., Talebpour, M., Fullerton, J., Ranjkesh, M., & Nooghabi, H. (2019). Identifying sports diplomacy resources as soft power tools. *Place Branding and Public Diplomacy, 15*(3), 147–155. doi:10.1057/s41254-019-00115-9

Adejumobi, S. (2000). Elections in Africa: A Fading Shadow of Democracy? *International Political Science Review, 21*(1), 59–73. https://doi.org/10.1177/0192512100211004

Asaaduzzaman, M., & Virtanen, P. (2018). Governance theories and models. In A. Farazmand (Ed.), *Global Encyclopedia of Public Administration, Public Policy, and Governance* (1st ed., pp. 1–13). New York, NY: Springer International Publishing. https://doi.org/10.1007/978-3-319-31816-5_2612-1

Beaugrand, C., & Geisser, V. (2016). Social mobilization and political participation in the diaspora during the "Arab Spring." *Journal of Immigrant and Refugee Studies, 14*(3), 239–243. doi:10.1080/15562948.2016.1212133

Beck, R. (2014, February 10). Express yourself. *N+1*. https://nplusonemag.com/online-only/book-review/express-yourself/

Buechler, S. (1995). New Social Movement Theories. *The Sociological Quarterly, 36*(3), 441–464. http://www.jstor.org/stable/4120774

Deos, A. (2014). Sport and relational public diplomacy: The case of New Zealand and Rugby world cup 2011. *Sport in Society, 17*(9), 1170–1186. https://doi.org/10.1080/17430437.2013.856588.

Ekman, J., & Amnå, E. (2012). Political participation and civic engagement: Towards a new typology. *Human Affairs, 22*(3), 283–300. doi:10.2478/s13374-012-0024-1

Farazmand, A. (2013). Governance in the Age of Globalization: Challenges and Opportunities for South and Southeast Asia. *Public Organization Review, 13*(4), 349–363. https://doi.org/10.1007/s11115-013-0249-4

Gilboa, E. (2008). Searching for a theory of public diplomacy. *The Annals of the American Academy of Political and Social Science, 616*, 55–77.

Gold, J. (1989, January 6–12). Enemy of the people. *LA Weekly*, 14–20.

Graziano, T. (2012). The Tunisian diaspora: Between "digital riots" and web activism. *Social Science Information, 51*(4), 534–550. doi:10.1177/0539018412456773

Hara, N., & Huang, B. (2010). Online Social movements. *Annual Review of Information Science and Technology, 45*(1), 1–56. https://core.ac.uk/download/pdf/213841424.pdf

Howard, P. N., Duffy, A., Freelon, D., Hussain, M. M., Mari, W., & Mazaid, M. (2011). Opening Closed Regimes: What Was the Role of Social Media During the Arab Spring? *SSRN Electronic Journal*. Published. https://doi.org/10.2139/ssrn.2595096

Jaw, S. M. (2017, February 1). All Gambians need to rebuild their country, even members of the old regime. *The Guardian*. https://www.theguardian.com/commentisfree/2017/jan/30/gambians-rebuild-country-adama-barrow-yahya-jammeh

Khamis, S., & Mili, A. (2018). *Arab Women's Activism and Socio-Political Transformation: Unfinished Gendered Revolutions* (Softcover reprint of the original 1st ed. 2018 ed.). Springer.

Kushkush, I. (2019, April 11). Sudan's diaspora helped bring Bashir's end near. *Quartz Africa*. https://qz.com/africa/1591956/sudans-diaspora-helped-bring-bashirs-end-near/

Laloupo, F. (2014). The African diaspora and the electoral process: What has changed? Building a collective sense of national identity. *Open Society Initiative for West Africa*. https://www.osiwa.org/wp-content/uploads/2015/05/05_afropolitan-A_diaspora.pdf

Lefor, L. J. (2020). *The New Normal: Digitization, Digitalization and E-Commerce in International Business*. Bloomington, Indiana: Authorhouse.

Little, W. (2014, November 6). Chapter 21. Social Movements and Social Change—Introduction to Sociology—1st Canadian Edition. In: *Pressbooks*. https://opentextbc.ca/introductiontosociology/chapter/chapter21-social-movements-and-social-change/

London Metropolitan University. (2014, April 3). *Football diplomacy: A new form of soft power*. Public Diplomacy and Global Communication 2013 (a). https://pdgc2013a.wordpress.com/2014/04/03/football-diplomacy-a-new-form-of-soft-power/

Mbaku, J. (2020). Good and inclusive governance is imperative for Africa's future. Https://Www.Brookings.Edu/Wp-Content/Uploads/2020/01/ForesightAfrica2020_Chapter2_20200110.Pdf. https://www.brookings.edu/wp-content/uploads/2020/01/ForesightAfrica2020_Chapter2_20200110.pdf

McAdam, D. (1996). Political opportunities: Conceptual origins, current problems, future directions. In D. McAdam, J. D. McCarthy, & M. N. Zald (Eds.), *Comparative perspectives on social movements: Political opportunities, mobilizing structures, and cultural framings* (pp. 23–40). UK: Cambridge University Press.

Meyer, D. S. (2004). Protest and political opportunities. Annual *Review of Sociology, 30*, 125–145.

Mo Ibrahim Foundation (2019). African Governance Report 2019—key findings. https://mo.ibrahim.foundation/iiag/gr-2019-key-findings

Nye, J. S. (2004). *Soft Power: The Means to Success in World Politics*. New York: Public Affairs.

Nye, J.S.J. (2006). Think again: soft power [online]. *Foreign Policy*. https://foreignpolicy.com/2006/02/23/think-again-soft-power/

Oola, S. (2011, May 13). Uganda: Understanding the Walk to Work protest. *Peace Insight*. https://www.peaceinsight.org/en/articles/walk-to-work/?location=uganda&theme=development

Østergaard-Nielsen, E. (2003). The politics of migrants' transnational political practices. *International Migration Review, 37*(3), 760–786. doi:10.1111/j.1747-7379.2003.tb00157.x

Quoteresearch, A. (2014, February 11). Rap is Black America's TV Station—Quote investigator. *Quote Investigator*. https://quoteinvestigator.com/2014/02/11/cnn-black/

Teorell, J., Torcal, M., Montero, J. R. (2007). Political Participation: Mapping the Terrain. In J. W. van Deth, J. R. Montero, A. Westholm (Eds.). *Citizenship and Involvement in European Democracies: A Comparative Analysis* (pp. 334–357). London & New York: Routledge.

Trunkos, J., & Heere, B. (2017). Sport Diplomacy: A Review of How Sports Can be Used to Improve International Relations. In C. Esherick, R. Baker, S. Jackson, & M. Sam (Eds.), *Case Studies in Sport Diplomacy* (pp. 1–17). West Virginia University: FiT

Publishing. https://fitpublishing.com/sites/default/files/pages_from_sportdiplomacy-011317-bw20.pdf

Tutlam, C., Akech, J., Mutambasere, S., Ramakhula, T., & Assim, U. M. (2019, May 16). Africa's democratic deficit: The role of the diaspora in bridging the gap between citizens and government. Https://Repository.Gchumanrights.Org/Handle/20.500.11825/996. https://repository.gchumanrights.org/handle/20.500.11825/996

Vertovec, S. (2004). Trends and impacts of migrant transnationalism. Centre on Migration, Policy and Society, 3, 1–80. Retrieved from http://www.cedir.fr/cedir2/wp-content/uploads/2012/07/VERTOVEC-Stephen-Migrant-Transnationalism-and-Modes-of-Transformation.pdf

Wilson Center (2007). Celebrity diplomacy: Challenges and opportunities. https://www.wilsoncenter.org/event/celebrity-diplomacy-challenges-and-opportunities

Zhang, W. (2010). China's cultural future: from soft power to comprehensive national power. *International Journal of Cultural Policy*, *16*(4), 383–402. doi:10.1080/10286630903134300

12 Relationship status

"It's Complicated"—Addressing relational dynamics between the African diaspora and citizen-residents in Africa

In the development of this book, I conducted a preliminary exploration of how citizen-residents in African countries and the African diaspora may perceive each other. This was inspired by personal and others' accounts of cultural clashes, false impressions, and business challenges upon re-entry into the homeland or host land, as well as the methodological approach applied and results derived from my 2015 doctorate dissertation, *Relationship Management of the "Brain Circulation" Phenomenon: The Case of the Ugandan Government and its Ugandan Diaspora in the USA*. In the 2015 case study, I adapted a relationship-management theoretical framework to gain insight into how the Ugandan government can motivate its Ugandan diaspora in the United States to invest in or contribute to Uganda.

This chapter explores some of the root issues of various relational dynamics, including misperceptions that set the groundwork for a future robust study, which would refer to Mpande's (2015) relationship management theoretical framework to gain insight on the relationship between the African diaspora and citizen-residents in the African homeland. Gaining an understanding of their relationship will help to determine appropriate public relational strategies and communication tactics, guidelines, policies, and innovative instruments that address underlying conflicts between the groups, and that also promote congruent values and norms that would ensure an appropriate cultural fit for their collaboration. Determining the relationship between these two groups is a phenomenon that has received little attention in development studies but is a critical area to explore in related fields.

For the development of this book, I constructed a qualitative questionnaire that I disseminated to 28 voluntary participants, who comprised three groups that I interviewed between 2019 and 2020: citizen-residents in different African countries, including Uganda and the Ivory Coast; diaspora members from ethnic and national backgrounds of Uganda, the Ivory Coast, Nigeria, Cameroon, the Sudan, Somalia, Ghana, and Egypt who currently reside in the United Kingdom, Canada, the United States, and Ireland; and returnees from the diaspora in their home country (Uganda). During the data gathering process, it is important to note that on many occasions, multiple interviews with different respondents were conducted throughout the

DOI: 10.4324/9781351031660-15

same day. Hence, to protect the participants' identities and to alleviate false assumptions that responses were offered by the same individual, all participant identities in this chapter have been given pseudonyms, as identified with an asterisk.

Departing from Mpande's (2015) adapted relationship management theoretical framework, this study adapted a broader co-orientational analytical approach to highlight an overview of the parties' perceptions of each other. Participants in the study for this book were asked to describe the perceptions and impressions they had of the other group (diaspora or citizen-residents), as well as perceptions that they believed the other groups had of them, based on the co-orientation analytical approach. A co-orientation questionnaire permits an analysis that reflects how each party perceives their relationship to be with the other party, as well as how they believe the other party perceives their relationship (Carrozzino-Lyon, 2012; Rhee, 2004; Brønn & Brønn, 2000; Trisler, 2010). According to Dozier and Ehling (1992), four co-orientation outcome states exist in the perception of relationships between multiple parties: a state of true consensus, a state of dissensus, a state of false consensus, and a state of false conflict (Mpande, 2015; Brønn & Brønn, 2000, pp. 12–13). Hence, a co-orientational model would reveal both parties' areas of agreement, congruency, and accuracy in their assessment of their relationship type and relational qualities. Such an in-depth analysis allows for a 360-degree perspective that better gives a holistic picture of a relationship, which would be assessed from both parties' perspectives as opposed to just one party's perspective—which is how most relationships are assessed.

These preliminary results set the foundation for an in-depth co-orientation framework analysis for a future robust study that would include more participants from different nations across Africa and across their diasporas to reveal greater insight into relational outcomes that can be identified through Hon and Grunig's (1999) categories of (i) relationship types (exchange, exploitative, communal, covenantal, contractual, or other) and (ii) relational qualities (relational trust, commitment, control mutuality, and relational satisfaction). These relational outcomes can be further analyzed through a co-orientational analytical framework to evaluate the parties' agreement, accuracy and congruency of their relationship types and relational qualities.

In this study, recurring data and similar responses led to emerging themes that revealed the types of misperceptions and stereotypical notions that may potentially fragment the relationship between some Africans in the diaspora and citizen-resident Africans in Africa. The summaries of perceptions and impressions that the African diaspora, citizen-residents, and returnees have about each other are presented below and illustrated with selected quotes for additional in-depth context. They are also summarized in Figure 12.1.

Please note that names were changed and modified with pseudonyms to maintain the anonymity of some participants, especially since different participants were also interviewed on the same day.

Perspective from some <u>Africans in the Diaspora</u> about <u>some Citizen-Residents</u> in Africa, in the context of collaborations towards Africa's development:	**Perspective from some <u>Citizen-Residents in Africa</u> about <u>some Africans in the Diaspora</u>, in the context of collaborations towards Africa's development:**
What impressions do some African Diaspora *have of Citizen-Residents* living in Africa? • Resilient and Hardworking • Uninformed about foreigners' realities	What impressions do some Citizen-Residents *have of the African Diaspora?* • Seeking sense of self • Misinformed about the African government • Not motivated sufficiently by governments
What impressions do some African-Diaspora *believe that Citizen-Residents in Africa have of the Diaspora?* • Morally bankrupt • Traitors • Uninformed about on-the-ground realities • Living the good life • Assume we think they are lazy	What impressions do some Citizen-Residents (including returnees*) *believe that the African Diaspora have of Citizen-Residents in Africa?* * returnees are citizen-residents who returned from the Diaspora and permanently reside in their African country • Traitors • Driven by self-interests • Well-intended, but misguided

Figure 12.1 Perceptions between the African diaspora and citizen-residents in Africa in the context of collaboration toward Africa's development

A. **Summary of perceptions and impressions from some *Africans in the Diaspora* about citizen-residents living in Africa in the context of positioning both groups for collaborations toward Africa's development:**

Q) What impressions do the African diaspora have of citizen-residents living in Africa?

Resilient and hardworking: Africans on the continent are extremely resilient in their ability to operate and address their daily needs "within an extremely dysfunctional system" (Mark*, personal communication, March 7, 2020). In light of that, there is a sense that they have unfulfilled dreams and passions, generally resulting from unemployment trends. It is clear that they are brilliant-minded and hardworking but lack opportunities to thrive and excel. This also means that some are "determined to do anything to survive and succumb to a culture of materialism that has taken root in many African countries" (Pierre*, personal communication, December 26, 2019).

Uninformed about foreigners' realities: "Some people back home [in our African countries] do not realize that discrimination occurs in the West and so newcomers … [to the host country] do not always have access to the best of opportunities, despite their levels of education or professional accomplishments back home. As a result, [our people back home in Africa] don't realize that the cost of living [in our host country] is high, and that less money remains after bills are paid" (Lanre*, personal communication, February 21, 2020).

Q) What impressions do the African diaspora believe that citizen-residents living in Africa have of the African diaspora?

Morally bankrupt: "Some people back in Africa also think that their counterparts in the West are morally bankrupt. The vices they hide to engage in at home are openly done in the West" (Jacques*, personal communication, December 26, 2019). "They perceive us as people who are stealing their jobs" (Fatoumata*, personal communication, February 1, 2020).

Traitors: "They think we betrayed the country by leaving; some think we should have stayed—not because of a civil war, but because of the economy. They don't understand that for some of us, the options were hard: stay with very basic necessities, or with a family business. They think we took the easy route to leave and not knowing how hard it is to be in a foreign land. So, where do I fit in?" (Dianne*, personal communication, February 1, 2020).

Uninformed about on-the-ground realities: "They think we have little knowledge of their on-ground realities and they disregard your views on issues, despite the fact that some of us may travel [home to our African country] frequently or were raised in the country" (Iris*, personal communication, December 26, 2019). "They question us, knowing that they lived through the struggle, and [so] who are we to say that we know better?" (Hassan*, personal communication, February 1, 2020).

Living the good life: "Many back home [in Africa] believe that the Diaspora have 'escaped' and are 'living the good life' that grants the diaspora a financially comfortable lifestyle and access to various opportunities. They perceive the Diaspora as having an 'I'm going to save my nation' mentality. I feel like my kids will not even want to help because they have been so far removed from everything … They don't perceive us in a good light" (Taye*, personal communication, February 1, 2020).

Assume we think they are lazy: "[Our people back home in Africa] think that we (the diaspora) think they are lazy" ((Jim*, personal communication, December 26, 2019).

B. **Summary of perceptions and impressions from *citizen-residents* living in Africa about their African diaspora counterparts in the context of positioning both groups for collaborations toward Africa's development:**

Q) What impressions do African citizen-residents have of their African diaspora counterparts?

Seeking sense of self: "Most of the Diaspora seem to have low self-esteem, are treated as inferior and not respected as proper citizens, are called names, and discriminated against racially, and considered as 'low-class' and as slaves. These drive many to trace their origins back in Africa" (Filo*, personal communication, January 11, 2020)

Misinformed about the African continent: "The diaspora tend to have derogatory ideas about Africans on the continent and this results in a failure to connect meaningfully and effectively. For those with little or no knowledge of home, they believe that Africa is a cursed and dark continent with devilish acts, bad governance, poverty, disease, etc." (Ora*, personal communication, January 11, 2020).

Not motivated sufficiently by governments: "Africans in the diaspora also have the impression that leaders in Africa are not doing enough economically, politically, socially to entice them to return and believe they will be better off in the diaspora. Leaders are not helping them and that is the major problem to be addressed" (Henri*, personal communication, January 11, 2020).

Advantaged: "Africans in the diaspora have many opportunities and better systems; we, on the ground, work with very little" (Steven*, personal communication, January 11, 2020).

Q) What impressions do African citizen-residents think that the African diaspora have of citizen-residents living in Africa?

Traitors: "They see us as traitors who sold their own black brothers into slavery and that has led to their suffering" (Louis*, personal communication, January 11, 2020).

C. **Summary Perceptions and Impressions from *returnees* (or citizen-residents living in Africa who returned from the diaspora to Africa) about their African diaspora counterparts, in the context of positioning both groups for collaborations toward Africa's development:**

Q) What impressions do African citizen-resident returnees have of their African diaspora counterparts?

Driven by self-interest: The diaspora can be an effective political lobby, but should be highly informed and not driven by their own personal agendas.

Well-intentioned, but misguided: Most diaspora mean well, as can be seen by the large amounts of remittances they send, but they should be focusing on interactions toward mutual respect, away from dependency.

Q) What impressions do African citizen-resident returnees think that the African diaspora have of them?

Failed to meet goals: If the diaspora are returning to their country, then this means that the diaspora may have not succeeded or met their goals or objectives in their host country.

This information stems from the data that was retrieved during participants in the study. Although this summary does not—nor should it—be used to generalize dynamics between all African diaspora and citizen-residents across the

African continent, it highlights commonalities of complex dynamics that exist between representatives of the two groups. Entrepreneurs seeking to start businesses, invest in their African home country, or contribute toward the development of Africa in various ways should also carefully consider how to mitigate some of these preconceived notions or misperceptions in their endeavors.

These findings are also important for policymakers and government agencies who may provide additional in-depth analyses to that characterize the relationship types and relational qualities between the African diaspora and their nation's citizen-residents. Mpande's (2015) adaptation of the relationship management framework offers policy makers, government agencies, and practitioners the tools to conduct thorough analyses between the two groups, as illustrated in Chapter 13. These analyses could inform practical initiatives to address potential underling tensions, promote mutual understanding, foster engagement and facilitate collaboration between the two groups

References

Brønn, P., & Brønn, C. (2000). A reflective stakeholder approach: Co-orientation as a basis for communication and learning. Bled, Slovenia: 7th International Public Relations Research Symposium. http://home.bi.no/fgl96053/bled2000.pdf

Carrozzino-Lyon, A. (2012). *Characterization and Communicative Analysis Of Wildlife Managers and Recreational Users of Virginia's Wildlife Management Areas* (Dissertation thesis). http://scholar.lib.vt.edu/theses/available/etd-06052012-132041/unrestricted/CarrozzinoLyon_AL_D_2012.pdf

Dozier, D. and W. P. Ehling (1992). Evaluation of public relations programs: What the literature tells us about their effects. In J. E. Grunig (ed.), *Excellence in Public Relations and Communication Management.* Hillsdale NJ: Lawrence Erlbaum Associates.

Hon, L., & Grunig, J. (1999). *Guidelines for Measuring Public Relations* [E-book]. Institute for Public Relations. https://www.instituteforpr.org/wp-content/uploads/Guidelines_Measuring_Relationships.pdf

Mpande, S. (2015). *Relationship management of the brain circulation phenomenon: The case of the Ugandan diaspora in the USA* (Publication No. 3718222) [Doctoral dissertation, Howard University]. ProQuest Dissertations and Theses Global.

Rhee, Y. (2004). The employee–public organization chain in relationship management: A case study of a government organization. http://www.instituteforpr.org/wp-content/uploads/2003_Rhee.pdf

Trisler, S. (2010). *Using Co-Orientation to Investigate the Views and Perceptions of Communications Held by the Public Relations Director and Superintendent in Two Indiana School Districts* (Master's thesis). http://cardinalscholar.bsu.edu/bitstream/123456789/193380/1/TrislerS_2010-3_BODY.pdf

Unit 4

Various challenges complicate nations' development agendas, particularly when the mutual cooperation and management of diverse relationships between vital stakeholders play significant roles in driving strategy and delivering key results. Although the African diaspora are amongst the key players in their African nations' development, their controversial national identities, relationships vis-à-vis citizen-residents in their homelands, and roles of engagement in the political and socio-economic spheres highlight a few challenges that hinder Africa's development—a matter of urgency for policy makers, nations, and key players to address.

In this unit, I present findings of the preliminary study that I conducted in the development of this book to offer insight into the dynamics between the African diaspora and citizen-residents in Africa. In Chapter 12, I reveal some of the dynamics and potential misperceptions that may describe the relationship between the African diaspora and citizen-residents across Africa and the implications in of their nation-building collaborative efforts. In Chapter 13, I explore how policy makers can implement critical analytical frameworks that incorporate cultural lenses to effectively engage the African diaspora in their African home nations. Specifically, I introduce my proposed adaptation of the relationship-management theoretical framework as a tool to assess and manage relationships between the African diaspora, citizen-residents, and their home country. I also refer to the importance of the co-orientational approach that I introduced in the previous chapter.

In Chapter 14, I propose recommendations and guidelines to strengthen networks and promote collaborations between the African diaspora and African citizen-residents, as well as to foster an enabling environment that promotes investments, entrepreneurial opportunities, and contributions from the African diaspora towards Africa's development. I also share guidelines for the diaspora to consider when seeking to invest in or relocate to their African home country. These recommendations and guidelines stem from various sources, including participants' interviews and literary analyses that I conducted in writing this book.

I conclude the book with Chapter 15, which explores the relevance of a pan-African approach in transforming paradigms to catapult Africa's development to newer levels of success.

DOI: 10.4324/9781351031660-16

13 Relationship-management theory

Harnessing relationships between the African diaspora and key stakeholders to motivate the diaspora to invest in or contribute toward their nations' development

Western and developing nations deploy different communicative strategies and channels to engage with their foreign audiences and build rapport. Less developed countries invest more in trust-building and credibility-enhancing strategies with foreign government audiences, or their "publics," more than their civil society (Mpande, 2015; Ndoye, 2009, p. 10). According to Ndoye (2009),

> *Western nations* tend to reach out to foreign publics using *public diplomacy* as a wartime exigency, a vehicle for the promotion of democracy, a means to expand modes of engagement and as a mouthpiece versus policy instrument; whereas *developing countries*, in the pursuit of their economic survival, are more inclined to use *international public relations* to directly reach out to *foreign government authorities*, not the *foreign countries' citizens*.
>
> (Mpande, 2015, p. 64; Ndoye, 2009, p.1)

Whereas most Western countries exercise public diplomacy with their publics and rely on non-governmental organizations (NGOs) to represent positive images to target foreign publics and reinforce their democracy, most developing countries extend public diplomatic strategies between government levels, not to the public, and invest in international public relations firms to brand their image and convey trust and credibility to Western foreign nations (Ndoye, 2009; Wang, 2005; Kunczik, 2003). Positive images are critical to ensure trust between nations, which influences their ability to secure and facilitate transactions of political, material, and international resources and capital (Mpande, 2015; Ndoye, 2009; Kunczik, 2003).

In light of this, how can African countries, in pursuit of their economic survival and in efforts to convey trust and credibility, use international public relations effectively with their citizens in foreign countries—namely, their diaspora? The African diaspora already use their soft-power skills and other attributes that position them as unofficial public relations practitioners when they engage with influential community leaders or government authorities in their host communities and home communities to foster development initiatives in Africa.

DOI: 10.4324/9781351031660-17

This chapter makes a case for why nations should consider implementing the relationship-management theoretical framework within their development agenda and in their outreach strategies to build positive rapports between the diaspora and citizen-residents. In the previous chapter, we identified misconceptions, perceptions, and stereotypes that some of the African diaspora and citizen-residents in African countries have about each other. Such sentiments heighten distrust that may discredit well-intentioned initiatives by either party. Given that the diaspora's contributions and financial investment in their African countries play a significant role in their nations' development, it is important that nations harness and maintain positive relationships with their diaspora and identify opportunities to ensure that relationships between all vital stakeholders—particularly between the diaspora and citizen-residents in Africa—are nurtured, protected, and harnessed effectively toward their nations' development.

Challenging normative public relations theories: A case for alternative "global" public relations theoretical perspectives

Relationship-management theory is a public relations theoretical framework that many public relations practitioners and researchers generally define through Ledingham's (2003) proposal: "the ethical and efficient management of an organization-stakeholder relationship, focused over time, on common interests and shared goals in support of mutual understanding and mutual benefit" (p. 190; Ledingham & Hung-Baesecke, 2015, p. 9).

The normative dimensions of many public relationship frameworks posited that two-way inclusive symmetrical styles of communication represent "excellent" models for public relations, which Kent and Taylor (2007) argue reinforce Western practices of generalizing excellence and less on relationship-building (Mpande, 2015). Instead, emphasis should be placed on how cultural practices in other nations affect public relations, and that "international public relations research should not be guided by efforts to prove that any single grand theory (or normative theory to use Vercic et al.'s terms) exists, but to understand the practice of public relations in other nations" (Mpande, 2015; p. Kent & Taylor, 2007, p. 13). Ultimately, there may be instances when symmetrical or asymmetrical communicative models between key stakeholders support optimal dynamics and relationship-building synergies between the diaspora and key stakeholders, effectively fostering brain circulation and supporting Africa's development.

Alternative theories to the normative theories of relationship management and excellence theories of public relations include Cancel, Cameron, Sallot, and Mitrook's (1997) contingency theory of accommodation.

> Deviating from arguments that the two-way symmetrical model in communications is optimal in organization-public relations, contingency theorists posit that 'true excellence' in public relations may, in fact, rely on one-way asymmetrical models, as a result of specific external and internal

> environmental variables that may lead to different levels of accommodation of publics on an advocacy-accommodation continuum in organization-public communication.
>
> (Mpande, 2015, p. 67)

Organizations may advocate for their own agenda, resulting in pure advocacy, one-way asymmetrical relationships. Generally, publics may perceive the one-way communication model as manipulative or exploitative. Hence, two-way symmetrical communication models suggest a more ethical and favorable communication model. However, two-way communication models may actually yield unfavorable outcomes, particularly if engaging with an audience with an immoral or unclear agenda (Mpande, 2015).

Mpande's (2015) study adopted a critical approach of *relationship management theory* to explore how the Ugandan government motivates its Ugandan diaspora in the United States to foster brain circulation and invest in their home country. Deviating from a normative approach of relationship management theory, Mpande's (2015) study employed a critical lens that pioneered an alternative theoretical framework to gain in-depth insight of how a state–diaspora relationship (representing an organization–stakeholder public relationship) could support a nation's development agenda. More specifically, the study explored the relationship between the Ugandan government and its US-based diaspora through a three-step public-relations framework that analyzed a) the influence of relationship antecedents, or external variables, on public relations strategies that the Ugandan government performed to motivate its diaspora to invest into Uganda; b) offline and online relationship cultivation strategies that the Ugandan government enacted with its diaspora: access, positivity, openness and disclosure, networking, shared tasks, and assurances (Hung, 2002; Hon & Grunig, 1999); and c) the relational outcomes that Hon and Grunig (1999) and various scholars presented as symmetrical or asymmetrical relationship types (symbiotic, exchange, communal, covenantal, exploitative, and contractual) and as relational qualities (relational trust, commitment, control mutuality, and relational satisfaction). Ultimately, Mpande's (2015) study acknowledged how both symmetrical or asymmetrical communicative models, integrated with social media, shaped strategies and influenced relationships between the Ugandan government and diaspora to promote brain circulation that would support Uganda's development.

Findings of Mpande's (2015) study implied that nations undergoing development must

> (1) cultivate multidimensional communication strategies with their diaspora resources; (2) ensure they adhere to the unique psycho-emotional needs related to trust, commitment, control mutuality, satisfaction, and feeling needed and valued by the home community; and (3) produce readily accessible documents and implement policies that facilitate diaspora investments in the national welfare (Mpande, 2015, abstract).

Mpande's (2015) study also introduced an alternative relationship management theory, within the context of international government public relations of a state–diaspora relationship, to support their home nations' development agenda:

> the ethical and efficient management of a State-Diaspora stakeholder relationship, focused over time, on common interests of socio-economic and political contributions and shared goals of national development, over time, in support of mutual understanding and benefit for interacting governments and their Diaspora publics.

However, this framework can be modified to address the specific organization and public when seeking to identify common interests in terms of contributions that address nations' development.

An overview of the alternative four-step relationship-management theoretical framework

The following key lessons and recommendations, derived from Mpande's (2015) study, introduce key components to include in a wholistic four-step relationship-management framework for nations to consider. Mpande's (2015) approach to the framework makes it a practical tool to guide key relationships between nation-states (organizations) and diaspora (publics) toward their development agenda (See Figure 13.1):

(i) Previous scholars that examined relationships through relationship-management theory generally focused solely on one of the three relationship components (antecedents, cultivation strategies, or outcomes), or on one variable within one of the components. Mpande's (2015) study demonstrates the *vitality in integrating all three relationship components into a sequential, four-step framework that explores each of the relationship components as independent research questions to generate a wholistic picture that provides clearer overall understanding of the relationship and identifies nuances.* A study on relationships must integrate both external and internal factors that influence both parties and considers how these variables may alter the relationship over time. Furthermore, data generated from one step of the framework may provide relevant insight and guide analyses at other levels of the framework to provide greater clarity and deeper understanding of the phenomenon in question.

(ii) Mpande's (2015) study contextualized the study to *consider relationship antecedents that are unique to a country's infrastructure (political, legal, economic structures), media, and cultural systems—including African cultural philosophies* of Kenya's *Harambee* (which means the whole country pulling together) and *Ubuntu* (a Ngusi Bantu term that means "I am because you are")—influenced relationship cultivation strategies between the government and

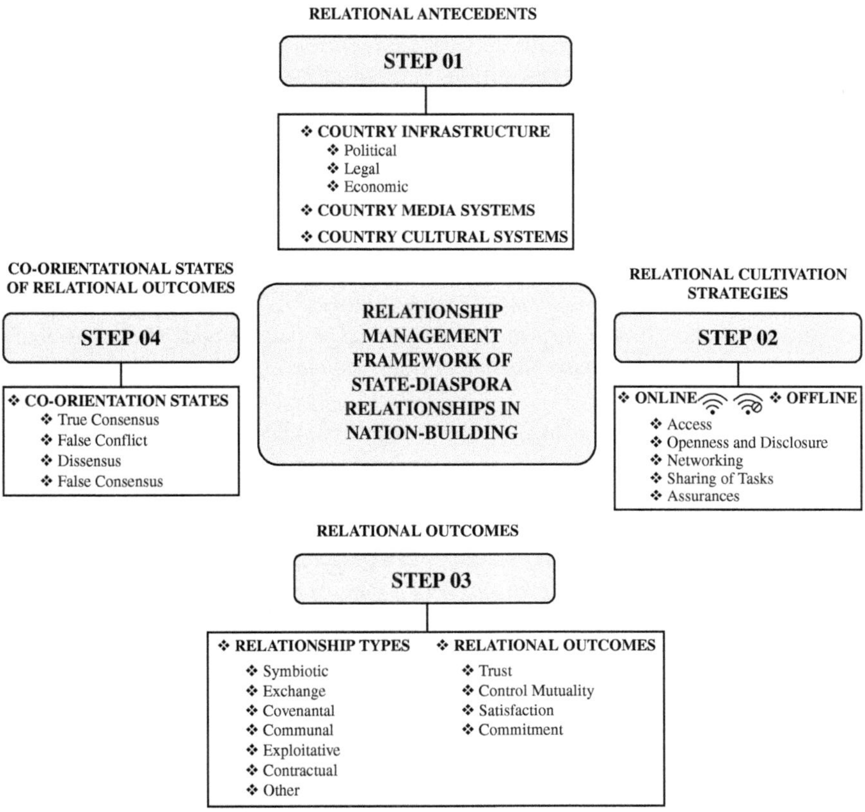

Figure 13.1 Relationship-management framework for state–diaspora relationships in nation-building (Mpande, 2015). Adapted from the works of Grunig (2002), Sriramesh and Vercic (2009), Hon and Grunig (1999), and Hung (2001)

its diaspora. This was referred to as *Harambuntu* so as to capture both sentiments. In Uganda, "*Twezimbe, Twegayite*" (Let us build our country) and "*Tu deyo yekka*" (Let us go back home) emerged as the common Luganda expressions used by government officials and diaspora communities in their collaborations to promote development. Development communication strategies and frameworks should incorporate the unique cultural dimensions of the groups, which reinforce identity connections with target audiences and can inform effective approaches to diplomatic behavior and relationship-building. A nation's diaspora is a unique stakeholder group that possesses one particular variable that distinguishes it from other foreign stakeholders: a similar cultural identity and resonance that inherently connects them to their heritage and homeland in psycho-emotional ways that transcend logic, science, and objective, hard facts. It would be important to consider how cultural ties with diaspora groups are leveraged, valued, and strengthened to fortify relationships that cater to each party's needs.

(iii) The advent of social media and virtual technology has drastically changed communication and relationships. Instead of focusing solely on how relationships are cultivated offline, Mpande's (2015) study also developed coding assessments to analyze how the Ugandan government cultivated its relationships with its diaspora using online tools, including websites and the social media platforms of Facebook and Twitter. In today's ever-evolving digital world, *it would be important for policy makers to assess how these relationship cultivation strategies are leveraged both offline and with digital platforms, including Instagram, Pinterest, LinkedIn, and other forms of online communication, which they use to cultivate relational strategies (access, openness and disclosure, networking, sharing of tasks, assurances) that may foster the brain circulation postulate.*

(iv) Previous studies on relationship-management theory may have also been limited by considering only one party's perspective to determine the quality of a relationship between an organization and its stakeholder public, or between two parties generally. Mpande's (2015) study emphasizes *the significance of assessing relational outcomes through a co-orientation framework that incorporates perspectives of both parties in a study to conclude: (i) the* types of relationships *that exist (e.g., symbiotic, exchange, covenantal, communal, exploitative, contractual), as well as (ii) the* quality of the relationships *(trust, control mutuality, satisfaction, commitment).* "Broom et al. and J. Grunig and Huang called for development of co-orientational measures that reflect *each* party's perceptions of the relationship, as well as what they believe the other party's perception of the relationship to be" (Rhee, 2004, p. 43). This is key because one party may falsely assume that their relationship with the other party is satisfactory or exploitative—although data may reveal that the other party harbors a contradictory perspective. Hence, shedding light on both parties' perspectives permits the researcher to gain a more complete, accurate picture. Policy makers who use a co-orientation framework may ultimately conclude if a false consensus, true consensus, or false conflict exists between the parties. This conclusion would guide effective data-driven interventions that address the reality of both parties' relationship to mitigate potential conflict. In the context of fostering brain circulation in a country, policymakers and practitioners should gain perspectives from both the country's government representatives and the particular stakeholder group (diaspora audiences, or representatives of a particular private corporation, public agency, development organization, or other target public) to shape their interventions.

(v) Mpande's (2015) study employed *multiple qualitative methods through textual analyses of websites, social media platforms, and interviews with members of the government and the diaspora that yielded insight on the complexity of the relationship.* A qualitative approach, as opposed to relying solely on quantitative methods, would offer richer context for the nature of some relationships.

> For instance, a quantitative study may limit analyses to merely conclude that a group perceives a relationship with its government to be asymmetrical, with little openness and disclosure and distrust. However, a qualitative exploration may further explain that the government chooses to control certain types of information to protect the interests of other stakeholder publics who may otherwise be vulnerable or prone to attack—unbeknownst to different stakeholder publics. However, assumptions that remain unaddressed may contribute to fragile relationships that challenge the parties' cooperation in the nation-building process. Hence, practitioners would need to determine how to effectively manage issues of discretion when cultivating relationship strategies between parties, while ensuring that their expectations and needs are met to fulfill a positive relationship. *Furthermore, a mixed methodology of both quantitative and qualitative methods may be most useful to generalize results amongst a larger subset of populations (quantitative), and also contextualize in-depth interpretations of data for better understanding of the phenomena (qualitative).*

There is also value in developing various relationship-management theoretical frameworks to manage different relationship cultivation strategies between various state actors, nonstate actors, or those that comprise both. For instance, in their study seeking clarity on the multiple meanings and conceptualization of "global health governance," Lee and Kamradt-Scott (2014) note that there exists a growing dilemma over power shifting between state and nonstate actors, reinforced by the rising prominence of nonstate actors leading and a rivalry that "erodes the capacity of states to govern" (para. 10). In our context, the state actors that Lee and Kamradt-Scott (2014) describe could be represented by the citizen-residents or government authorities, and the "non-state actors" they refer to could be represented—in our context—by the African diaspora. The dilemma surrounding these groups' power shift contributes further to the tensions and fragile relationships between them, as we have described in earlier chapters. Understandably, it may become increasingly difficult for state and nonstate actors to define their respective parameters and scope of responsibilities.

Hence, implementing the relationship-management theoretical framework with the co-orientational analysis may reveal that one party perceives their relationship type to be *noncontractual* and describes the quality of their relationship as that of *relational dissatisfaction*—unbeknownst to the other party. Policymakers who have access to data that describes the relationship types and qualities of relationships between these groups, or state and nonstate actors, can pragmatically implement conflict-resolution strategies or practical interventions through policies, frameworks, or guidelines that clearly articulate how each group should govern in particular contexts, without infringing on the other group's boundaries. Some solutions and recommendations to promote and enhance a positive relationship may also stem directly from each group, derived from their in-depth qualitative responses to interviews or other data-gathering mechanisms.

In Chapter 12, we learned that the sample groups from both the African diaspora and citizen-residents in African countries expressed a frustration that the "other group" does not understand the group's "realities." The qualitative nature of the questionnaire revealed more context about each of their "realities." We also learned that each group may have harbored complexes about the other, suggesting a distrust of the other party's level of knowledge and the other party's ability to be effective in implementing development solutions in Africa. Additional analyses and inquiries in a robust co-orientational analysis would reveal the relationship type such data describes, as well as the relational quality. Inserting such rich data within a relationship-management framework of a more thorough, robust study offers an opportunity for policy makers and practitioners to shape institutionalized approaches and policies that support their collaborations.

The following chapter will reveal additional recommendations and guidelines, offered by the diaspora and citizen-resident participants in the preliminary, exploratory study of this book. The study introduced a co-orientational approach to shed light on how each group perceived the other and how they believed they were perceived by the other group. In the study, participants also offered recommendations and guidelines to enhance positive relationships between the diaspora and citizen-residents, and how nations can foster an enabling environment to encourage the diaspora to invest in or contribute to their African nation's development.

References

Cancel, A. E., Cameron, G. T., Sallot, L. M., & Mitrook, M. A. (1997). It Depends: A Contingency Theory of Accommodation in Public Relations. *Journal of Public Relations Research*, *9*(1), 31–63. https://doi.org/10.1207/s1532754xjprr0901_02

Ledingham, J. A. (2003). Explicating relationship management as a general theory of public relations. *Journal of Public Relations Research*, *15*(2), 181–198. doi:10.1207/s1532754xjprr1502_4

Ndoye, I. (2009). Crafting the image of nations in foreign audiences: How developing countries use public diplomacy and public relations? *N.d*, 1–13. https://instituteforpr.org/wp-content/uploads/ImageInForeignAudiences.pdf

Hon, L. C., & Grunig, J. E. (1999). *Guidelines for Measuring Relationships in Public Relations*. Gainesville, FL: the Institute for Public Relations. http://www.aco.nato.int/resources/9/conference%202011/guidelines_measuring_relationships[1].pdf

Hung, C. F. (2001). *Toward a normative theory of relationship management*. Gainesville, FL: the Institute for Public Relations. http://www.instituteforpr.org/wp-content/uploads/2001_Hung.pdf

Hung, C. F. (2002). *The Interplays of Relationship Types, Relationship Cultivation, and Relationship Outcomes: How Multinational and Taiwanese Companies Practice Public Relations and Organization-Public Relationship Management in China* (Dissertation thesis). Available from ProQuest Dissertations and Theses database. (UMI Number 3115706)

Kent, M., & Taylor, M. (2007). Beyond excellence: Extending the generic approach to international public relations: The case of Bosnia. *Public Relations Review, 33*(2007), 10–20. doi:10.1016/j.pubrev.2006.11.002

Kunczik, M. (2003). Transnational public relations by foreign governments. In K. Sriramesh & D. Vercic (Eds.), *Handbook of global public relations* (pp. 399–424). Mahwah, NJ: Lawrence Erlbaum.

Ledingham, J., & Hung-Baesecke, F. (2015). *Relationship Management: The Core Focus of Public Relations*. ResearchGate. https://www.researchgate.net/publication/322567510_Relationship_Management_The_Core_Focus_of_Public_Relations

Lee, K., & Kamradt-Scott, A. (2014, April 28). The multiple meanings of global health governance: A call for conceptual clarity. *Globalization and Health*. https://globalizationandhealth.biomedcentral.com/articles/10.1186/1744-8603-10-28

Mpande, S. (2015). *Relationship management of the brain circulation phenomenon: The case of the Ugandan diaspora in the USA* (Publication No. 3718222) [Doctoral dissertation, Howard University]. ProQuest Dissertations and Theses Global.

Rhee, Y. (2004). The employee–public organization chain in relationship management: A case study of a government organization. Institute for Public Relations website: http://www.instituteforpr.org/wp-content/uploads/2003_Rhee.pdf

Sriramesh, K., & Vercic, D. (2009). A theoretical framework for global public relations research and practice. In: K. Sriramesh & D. Vercic (Eds.), *The Global Public Relations Handbook: Theory, Research, and Practice* (pp. 1–25). New York, NY: Routledge. https://meistra.files.wordpress.com/2014/10/krishnamurthy-sriramesh-dejan-vercic-the-global-public-relations-handbook-revised-and-expanded-edition-theory-research-and-practice-communication-routledge-hardcover-2009.pdf

Wang, J. (2005). Localizing public diplomacy: The role of sub-national actors in national branding. *Journal of Place Branding*, *2*, 32–42.

14 Guidelines and recommendations to foster African diaspora engagement with their African homelands

Enabling an environment that promotes collaborations between the diaspora and citizen-residents in Africa requires the leverage of formal and informal systems, mechanisms, policies, and initiatives that need to be refined, established, or initiated between both groups. I identified and compiled this study's participants' data into various themes and categories. Contextualizing the data with additional research culminated in recommendations to foster African diaspora engagement with their African homelands. The four categories of recommendations are (a) promote collaborations between the African diaspora and African citizen-residents in Africa; (b) foster an enabling environment that promotes investments and entrepreneurial opportunities in Africa from the African diaspora; (c) strengthen networks between the African diaspora and citizen-residents in Africa, and (d) tips for Africans in the diaspora seeking to contribute to, invest in, or relocate to Africa.

A). Promote Collaborations between the African diaspora and African citizen-residents in Africa

Based on emerging themes from my participants' data, supported by any additional research analyses I conducted, below are eight recommendations to promote effective collaborations between the African diaspora and African citizen-residents in their joint efforts in nation-building (See Figure 14.1):

1) **Eliminate complexes by changing existing mindsets and misperceptions:**
   - (i) *Manage the social identity complex (African/diaspora identity):* The mentality of "I am an African in the Diaspora" creates a barrier between "diaspora" and "home" because it adds to complexes, increases complexities, and misunderstandings. Instead, there should be a reassertion that people on the ground in Africa and Africans in the diaspora share a collective identity and sets of unique experiences that should leverage on unification.
   - (ii) *Ban the "saviors' complex":* Change the perception of needing to "save" African communities on the grounds that one may perceive

DOI: 10.4324/9781351031660-18

Figure 14.1 Promote collaborations between the African diaspora and African citizen-residents in Africa

them as "helpless" or "dependent." Instead, this mindset should be replaced with an approach to putting an end to injustices and oppressive behaviors that take advantage of those in Africa. One should aim to empower those on the ground by helping them secure access to resources that complement the resources they already possess.

(iii) *Remove superiority and inferiority complexes:* Everyone—including those in the diaspora and citizen-residents in Africa—offers a valuable contribution that is not restricted solely to those with formal education or exposure to international opportunities. The diaspora should not use their opportunities and access to materials or to privilege to mistreat, belittle, or exploit those on the ground; instead, they should use their opportunities to contribute to serving and investing in those at home. Simultaneously, those on the ground should not exploit the goodwill of the diaspora by engaging in behaviors that would breed distrust when funds are sent home. Ultimately, there should be humility from both groups in seeking to solve problems on the continent.

2) **Leverage social media platforms and ICT to strengthen connections and networks:**

Social media groups are useful to connect those in the diaspora with those back in the Motherland so they can learn and explore opportunities and collaborations. Strengthening ties between groups in the diaspora and in the West is helpful, particularly for those seeking access to niche communities on the ground in Africa. Social media platforms are also useful in allowing both groups to penetrate already-established networks and organizations in the short term to learn more about issues or about policies. For instance, the social media group Sudan Malaria invites anyone who has insight into the Sudanese malaria problem to go in and contribute to discussions informally. That is also a way to start learning about issues on the ground, prior to making life-changing decisions to relocate. One can also join business-oriented groups and niche networks to understand priorities around small businesses—especially for people of color—or those interested in international development. Social media platforms can also host special events featuring different speakers from Africa and those from the diaspora with certain skillsets to discuss business or self-development opportunities in Africa.

3) **Plan short-term visits on the ground:** Prior to deciding to relocate to Africa permanently, it would be valuable for the diaspora to visit their African homelands frequently to gain first-hand experience of what the country has to offer. They could also engage with citizen-residents on the ground and identify niche markets or opportunities to assess where and how one can make valuable contributions. Based on research, it may be possible to reside in the host country, yet still actively engage in projects back home.
4) **Manage cultural differences:** It is important to ensure that there is a strong degree of cultural fit and an alignment of core values between the community with which the diaspora want to engage in partnerships and do business. Cultural differences are to be expected, including ethnic biases or male-dominated attitudes that accompany patriarchal societies. However, one should be honest about one's tolerance level of cultural differences and be prepared to make adjustments as appropriate. Ultimately, the African diaspora and citizen-residents in Africa have to be willing to put their differences aside and find ways to collaborate and cooperate.
5) **Be open to each group's ideas of innovation:** Africans on the ground should not always resist ideas from their Western counterparts by insisting that "this is how we do things here." They should be open to solutions that may deviate from their conventional norm. Simultaneously, the African diaspora should also respect that people back home (across Africa) also have their own solutions. Both groups should recognize that solutions are not always one-way; instead, they should be open to collaborations together.

Also, one should realize that there is no need to always reinvent the wheel. Different people from different cultures and countries could adopt and tweak solutions that are tailored to their country. Someone may have experienced challenges in other countries and already identified solutions and strategies that others can apply to their own local contexts to arrive at the same destination (participant, personal communication, December 21, 2019).

Hence, knowledge transfer is as valuable—or more valuable—than financial remittances as a means of collaboration. Financial remittances should be used, instead, to learn skills or trades to promote more self-sufficiency.

6) **Engage in transparent dialogues and communication to address misconceptions:** Honest, transparent dialogue is important for both citizen-residents at home and those in the diaspora to discuss their opportunities, achievements, challenges, limitations, and hardships. This will help to dispel myths that the grass is greener on the other side, as problems exist everywhere. Both groups can also address any misconceptions or misperceptions about each other to identify opportunities that support and fulfill each other's needs.
7) **Be Africa's ambassador:** We should serve as ambassadors for the African market and help to globally promote more goods, products, and services that hail from the African continent and from Africans. We should also promote the opportunities of conducting businesses in Africa. Hence, we need to change the perception that doing business in Africa is "hard," risky, and ripe with corruption, or that business opportunities and jobs in Africa are impossible to find unless one has connections. Doing business in Africa is not different from doing business in any part of the world. Similar to all businesses everywhere, relationships in Africa also need to be cultivated.
8) **Strengthen trust:** It is important for both groups to ensure and strengthen their ability to trust each other. One way to build trust is to maintain integrity and to do what one says one will do. For example, if there are projects that both groups agree to develop together, they should ensure that they follow through on agreements.

B). Foster an enabling environment that promotes investments and entrepreneurial opportunities in Africa from the African diaspora

An enabling environment that motivates investment and entrepreneurialism in the interests of Africa's development agenda requires the leverage of formal and informal systems, mechanisms, policies, and initiatives that need to be continually refined, strongly established, adaptive to the global and local context, and responsive to the needs of the market. The following recommendations are targeted primarily towards African governments, and stem from emerging themes of participants' data, supported by analyses from additional sources (See Figure 14.2):

1) **Strengthen democracy and governance that enhance peaceful climates:**

Figure 14.2 Foster an enabling environment that promotes investments and entrepreneurial opportunities in Africa from the African diaspora

It is important to have a strong democracy and a governance system that reinforce anti-corruption measures and obedience to the rule of law. This also means ensuring that credible elections are held so that politicians are upheld to performance metrics, as opposed to rigged elections or election officials' reliance on bribes. Reinforcing a democracy also offers more freedom and protection from human-rights violations. This includes ensuring a democracy that will not criminalize journalists, bloggers, and others for freedom of expression. Strengthening governance and ensuring accountability mechanisms guarantees the security of lives and communities' properties to the best extent possible. Hence, it is also important to ensure and prioritize political stability. Peacebuilding efforts need to be strengthened for one to feel safe to relocate to the homeland and to open up health clinics, businesses, and essential services that can only thrive in conflict-free environments and address the needs of the community.

2) **Develop government and state ministry-sponsored programs for diaspora investments:**

The state and the various ministries that are responsible for immigration, tourism, and foreign affairs must provide flexible and adaptable programs and policies of special dispensation for returning Africans in the diaspora. This will include a dedicated foreign office to register and process data and information effectively and efficiently. There should also be adequate technology provided that can support innovative investments and businesses. Policies, including rebate, free zone policies, tax exemptions, agriculture inputs, and machinery could also be featured in programs that incentivize diaspora investments. Governments can also sponsor short-term programs for Africans in the diaspora to work and live (less than eight weeks) as a way of easing the diaspora into the culture and system. Embassies could hire consultants and specific specialists who can serve as points of contact to meet with diaspora members who are interested in learning more about investing in and/or contributing to investments back home. Such consultancies can also be set up by the diaspora. Their objective would be to effectively describe clear and transparent processes for investments that may address fears the diaspora harbor about making risky investments or losing money on investments.

3) **Develop network programs, knowledge, and resource hubs for investment processes:**

   It would be vital to develop information hubs that simplify the processes for business registration, identify "quick-win" business opportunities for investors, and provide detailed guidelines for investments. Similarly, it would be valuable to develop a safe, secure, and accessible repository that organizes information on the knowledge, skills, abilities, and aptitudes of practitioners, researchers, policy makers, and other specialists, documenting, packaging and institutionalizing information on best practices for various purposes. Critical information for investment purposes could include guidance on avoiding cumbersome registration processes for business; ways to identify "quick-win" business opportunities for investors; free zone areas for manufacturing; and provision of a corruption-free environment for the processing of all activities. For those seeking to re-acculturate or plan visits to their home country after years of absence, information would also consist of clear instructions and guidance for resettling, residence, safety, transport methods, cultural differences, and faux pas, weather, health risks, shopping areas, and social opportunities for expatriates.

4) **Strengthen infrastructure and secure systems that facilitate an effective exchange of goods, services, and mobility:**

   It is important to develop easier systems to support the transfer of goods and services, including money. This includes a remittance system that facilitates sending and receiving remittances in both directions, which would be necessary when purchasing goods and services from abroad. The remittance systems should also be more financially inclusive of refugees and offer opportunities for those that lack access to banks. The highly anticipated African passport would also be a valued feature to facilitate movement across regions and strengthen business opportunities. Developing stronger infrastructure also grants better access to healthcare, education systems, and transportation to support other sectors.

5) **Market promotions and incentives from governments:**

Incentives that are afforded to foreign investors should also be afforded to citizens or residents who are investing money in the country, as there have been cases of preferential treatment towards foreign investors. Governments play a big role in engaging and attracting the diaspora. Hence, governments should reduce bureaucratic red tape that could discourage the diaspora from investing in opportunities. Instead, they should invest more in organizing network events and concrete initiatives through their embassies, advertising national diaspora bills and diaspora bonds, and interacting directly with the diaspora to promote initiatives that cater to the diaspora who seek opportunities to connect to Africa.

C). Strengthen strategic networks between the African diaspora and citizen-residents in Africa

Africa's nation-building process requires a coordinated, collaborative effort that reflects the shared values, principles, and goals of all stakeholders of the global community. In particular, African governments, citizen-residents, and diaspora groups comprise valuable networks, or an "interconnected group of people linked to one another in way that makes them capable of beneficial cooperation, which can take various forms, including the exchange of goods and ideas" (Grewal, 2008, p. 20).

Recurring responses among the respondents of this preliminary study included "networks" and the leverage of social media. Below are a few strategies to leverage networks between citizen-residents in Africa, the African diaspora, and the African government to effectively direct efforts towards their shared goal of revitalizing their nation (See Figure 14.3):

1) **Hone the responsibility of "leading social groups" of networks:**
   Deutsch (1966) acknowledges "leading social groups" as those that would need to

   > "be 'above' some of the main groups to be led, at least in terms of current prestige, and usually in the long run in terms of economic, political, and social opportunities, skills, wealth, organization and the like, so that a member of another group would have the sense of 'rising in the world'… or 'moving vertically in society."
   >
   > (p. 102)

   This also suggests that the voices and perspectives of these "leading social groups" or individuals within these groups are influential in society. They would generally represent a dominant group whose views or ideologies may be more rapidly and largely disseminated through technology and communicative platforms. In the contemporary technological era, these leading social groups may be recognized as influencers, celebrities,

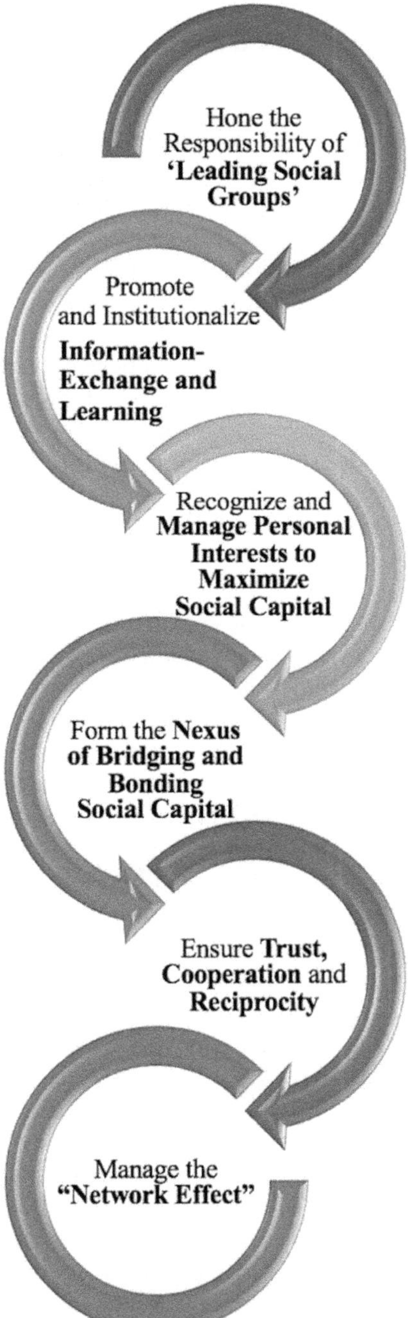

Figure 14.3 Strengthen strategic networks between the African diaspora and citizen-residents in Africa

or community leaders who amass large numbers of followers on social media platforms and may easily infiltrate other influential communities and networks. Given their visible platforms, these leading social groups should responsibly use their influence to motivate their local and global communities to become actively involved in issues related to socioeconomic or political development in their nation, concerning investments opportunities, governance, or human rights.

Social media platforms have more easily enabled some of these "leading social groups" to bypass third parties or traditional media gatekeepers who may control the production and dissemination of information. The advent of digital communication and social media positions these groups to more directly access other social leading groups in media, politics, and other spheres of influence and foster collaboration on the national development agenda. With strong networks, leading social groups of one community who may be restricted in using social media platforms may rely on their counterparts who are leading social groups of other communities to collaborate and disseminate their message.

2) **Promote innovative information exchange and learning to institutionalize best practices:**

Information and learning play a central role in networks. Information represents resources, or forms of input in the decision-making, production, or bureaucratic process (Branam, 2006, p. 12). Encouraging the opportunity to deviate from repeated learnings of practices allows networks to learn from alternatives. Just as "a new kind of social life developed around the reading and exchange of books and printed papers" (Tarrow, 2011, p. 45), new social lives have develped around online communities and networks.

Combined with traditional forms of learning, new digital platforms permit civil communities, governments and diaspora members to gain exposure to new practices and alternative ideas that could be exchanged and implemented. Such innovation of information-exchange also places value on the source of information-gathering. Heterogeneous, or diverse sources in a network contribute towards members' learning and education of new innformation that is critical in fostering a community and building the nation. Best practices that derive from such information exchange could institutionalized into nation-building.

Ultimately, members gain a two-fold benefit for innovative learning and information-exchange. First, as network members normalize a receptive approach of innnovative practices of information-exchange and learning in their pursuit of nation-building, they position themselves to readily-adopt new technologies that enhance the way they collaborate. Second, the information that is generated and exchanged represents innovative development solutions and other useful content to become implemented in the national develeopment agenda.

3) **Recognize and manage personal interests to maximize social capital in networks:**

Social capital is a significant value that can be a private and public good for network members and participants (Grewal, 2008). As a private good, social capital benefits the individual who is personally invested in creating, building, and finding value in the relationships that she or he personally invests in. The individual benefits from social capital as a public good because the value of social capital is only maximized if the people in his/her network are also just as well-connected to others outside of the circle (p. 20). Consequently, the degrees of seperation between well-connected individuals are lessened considerably.

However, "personal self-interests" usually present a social dilemma that stifles cooperation and focuses more on immediate private, personal interests, and less on the long-term, public, and community at large. These self-interests suggest different motives in joining a network, which may also clash with those of other members. For instance, a participant in this preliminary study noted that while governments in Africa may encourage entrepreneurship, there is the sense that some people in agencies may withhold paperwork to alleviate competition from some diaspora members because they recognize that there are not many opportunities for locals in the country, (even though) everyone is a national (participant, personal communication, 2020). Such perceptions—whether actual or perceived—challenge cooperative or collaborative opportunities between government officials, citizen-residents, and diaspora members of a network.

It is critical, therefore, that different self-interests, motives, and agendas are carefully assessed and that expectations are managed to ensure that the value of social capital is maximized among the African diaspora, citizen-resident groups, and government officials. The social-psychlogical theory, which refers to the instrumental model (use of desirable incentives or sanctions) and social motivation model (use of predisposed attitudes), could be applied to explain individuals' different motives in joining a network. Identifying these motives could drive the formation of specific networks that invite those with similar mindsets and values to ensure uniformity and shared agreements among members.

4) **Form the nexus of bridging and bonding social capital:**

By *bridging* social capital, members of a network can benefit from the value of access to external information and heterogeneous source of assets that is accessible throughout the network. Members can form communties or valuable networks and thereby facilitate an exchange of goods and ideas that fulfill concrete objectives in promoting socio-economic development in the African country. *Bonding* social capital, however, is more homogeneous and reinforces a mobilized identity. Bonding capital accentuates members' common, shared heritage in their African nation.

Hence, leveraging ways to bridge and bond social capital supports the dual nature of a cultural and "development" network that reinforces members' mobilized identity and motivates their collective action towards a greater purpose.

For instance, African diaspora networks based on shared interests in a particular industry or sector may form to encourage diverse members of the diaspora to collaborate and identify ways to contribute funds, leverage skills, and develop that sector. One type of network may restrict membership solely to African diaspora members in a host country, or exclusively to citizen-residents in the same home country, to improve sectors in their home country. Alternatively, another network may be formed between African diaspora members and citizen-residents in home countries to influence governments' abilities to effect change in several sectors. Regardless, the goals and objectives of these networks would influence the nature of these networks, their membership criteria, and the quantity and types of resources that members have access to—all of which may impact the degree to which bridging and bonding social capital occurs.

But both approaches of leveraging social capital present opportunities for African governments, citizen-residents, and the diaspora in efforts to contribute towards or invest in Africa's development. It would be critical for networks to articulate their goals and ensure that members also feel a shared ownership of a network that is inclusive.

5) **Ensure trust, cooperation, and reciprocity of networks:**

Another important characteristic of networks that Sikkink (2009) highlights is "their ability to build trust and confidence among network participants" (Sikkink, 2009, p. 230). Tilly (2010) also highlights the significance of trust in social relations, which he acknowledges as a "relation in which at least one party places a valued enterprise at risk to the malfeasance, mistakes, or failure of another party. Trust is often, but not always, mutual" (Tilly, 2010, p. 272). Tilly's (2010) issue of mutuality supports Putnam's (2001) emphasis that "a society characterized by generalized reciprocity [(unspecified, returned favors)], is more efficient than a distrustful society, for the same reason that money is more efficient than barter" (Putnam, 2000, p. 21.)

Such trust can be reinforced through regular communication that reflects a transparent agenda and fosters an exchange of information among members. Responses indicated that trust was important for both the African diaspora and citizen-residents to collaborate and ensure that they could engage in nation-building activities. A participant also reinforced the importance of ensuring that promises and agreements were fulfilled between citizen-residents and African diaspora in their efforts to collaborate (personal communication, January 12, 2020). Additionally, clear rule adherences, performance, role designations, and discussion of mediating standards that maintain the functionality of the network are also vital components to foster trust and cooperation (Tyler, 2010; Grewal, 2008). A core group of designated network leaders should establish norms and protocols that form the basic organization of the group, yet also motivate members to offer contributions and engage in ways that reflect a reciprocity and shared ownership.

6) **Manage the "Network Effect":**

John's (2010) idea of the "network effect"— that "the value of a network for its users increases as the network expands"—is flawed. The number of people joining a network does not necessarily equate to a uniform message or equitable platform that is representative of the powerful minority or the powerless majority. It is important the African diaspora and citizen-residents in Africa focus on developing groups that have a strategic, cohesive, unified message; otherwise, they risk an expanding network of plural groups that lack direction, which ultimately weakens the value of their "strength," despite the numbers.

However, there are various indirect benefits that stem from a growing network. Increased value, derivative of size, is also linked to its attractive quality through its "power to draw other users into the network from other networks" (Grewal, 2008, p. 40). Hence, it would be essential to reduce diminishing effects of the value of the network and to ensure that it maintains its goals in reinforcing a collective unit among the diaspora, citizen-residents, and government for effective collaboration.

D). General tips for Africans in the diaspora seeking to contribute to, invest in, or relocate to Africa

The following recommendations, tips, and advice stem from emerging themes of this study's participants' data, supported by analyses from various sources. The following information is derived specifically from Africans in the diaspora who actively engage in opportunities in their African homelands, or former residents of the diaspora and who are currently returnees in their African home country (see Figure 14.4):

1) **Learn the global trends in Africa's development agenda:** These include the roles of China, Russia, the United Kingdom, or other countries in Africa's development. As diaspora, be active in economic and trade engagement, driving policy as opposed to being driven by policy. Be actively engaged in driving conversations and policies that hold people accountable and speak out against issues that you know may not be in the best interests of Africans. Start businesses and mentor others, as opposed to being a critic of initiatives. "If you are going to criticize, be a part of the engagement" (participant, personal communication, January 23, 2020).
2) **Develop entrepreneurial organizations or support already-existing organizations in Africa.** It is critical to create or provide job opportunities across the African continent, based on the imminent need to address unemployment among a growing youthful population. Graduates from universities seek employment upon completion of their studies,

Figure 14.4 General tips for Africans in the diaspora seeking to contribute to, invest in, or relocate to Africa

yet struggle to join the labor market or a labor market that adequately responds to their skillsets.

3) **Be intentional about investing in women, the youth, and marginalized groups.** Explore training incubation and programs that provide resources, especially for entrepreneurship opportunities that can empower women and youth to be self-sufficient. Women across African countries are the backbone of their nations' economy and play an integral role in their households, yet remain on the periphery of the labor market, face barriers that limit their participation in the market and are excluded from access to economic or social capital. Africa also has the youngest population in the world, and they need to be integrated the labor market, particularly after completing their studies. Investments in all these groups also address unemployment challenges that add constraints to the economy.

Investments also refer to knowledge transfer. Knowledge transfer is as valuable as—or more valuable than—financial remittances as means of collaboration. Financial remittances should be used to learn skills or trades to promote more self-sufficiency.

4) **The diaspora should consider relocating to Africa through a series of phases**, or frequent short-term trips, as opposed to making a one-time permanent move to an African country, especially if you are not familiar with the country. One may discover ways to retain a base in one's Western host country. This will support gaining on-the-ground realities and conducting first-hand research that is necessary to understand the culture as well as the overall business and investment climate. This would also help to inform the diaspora about how to be financially prepared and to understand the economic climate, prior to making a move to another country. One may underestimate the cost of living, cash flow expenses, and other financial requisites that would be vital if one were to start a business, or is in search of a job.
5) **Students should join or volunteer in relevant university-sponsored programs in their host countries.** Many programs exist in universities, including Engineers without Borders. These programs offer students to gain exposure to and practical experience in development work in developing countries while at school. These opportunities allow them to broaden perspectives, network with others, and gain valuable insights that can inform their academic degree, educational experiences, and profession, as well as foster key relationships that will guide their career development. This option may be easier for professions in the trade and private sector than it may be for those seeking to enter politics in their home country, because one would have to be on the ground to understand the nuances governing the political nature of relationships. Other programs for students and professionals to join may be broader, including the African Leadership Network, an organization meant to re-educate the younger generation of Africans. For instance, the Network has been working on building universities in Africa and to transform the rhetoric about Africa.
6) **Professionals or new entrepreneurs should join relevant programs within the host country that support business investment resources.** For instance, in the United States, the diaspora should identify ways to be involved with the United States Chamber of Commerce. Similar equivalents in other host countries are important to support the diaspora's ability to actively contribute to their particular industry, promote interest in local business opportunities, and identify ways to be active in the global and local communities.

An enabling environment for the African diaspora that would permit them to invest in their home nations' development depends on the capabilities of the state, which sets a foundation and framework for many of the infrastructure developments and industrializations that can ignite growth in development sectors. This foundation also sets the tone of governance to combat corruption and ensure that the climate is politically and economically stable and attractive for investment. An enabling environment for investment also rests on the relational dynamics between the diaspora and their governments, as well as citizen-residents.

Additional features that could support an enabling environment include strong, well-managed, strategic networks for collaboration. Effective networks rely on trust and information-sharing, reciprocity, and exchange. Information resources also need to be supported through well-designed knowledge management repositories and systems that institutionalize best practices for investments. Such information could also identify key re-acculturation strategies for the African diaspora who are seeking to penetrate new environments in their African home countries.

But it also depends on the African diaspora to be proactive and intentional about becoming actively involved in their nations' welfare. This requires the diaspora to continuously study global trends in their African home countries and identify resources in their host countries that would help them to strategically plan and pursue opportunities to contribute towards their communities in their African home countries.

References

Braman, S. (2009). *Change of State: Information, Policy, and Power* (Illustrated ed.). Cambridge, MA: The MIT Press.

Deutsch, K. W. (1966). *Nationalism and Social Communication: An Inquiry into the Foundations of Nationality* (2nd ed.). Cambridge, MA: MIT Press.

Grewal, D. (2008). *Network Power: The Social Dynamics of Globalization*. New Haven: Yale University Press.

John, R. R. (2010). *Network Nation: Inventing American Telecommunications*. Cambridge, MA: Belknap Press: An Imprint of Harvard University Press.

Putnam, R. D. (2001). *Bowling Alone: The Collapse and Revival of American Community* (1st ed.). New York: Touchstone Books by Simon & Schuster.

Sikkink, K. (2009). *The Power of Networks in International Politics*. Ithaca, NY: Cornell University Press.

Tarrow, S. G. (2011). *Power in Movement: Social Movements and Contentious Politics (Cambridge Studies in Comparative Politics)* (3rd ed.). New York: Cambridge University Press.

Tilly, C. (2010). Cities, states, and trust networks: Chapter 1 of cities and states in World History. *Theory and Society*, *39*(3–4), 265–280. doi:10.1007/s11186-010-9119-z

Tyler, T. R. (2010). *Why People Cooperate: The Role of Social Motivations*. Princeton; Oxford: Princeton University Press.

15 A critical road ahead in Africa's development

Reflexive highlights

My upbringing has played a significant role in my work within the context of Africa's development across diverse sectors and industries, ranging from media and entertainment, business and international development to academia over the past two decades, directed toward Africa's development. My 2015 doctorate dissertation, conference papers, articles, and presentations on the African diaspora, cultural identities, African political thought, African development, and various subjects led to the germination of this book, whose process started in late 2016 and will be published in 2021. This book expanded further upon theoretical frameworks and concepts, responded to a few gaps in the 2015 dissertation, and explored new ground for further research.

This book illuminated a few fundamental key take-aways that I have summarized below, regarding necessities in approaching Africa's development: (i) a decolonizing of the mind and implementation of critical analytical frameworks to foster innovative and meaningful development; (ii) the role of culture and indigenous knowledge in Africa's development; and (iii) strong governance and combat of corruption in order to builds industrialization and set a foundation for a strong infrastructure. As a result, the book also increased the urgency of a call-to-action for global scholars and practitioners across various disciplines to collaborate on ways to develop and implement alternative paradigms and produce transdisciplinary within contexts of African development.

Writing this book during the "Year of 2020" also heightened the relevance of my critical approach and perspectives in discussing Africa's development, diasporic identity, and ethnic and racial media portrayals. Against the backdrop of the dramatic underpinnings revealed in the Year of 2020, this book, therefore, raises a few thought-provoking questions regarding the relevance of pan-Africanism in the 21st century.

I hope that you may join me on this contemplative journey about the road ahead toward Africa's development!

DOI: 10.4324/9781351031660-19

1) Approaching Africa's development necessitates a decolonizing of the mind and implementation of critical analytical frameworks

Although not new information to me, all my research in this book merely reinforced that in addition to other factors necessary for increasing sustainable development, Africa's sustainable development is dependent on emancipation from colonial legacies that still exist.

Through research and analysis, one can identify colonial legacies that exist across a spectrum of subjects interrelated to sustainable development, some of which include identity politics and nationalism; the formulation of some socioeconomic development models and paradigms to develop nations' industries growth sectors; development communication and media strategies; and relationship-management frameworks to foster stakeholder engagement, coordinate international public relations, and strengthen international diplomacy between vital actors in the development agenda. This book attempted to present a critical transdisciplinary approach in addressing the African diaspora's role in their African countries' national development agenda. In so doing, it was important to reveal how colonial strongholds have been hegemonized across this vast range of development subjects.

The problem is exacerbated when normative ideologies remain unquestioned, are regarded as universal truth, and are reiterated as "excellent" or "best practice" models in education programs and in organizations. "The Western tradition of knowledge is only valid and useful for some ends; for others it is unworkable" (Ndhlovu, 2015; Suárez- Krabbe 2009). This is not to reject the value of Western theories, but to situate their use appropriately in time, place, and geographical context. This is to also acknowledge other valid non-Westernized knowledge systems and epistemologies that would be more applicable and more relevant to address other societal and global dynamics. Otherwise, one risks perpetuating and maintaining a social order of power imbalances and hierarchical societal structures that unfairly allocate and distribute resources; continue to disenfranchise marginalized communities; limit socioeconomic progression that will impoverish the disadvantaged; and result in other adverse impacts on developing communities.

But it takes a desire and a will for one to acknowledge that colonial strongholds did not just dissipate once African countries gained their independence. Hence, the approach toward development requires a conscious effort to pursue the liberation of a mindset that remains subconsciously clutched within hegemonic ideals. So whether one is a citizen-resident living in Africa, the diaspora, or a representative of another cultural group that comprises the global community of stakeholders and vital actors in Africa's development, all individuals should adopt a collective psycho-emotional commitment and willingness to discover and pursue alternative paradigms that could be implemented toward building our African nations.

One approach toward decolonizing one's mindset is to intentionally apply a critical lens toward theoretical frameworks and interventions for Africa's development agenda. This would generally require that one questions taken-for-granted assumptions and sources of knowledge production systems and structures; carefully identifies and assesses the power dynamics of all the actors that are involved in the phenomenon under investigation; links these observations to society-level patterns and trends; develops appropriate interventions to mitigate harm and risks; and offers sustainable solutions that are contextualized to suit the local environment and emancipate the disadvantaged, or marginalized populations. It also requires suspending biases that restrict information power to an elite few. For the diaspora seeking to contribute toward their African home country, it is important to advocate for and include key citizen-residents— particularly the beneficiaries of the development program—in key leadership roles in their own development processes. Their insights, cultural values, unique perspectives, and daily experiences provide vital data for technology (the know-how) and the product (solution).

Hence, the diaspora who seek to invest in, pursue entrepreneurialism in, or otherwise contribute to their African home country's development should understand how ideological values inform the types of developmental frameworks and models that are applied to address development issues. Those ideological frameworks shape and inform how they perceive and define the parameters surrounding development opportunities that they seek to invest in. These frameworks shape their entrepreneurial endeavors' missions, organizational values, and cultures; guide their collaborations with stakeholders; inform the structure of their programs; and guide their activities and technical ways of problem-solving. These ideologies shape the way the media frames the development phenomenon issues that inform the communication and outreach strategies, systematic processes, and behavioral theories that design and implement communication activities. These activities promote the desired sustainable social and behavioral change at individual and community levels. These ideologies also shape how resources are allocated and distributed. In short, the diaspora's approach toward contributing to their African country's development agenda necessitates their ability to discern, challenge, and, when relevant, reject normative paradigms and ideologies that presume to be the sole, fundamental principles that guide strategic planning and activities in communities, which ultimately shape individual and collective responses. There is an urgent need to explore and embrace new ideologies and methodologies that more accurately identify and contextualize unique approaches toward their nations' development plans.

2) Integrating the role of culture and indigenous knowledge in development agendas

Numerous studies from development specialists and researchers, including Andrews (2009), reinforce the necessity of incorporating culture and directly involving recipients of the development aid process as valid participants in socioeconomic development (Mpande, 2015).

Culture plays a key role in preserving indigenous knowledge that provides guidance, core values, a framework of best practices, and the basis of rules, norms, and processes to address challenges, strengthen problem-solving, and foster development. Development within the African content is linked to a participatory-focused paradigm that relies on collective behaviors and communicative channels that support the ideologies, methodologies, tools, and dissemination of messages that are required to effectively build, sustain, mobilize, and develop communities.

The Green Belt Movement (GBM), pioneered by Nobel Peace Prize winner Wangari Maathai, epitomizes the integration of culture in a development model that empowered local communities in Kenya to plant trees and preserve their environment for sustainable livelihood amidst challenges that threatened their survival. The GBM illustrated a unique, culture-based strategy and people-centered approach that positioned culture as a vital requisite; empowered women who had been marginalized as change-agents; and relied on women's indigenous knowledge and resilience to "combat the problem … at local and structural levels" (Mpande & Muneri, 2018, p. 108). By evolving from a movement aiming to preserve the environment to a platform that "articulated a new form of democracy for a marginalized community" (Mpande & Muneri, 2018, p. 109), the GBM demonstrated the interconnectivity of sustainable development as being economic, political, cultural, and social (Mpande & Muneri, 2018).

Wright (2020) also emphasizes the value of acknowledging indigenous knowledge as a vital resource in development and in empowering marginalized groups, such as women, as change-agents in the development agenda (personal communication, January 23, 2020). Within the business context of her company, Shea Yeleen, Wright (2020) acknowledges women in the local communities in Ghana as subject-matter experts whose knowledge and lived experiences of the culture is vital to the business model and has far-reaching impacts on developing the community:

> There is the [perception] issue that women in rural areas can't create anything of quality because they haven't been traditionally educated. Oh, they've been educated. It's just not books … it's a different education. They know more about [this business] than anyone because it's something that's built into their culture and sometimes we don't acknowledge the importance of culture.
>
> (Wright, personal communication, January 23, 2020)

Hence, practitioners, researchers, and policy makers should develop inclusive frameworks that involve community members as stakeholders and partners, and that are tailored to suit the unique cultural context of the environment.

It is also important to recognize the role of culture in development within relationship-building between key stakeholders. Based on my research data, a strong culture fit is a vital tool in development, which requires a congruence of norms and values between citizen-residents in Africa and the African diaspora in their collaboration toward their nations' development.

3) Approaching Africa's development necessitates strong governance

Governance in Africa is inextricably linked to all areas of Africa's socioeconomic, political, and cultural development. It is easy to want to blame all the challenges and limitations underlying Africa's development on colonial ills and perils. However, while tracing the link between development issues and colonial history is certainly valid, other intracontinental factors and dynamics should be held accountable for Africa's development. Rotberg (2014) attributes many problems in Africa to the "continent's legacy of bad governance. In the post-independence period, authoritarian strongmen took control of many countries, enriching themselves and their cronies by exploiting the peoples labor and their country's resources" (Introduction). We will refrain from a debate about whether most of Africa's development challenges should be attributed to colonial legacies or to a legacy of bad governance. But we will draw attention toward a generally agreed observation: citizens expect their nation-state and leaders to effectively and efficiently deliver and provide political, social, and economic goods and services for their nation's welfare. In particular, these goods and services pertain to safety and the rule of law, participation and human rights, sustainable economic opportunities, and human development. The ability to effectively engage the private sector and other key stakeholders in the provision and delivery of these goods is also an indicator of governance.

Hence, Africa's development also rests on the accountability of leaders who can set a moral tone for the country that reflects integrity and replaces corrupt administrations with those that are law-abiding and perceived as trustworthy; provides political stability and ensures security for its people—particularly the vulnerable; assures a proper allocation of resources toward building stronger infrastructure; fosters enabling environments for investment and invests in their nation's human capital. For instance, many would trace daily struggles of police brutality and injustice, bribery, medical and educational deficits, ethnic factions, child soldiering, or crimes against humanity to either bad governance or corruption practices, that may lead to rebellions, coup d'états, or wars. Would a driver who is bribed for money at every traffic light by a different police officer and beaten to death in jail because he refuses to pay the officers, or a young girl who is unable to continue her education because of exorbitant tuition fees or teacher pay strikes, more quickly point their fingers toward the state of governance and corruption in the country, or to their nation's colonial history?

Governance and leadership play fundamental roles in setting the moral tone, as well as in providing the architectural framework, base, and foundation for the systems, processes, and infrastructure to create and facilitate opportunities for the African diaspora, citizen-residents, and relevant stakeholders to develop Africa's sustainable future.

4) Approaching Africa's development necessitates pan-Africanism ... true or false?

The "Year of 2020" was undoubtedly one of the most crucial, life-transformative years of the past few decades. The thunderous wake of the global Covid-19 pandemic and global protests against racial injustice and police brutality stirred a cascade of polarizing thoughts and gripping emotions, leaving the global community to reel from the devastating impacts. Of significance, some of these impacts also revealed glaring disparities, particularly between racial and ethnic minority groups and Caucasian groups, begging many notable questions, and in particular, one that is relevant to our context: Is pan-Africanism relevant in addressing some of the more recent challenges related to health, socioeconomic, and racial inequities that impact human welfare in Africa and the global community?

Covid-19 racial/ethnic and systemic health and social disparities

Research has revealed evidence that suggest correlations between inequities in terms of social determinants of health and increased risk of illness and death from Covid-19 in racial and ethnic minority groups, cited by the Centers for Disease and Control Prevention. According to research, discrimination in health systems and various systems place chronic and toxic stress particularly on racial and ethnic minority groups that "[shape] social and economic factors that put some people from racial and ethnic minority groups at increased risk for COVID-19" (CDC, 2020, para. 3). Additional disparities that the CDC (2020) note could also be applicable globally include (i) limited or self-restricted healthcare access and utilization, influenced by cultural and linguistic barriers; (ii) occupation, in which racially disproportionate representations of racial and ethnic groups worked in jobs that exposed them further to the virus and in which they could not work remotely or online or take paid sick leave; (iii) educational, income, and wealth gaps that placed pressure on those with lower-quality education, lower school completion rates, college entrance barriers, and resulting lower-paying jobs, which resulted in occupations that increased their exposure to the virus; and (iv) housing, reflected in urbanization or crowded conditions that illustrated more where racial and ethnic minority groups lived, making it difficult to obey social distancing rules and other prevention tactics, and those whose cultures encouraged shared households or faced probable risk of eviction and homelessness, or the continued risks of shared housing.

Notably, the band for solidarity occurred during Covid-19 during the controversial suggestion by two French doctors to use African countries as testing sites for a Covid-19 vaccine, despite the lower cases of Covid-19 deaths across the continent that were reported at the time. Raising alarm and sparking global outrage, many expressed fury and disbelief, including global celebrities, political leaders, and international organizations who expressed offense at the idea of repeating history and using Africans as medical guinea pigs. Director-General of the World Health Organization (WHO), Tedros Adhanom Ghebreyesus, famously and publicly condemned the French doctors for reflecting a colonial mentality that insulted the Black community when they sought to position Africa as a testing ground for a vaccine, adding that "it was a disgrace, appalling, to hear during the 21st Century, to hear from scientists, that kind of remark" (BBC News, 2020, para. 6), prior to assuring the entire global community that such an approach would not occur.

Global protests against police brutality and racism

Global race protests in 2020 after the George Floyd lynching in the United States and cases of police brutality forced many organizations and individuals around the world, particularly African migrants, to confront brutal realities about present-day race relations they may have had limited exposure to or lesser understanding of, or had seldomly discussed openly in public spaces.

The year of 2020 brought to light some prominent deep-seated core beliefs and ideologies that were rooted in nations' political and socio-economic history. Throughout the year, several states in the United States witnessed the removal of the US confederate flags and replacement of some street names. Several countries similarly witnessed the removal of statues and figures of slave owners across Europe, and protests in solidarity across Europe and other parts of the world sought to confront or end racism. Suddenly, audiences turned to diversity and inclusion offices in corporations, institutions invested in initiatives to promote anti-racism in their work environment, general publics sought to understand or criticize subjects like critical race theory, while students gained interest in Africana studies. There was increased enrolment in historically Black colleges and universities (HBCUs) and increased sales of New York bestseller books from Oprah's Book Club, including *Caste: The Origins of our Discontent* by Isabel Wilkerson; *So You Want to Talk About Race* by Ijeoma Oluo; and *Why Are All the Black Kids Sitting Together in the Cafeteria?* by Beverly Daniel Tatum. In short, it seemed that those that had never questioned race or race-related matters urgently sought historical context about race and contemporary events, such as the Black Lives Matter global movements, relevant online social hashtags, or Instagram posts with Black squares.

The domino effect of racial consciousness also spilled over to more recent flashbacks, when some questioned if there was some truth and validity, after all, to several controversial global headlines when some public leaders publicly addressed racism. Colin Kaepernick was dropped in 2016 from the National

Football League (NFL) for kneeling during the national anthem in protest against racism and police brutality and systemic oppression in the United States. In 2020, several media platforms referred to the significance of his protest and its resurged relevance in the wake of race-related events and discourse. Similarly, radio stations and online interviews with Dr Arikana Chihombori-Quao celebrated the medical doctor, activist, and former African Union representative to the United States from 2017 to 2019, who had implored African nations to liberate themselves from contemporary economic strongholds of former European colonies.

Meanwhile, social media campaigns flooded social media timelines, urging the collectivism of the African diaspora to support the protests within Africa, with hashtags ranging from #endsars to end police brutality in Nigeria and #aminext to end gender-based violence in South Africa to #congoisbleeding to end child labor in Congo and more.

In short, the Black Lives Matter protests, Covid-testing criticisms against Africans, and intracontinental campaigns against human rights all have one theme in common: the call for solidarity and collaboration among Africans in Africa and the broader African (Black) diaspora was critical to dismantle imbalanced power structures and liberate social ills from grips of all forms of abusive, oppressive power.

More questions about Black and African unification circulated:

- Could Africa learn lessons from the Ebola crisis and other health pandemics to solve the Covid-19 pandemic? Hope sparked when innovative responses from Senegal and other countries also made scientific medical breakthroughs with testing mechanisms (see Unit 2).
- Although one-size-fits-all answers cannot be applied throughout Africa because each country reflects its own unique socioeconomic conditions, are there best practices that can be identified and contextualized to the locale?
- Is there a continental strategy for the African continent to address the surge and spread of the coronavirus?

By the time this book is published, the Ebola crisis and previous pandemics would have most likely presented a framework for a response that many African countries have also adopted. It remains to see how effective it is and, hopefully, if it can serve as a new blueprint for future pandemics.

After all, can the rest of the world also look to Africa for best practices and lessons learned? Are these the beginnings of a resurgence for a pan-African approach?

Pan-Africanism: To be or not to be?

So, given that the Year of 2020 recognized a need for racial, socio-economic, and cultural unification for Africa and the African diaspora, is this where pan-Africanism highlights its relevance in addressing these issues? Or is this where we assert that pan-Africanism remains a utopic ideal that cannot be realized?

Pan-Africanism has been the subject of numerous debates over years that are still ongoing. First, there are different schools of thought to approach pan-Africanism, as Okhonmina (2009) articulates, echoed by various scholars, which position different African countries to define and prioritize different roots issues of development challenges and solutions that make it difficult for them to unify. An Afrocentric perspective traces pan-Africanism nationalism to distinct eras in history covering the B.C. period, whereas Eurocentric perspectives begin from a mid-19th-century perspective that can be illustrated "through revolutionary Pan-African Nationalism against slavery between the fifteenth and nineteenth century to the intellectual, geopolitical, scientific, and cultural Pan-African Nationalism of the twentieth century culminating in the proposal of the United States of Africa" (Okhonmina, 2009, p. 87).

Emphasizing political integration in Africa, pan-Africanism referred to an Afrocentric perspective that focused on Africa's struggle against foreign domination and various African leaders' fight for independence. Over the following decades into the 1980s, pan-Africanism evolved into various initiatives and movements and has also been institutionalized in different organizations. The Black Power movement, Afrocentric movements, Kwanzaa, and the Pan-African Congress Movements gained prominence throughout the United States. Notably, African approaches to intellectualism and culture emerged and sought to replace long history of dominant Eurocentric ideologies in intellectual and cultural systems (Kuryla, 2020). However, by the 21st century, pan-Africanism was more strongly linked to unification in African countries, particularly Sub-Saharan Africa (Kuryla, 2020).

In the 21st century, pan-Africanism "asserts that the fate of all African peoples and countries are intertwined" (Musewe, 2014, para. 4). Some scholars encourage a renewed mindset to address creative means of a new economic and democratic model so that a pan-African ideology can address issues of poverty and include Africa in the global economy.

Ultimately, in some contexts, pan-Africanism argues against a responsiveness to colonialism, racism, and neocolonialism; in others, it advocates for economic and political unification. For some, political and economic unity in Africa should not be based on race, especially since "economics rather than race are the underlining factor in the European enslavement of Africans" (Okhonmina, 2009, p. 88; Williams, 1961, p. 51). Similarly, Sulayman Nyang, former professor and former chairman of the African Studies Department at Howard University in Washington, D.C. and a former deputy ambassador and head of chancery of the Gambia Embassy in Jeddah, Saudi Arabia, illustrated the concept of pan-Africanism in his 2005 essay on US–African Relations that addresses the racial perspectives that account for the relationships between Black Americans and Africans. Nyang (2005) notes that from the pan-Africanists' perspective, liberation was not based on the replacement of White leadership with Black leadership in the African National Congress (ANC). Instead, liberation stemmed from pan-Africanists as agents of cultural and economic means of production (Nyang, 2005).

But fast-forward to the 21st century, and many have been disillusioned by pan-Africanism for its struggle to mobilize African countries against internal divisions of culture, race, and ethnicity. Declaring pan-Africanism to be "dead," some critics cite an inability for African nations to hold each other accountable against corruption, an inability to achieve solidarity, and an inability to carve their own approach toward democracy. Musewe (2014) shoots down the ideal of African unification and compares the approach to that of the European Union, which sheds "no common standards of behaviour as within the EU for example. There is no common purpose when it comes to the alleviation of poverty, leadership accountability and governance" and that the only common factor of Africans is their residence on the same continent (para. 7).

Instead, Musewe (2014) advocates for the emergence of a new beginning for Africa:

> In my opinion, the destiny of Africans is solely dependent on the emergence of new political forces within Africa. We must see the emergence of a new generation of African leaders that focus on local development. We need to see the establishment of new accountable political institutions within countries and a new narrative of self-sufficiency and sustainable development. Only after that can we begin to look at Africa as a whole.
> (para. 9)

And maybe Musewe (2014) has a point. As the world changes, so do the transcultural and transnational experiences that shape our new realities. Perhaps we need a brand new, fresh lens through which to view pan-Africanism. We may not be able to go back to the past, but the past can help to inform our present, equipping us with valuable lessons learned and best practices as we approach new paradigms of development.

How can such a new lens address the simultaneous pulls of shared struggle, triumph, perseverance, resilience, and innovation in Africa? How can Africa position itself to commit toward a mission that seeks to redefine a human freedom that all countries can hold each other accountable to? What would it cost or require for Africa to give up, exchange, reject, and embrace to further operationalize a liberation of socioeconomic, cultural, and political strongholds and pursue innovative solutions—both theoretically and pragmatically? And most importantly, is Africa prepared to pay that price for this human freedom? Much attention has been paid to the "new normal" post-2020 through a digital revolution of innovative technology and "new ways of doing business." But truthfully, at the heart of any "new normal" lies new ideologies that prompt new value systems, new attitudes, new thoughts, new actions, new behaviors, and a new reality.

So, perhaps a better question is this: Is Africa positioned to commit to a "new normal"?

References

Andrews, N. (2009). Foreign aid and development in Africa: What the literature says and what the reality is. *Journal of African Studies and Development, 1*(1), 8–15. http://www.academia.edu/202805/Foreign_aid_and_development_in_Africa_What_the_literature_says_and_what_the_reality_is

BBC News (2020, April 6). Coronavirus: Africa will not be testing ground for vaccine, says WHO. https://www.bbc.com/news/world-africa-52192184?at_custom4=7FB20E24-7837-11EA-8A08-21E047744363C&at_custom2=twitter&at_custom3=%40BBCWorld&at_campaign=64&at_medium=custom7&at_custom1=%5Bpost+type%5D

Kuryla, P. (2020, October 21). Pan-Africanism: History, achievements, & facts. *Encyclopedia Britannica*. https://www.britannica.com/topic/Pan-Africanism

Mpande, S. (2015). *Relationship management of the brain circulation phenomenon: The case of the Ugandan diaspora in the USA* (Publication No. 3718222) [Doctoral dissertation, Howard University]. ProQuest Dissertations and Theses Global.

Mpande, S., & Muneri, T. (2018). The Green Belt movement and its rhetoric of African development communication. In: E. Mutua, A. Gonzalez, & A. Wolbert (Eds.), *The Rhetorical Legacy of Wangari Maathai* (pp. 95–111). Washington D.C.: Lexington Books.

Musewe, V. (2014, August 21). The ideal of Pan Africanism is dead. *Lesotho Times*. http://lestimes.com/ideal-pan-africanism-dead/

Ndhlovu, F. (2015). A decolonial critique of diaspora identity theories and the notion of superdiversity. *Diaspora Studies, 9*(1), 28–40. doi:10.1080/09739572.2015.1088612

Nyang, S. S. (2005). US–Africa relations over the last century: An African perspective. *US-Africa Relations over the Last Century: An African Perspective, 72*(4), 913–934. https://muse.jhu.edu/article/527431/pdf

Okhonmina, S. (2009). The African Union: Pan-Africanist aspirations and the challenge of African unity. *The Journal of Pan African Studies, 3*(4), 85–100. https://www.researchgate.net/publication/242743445_The_African_Union_Pan-Africanist_Aspirations_and_the_Challenge_of_African_Unity

Suárez Krabbe, J. (2009). Introduction: Coloniality of Knowledge and Epistemologies of Transformation. *KULT. Postkolonial Temaserie, 6*(Special Issue), 1–10.

Williams, E. (1961). *Capitalism and Slavery*. New York: Russel and Russel.

Index